The Path of the Devil

The Path of the Devil

Early Modern Witch Hunts

Gary Jensen

ROWMAN & LITTLEFIELD PUBLISHERS, INC.
Lanham • Boulder • New York • Toronto • Oxford

ROWMAN & LITTLEFIELD PUBLISHERS, INC.

Published in the United States of America
by Rowman & Littlefield Publishers, Inc.
A wholly owned subsidiary of The Rowman & Littlefield Publishing Group, Inc.
4501 Forbes Boulevard, Suite 200, Lanham, Maryland 20706
www.rowmanlittlefield.com

Estover Road
Plymouth PL6 7PY
United Kingdom

British Library Cataloguing in Publication Information Available

Library of Congress Cataloging-in-Publication Data

Jensen, Gary F.
The path of the Devil : early modern witch hunts / Gary Jensen.
p. cm.
Includes bibliographical references and index.
ISBN-13: 978-0-7425-4696-7 (cloth : alk. paper)
ISBN-10: 0-7425-4696-9 (cloth : alk. paper)
ISBN-13: 978-0-7425-4697-4 (pbk. : alk. paper)
ISBN-10: 0-7425-4697-7 (pbk. : alk. paper)
1. Witchcraft—History. I. Title.
BF1566.J46 2007
133.4'309—dc22 2006002136

Printed in the United States of America

∞™ The paper used in this publication meets the minimum requirements of American National Standard for Information Sciences—Permanence of Paper for Printed Library Materials, ANSI/NISO Z39.48-1992.

Contents

Preface

One of the most popular books assigned as supplemental reading in introductory sociology, deviance, and theory courses in sociology in the 1970s and 1980s was Kai Erikson's (1966) classic, *The Wayward Puritans*. Erikson's work dealt with three waves of ritualistic punishment in New England, including the Salem witch trials, and is the best known of a relatively small number of works by sociologists dealing with issues relevant to the larger episode referred to by most historians as "the early modern witch craze." Additional sociological treatments of the topic can be found in a small set of articles (Currie 1968; Chambliss 1976; Ben-Yehuda 1981; Andreski 1982; Sebald 1981, 1989; Goode and Ben-Yehuda 1994b), a chapter in a larger work (Stark 2003), and a few monographs (Sebald 1978; Weisman 1984; Ben-Yehuda 1985; Andreski 1989; Oplinger 1990; Goode and Ben-Yehuda 1994a; Geis and Bunn 1997).

In contrast, theory and research on the topic by historians has been growing at a rapid pace, with over twice as many books on the topic published in the 1990s alone than the total for sociology in the forty years since Erikson's work was published. The study of the witch craze has become a major specialty among historians, but comparatively little has been published on the topic by sociologists. This neglect may reflect the fact that sociology has become a highly specialized discipline, and the phenomena of interest fall "between the cracks." The episodes encompassed have some of the features of *collective behavior* and *social conflict*, but involved institutional mechanisms that locate it in the specialty involving *law and social control*. And, when the discussion turns to the social construction of the stereotypical witch, the punishment of women as witches, variations in witchcraft, and possession, then it falls within the study of *deviance*.

This study of *The Path of the Devil* demonstrates that the early modern witch craze is an ideal topic for illustrating (1) the different features of the historical episode that are "highlighted" when different sociological concepts are applied (e.g., deviance, social control, collective behavior, social conflict), (2) the application of different types of sociological theories (e.g., functionalist vs. conflict theories), (3) the issues involved when scholars move toward greater precision and begin to "operationalize" variables, and (4) the issues that can be addressed through the compilation of quantitative data and statistical analysis. These are topics that are relevant to basic introductory courses in sociology and a wide variety of advanced courses.

The monograph is intended to illustrate the utility of bridging work in often insular academic specialties within sociology as well as across disciplines. The specialists within sociology that should have some interest in the work include scholars and teachers covering women's studies, gender, theory, deviance, law and social control, contentious politics, social conflict, medical sociology, collective behavior, social change, minority groups, and religion (among others). The range of topics addressed in the book should give the work interdisciplinary appeal as should the fact that it draws heavily on the large body of literature mentioned.

Chapter 6 attempts the most far-reaching integration of disciplines and specialties by integrating historical observations with psychological perspectives on scapegoating, ideas borrowed from criminology, and themes under development in the study of collective behavior as "contentious politics." The chapter builds on Charles Tilly's proposition that forms of social conflict vary among social settings to "explain" societal and temporal variations in witch hunts with specific attention to the relationships among war, rebellion and witch hunts.

The Path of the Devil has some of the properties of a "scientific" monograph because it incorporates the results of a project funded by the National Science Foundation (Temporal and Spatial Variations in Early Modern Witch Hunts, 1993–94). Indeed, a major emphasis in the work is that a casual inspection of general trends cannot untangle complicated relationships, and that some specific empirical issues necessitate a multivariate analysis. Most of the statistical detail is confined to two chapters and, when provided, is not unduly complex. Some data are presented in chapters 6 and 7, but in a fashion that should be within the grasp of most readers and certainly college students.

Chapter 7, "The Salem Witch Hunt: A Perfect Storm," focuses on the witch hunt of particular interest to students in the United States. "New" theories about the timing of the Salem episode have been proposed in recent years, one deemed to be "meticulously researched," attributing the episode to "sleeping sickness." Moreover, a sizeable number of students are familiar with the argument that the Salem craze was linked to ingestion of a type of mold (ergot) that grows on rye and can cause hallucinations. Although information that has a "scientific" aura is presented to back such biological arguments, no actual systematic analysis is presented in either case. When data cited as support for these two biomedical theories are compiled and analyzed in chapter 7, neither fares very well. In contrast, most features of the Salem witch hunt are quite consistent with the general sociohistorical observations arrived at in the study of the European witch craze. In fact, the title for the chapter reflects the fact that the generalizations and observations presented in earlier chapters can be illustrated using information about the Salem–Essex County trials. A perfect storm occurs when a variety of circumstances converge to generate an unusually dramatic event.

The final chapter deals with questions that are raised by most audiences to any discussion of "witch hunts": Was McCarthyism an instance of the same phenomenon in more modern times but in a different form? Are there any parallels between the search for witches and Satanists in preschools and the early modern witch hunts, including Salem? Are attacks on women as witches still occurring in modern times? "Metaphorical" comparisons are commonly proposed when considering modern versions of witch hunts, but it is intriguing to ask whether any evidence would point to any of these modern episodes as "more than a metaphor." In short, is there any evidence that empirically discerned relationships found in the study of the early modern witch hunts apply to modern witch hunts?

This work has taken over twenty years to complete and began with an opportunity provided by Women's Studies and the Curriculum Integration Project at the University of Arizona, a project funded by the National Endowment for the Humanities. In 1982, I was supported for a summer together with several other faculty with the charge to integrate more materials by, about, and for women into my classes. This experience not only affected the content of my classes but led to a new research agenda involving the study of witch hunts. I owe special thanks to Myra Dinnerstein, Judy Nolte Lensink, and Patricia MacCorquodale for including me in that program. I also received small grants from the Social and Behavioral Sciences Research Institute at the University of Arizona and the University Research Council at Vanderbilt University to begin the study. These grants led to a grant from the

National Science Foundation (NSF) to study "Temporal and Spatial Variations in Early Modern Witch Hunts." Two students worked on the NSF project as graduate research assistants, MaryAltani Karpos and Jim Wilson. Jim Norris was an undergraduate research assistant and compiled data on the movement of Jews. Finally, Soma Chaudhuri, a graduate student at Vanderbilt, is extending the study to encompass India, and some of the observations in chapter 8 are based on the literature she is assembling on attacks on women as witches in India. I would also like to thank Doug McAdam and Darrell Steffensmeier for their insightful comments and Charles Tilly for his sage advice on publishers.

I owe the most to my wife, Sheila, who had to hear me retell the story about the early modern witch craze over and over again when colleagues would ask about my research project. People are fascinated by the study of witches and witch hunts, and what should have been a short depiction of my project typically led to an hour-long conversation and endless new questions. I cannot count the number of times I was asked to repeat the story, and I appreciate her patience with a project that took far longer than I ever intended.

CHAPTER ONE

Early Modern Witch Hunts

Newes from Scotland, 1591. Reprinted by permission of Special Collections, University of Glasgow, Scotland.

For over three hundred years, we knew where the Devil was. From the mid-fifteenth through the early eighteenth centuries, he traveled routes of economic, social, and religious exchange from northern France, Switzerland, and Germany through England and Scotland to the Puritan New England colonies. He made late excursions into Hungary, Poland, Russia, and Scandinavia as well. He was not actually observed in his travels. Rather, Satan was known through his contracted coconspirators, the witches. He had entered into similar contracts with other enemies of Christian society but found a new and receptive market among women in early modern Europe. Satan contracted hundreds of thousands of women into his service, and Christian society found and executed somewhere between fifty thousand and one hundred thousand of them.

The battle between Christian society and Satan's servants experienced ebbs and tides until the early to mid-1700s when the Devil apparently abandoned the large-scale use of such contractual arrangements as a source of organizational power. Popular belief in witches and witchcraft continued, but the pursuit of heretic witches as "servants of Satan" (Klaits 1985) came to an end. Occasionally, Christian leaders see signs that Satan is attempting to resurrect his old arrangement with women, as witnessed by Pat Robertson's detection of child-killing, lesbian witches among supporters of the Equal Rights Amendment in the United States in the mid-1990s (Buchwald 1994).

These first few paragraphs summarize the *demonological* interpretation of a historical episode that continues to capture scholarly and public interest—the early modern witch craze, spanning the fifteenth through the early eighteenth centuries. The view that the pursuit and execution of witches was a vigilant response to a real threat to Christian society was the official interpretation of what was happening at the time as well as one scholarly version of the story as recently as 1925 (see Summers 1926). Judging from numerous late-night religious programs and the readiness of the media to focus on even the slightest hint of Satanism, cults, or witchcraft in crime stories (Richardson, Best, and Bromley 1991), some segment of the public still shares this view. In the recent case of the murder of a pregnant woman and her unborn child in California, lawyers for the defendant husband could count on some people to believe that it was a ritual murder involving hidden enemies worshiping Satan. Similarly, parents and prosecutors involved in the most costly trial in California history, the McMartin preschool case, were quite ready to accept that rituals involving a coven of witches might be behind the fantastic tales told by some of the children. Due process of law helps keep such tendencies from escalating into major witch hunts, but the underlying suspicions and fears reveal themselves periodically.

The witch label has been used for centuries as a stigmatic label when demonizing women as enemies or countering female challenges to male authority. Moreover, a less overtly political version of the witch endures as a symbol in American popular culture. The popular witch is symbolized on police cars in "Witch City"—Salem, Massachusetts—as an old hag on a broomstick, complete with peaked hat and flowing cape. Other versions can be found on decals for the high school athletic teams in Salem, named the "Witches." The local post of the Salem VFW also uses her as a symbol.

The witch is the female symbol for Halloween, and her costume remains one of the most popular costumes for trick-or-treating. However, this commercial version of the witch was not fully assembled until the worst phases of the early modern witch craze were past. During the craze, witches were depicted in the nude or in garments appropriate to time and place. It is not until the end of the craze that the symbolic witch was assembled, complete with the peaked hat. When real people were being hanged or burned, the characteristics of witches were the characteristics of real people. The Halloween witch is an enduring cultural artifact created out of materials assembled by the end of the early modern witch craze to represent women as enemies of Christian society.

The tercentenary of the Salem witch hunts was celebrated in 1992 with the dedication of a memorial to honor the victims of the witch trials (see figure 1.1). According to the 1992 *Salem Visitor's Guide*, the memorial was designed "to create a reflective environment invoking the lessons of human rights and intolerance." That memorial serves as a reminder of a quite different interpretation of the historical pursuit of witches than the pursuit of real heretics, one symbolized in the contemporary use of the notion of a "witch hunt." The concept of a "witch hunt" is likely to be invoked when someone believed to be innocent is pursued relentlessly based on what appear to be contrived, vague, and ill-founded accusations. A "witch hunt" is even more likely to be suspected when alternative motives for such a pursuit are suspected. Standards of justice now taken for granted were not in place for those accused in Salem, and traditions that ordinarily protected the accused were ignored in the panicky search for witches and their leader.

Although a sizable segment of the population may believe in an enduring reality of conspiracies involving Satan and his heretic witches, the notion of a "witch hunt" implies that the pursuit of such enemies is based on fantasy and hidden motives. Other words used to refer to the historical pursuit of the satanic witch carry similar connotations. Historians and others refer to the pursuit of Satan and his witches in the fifteenth through the seventeenth centuries as the early modern "witch craze." The notion that this enduring

Figure 1.1. The Salem Witch Trial Memorial. The Salem Memorial, located adjacent to the Peabody Museum and Essex Institute, was dedicated during the tercentenary of the Salem witch trials as "a reflective environment invoking the lessons of human rights and intolerance." The stone "seats" are engraved with the names of the victims. The Salem trials occurred near the end of over two hundred years of trials that had swept Europe, taking the lives of between fifty thousand and one hundred thousand people, primarily women. The trials were conducted based on a belief system now called "demonology," merging folklore with pseudoscientific, quasi-legal conceptions of the relation between the natural and supernatural worlds. (Author's photograph.)

and often explosive hunt was a *craze* implies that it falls within the same general category of collective behavior as fads, manias, and panics. Other words such as *scapegoat* and *persecution* are intimately intertwined with the notion of a witch hunt as well, all based on interpretations quite different from the "official" view of the witch hunts at the time. However, as will be elaborated in chapter 2, such words are not simple substitutes for one another. Rather, they reflect distinct theories about the nature of witch hunts.

Historical Studies

In a 1973 seminar, H. C. Erik Midelfort noted that "scholarly studies of witchcraft have been sprouting lately like mushrooms in a fairy ring" (see

Midelfort 1979). This surge turned out to be an enduring trend: more than twenty years later, Peter Burke (1993) observed that "witchcraft has moved from the periphery of historical attention to a place near the centre" (435). Another surge of studies since the mid-1990s has reinforced the trend, and the fairy ring keeps growing.

A huge body of scholarship describes the path of the devil and the company he kept during the early modern period (roughly the fifteenth through the seventeenth centuries), most of it authored by historians. Detailed summaries of data are available for southwest Germany (Midelfort 1972), Switzerland and parts of France (Monter 1976; Muchembled 1977), England (Ewen 1929; Macfarlane 1970a, 1970b), Scotland (Black 1938; Larner 1981; Goodare 2002), Italy (Martin 1989), the Netherlands (Gijswijt-Hofstra and Frijhoff 1991), Hungary, Sweden, Estonia, Norway, Portugal (Ankarloo and Henningsen 1993), Bavaria (Behringer 1997), and New England (Boyer and Nissenbaum 1974; Demos 1982; Weisman 1984; Karlsen 1987; McMillen 1990; Robinson 1991; Rosenthal 1993; Carlson 1999; Roach 2002; Norton 2002). These detailed works on specific settings are complemented by numerous monographs summarizing and interpreting research on witchcraft and witch hunts (see, e.g., Weissman 1984; Klaits 1985; Quaife 1987; Scarre 1987; Ginzburg 1991; Barstow 1994; Brauner 1995; Levack 1995; Willis 1995; Breslaw 1996; Briggs 1996a, 1996b; Purkiss 1996; Barry, Hester, and Roberts 1996; Bostridge 1997; Reis 1998; Carlson 1999; Gibson 1999; Gijswijt-Hofstra, Levack, and Porter 1999; Meltzer 1999; Thurston 2001; Ankarloo and Clark 2002; Stark 2003; Behringer 2004) and a twelve-volume anthology bringing together a wide range of scholarly articles on the topic (Levack 1992).

Several trends in historical scholarship help explain the surge in studies of the early modern witch craze, some reflecting general trends in the humanities and social sciences. One of the most relevant is the growth of feminist theory and research together with growing interest in scholarship for and about women in a wide range of academic disciplines. It is widely noted that women appear to have been the main targets of witch hunts and that a significant proportion of the men who were tried or executed were related to these women, but that fact has taken center stage in several recent studies (e.g., Larner 1981; Karlsen 1987; Barstow 1994; Willis 1995; Breslaw 1996). The most common estimate of the percentage of women among people accused or executed as witches is 80 percent. There is variation, with males more common in Estonia and Russia and equally represented in Finland (Ankarloo and Henningsen 1993), but most studies estimate somewhere between 70 and 90 percent of the targets were women (see Barstow 1994 for a summary). A study of medieval trials suggests that males were the likely targets of early trials, but that a shift to females had occurred by the fifteenth century (Kieckhefer 1976). Rodney Stark (2003) cautions us to remember that men were victims as well and that it is misleading to focus exclusively on variables such as misogyny that apply primarily to the explanation of female victimization. On the other hand, by the time the major panics were under way, women were greatly overrepresented, and men were typically caught up in the process as relatives or as suspects named by women under torture.

The charges giving rise to the most intense witch hunts reflected the demonological theory that witchcraft was heresy, that people found guilty of witchcraft had entered into a contract, a pact, with Satan, and that women were the most likely to succumb to Satan's bargain. During the most intense witch hunting, female deviance was accorded a peculiarly patriarchal interpretation. Women were punished for witchcraft, but their ability to engage in such activity was a reaffirmation of male power via Satan. In fact, Anderson and Gordon (1978: 175) suggest that the satanization of witchcraft was a "masculinizing" of witchcraft that made it more acceptable as a truly serious problem to male authorities (see figure 1.2).

Throughout the Salem witch trials in colonial Massachusetts, both the afflicted girls and the women accused of witchcraft were queried for any clue that would lead to a male leader. George Burroughs, a charismatic and controversial ex-minister of the Salem Village parish, was suspect and named in the fantasies and confessions of several of the young girls and women. Five men were executed in the Salem witch trials, versus fourteen women. Burroughs was the only one neither related to an accused witch nor actually living in Salem Village. As the only minister to stay in the province of Maine during the Indian raids, he was arrested while garrisoned with the people of Wells, Maine. Two months later he was hung, insisting to his last words "that there neither are nor ever were witches" (Mather 1693: 128–-29). Although women were the common victims of witch hunts, they were rarely credited with independence or any real power independent of Satan. Rather, they were depicted as seduced by a male demon.

The mythical structure of heretical witchcraft was organized in patriarchal form, with women following a male leader. Moreover, some historians claim that its control took the form of institutionalized (and hence patriarchal) ritual violence against women. Anne Llewellyn Barstow (1994) argues that it is hard to explain the sexually sadistic nature of the torture and execution of women during the witch craze without introducing the idea that the witch wars were instances of institutionalized *sexual* violence against women. Torture was often directed at a woman's sexual organs, and an accused woman

Figure 1.2. A peculiar form of patriarchy. The Western demonological conception of an organized conspiracy of witches "masculinized" witchcraft and depicted it in a form consistent with the patriarchal organization of the religious and political systems of the time. Women were conceived of as capable of entering into organized relationships that threatened society, but a male demon was the real culprit. Thus, women were both accorded significance as a hidden source of power and depicted as weak and submissive at the same time. (Satan holding court for newly anointed witches; from Gerard d'Euphrates' *Livre de l'histoire et ancienne cronique*, printed by E. Groulleau, Paris, 1549. Reprinted with permission of Dover Publications.)

might be raped in prison or have breasts cut off. Men were subject to horrible tortures as well, but they were in the minority during most of the witch wars.

A second, but related, trend in historical scholarship reflected in witchcraft–witch hunt research is what Peter Burke (1993: 435) calls the movement to "write history from below." Several reviews of research on witch hunts have noted the importance of studies focused on the routine, village-level interactions and disputes that gave rise to charges of witchcraft (e.g., Macfarlane 1970a, 1970b; Thomas 1971; Boyer and Nissenbaum 1974; Monter 1976; Demos 1982; Karlsen 1987; Briggs 1996b). Although changes and variations in legal codes, religious and political conflicts, and beliefs systems at a societal level are relevant to understanding dimensions of the witch craze, studies of the "microlevel" conflicts generating accusations and the history of relationships among the parties involved have generated new ideas about the larger, "macrolevel" social forces at work.

The "cliometric" or quantitative history discussed by Fogel and Elton (1983) in *Which Road to the Past?* is well represented in the study of witch hunts. As Burke (1993) points out, the local and regional works have been distinct in their use of quantitative methods to "map the distribution of trials over time and space" (436). They have also been distinct in providing detailed data on the characteristics of parties involved in witch trials and the characteristics affecting transitions in the course of a witch trial (see Karlsen 1987; Martin 1989). The local and regional studies listed earlier have compiled considerable data on dimensions of witch trials over time and space that allow precise conclusions about the relationship of variables such as war to witch hunts, conclusions that challenge or qualify theories focusing on broad correspondence of eras (Midelfort 1972; Monter 1976; Demos 1982).

One of the most cited of the regional studies mapping the distribution of witch hunts over time and space is H. C. Erik Midelfort's (1972) study of *Witch Hunting in Southwest Germany, 1562–1684*. Midelfort's data span the fifteenth through the seventeenth centuries, providing detailed information on both small panics and large epidemic episodes. Witch executions were most intense during the span of time encompassing the Thirty Years War but sputtered out following that war. The number of communities with trials peaked in that same span of time, but with a resurgence in the last half of the seventeenth century. By examining relatively precise fluctuations in witch trials, Midelfort challenges theories that would attribute witch hunts to war and raises questions about a variety of possible correlates that could not be addressed without such detail. The general course of historical research on the topic has involved debates requiring an ever-increasing degree of temporal and spatial precision.

Historical Sociology

The general growth in scholarship by historians with features that make their work quite "sociological" has been accompanied by a general growth in scholarship by sociologists focusing on "social history" as well. "Comparative and Historical Sociology" was founded as a disciplinary specialty within the American Sociological Association (ASA) in 1988. Issues of that association's journal, the *American Sociological Review*, are as likely to include articles categorized as "historical studies" as any other topic. Indeed, the 1993 winner of the ASA Distinguished Scholarship Award was Jack Goldstone's (1991) *Revolution and Rebellion in the Early Modern World*, a monograph incorporating quantitative methods into the study of rebellion and revolution in three societies.

The increasing use of quantitative methods in the study of history by historians, sociologists, and other social scientists and, specifically, in research by historians on the witch craze is not paralleled by any corresponding trend in sociological scholarship. What attention the topic has received in sociology has been theoretical and discursive (Erikson 1966; Currie 1968, 1973; Chambliss 1976; Sebald 1978, 1981, 1989; Ben-Yehuda 1980, 1981, 1985; Andreski 1982, 1989; Oplinger 1990; Goode and Ben-Yehuda 1994a, 1994b; Geis and Bunn 1997). Among sociologists, Weisman (1984) has presented data on characteristics of people involved in the colonial witch trials over time, and Stark (2003: 201–88) has summarized data on witch trials among societies.

The paucity of work is somewhat surprising since sociology is the discipline most closely identified with the study of topics that would seem to include witch hunts, such as deviance, social control, and collective behavior. It is also surprising given the fact that sociology is more likely to be viewed as a "quantitative" social science than history. Yet, only one work by a sociologist incorporates any quantitative data or methods into the study of the topic (see Weisman 1984), and that study focuses exclusively on witch trials in New England, with five tables on characteristics of the persons involved.

As will be elaborated later, part of the explanation of the relative neglect of the topic among sociologists may rest with the fact that early modern witch hunts do not fall in any one area of specialization within sociology. Sociology is a highly specialized discipline, and scholars in each area tend to concentrate on topics dominating the professional journals and conference debates in that area. The fact that the wave of witch trials and executions in the early modern period is referred to using the words *witchcraft*, *witch hunt*, and *witch craze* reflects the fact that the phenomenon itself can be conceptualized in different ways. Indeed, when ideas from distinct specialties are considered, they lead to a better understanding of the phenomenon.

Three Sociological Specialties

The rest of this chapter will begin a dialogue, shifting back and forth between concepts and issues in three sociological specialties and historical scholarship on the early modern witch craze. Although it is difficult to think of an area of sociology that would be totally irrelevant to the study of the witch craze, three specialties are particularly relevant and correspond to different features of the historical episodes under consideration: witchcraft, witch hunts, and the witch craze. The corresponding sociologies are (1) deviance, (2) social control, and (3) collective behavior.

The best-known works by sociologists specifically dealing with witch hunts fall within the first two categories. The two areas overlap, and some sociologists combine them into a broader specialty, deviance and control. However, recent treatments of social control have gone well beyond prior definitions that limited that field to the study of "reactions to deviance." Led by Jack Gibbs and Donald Black, the study of social control has grown increasingly independent of the study of deviance. Finally, the reference to the early modern witch hunts as a *craze* requires discussion of the applicability of the study of collective behavior to the topic, and that specialty will be considered last.

Witchcraft and the Sociology of Deviance

"Deviance" is a concept used by sociologists to encompass a variety of forms of human conduct that have been defined or reacted to by some members of a social system as wrong, bad, immoral, illegal, or worthy of condemnation and punishment. The concept encompasses phenomena that have been and are referred to using words laden with moral, religious, psychological and medical overtones such as *depravity*, *pathology*, *corruption*, *perversion*, *abnormality*, *evil*, *immoral*, *sinful*, *bad*, and *sick*. As a word in ordinary human language, *deviance* can take on similar negative connotations. However, the concept is preferred by sociologists over other words that are laden with stronger judgmental overtones or that embody a particular causal interpretation.

Sociologists differ in the features of deviant phenomena that interest them: some focus on conduct that violates norms, and others focus on the development and application of normative definitions themselves. Embracing the most common definition of *deviance* adopted by sociologists, *deviant behavior* specifically is conduct that violates definitions of appropriate and inappropriate conduct shared by the members of a social system. While allowing for relativity, deviance is defined in terms of potentially measurable normative standards of members of a system. Thus, although it is common to note that "deviance is in the eyes of the beholder," the normative definition requires that definitions must be shared to some degree (i.e., that they are "social"). Definitions that come to be embodied in legal codes and define conduct as criminal have been particularly central to the sociology of deviance, and those accepting such a "realist" tradition assume that there are real measurable variations in conduct that violate such codes. From this perspective, the witch craze would be conceived of as a surge in some form of conduct such as witchcraft, religiously prohibited forms of magic, or Satanism.

An alternative to the normative definition has been a "reactive" one, exemplified by definitions such as "conduct that is subject to social control" (Black 1976: 9), "behavior that people so label" (Becker 1963: 9), and "a property *conferred upon* these forms by audiences which directly or indirectly witness them" (Erikson 1962: 308). From this perspective, the focus is not on what people are "doing" or have done so much as it is on how people and conduct come to be defined or labeled in certain ways.

Some of the advocates of such a position are called *social constructionists* (see Goode 1994) since they are interested in how phenomena come to be defined as problems—that is, how problems are "constructed" by people and groups making claims or "framing" the problem. James Richardson, Joel Best, and David Bromley (1991) stress that the most basic questions asked by constructionists are "Who is making claims? Why are they making them? What do they say? and How do others respond?" (4). As will be discussed in the next section, the focus is more on social control than on the conduct itself.

Considerable debate concerns the best, least biased, or most sociological definition of deviance, with strong critiques and countercritiques leveled by advocates of reactive versus normative definitions (Goode 1994; Gibbs 1966, 1981, 1989). As Erich Goode (1994) points out, advocates of a radical reactivist perspective tend to view the actual conduct leading to social control as unimportant. The important subject matter is the invention, selection, and manipulation of beliefs that define conduct as bad, sinful, criminal, or the like and the selection of people into those categories.

The reactivist conception of deviance is particularly applicable to the study of situations where the actual conduct involved does not violate widely shared normative standards or where conflicting norms arise. Even for conduct where there is widely shared and strong consensus on the impropriety of the conduct (intentional killing), other beliefs, definitions, or norms defining "mitigating circumstances" (e.g., self-defense, "in the line of duty," mental capacity, etc.) affect the way in which the conduct is categorized.

When dealing with categories of criminal conduct, the reactivist focuses on (1) the moral enterprise involved in constructing, interpreting, and changing legal definitions, including the strategies used, and (2) the actual enforcement, application, and negotiation of those definitions in practice. When categories of crime are created, changed, or abolished, the central question becomes "Whose normative standards, values or interests were represented in that change?" A common strategy to justify categorizing a situation as a new "problem" is to claim that it fits in old categories that are widely accepted as deviant. Satanizing, demonizing, or diabolizing practices and people that are disliked is one such tactic.

Most historians studying the witch craze end up with some version of a reactivist or constructivist perspective. Since the people charged with witchcraft could not or did not engage in many of the activities of the heretic or satanic witch, why would such a stereotype be invented and applied to these people? What led to such a conception, and why were people hunted and made to fit the category? As noted earlier, the modern notion of a witch hunt has come to refer to situations where targets are not guilty of any wrongdoing but are the victims of scapegoating or persecution. The focus of most of the historical research mentioned earlier is on witch prosecutions and witch trials, not on witchcraft and witch behavior. In fact, the episode is commonly referred to in terms of persecution and scapegoating because it is presumed that witchcraft and witch behavior had little to do with the witch hunts.

However, historians also ask questions about actual conduct that would have been widely defined as sinful in a Christian setting. "Were there really witches?" (Midelfort 1974) and "Were the Salem witches guiltless?" (Wendell 1892). Was there a surge in Satanism, black witchcraft, and other forms of heretical, deviant conduct? Is there any basis in real-world conduct, or was the witch craze directed at "mere phantasms" (Midelfort 1968: 376)? Some of the terms used in the study of the witch craze (*witchcraft*, *witches*, and *witch cults*) focus our attention on real behavior and the people or groups that engage in it. In fact, in a critique of the dominant historical treatment of the Salem witch hunts as persecutions of totally innocent people, Chadwick Hansen (1969: x–xi) argues that the possessed were not frauds but were mentally ill and that many of the accused did practice witchcraft.

From 1929 until 1974, the article on witches in the *Encyclopaedia Britannica*, written by the Egyptologist Dame Margaret Murray (1921, 1931), depicted the witches who were pursued during the early modern witch craze as a continuation of pre-Christian fertility cults worshiping pagan goddesses. In essence, the witch hunts were a response by the church to a cult with practices and beliefs that violated what were supposed to be widely shared norms of appropriate religious conduct. The development of commercial enterprises in contemporary Salem by people identifying themselves as "Wiccans" or practitioners of "The Craft" reflects the conception of the activities of those accused of witchcraft as linked to ancient systems of religious belief that were demonized by Protestant and Catholic establishments.

The Catholic priest-historian Montague Summers ([1926] 1987) reaffirmed Murray's view, claiming that the confessions of witches and other heretics in medieval and early modern times revealed the "hideous and horrible fact" (10), that Satanism was real and constituted a grave threat to the Christian world. In a later work, Julio Caro Baroja (1964) describes *The World of the Witches* and entertains the possibility that some form of organized witchcraft did exist.

Norman Cohn's (1975) *Europe's Inner Demons* is typically cited as dealing a key blow to the theory that the witch craze was directed at real witch cults. Cohn argues that the image of the witch cult, with its nocturnal meetings, sexual orgies, cannibalism, and worship of bestial deities, was nothing more than the elaboration of the stereotype that had been applied to Jews, early Christians, and a variety of heretical sects in medieval times. The fact that people would confess to such activities was a result of torture, suggestion, and reinforcement of beliefs about satanic heresy developed in prior persecutions.

Richard Kieckhefer's (1976) studies of European witch trials from 1300 to 1500 led him to the same conclusion. The witch stereotype is an "elite" or "learned stereotype" derived from earlier trials and reinforced through confessions under torture. Beliefs that were organized into an official "demonology" were combined with popular beliefs about witchcraft to define an organized conspiracy of witches that were aligned with Satan. Both Kieckhefer and Cohn were instrumental in shifting the focus in the study of witch hunts to the Renaissance and early modern history as opposed to medieval history and, to use Leland Estes's (1983: 277) word, a common view of judicial and literary elites as "gatekeepers" for the craze.

In recent publications, the historian Carlo Ginzburg (1991, 1993) argues that it would be a mistake to view all beliefs about witch cults as total fabrications. He notes that some aspects of witch beliefs associated with the witch hunts were derived from real groups of women who believed themselves to have special powers. But, quite contrary to the satanic witch pursued during the witch hunts, they were members of fertility cults that sought to protect fields from witches who would destroy potential crops. Ginzburg argues that beliefs about night-flying witches and the witches' Sabbath were inverted versions of the activities and beliefs of real groups.

Rejecting Ginzburg's as well as Murray's arguments, Robert Muchembled (1993) proposes that there was an underlying reality to the target of attack, but that it had "nothing to do with any organized non-Christian cult, even of a residual or mythic kind" (148). Rather, he believes that the witch hunts were an attack by representatives of elite culture on popular culture of the time. He proposes that features of peasant and village culture were "diabolized" by religious and political elites through "the myth of satanism" in the attempt to acculturate peasants in rural areas. The notion of nighttime Sabbaths "diabolized the hours of night," a time of youthful revelry, dancing, and amusement in peasant culture. Peasant beliefs that some people with special powers could tap into a polytheistic "plurality of forces" were transformed "into the realm of diabolism." In short, Muchembled views witch hunts as attempts to stamp out peasant paganism and cultural practices.

For Muchembled, the witch hunts represented a "conflict of cultures," with peasant women a central focus because they were crucial to the transmission and perpetuation of that culture. Peasant women with special knowledge or who were believed to have special powers had to be rooted out, and they became central targets of witch hunts. In addition to its fit with the selection of some types of women as targets, Muchembled suggests that this interpretation is consistent with the fact that, over time, witch hunts moved from the religious and cultural core of European society to more peripheral settings. Witch trials spread as elite culture spread, with middle-level officials playing the key role in the attempt to stamp out peasant culture. Moreover, he argues that witch hunts were not associated with war and civil disturbances but, rather, with differentiation and economic change that increased both peasant use of magic as well as attempts to suppress such conduct.

The view that gender-linked differences in behavior resulted in witch hunts as a means to challenge female folk medicine and beliefs was proposed over thirty years ago by Ehrenreich and English (1973) in *Witches, Midwives and Nurses*. Advocating a feminist perspective, they argue that common practices by midwives and wise women were diabolized in the establishment of religious, political, and economic patriarchies. Although only a small section of their book deals with witches, the argument is quite similar to that proposed by Muchembled. However, as will be discussed in chapter 6, the emphasis on midwives as potential suspects for diabolic witchcraft has received little support in research.

The main thrust of historical scholarship has been away from views that there were any real surges in witchcraft, witch cults, or witches towards a reactivist-constructionist view of the episode. From such a perspective, the early modern attack on witches is more commonly depicted as a struggle among groups with conflicting belief systems, as mass persecution based on an elite demonological belief system, as a strategy for controlling threatening groups, or as a convenient scapegoat for tensions generated by social, economic, and demographic change.

Contemporary treatments of Satanism in the sociology of deviance take a constructionist position as well (see Richardson, Best, and Bromley 1991). In contemporary American society, Satanism has been linked with everything from rock music to missing children. Yet, when thoroughly investigated, there is little or no evidence of any major surge in Satanism as the explanation for missing children or the sexual abuse of children. Moreover, no one has found a correlation between heavy metal music and satanic practices among youth. However, constructionists note that growth in and the visibility of satanic churches has provided a real-world foundation for the anti-Satanists' claims. As was the case with the witch craze, bits and pieces of reality are assembled together with historical stereotypes of heretics and hidden internal enemies into a "problem" that grows more serious as new problems are linked to it.

Several explanations of why the craze occurred when it did have definite parallels with sociological theories of crime and criminal conduct. For example, Muchembled's (1993) explanation of witch trials parallels "cultural conflict theories" of crime in sociology. Culture conflict theorists argue that high crime rates for some groups are generated by the ability of more powerful groups to impose their values and norms on others via legal definitions and processing (e.g., see Sutherland, Cressey, and Luckenbill 1992; Vold and Bernard 1986; Miller 1958). Categories of people with relatively little power are more likely to engage in activities that conflict with the law than those who can shape the law. Muchembled's attribution of witch hunts to a "conflict of cultures" entails exactly such a criminogenic situation. Activities and the beliefs they reflect in peasant culture conflicted with elite culture. Legal codes and processes were shaped by elites to attack peasant culture. When applied to conduct, such theories imply that crime rates will be high when power shifts occur, when some groups move to extend their control over others, or when groups with different normative systems and unequal power are brought into contact with one another. Stark (2003: 232–51) proposes that religious conflict increased intolerance of nonconformity, which was, in turn, reflected in the war with witches. Marxist versions of "conflict theory" have been very popular in sociological criminology and embody a similar logic (e.g., see Quinney 1977; Chambliss and Mankoff 1976). However, they focus on economic differentiation and conflicting group interests rather than normative or cultural conflict. Since such conflict theories have been applied to witch hunts, they will be discussed further in chapter 2.

A major competitor with culture conflict theory in sociological criminology has been "strain" theories of deviance. Theories focusing on deviance as a product of frustration, powerlessness, or some form of stress or strain fall within this general category. *Cultural conflict theories* attribute high rates of deviance to struggles for dominance among groups with conflicting norms or conflicting interests, while *strain theories* posit that forms of deviant conduct are adaptations to problems generated by one's location in the social system. This type of theory has been particularly popular in the explanation of juvenile delinquency, but it is applicable to a variety of other types of deviance as well. For example, Robert Merton (1957) argues that in contemporary American society, high rates of "innovative" deviance will be found among lower-class people who lack the means of attaining widely shared success goals by legitimate means. Some views of witchcraft fit this imagery. A reputation as a witch or knowledge of witchcraft could be classified as a "deviant adaptation" to lack of access to other sources of power and status. Hence, any circumstance or change that increased the number of people in such circumstances could increase the number of people attracted to such adaptations. This type of explanation is quite different from that proposed by conflict theorists in that the witch and witchcraft would not be viewed as approved activities that are under attack by elites or powerful groups with different perspectives. Rather, witchcraft would be viewed as a limited, and generally discouraged, response to stress and strain.

Some witchcraft scholars in the early modern period argued that the women charged with witchcraft were women suffering from what would now be called mental illness and were easily deluded by Satan into believing they were witches (e.g., Weyer [1563] 1991; Scot [1584] 1930). Thus, if surges in witchcraft or the number of people who believed they were witches are indicative of surges in mental illness, then theories relevant to fluctuations and variations in mental illness would be relevant to witch hunts as well. Circumstances currently identified as correlates of mental illness such as environmentally induced stress, socioeconomic disadvantage, and disruptions in the life course (see Goode 1994 or Clinard and Meier 1989 for reviews) may have been correlated with surges in activities and beliefs that made one liable to charges of witchcraft.

Stark (2003: 211) has expressed strong reservations that mental illness was involved because court records show witchcraft and mental illness to be recognized as distinct categories. However, he also states, "This is not to suggest, of course, that many of those selected as 'witches' weren't quite peculiar." Of course, this qualification also means that increases in peculiar behavior or the proportion of the population exhibiting peculiar behavior could play a role in facilitating charges of witchcraft.

A third brand of sociological theory addressing variation in actual deviant conduct focuses on variations in degrees of social organization-disorganization at the societal level and variations in social bonds at the individual level as key variables (Hirschi 1969; Briar and Piliavin 1965; Toby 1957; Reiss 1951). Such theories posit that deviant conduct is more common among socially marginal people than those who have strong ties to others in the system and that high rates of such conduct are found in settings where social bonds among people are either absent or deteriorating. Circumstances that increased the number of marginal people or contributed to the deterioration of communal bonds would give rise to high rates of violence, property crime, and other forms of deviant conduct. This type of theory has been applied to activities ranging from accidents to serious criminal conduct (see Gottfredson and Hirschi 1990).

As a general brand of theory, social bond theory is paralleled in some historical theories of witchcraft as well. Macfarlane (1970a, 1970b) and Thomas (1971) focus on the breakdown of village-level responsibility for the destitute that, when combined with an increase in women who had to depend on charity from neighbors, led a rising number of women to rely on the role of witch as a source of power. Such circumstances would increase the odds of witchcraft accusations. From this perspective, the number of witches increased during the transition from communal responsibility for the indigent toward a system of state responsibility.

Numerous additional themes in the sociology of deviance could apply to features of witchcraft and witch hunts, but one theory in particular can aid in the explanation of changes or shifts in the nature of deviants as internal enemies. Although most sociological theories of crime have focused on the explanation of offender conduct, one of the most recent theories of crime focuses on the explanation of victimization. "Routine activities" or "opportunity" theory (Cohen, Kluegal, and Land 1981; Cohen and Felson 1979) explains rates of victimization in terms of the attractiveness, availability, and guardianship of potential victims. Although that theory focuses on the victims of crime, it can also be applied to the targets of punishment, persecution, or scapegoating. Several historians have noted that the pursuit of witches was less intense when traditional groups periodically assaulted as internal enemies were available. For example, Midelfort (1968) proposes, "With Jewish or Moorish elements to eliminate, Spain could hardly waste time on witchcraft" (381). Barstow (1994) argues that as internal religious heretics "were tamed, the inquisitors, especially in Germany, turned on fringe groups such as witches" (62). Martin (1989) suggests that with the lessening of the intensity of Protestant-Catholic conflict, the Catholic Church "began to look within itself rather than to any external threat, and there it found a mass of pagan ritual and superstition" (218). One plausible explanation for the shift of attention from Jews, lepers, and other heretics to women as witches is that traditional targets were less available and/or protected by elites. The stereotypical traits of more traditional enemies were carried over to the new heretic witch (a theme explored further in chapter 6).

Witch Hunts and the Sociology of Control

In 1968, H. C. Erik Midelfort noted that the difficulty in proving the existence or nonexistence of organized witchcraft as the foundation of the witch craze led historians to concentrate on other aspects of witchcraft. Most assumed there was no real witch cult and moved on to study demonology as a belief system and witch trials as another instance of the search for heretics growing out of religious conflicts and struggles in the early modern period. In short, the study of witch hunts shifted largely to the study of "social control."

Although the concept of social control has been used by sociologists for most of this century (see Gibbs 1989: 55–56), there is no consensus on the definition of the concept to guide either theory or research, and social control has not received the same elaborate development of competing perspectives as that which characterizes the explanation of deviant conduct. However, within the last several decades two theorists have proposed definitions, conceptual distinctions, and propositions that deal specifically with social control as a distinct specialty within sociology, Donald Black (1976, 1979, 1983, 1984, 1989, 1993) and Jack Gibbs (1981, 1989, 1994).

Both theorists distinguish between the sociology of deviance and the sociology of social control but take different paths in approaching that distinction. Black argues that the study of social control is distinct from the study of deviance because of the dependent variable selected. When variation in "reactions to deviance" is the subject matter to be explained, social control is the dependent variable, and the theory to explain it is a theory of social control (Black 1984, 1989, 1993). In *The Behavior of Law*, Black (1976) defines *social control* as "the normative aspect of social life, or the definition of deviant behavior and the response to it, such as prohibitions, accusations, punishment, and compensation" (2). In later work, Black (1984) argues that "social control is present whenever and wherever people express grievances against their fellows" (5). Variations in reactions to deviance or the manner of expressing and resolving grievances are the focus of the sociology of social control as distinct from the explanation of deviant conduct itself.

Gibbs would agree that social control is the dependent variable in a theory of social control but advocates a far more fundamental distinction. In fact, he rejects the view that the study of social control is the study of reactions to deviance and advocates a much broader conception (1981: 78): *Social control* is an attempt by one or more individuals (the "first party") to manipulate the behavior of another individual or individuals (the "second party") *by or through* another individual or individuals (the "third party") by means other than a chain of command (i.e., one party merely giving orders to another through a third party). Thus, social control is distinct from direct or proximate control attempts involving two parties (e.g., a request for aid, a demand for money, etc.) and sequences of proximate control as in a chain of command. Such attempts can take several forms, with numerous subtypes within each category. Details on all of the types and distinctions among types and subtypes are quite intricate and will not be dealt with in this work. However, it is clear that social control is not to be equated with reactions to deviance.

Gibbs rejects definitions of social control that limit it to reactions to deviance for two reasons. For one, a variety of phenomena typically thought of as some type of social control are not reactions to deviance, such as propaganda, advertising, education, strikes, protests, and governmental regulations. Second, not all reactions to deviance qualify as social control. For example, acts of self-defense or individual vengeance would not necessarily qualify as "social" control. To qualify as social control in terms of Gibbs's definition, the victim must respond with the intent of manipulating the behavior of a second party through a third party. If a person responds to an attack on person, property, or others in order to "set an example," the conduct would qualify as a type of vicarious social control (deterrence). If the purpose is to enforce norms or establish justice, the victim becomes an *agent* of social control, and it is the group that is attempting to manipulate second parties (potential deviants) through third parties (the victim). Thus, attempts at social control are purposive or goal oriented—attempts to change or manipulate the behavior of others in a desired direction.[1]

Gibbs's elaboration of a variety of types and subtypes of social control and his emphasis on the three parties in control situations can be applied to the description of some features of the witch craze and to identifying differences among theories of witch hunts. Historians who focus on village-level social interaction (Macfarlane 1970a, 1970b; Thomas 1971; Demos 1982; Briggs 1996a, 1996b) describe the encounters that fuel accusations of witchcraft in terms that correspond with Gibbs's distinction between attempts at direct or "proximate" social control and "referential" social control. "Trick-or-treat" situations generating ill will between some women and members of the community often involved rebuked requests for aid (i.e., failed attempts at proximate control). Such rebukes were often followed by curses. Curses are instances of attempted referential social control. A curse by the rebuked (the first party) is an attempt to affect the charitable behavior of the person solicited (the second party) by invoking the threat of intervention by a third party (e.g., God or Satan). Subsequent misfortune could lead to private vengeance (attempts at proximate control). But, with the development of courts to handle grievances and to process heresy, accusations could be brought to a third party (the church or state) that could be prompted to take action against the accused ("allegative" social control).

Most theories of witch hunts introduce motives and relationships that add additional types of social control to the scenario. Theories that view witch hunts as male attempts to control all or some types of women by punishing symbolic examples are proposing a type of "vicarious social control" wherein punishment is used by the first party to control a second by punishing a third. Theories that propose witch hunts as elite attempts to stamp out peasant culture by punishing those women symbolically representative of it are also emphasizing vicarious social control, but the motives and the specific parties are different. Other theories, discussed more fully in chapter 2, are mentioned here to illustrate the utility of Gibbs's conception of social control and its subtypes for discussing witch hunts. Theories differ in terms of the key features of his definition: the motivation and allocation of the parties involved to the three roles defining social control.

Gibbs's delineation of types of social control is useful for describing the interactions generating witchcraft charges as well as theories of witch hunts, but propositions involving those types apply to the witch craze only at a very general level. For example, Gibbs proposes that successful "proximate" control requires nearly complete consensus on appropriate and inappropriate conduct, including claims and requests. A decline in normative consensus will increase the frequency of attempts at referential control relative to proximate control. Such a notion is central to Macfarlane's and Thomas's theories of witchcraft charges. Requests for aid are less likely to be honored with an erosion of communal norms of charity, and those categories of women who were aided in the past were forced to rely on techniques of referential social control. An increase in size and social differentiation coupled with declines in normative consensus will lead to further shifts toward allegative, vicarious, and other forms of social control. However, none of these propositions has a clear bearing on fluctuations in witchcraft accusations and trials, just as the theories that can be restated in terms of such notions relate only to very broad trends in such phenomena.

Black's work is filled with propositions that appear to have some bearing on features of the witch craze. In fact, he cites the witch craze to support a variety of propositions about the behavior of law and social control. For example, the characteristics of targets of witch trials are (in some ways) similar to the defendants in criminal cases, and Black (1976: 56–59) cites the selection of relatively defenseless women as support for the proposition that law is more likely to be directed at people who are powerless. He cites Currie's (1968: 13–14, 19) findings that witchcraft confessions were more likely on the continent with royal witch finders than in England with local witch finders as support for the proposition that self-application of the law (i.e., confession) increases with the relational distance or authoritativeness of the prosecution (Black 1993: 70). The same proposition is claimed to apply to the relation between the accused and the accuser (73, n. 14).

Several studies of early modern witch hunts have proposed that the conception of the victims as "powerless" is an oversimplification. In *The Devil in the Shape of a Woman*, Carol Karlsen (1987) documents the fact that "most witches in New England were middle-aged or old women eligible for inheritances because they had no brothers or sons" (116). She adds, "As older women, in most cases poor, middling, or unexpectedly well-off women, some of their attitudes were construed . . . as evidence of witchcraft" (119). Women who "stood in the way" of the orderly transmission of property from one generation to another and who violated gender norms were at high risk of charges of witchcraft.

In reference to European witch hunts, Marrianne Hester (1996) notes that "laboring women, widowed and possibly older, and poor women were vulnerable to charges of witchcraft but that women who were in competition with men in areas such as brewing were also vulnerable" (305). In *Malevolent Nurture*, Deborah Willis (1995) observes that women who constituted a threat to patriarchal interests of men also constituted a threat to women who were attempting to live up to expectations for them as mothers. Most accusations were anchored in conflicts involving women: "Village-level quarrels that led to witchcraft accusations often grew out of struggles to control household boundaries, feeding, child care, and other matters assigned to women's sphere" (13). The shared characteristic of those women most likely to be accused of witchcraft was that they wielded some power and, thus, could constitute a threat to both men and women in a gender-structured economy.

Black's (1993: 144) theory of "moralism," which he defines as "a tendency to treat people as enemies," would certainly seem to apply to the witch hunts. He argues that one dimension of moralistic social control is "punitiveness," or "the infliction of pain and deprivation" (148), and he proposes that "the frequency and severity of punishment by third parties increases with social inequality and the breakdown of intimacy," citing the burning of witches, heretics, and others at the stake as examples. He goes on to claim that "these practices declined as inequality and the social remoteness of third parties attenuated" (149). However, such a proposition is contrary to other theories wherein witch hunts were attempts by patriarchal society to keep women "unequal." Black's proposition implies that the persecution of witches would grow in intensity with increases in inequality, while other theories imply that persecution increased in intensity as women made gains relative to men. If declines in gender inequality prompt witch hunts and such hunts function as repressive countermeasures to reinforce gender inequality, then witch hunts and gender inequality would be related to each other in a manner opposite to that proposed by Black. In short, it can be argued that it is when women are gaining power (i.e., inequality is declining) that women are most likely to be a threat in need of control.

Black's proposition that control grows more punitive with social distance is problematic when applied to witch hunts as well. Witches were intimate enemies. They were, in general, known to those bringing charges against them. Even their categorization as heretics places them in a closer relationship to their prosecutors than external enemies. In fact, it could be argued that the most moralistic and vicious forms of punitive violence are reserved for intimate enemies, the traitors and heretics among us, rather than for more distant enemies.

In summary, Gibbs's conceptual distinctions in the sociology of social control facilitate a description of the sequence of control attempts involved in microlevel encounters leading to witch trials and facilitate a comparison of theories that involve contending parties and specific motives. Moreover, since the witch hunts occurred within institutional legal machinery, propositions about the relative frequency of different types of control with increasing societal differentiation will apply in a general sense as well (i.e., proximate to social; referential to vicarious and allegative; informal to formal; etc). The sociology of social control is not sufficiently precise at present to generate specific hypotheses or predictions about the timing, content, and targets of witch hunts. Theories of social control that have been applied specifically to witch hunts will be addressed in chapter 2.

The Witch Craze and the Sociology of Collective Behavior

Reference to the pursuit of heretic witches as the "witch craze" implies that, in addition to treating the topic as a form of deviance or a type of social control, it can also be encompassed by the specialty dealing with collective behavior. Indeed, Ben-Yehuda (1981) states that "In one respect, the European witch craze is one instance of a larger analytic category of so-called 'Collective Behavior'" (335). However, we encounter serious conceptual problems when we try to place the early modern surges of witch trials and executions into traditional definitions of collective behavior or types of collective behavior. For example, it might be more appropriate to refer to the early modern "witch panic" since *crazes* are generally defined as a surge in the pursuit of something loved or valued (Bainbridge 1997: 370). In contrast, *panics* encompass surges in behavior aimed at escape, avoidance, or protection from something feared. On the other hand, one of the unique properties of the early modern witch hunts was that they were attempts to deal with something feared through the use of formal control mechanisms. In that sense, people were attempting to control something they feared through institutional machinery. Witch hunts had some properties like panics, but they still do not fit comfortably under that rubric. The early modern witch hunts have some of the properties of collective behavior, but they still fall outside the field when standard definitions are considered.

In his classic work on collective behavior, Neil Smelser (1962: 73–74) specifically excludes "collective reaffirmations of values, rituals and ceremonies" from his theory because such collective activities are "institutionalized." Thus, functional theories that depict witch hunts as episodic, collective rituals, reaffirming collective values (see Erikson 1966), would be excluded from the domain of collective behavior as conceived by Smelser.[2] Collective behavior encompasses transitory joint action "assembled as quick solutions for problems arising out of structural strain" (74). Witch hunts occasionally took the form of transitory mob action, but such episodes appear to have been quite rare. Rather, witch hunts were carried out according to rules institutionalized in the fifteenth century, if not earlier. Thus, witch hunts can be conceived of as collective ceremonies that occur in an episodic, "panic" fashion, especially when officials are receptive to hearing accusations. They spread among communities in an epidemic style, and, at the microlevel, charges escalated when institutional officials processing such charges defined witchcraft as diabolic and allowed torture. Thus, the epidemic had "paniclike" properties, but they were a product of periodic incorporation of witchcraft into institutional control machinery. Reference to early modern "witch hunts" captures the central features of the phenomenon quite well, but the historical phenomenon has been referred to under rubrics ranging from the witch craze and witch panics to witch hunts and witch wars.

Smelser's notion of "contagious beliefs" might strike some scholars as relevant to the explanation of witch hunts, but the focus of theories of collective behavior on the crowd, the public, masses, and mobs limits their relevance as well. The beliefs that witches were contractual participants in organized conspiracies led by Satan transformed neighborhood microproblems into heresy and justified a collective institutional response. However, it was religious and political elites who shaped, encouraged, and institutionalized such beliefs. They were institutionalized in papal bulls, demonological treatises, witchcraft pamphlets, and in both secular and religious legal procedure. Thus, although the beliefs involved in witch hunts drew on popular folklore, it was elites who organized them into a demonological belief system, emphasizing heretical conspiracies led by Satan. Reiterating the role of elites in the generation of witch panics, Midelfort (1981) states that "it was the fateful intervention of learned and thoughtful lawyers and theologians with their panic-stricken demonology that sent thousands of women to their deaths" (31). Unlike the collective behavior of the masses, the collective panics of elites are likely to be carried out through legitimate institutional channels; hence, the imagery and definitions characterizing theories of collective behavior do not apply in their present form. The most severe witch hunting followed the elite invention of demonology that helped transform village-level conflicts into demonic schemes.

Numerous theories of witch hunts posit some form of stress or strain as part of the causal impetus for witch hunts, and such categories of causal forces are common in theories of collective behavior. Smelser's theory of collective behavior focuses on some sort of "structural strain" as a necessary condition for collective behavior. However, that parallel does not allow a direct application of a theory of collective behavior to witch hunts. With no specification of the range of variables that qualify as empirically discernible sources of strain and no specification of the outcome of strain, the theory does not generate any testable predictions in advance of analysis.

Erich Goode and Nachman Ben-Yehuda's monograph on *Moral Panics* (1994b) and an article elaborating on that concept in the *Annual Review of Sociology* (1994a) are examples of the treatment of witch hunts as a type of collective behavior. They categorize witch hunts together with a variety of other episodic surges of public concern that Stanley Cohen labeled "moral panics." Such episodes include wavelike surges of public concern and hostility generated by "a particular issue or perceived threat—which, as measured by concrete indicators, turns out not to be especially damaging" (Goode and Ben-Yehuda 1994b: 4). Such episodes "arise in troubled times, during which a serious *threat* is sensed to the interests or values of a society." The witch craze is identified as one such historical episode.

They identify three types of theories of moral panics: (1) grassroots, (2) elite-engineered, and (3) interest group theories. In grassroots theories, panics "originate with the general public. . . . [A] kind of diffuse anxiety or strain simply explodes at the appropriate time, given the requisite triggering event" (1994a: 161). In elite theories, small but powerful groups encourage such panics, typically as a diversionary tactic to detract attention away from other problems for which they could be held responsible. From interest group perspectives, groups other than elites can be involved in the generation of panics "to make certain that certain rules take hold and are enforced" (165). They believe that moral panics grow out of grassroots anxieties but that the timing and content of their expression in the form of a moral panic are shaped by elites and interest groups. Moral panics occur when public anxiety surges and it is in the interests of elites or other groups to encourage panic. Of course, there is no advance specification of time variant or measurable circumstances that should increase the probability of such collective episodes.

Although witch hunts do not fall unambiguously within the limits specified in traditional definitions of collective behavior, certain aspects of such hunts fall within the broader perspective on such behavior referred to as *contentious politics* (McAdam, Tarrow, and Tilly 2001; Aminzade et al. 2001). Doug McAdam and his colleagues specify the properties of an episode of contentious politics as "episodic rather than continuous, occurs in public, involves interaction between makers of claims and others, is recognized by others as bearing on their interests, and brings in government as mediator, target, or claimant" (5). This depiction fits witch hunts quite well. They are episodic, occur in public arenas, involve makers of claims and others, are recognized by others as bearing on their interests, and involve governmental institutions as mediator or claimant.

The advocates of this new approach to the study of collective behavior argue that it challenges the boundary between institutionalized and noninstitutionalized conflict as well as the tendency toward compartmentalization of topical literatures. The study of early modern witch hunts requires crossing these same boundaries. Witch hunts are episodic, crazelike episodes involving contentious conflict carried out within an institutional framework. A thorough understanding of witch hunts requires that numerous boundaries be crossed for the simple reason that the phenomenon does not fall clearly in any single sociological specialty.

A dynamic, interactive framework has been proposed for analyzing mobilization in contentious politics (McAdam et al. 2001: 45). Since episodes of contentious politics are defined as involving at least one set of state actors and one insurgent group, it is not clear whether less differentiated episodes of contention at the village level are encompassed by the concept. Yet, many of the ideas invoked as part of the dynamic framework can be applied to the study of witch hunts. For example, for a witch hunt to begin, certain conflicts or events have to be collectively framed through a process of collective attribution. People with the power to open or close the institutional floodgates played a key role in transforming village-level interpersonal conflicts into a very specific form of religious heresy. When such a framework was invoked conflicts and charges of witchcraft escalated. As McAdam et al. note, "Entire episodes, their actors, and their actions are interactively framed by participants, their opponents, the press, and other third parties" (45). As will be elaborated in chapter 7, the initial processes leading to the Salem trials required eliminating some interpretations of the afflictions exhibited by girls and young women and framing the problem as an episode of traditional heretical witchcraft. This interpretation was facilitated by a contentious faction of Salem villagers and reinforced by the sermons and proclamations of prominent religious leaders at the time. They did not have to invent such a collective frame since it had been constructed and episodically invoked for at least two centuries.

At present, advocates of the study of contentious politics have been searching for common principles underlying disparate forms of collective behavior. One of the most dramatic claims in scholarship on collective behavior in the 1990s was expressed in Jack Goldstone's (1991: 46) *Revolution and Rebellion in the Early Modern World*, where he proposes that social structures are "near-fractal," showing similar features on macro-micro scales. This theme is reiterated more recently in a study of prison riots by Goldstone and Useem (1999) where they propose that "the principles of social organizations repeat themselves on different scales" (986). More specifically, they propose that the same principles that apply to a state-centered theory of rebellion and revolution can be applied to small-scale surges of collective behavior, such as prison riots. Their most basic proposition is that the principles underlying collective behavior against authorities appear to be fundamentally the same whether one is examining revolution against monarchies and empires or riots against prison authorities (986).

Since both rebellion and prison riots are directed "against authorities," it is certainly plausible to propose that similar circumstances, operating at different fractal scales, generated these two forms of collective behavior within their respective social systems. However, Goldstone also speculates that outbursts of witch hunting in England might be explained by his theory. Speculating on English witch hunts, Goldstone asks, "Could greater popular insecurity during the period of population expansion have contributed to the paranoia? Could greater elite assurance and stability after 1650 have contributed to elite suppression of popular superstition?" (347). The presumptive answer to these questions, given the statements about fractal scales, is that the same circumstances that produced rebellion and revolution in England produced the English version of the early modern witch craze. Since the largest witch hunt occurred in the span of years encompassing the English Civil War, it was reasonable to make such a suggestion.

Goldstone speculates that civil war and witch hunts are generated by similar circumstances, but other social historians have proposed a complex variety of relationships between war and witch hunts. Some discussions suggest a direct positive relationship, with war operating as a type of crisis, encouraging the symbolic and/or cathartic persecution of witches as scapegoats. For example, Nachman Ben-Yehuda (1981) states, "The coincidence of the termination of the craze with the termination of the Thirty Years War in the Peace of Westphalia is not just a chance occurrence. This peace, no doubt, gave official recognition to religious pluralism and symbolically ended the European struggle to redefine the social system morally" (23). This argument parallels Hugh R. Trevor-Roper's (1967) speculation that "if the universal scapegoat of the Black Death in Germany had been the Jew, the universal scapegoat of the Wars of Religion will be the witch" (111–12). Stark (2003: 201–88) takes a similar position on war and witch hunts, arguing that religious wars were one of the major causal forces generating witch hunts. Mary Beth Norton (2002) elaborates a similar line of argument about the Indian wars and the Salem witch trials.

The relationship between war and witch hunts has been depicted as quite variable as well, depending on the specific operationalization of war. The quote just cited from Ben-Yehuda (1981) implies a positive association between war at one level of analysis and the witch craze, but he also observes that invading armies halted the persecution "in many cases" and that "the internal stresses, insecurity, and instability experienced by persons living in the stricken areas during the invasions of various military groups and armies provided fuel to the burning furnace of the final phase of the witch craze" (23). In *Witches and Neighbors*, Robin Briggs (1996b) introduces yet another complication by proposing that "when outbursts of witchcraft persecution can be related to warfare, it is usually on the fringes of conflict or when its impact was less overwhelming" (308). War on the fringes of a social system might constitute a type of "diffuse" external threat, prompting collective anxiety and uncertainty about individual and communal survival and, hence, increasing the probability or severity of witch hunts. When all of these complexities are considered together, it is far from clear what relationship should be expected between war and witch hunts. Trevor-Roper, Ben-Yehuda, and Stark lead us to expect a positive relation between war and witch hunts, and Briggs leads us to expect that distant wars might be positively related.

A third position has emerged as the dominant position among those historians who have compiled numerical data on witch trials and executions: war tends to inhibit witch hunts. John Demos (1982), Erik Midelfort (1972), E. William Monter (1976), and Ruth Martin (1989) all suggest that both war and internal rebellion tended to inhibit witch hunts and that witch hunting was a "peacetime" activity. If war is defined in terms of actual warfare, then it makes sense to argue that war inhibited witch hunts. Witch hunts were not vigilante actions but, rather, were carried out through state and ecclesiastical legal machinery (Levack 1987). They required support from the church and/or state and the expenditure of considerable time and resources. Invasion as well as internal warfare would disrupt such machinery and the inclination to use it. In short, involvement of a social system in structured conflict should decrease the probability that resources will be invested in the search for hidden, internal enemies.

In contrast to Goldstone's view that these distinct forms of collective action might all grow out of the same social conditions, some theorists argue that there are distinct circumstances relevant to different types of collective behavior. For example, Thomas Schoeneman (1975) argues that witch hunts were "revitalization movements" led by powerful individuals and organizations seeking "to maintain the powers-that-be by settling the blame for social ills and misfortune on rival, deviant, and/or unassimilable groups within or near cultural boundaries" (534). Schoeneman's conception is similar to Gusfield's (1986) idea of prohibitionist movements in the United States as reactionary, symbolic crusades in which established status groups attempt to defend their values in view of mounting threats from growing immigrant groups. Gusfield's theory is relevant to the application of other sociological theories to witch hunts because Prohibition is viewed as an example of "status politics" in contrast to "class politics." Drawing on prior political theory, Gusfield notes that class conflicts occur during "periods of economic recession" as compared to status conflicts that occur during "periods of relative prosperity." He footnotes Lipset's (1955) statement that "the political movements which have successfully appealed to status resentments have been irrational in character and have sought scapegoats which conveniently serve to symbolize the status threat" (168). The Reformation and Counter-Reformation involved struggles over values, and one theorist has suggested that the Catholic intensification of witch hunting during the Counter-Reformation was, in part, a Catholic reactionary movement, rejecting Protestant critiques of witch hunts (Midelfort 1971). If (1) witch hunts are more likely to grow out of status conflicts than class conflicts and (2) prior observations about the conditions under which the two types of struggles occur are correct, then witch hunts should not be a mutual, positive correlate of rebellion and revolution. In fact, several historical studies have suggested that overt internal strife inhibits witch hunting.

Charles Tilly (e.g., 1984, 1986, 1992, 1993) also implies that different forms of collective behavior occur under different circumstances when he proposes that "alternative paths of state formation . . . led to different forms of resistance and rebellion" (1992: 66). Major revolutionary situations such as those in France required the convergence of popular rebellion "with the manoeuveres of great lords against pre-eminence" (1992: 150). The heartland of the witch craze, southwestern Germany, was characterized by what Tilly (1992) calls "intensely fragmented sovereignty" (41). Not only was sovereignty intensely fragmented, but the Peace of Augsburg in 1555 made religious allegiance a matter of local sovereignty, with dissenters free to pack up their bags and move their allegiance elsewhere. Thus, not only might war and rebellion inhibit witch hunts (by clearly defining enemies and disrupting institutional machinery for hunting witches), but war and rebellion may require the convergence of conditions that structure and direct the identification of enemies as well. Rebellions against clearly defined, discernible enemies in a struggle for power in the real world (e.g., France) occur under conditions that might lead to the search for imaginary enemies in less organized systems. In sum, Tilly's arguments about structured conflict are contrary to Goldstone's speculation that episodes as distinct as witch hunts and rebellions are generated by one and the same conjunction of conditions.

Tilly's depiction of important social changes in early modern Europe can also be applied to certain features of witch hunts and their historical context. For example, in *Coercion, Capital and European States*, Tilly (1992: 53) describes the early modern period (approximately 1400–1700) as "the age of brokerage." Wars were fought increasingly by mercenary forces supplied by contractors as opposed to the retainers, vassals, and militia who owed personal services to monarchs in the prior era of "patrimonialism." Allegiance was no longer based on a common connection to place, shared history, or a history of social exchange; rather, allegiance could be bought and sold. The age of brokered allegiance in war making was followed by "nationalization" with troops drawn from the sovereign's own citizenry. Loyalty became a matter of citizenship in a nation-state.

The heretic witch involved imagery that fits quite well with a depiction of this historical period as the age of brokerage. The demonological conception of the witch (required for witch hunts to reach epidemic levels) incorporated the view that the allegiance to Christianity could be "brokered" by Satan. Souls could be bought and sold, and women could become God's enemies through pacts or contracts in which they exchanged allegiance for sex, money, or power. Just as mercenary armies contracted their allegiance for money, Satan contracted legions of women to mount his attack on Christian society. It is not surprising that witchcraft was transformed from folk magic into a brokered conspiracy in an era of portable and contractual allegiances.

The notion that different types of collective behavior and social conflict vary in wavelike fashion among systems and within systems over time is central to "long-wave" or "world systems" theories in history, economics, political science, and sociology (e.g., see Braudel 1972a; Wallerstein 1974, 1980; Modelski 1978, 1987; Modelski and Thompson 1989; Bergesen 1983; Goldstein 1988; Berry 1991). Long-cycle theorists focus on the nature, causes, and consequences of large-scale changes in the political economy, with the relation between economic cycles and global war a major focus. Major power wars are deemed to occur near the peak of the expansion or "upswing" phase of fifty-year-long waves of alternating growth and contraction.

Although global war receives considerable attention, some cycle theorists speculate about the different forms that conflict and/or collective behavior might take at different times in the cycle. For example, Braudel (1972b: 897–99) associates anti-Semitic violence and crusades with economic depression, while global wars are linked to economic booms. Similarly, Berry (1991) suggests that during contractions or depression, "Those who find it difficult to cope with circumstances that appear beyond their control look for someone to blame," and "These are years of 'devil' theories: someone or something must be blamed" (174). Scapegoating, religious revivals, and antipapist, utopian, social reform, and millenarian movements all are thought to have "jelled in a period of depression." Finally, Goldstein (1988: 264) notes that Lasswell's theory about the psychological effects of economic prosperity and economic depression is consistent with the idea that wars occur on upswings, while scapegoating and internal hostilities peak during times of depression. Of course, such arguments imply the exact opposite relationship between economic conditions and witch hunts as that proposed by Schoeneman and Lipset.

To summarize, three different approaches to collective behavior and collective conflict imply a negative correlation between wars and witch hunts. However, the process generating that negative relation varies, as do the predictions that would be derived about the predominance of witch hunting during upswings and downswings. From one perspective, war is structured conflict with overt contenders for power in the real world and inhibits the invention and search for hidden internal enemies. From another perspective, reactionary status struggles and scapegoating peak during times of prosperity, while long-wave theorists suggest that such forms of collective behavior are linked to periods of economic recession, depression, or decline. Thus, although a minor topic in some approaches to collective behavior and collective conflict, perspectives in that field of study generate quite distinct implications for the explanation of witch hunts when they are addressed. It may be that different types of collective behavior or "repertoires of contention" occur at different times and under different circumstances. Local village-level conflicts reflected in charges of witchcraft may be most common in settings and times when there are not clear and present enemies. Thus, prison riots and revolutions may share far more in common with each other than they do with episodes of witch hunting.

Conclusion

This chapter does not exhaust all of the sociological topics that have some bearing on the early modern witch hunts. Theory and research in the "sociologies" of gender, culture, religion, stratification, social change, population, medicine, work, and a variety of additional areas could be applied to the topic as well. The sociologies of deviance, social control, and collective behavior were chosen because they correspond with features of the different conceptions of the phenomena as a dependent variable: (1) a type of individual or group behavior violating religious or legal norms, (2) institutional attempts to control witchcraft, and (3) surges in persecution or scapegoating, or a series of crazes or moral panics (see figure 1.3).

The subject matter can be viewed through numerous conceptual "lenses" and different features highlighted by different conceptual filters. For example, although it might be a sociological oxymoron (given the definition of collective behavior as "noninstitutionalized") to refer to the early modern witch hunts as a "craze" or "panic" in the form of "institutionalized ritual violence," such a conception captures some features of the phenomenon. Although crazes and panics fall in the same broad category of collective behavior as rebellions and revolutions, there are strong precedents for proposing an inverse relationship between witch hunts and other forms of conflict. Collective conflict and collective behavior with clearly discernible enemies may preclude or at least inhibit the search for imaginary enemies. Or, as Gusfield, Tilly, and others imply, the circumstances that generate one may be quite different from the circumstances that generate another.

Although there is a strong consensus that the image of organized heretic witches led by Satan was a learned, elite myth and that those prosecuted were often innocent of any deviant conduct, several theories are based on the

A Type of Deviance or Deviant Behavior

WITCHCRAFT: Individual and group behavior intended to influence natural events and experiences through the use of special knowledge of supernatural forces or hidden spiritual forces governing nature. An individual who regularly engages in such activity and adopts an identity based on that practice is a witch. Witchcraft falls in the sociological study of deviance when it is defined or reacted to as a violation of shared religious or social norms.

A Type of Social Control

WITCH HUNT: Organized attempts to control people or groups by lodging accusations of deviance through institutional control mechanisms. Such hunts are earmarked by accusations that are difficult to prove or disprove and by motives other than those publically professed.

A Type of Collective Behavior

WITCH CRAZE: Commonly used term to refer to surges of collective, contagious, escalating, and emotion-laden behavior intended to control witches and witchcraft.

Figure 1.3. Different features of the topic are highlighted when conceived of as deviance, social control, or collective behavior.

assumption that people with histories of contentious conduct or practitioners of folk magic were liable to attack. Thus, conduct is relevant to some degree but not in the imaginary demonic form conceived by elite demonologists. Moreover, many victims are drawn into the craze through mere association with others who were charged or based on accusations made under torture. Finally, many of the same conditions that could increase witch hunts through heightened intolerance or threats to elites could increase the availability of targets (i.e., the frequency of contentious conduct, the prevalence of people entering into trick-or-treat situations, the prevalence of practitioners of folk magic, etc.). Most theories, including those summarized in the next chapter, do not require increases in potential targets or targeted behaviors to explain witch hunts. Yet, the general conditions identified by theories that attempt to explain variation in deviant conduct are quite similar to those conditions identified as relevant to witch hunts as a panic or witch hunts as social control—cultural conflict, strain, or disorganization induced by "troubles," problems, changes, shifts, or transformations in emerging nation-states.

In chapter 2, three general brands of theory that have dominated both historical and sociological scholarship on the witch hunts will be outlined, all focusing on witch trials as instances of variation in social control. Several theories introduced in this chapter will be examined further and classified in terms of their focus on witch hunts as a form of (1) ritual sacrifice, (2) strategic persecution, or (3) scapegoating. The theories are basically theories of social control in that they each involve the three-party interaction central to Gibbs's definition of "social" control and were carried out through formal institutions designed to control behavior and people. Yet, surges of witch trials also take on the some of the characteristics of panics and other forms of collective behavior. Moreover, witch hunts can reflect surges in the visibility and prevalence of the types of people and behavior that generate charges of witchcraft. One of the reasons that such episodes capture the attention of such a wide audience is the fact that they can be viewed in so many different ways, but that fact also makes the subject matter somewhat illusive to academic specialists. Chapter 2 will take steps toward examining actual empirical issues in the study of early modern witch hunts by condensing, simplifying, and contrasting theories.

Notes

1. Black has been inconsistent on the issue of motivation. For example, he declares that his concept of social control entails no assumptions about "the subjective meanings of social control for those who exercise it or experience it" (1983: 34, n. 1). Yet, in that same work and others (1984, 1993), he elaborates the view that some forms of crime are instances of social control ("self-help") in that they are responses to deviance or expressions of a grievance. He gives no clue as to how crime can be shown to be "an expression of grievance" without considering the subjective meanings of the experience to those involved. The examples that Black uses are situations where behavior that violates criminal law "is moralistic and involves the pursuit of justice" (34), and he deems conduct that involves such grievances to be a form of "social control," even when the conduct is "an immediate response to the offense." Motives and meanings appear to be crucial to differentiating between crimes that are instances of social control and those that are not. However, Black seems to believe that concepts and theories ignoring motives and subjective meanings are somehow sociologically superior to those that incorporate such notions, and he continually declares that his theory does not require attention to such issues.

One characteristic of Gibbs's definition that sets it apart from Black's work is his emphasis on social control as attempts at manipulation via a third party, whether that third party is an actual person or a reference to "society," "expectations," or "norms." It is this third element that distinguishes *social* control from external behavioral control or simple interpersonal responses or reactions. Although Black distinguishes self-help as a form of social control from social control "through third parties such as police officers or judges," his only justification for including it as a type of social control is that it can be a response to deviant behavior (i.e., an expression of a grievance). However, only some forms of self-help would qualify as social control under Gibbs's definition: attempts by the grieved to manipulate the behavior of the offender through or by a third party, or attempts to manipulate the behavior of others through a response to the offender. A mere expression of anger or vengeance would not qualify as social control for Gibbs.

Black seems to recognize the necessity of emphasizing the "social" dimension of social control in his examples even though his definition of crime and self-help as social control is not specifically social (i.e., "an expression of a grievance"). If an animal kills another in self-defense or in defense of territory, pack, or young, it is not "social" control. The same situation involving humans is not "social" control, according to Gibbs's delineation. Gibbs's definition would exclude mere self-defense or defense of others. In short, while Black excludes social control via third parties as instances of crime as "self-help" by definition, there are three parties involved in all situations where the conduct is a expression of a grievance. Grievances can only be distinguished from anger, rage, or self-defense by invocation of a third party, whether real or imaginary.

2. According to Smelser (1962: 75), "Empirically some types of behavior are on the borderline between collective behavior and ceremonial behavior," and he cites lynching as an example. As a hostile outburst associated with economic and status deprivation, it qualifies as collective behavior; but when conceived of as a quasi-institutionalized form of justice or a collective ritual to reaffirm a value system, it does not.

Witch hunts were conducted through religious and secular courts and are further from the borderline in terms of Smelser's definition than lynching. However, by precluding such phenomena from the study of collective behavior, the craze- or panic-like behavior of elites is pushed into other substantive arenas where it is defined as a political strategy. Although mobs panic and riot, elites process their crazes and panics through institutions and legal-cultural belief systems.

CHAPTER TWO

Explaining Witch Hunts

Sacrifice, Persecution, and Scapegoat Theories

Ein erschröckliche geschicht/so zu Derneburg in der Graffschafft Reinsteyn/am Hartz gelegen/von dreyen Zauberin/unnd zwayen Mañen/In etlichen tagen des Monats Octobris Im 1 5 5 5. Jare ergangen ist.

Die alte Schlang der Teüffel/dieweyl er Got/und zůvoran den Sun Gottes/unsern Herrn Jesum Christum/und das gantze menschliche geschlecht/fürnemlich umb unsers Haylands Christi willen hasset/hat er sich bald im anfang/und kürtzlich nach der erschaffung umb dz weibsbild/als umb die/welcher same seinen kopff zertretten solt/angenom̃en/dieselbigen durch sein hinderlist und lugen/zů dem jämerlichen fal/deß unglaubens vñ ungehorsams wider Got gebracht/Darauß das gantz menschlich geschlecht/in ewige verdamnuß vñ verderben komen were/so Christus unser Hayland/den zorn des Vatters nicht weck genomen/und das gericht wider uns auffgehaben het. Nu behelt der alte Feind gleichwol alten haß wider Christum/und uns/für vñ für/und helt auch sein alte weyse/er setzet sonderlich dem weiblichen gschlecht hart zů/als dem schwecheren werckzeug/damit er sie von Christo wegreysse/vñ in ewige verdamnuß füre/vñ wie er zů Eua sprach/sie wurden werdē wie die Götter/Also bläßt er noch das gifft in der weyber hertzen/lernet sie zaubern/auff das er sie klůg mache/das sie mehr wissen dann andere leüt/und also den Göttern gleich werden/damit macht er sie im anhengig/und zů Teüffels dienerin/ja auch zů Teuffels breüten/wie dise jämerliche geschicht/welche warhafftigklich also wie unden angezaiget/am Hartz ergangen ist/Die derhalben also gemalet vñ geschriben/im druck auß gangen. Auff das doch die rohe lose welt/zů Gottes forcht erwecket/und von dem Gottlosen wesen abgeschreckt werden/ Dann Gott der allmächtige derhalben solche Exempel uns sehen laßt/das er damit unsere harten hertzen durch dise erschröckliche exempel / zur forcht Göttliches gerichts/und straffe erwecke/man mag es malen/predigen/singen und sagen/vñ wie man jmer kan den leüten einbilden/damit der laydige hauffe ein wenig zů Gottes forcht/gehorsam/und zucht gezogen werde/besonder zů disen letsten zeyten/in welchē der listige Sathan/dieweyl er mercket/das der tag des gerichts sich nahet/gar rasend toll und unsinnig ist/und bede durch sich und seine gelider/ grewlicher weyse/wider Christum und sein armes heüfflein wüttet/Die ellende welt aber dargegē so frey sicher in allem můtwillen dahin lebet/als ob der Teuffel vor langst gestorben sey/und kain Got/kain gericht oder straff/verhanden were/Der Almächtig Got und vatter/unsers Herrn Jesu Christi/wölle dem grimigen feinde wehren/sein armes heüfflein vor im und seinen glidern schützen und handthaben/seinem und der seinen wütten und toben/einmal ein ende machen/durch Jesum Christum Amen.

¶ Folget die geschichte / so zů Derneburg in der Graffschafft Reynstein am Hartz gelegen/ergangen ist/ Im October des 1 5 5 5. Jars.

From a broadside newsletter, Derneberg (Harz), 1555. Reprinted with permission of Dover Publications.

Attempts to explain early modern witch hunts or other dramatic, epidemic surges in punishment are bound to invoke the concept of a "scapegoat" at some point in an analysis. Yet, the concept itself is rarely discussed, and the process of scapegoating is taken for granted. It is an ancient concept borrowed and modified from Jewish ceremony on the Day of Atonement. In its original form, the high priest presented two goats to Jehovah before the tabernacle door, casting lots to decide which was to be slain as a sin offering (*For Jehovah*) and which was to be sent into the wilderness (*For Azazel*). The latter goat, a "scapegoat," is given the burden of the people's sins to carry away.[1]

Of course, views that certain historical episodes or events are instances of "scapegoating" are based on historical hindsight and current knowledge about the "real" causes of problems and the "real" motives of those making such accusations. Because the dominant belief in modern times is that Jews were not responsible for the Black Death in the mid-fourteenth century, blaming them is readily conceived of as a displacement of anxiety onto a minority group, as an elite diversionary strategy to avert blame for problems that they could not solve or as an excuse for persecution. Because ornery women could not have appeared as specters and caused the many strange misfortunes experienced in their villages, it appears eminently logical to look for other reasons that they would be blamed. Scapegoats "carry away" the people's burden and may be adopted as one strategy in a repertoire of contention.

The concept of persecution is often introduced together with scapegoating as another crucial consideration in the explanation for witch hunts. Indeed, modern use of the term *witch hunt* incorporates elements of both persecution and scapegoating. In "Witchcraft Past and Present," Christina Larner (1984) defines a *witch hunt* as "pursuit of a group of persons for their supposed characteristics or beliefs rather than for anything they have done" or "the relentless pursuit of an individual by a group through artificial or contrived charges" (88). In *The Scapegoat*, René Girard (1986) argues that terms such as *persecution* and *scapegoating* are related as part of a universal underlying structure to mythology that he calls "a persecution text." He uses the myth of Oedipus as an example of a typical persecution text. Oedipus is blamed for the plague in Thebes because he killed his father and married his mother. He must be banished to end the epidemic. Moreover, he has numerous "signs" of a potential victim: He was abandoned as an infant. He limps. As a foreigner, he is a stranger, but a stranger with some power and, hence, a real threat. He must be punished to end the plague. The attribution of blame for a crisis (the plague) to unintentional incest and patricide by Oedipus (an innocent victim or scapegoat) requires punishment (ritual violence), and Oedipus has the type of differentiating characteristics that make people liable as targets of unjust persecution.

Girard makes the dramatic claim that "all human language, and other cultural institutions, in fact, originated in collective murder" (193). *To persecute* originally meant "to prosecute," and *martyr* meant "witness." The conflicts involved in early Christianity transformed the meaning of the terms to refer to unjust acts of collective violence against innocent or heroic victims (202). Similarly, the study of "stereotypes of persecution" forces us "to turn to words that are related" such as *crisis*, *crime*, *criteria*, and *critique*. All four words are derived from the Greek verb *krino*, "which means not only to judge, distinguish, differentiate, but also to accuse and condemn a victim" (22).

A third concept relevant to the explanation of witch hunts is sacrifice. One goat is sacrificed to atone for the people's sins, and another is sent away into the wilderness. In Christian religious ceremony, sacrifice is linked to historical episodes of institutional ritual violence and persecution. Christ is "the Lamb of God" who bears the burden and carries away the sins of the world by willingly sacrificing his life. He is not responsible for those sins but accepts his role as a savior whose duty is to bear the brunt of blame for humankind and allow them a new start. From one view, his crucifixion was a willing sacrifice. From another it was an instance of persecution in which ruling elites targeted the leader of a growing heretic threat, not so much for anything he had done as for his beliefs. To the degree that his crucifixion diverted blame for worldly ills, it could be seen as an instance of diversionary scapegoating. If Jesus provided a convenient target for displacing mob anger and collective anxiety, then he was a scapegoat in yet another sense of the word. Of course, from the standpoint of those responsible for society's well-being, he was a criminal processed through institutional machinery to maintain law and order and to deter others from similar transgressions.

Contemporary attempts to explain witch hunts rarely view them as instances of ecclesiastic or secular law enforcement—that is, a response to an alarming increase in real witchcraft. Rather, contemporary accounts focus on witch hunts as (1) a functional ritual ceremony necessitated by disruptions, crises, or social changes that threaten the survival of the community as a corporate entity; (2) strategic persecution encouraged by elites and directed at representatives of threatening groups; or (3) a diversionary strategy for diverting blame or cathartic displacement of anger and anxiety onto a scapegoat.

Elements of all three types of theories may end up encompassed in one discussion, but, as will be argued, certain emphases and themes are unique to each. Indeed, Girard's treatise on scapegoating, collective violence, and persecution as central to the structure of language and mythology suggests that theories about institutionalized ritual violence may share a common structure and refer to different nuances of the same phenomenon.

However, there are also differences among the concepts of sacrifice, persecution, and scapegoating that can be used to highlight unique aspects of each theory. For example, Kai Erikson's (1966) *Wayward Puritans* exemplifies themes that, although not directly invoking a metaphor of "sacrifice," come very close to it in the process of highlighting the ritual ceremonial aspects of witch hunts. William Chambliss's (1976) neo-Marxist challenge to Erikson's theory and a variety of historical studies stress "persecution themes" that are similar in some ways to scapegoating theories, but distinguished by their focus on witches as "symbolic" of threatening groups. Finally, a variety of theories treat witch hunting as scapegoating—the diversion of blame or the cathartic displacement of anger through blame. Most scapegoat theories also involve notions of persecution, with some versions focusing on the scapegoats as serving general system needs rather than the interests of specific groups.

Witch Hunts as Sacrificial Ceremonies

The general public and most undergraduates are likely to view criminal behavior and much of the realm of "deviant behavior" as encompassing "bad" or "evil" activities, qualifying as "dysfunctional" social problems to be countered by vigorous efforts at governmental control. As part of a counterargument to such conventional and "commonsense" logic, sociologists are inclined to "set them straight" by discussing the "positive functions" of crime or deviance, drawing on Durkheim's discussion of crime as a "normal" characteristic of social systems. Most, if not all, introductory deviance or criminology texts and readers include a discussion or list of "the functions of deviance" (e.g., Schur 1979: 70; Landis 1980; Hagan 1985; Farrell and Swigert 1988: 36–37; Bynum and Thompson 1989: 21–22).

Although textbooks on deviance go on to challenge all sorts of theory and research on grounds of conceptual, empirical, and methodological problems, discussions of the "functions of deviance" are presented in a cursory, ritualistic fashion with no attention to validation. Even textbooks for advanced classes in the sociology of deviance show little concern about clear delineation of concepts or the development of clear propositions or hypotheses about the phenomena encompassed. For example, sometimes it is the *rejection* or punishment of the deviant that is used to illustrate the functions of deviance (e.g., rejecting the deviant contributes to group solidarity and reaffirmation of norms). In other examples, deviant behavior itself is depicted as functional (e.g., deviant behavior can lead to social change or function as a "safety valve"). For example, one of the propositions in Dentler and Erikson's (1959) "The Functions of Deviance in Groups" is that "groups will resist any trend toward alienation of a member whose behavior is deviant" (102). Erikson (1966) depicts his explanation of the waves of ritual punishment in New England as an extension of this earlier work with no explanation of how banishment and execution (the ultimate rejection of deviant members) can qualify as resistance to alienation of deviant group members (see Roshier 1977 for a more elaborate critique).

In his discussion of "hidden" procedural rules in the sociological study of deviant behavior over thirty years ago, Travis Hirschi (1973) pointed out that sociologists embrace paradox and irony to such an extent that "assertions considered paradoxical or ironic are not required to meet the standards applied to straightforward hypotheses" (161). He noted that discussions of the "functions of deviance" provide numerous illustrations of this bias. The notions that deviance has functional consequences and that such functions are relevant to explaining its persistence are ironic and paradoxical in view of common folk beliefs and conventional wisdom. Sociologists' fondness for irony and paradox has led to the reiteration of arguments that are rarely scrutinized for clarity or consistency.

Since discussions of the functions of deviance can be viewed as attempts to stimulate unconventional thinking and objectivity, it may be unfair to expect a clear specification of what it is that serves such functions and the type of consequences of that phenomenon that can be considered "functions." However, it is not unreasonable to hold such expectations for works that purport to provide scholarly support for specific functional theories. When competing theories are examined, their differences and the underlying causal logic unique to each has to be specified.

A useful tool for clarifying functional theories is Arthur Stinchcombe's (1968: 80–93) analysis of the logic of functional explanation. Stinchcombe notes, "By a functional explanation we mean one in which the *consequences* of some behavior or social arrangement are essential elements of the *causes* of that behavior" (80). The elementary causal structure of a complete functionalist logic is reproduced in figure 2.1. According to that logic, some type of threat or tension undermines a "homeostatic" condition of a social system. The decline in that condition leads to a response or reinforcement of an existing response that reinstates or reinforces that homeostatic condition. Functional explanations are, therefore, complex causal theories "with a special causal priority of the consequences of the activity in the total explanation" (100).

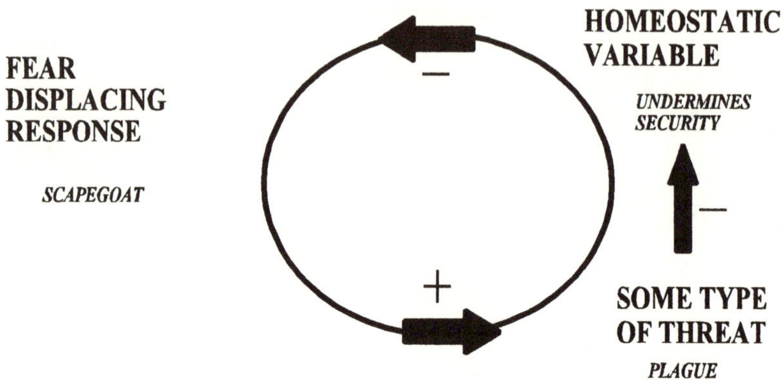

Figure 2.1. The logic of functional explanations (based on Stinchcombe 1968). Most theories of witch hunts follow a similar logic. Some type of threat, either to society or to some members of a society (e.g., plague), leads to a decline in security. The minus sign between the threat and the homeostatic variable means as the threat increases, security decreases. People do not like such a state and begin searching for a response (e.g., scapegoating). The minus sign between security and the response means that as security declines, the search for a response increases. Finally, for the response to function as expected, it has to reestablish security (the homeostatic condition)—hence, the positive sign between the response and the homeostatic variable. In the example, scapegoating increases and security increases (i.e., a positive relationship). A variety of different threats, homeostatic variables, and responses can be found in the witch hunt literature.

The best-known work in sociology dealing with witch hunts from a functionalist perspective is Erikson's (1966) *The Wayward Puritans*. Erikson includes the witch hunts in Salem, Massachusetts, in 1692 as one of three surges in ritualistic punishment that stemmed, he argues, from various threats to communal survival and solidarity. Surges in ritualistic violence or punishment such as witch hunts allegedly functioned to redefine or reaffirm the boundaries of the community. He builds his argument on the approximate coincidence of certain crisis-generating events with three "crime waves": the persecution of Anne Hutchinson, the persecution of the Quakers, and the Salem witch hunts. His basic theoretical model is a Durkheimian functional model in which a tension threatens a "homeostatic" condition of a social system (e.g., survival, moral consensus, solidarity), resulting in ceremonial social control rituals that function to reestablish homeostasis (Jensen 1988).

While the targets of witch hunts are clearly unwilling victims, Erikson's theory contains connotations of ritual sacrifice. Ritual violence is depicted as serving functions for the whole community, and the deviant is depicted as playing a role that, when empty, is filled by new deviants as needed by the system. Erikson (1966) argues that episodes such as the trial of Anne Hutchinson should be seen "as a ceremony and not a test of guilt, as a demonstration rather than an inquiry. . . . The various participants seemed to be moving in cadence, joined together in a kind of ceremonial chant" (103–4). Societies "need" deviants, and, although they may not be aware of it, offenders "manage to fashion" a stable rate by moving into those roles when they are empty (179). Deviants respond to "rules" in much the same sense as "a participant in a festival" (29).

The emphasis on roles, cadence, and ceremony, with people marching into deviant roles when the system needs them, carries with it connotations similar to notions of ritual sacrifice. When needed for a ceremonial sacrifice, someone will come forward into the role and carry away the sins of the world. If new deviants are needed, they can be found in ample supply waiting on the margins. Deviants are participants in a game that ultimately serves the wider system's needs "by patrolling the outer edges of group space and by providing a contrast which gives the rest of the community some sense of their own territorial identity" (Erikson 1966: 196). In short, badness is depicted as having "good" consequences.

In fact, ceremonies that define morality by highlighting deviance are so essential to system survival that, in the absence of one type, society will shift to another. Erikson draws on Emile Durkheim's "society of saints" discussion to propose that there is a constant level of deviance in society. In *The Rules of Sociological Method*, Durkheim (1958) argued that in a society of "exemplary individuals" where "properly so-called" crimes are unknown, "faults which appear venial to the laymen will create there the same scandal that the ordinary offense does in ordinary consciousness" (68–69). Because deviance-highlighting ceremonies are functional, the members of this "society of saints" shift to deviation and become "deviants" whose transgressions would not be noticed were there more traditional deviant members available. Erikson argues that were a community to "lop off its most marginal people, it is unlikely that the volume of deviation in the community would really be reduced. Either new ranks of offenders would move into the vacuum in place of their departed fellows . . . or the agencies of control would focus on a new target area" (26–27). This line of reasoning leads Erikson to propose that "the amount of deviation experienced by a community will remain fairly stable over time" (27).

On the surface, the argument that the amount of deviation will remain relatively stable over time seems to be contradicted by the argument that there are "crime waves" induced by "unsettling historical change" (70) or that such waves are an "index to social disruption and change" (153). How can deviance be "fairly" constant and also wavelike? The answer is that it is *shifts* in relative attention to different forms of deviance that generate "crime waves" and that such shifts are most likely to occur during periods of social disruption and change. The changes or "occasions" that trigger such shifts can take several forms. Erikson specifically mentions realignments of power within the group and the appearance of new adversaries or enemies outside of the group as possibilities.

Erikson's description of the different problems confronting the Puritan community over time leads into a statement about "The Shapes of the Devil" (the title of his chapter 3):

> As the wilderness took on this new character, it seemed that even the Devil had given up his more familiar disguises. He no longer lurked in the underbrush, for most of it had been cut away; he no longer assumed the shape of hostile Indians, for most of them had retreated inland for the moment; he no longer sent waves of heretics to trouble the Bay, for most of them lived quietly under the protection of toleration; he no longer appeared in the armies of the Counter-Reformation, for the old battlefields were still too far away to excite the imagination. But his presence was felt everywhere, and when the colonists began to look for his new hiding places they found him crouched in the very heart of the Puritan colony. (157–58)

The "shape" of deviance, like the shape of the Devil, appears as "waves" of attention even when the total volume of all forms of deviance that could be attended to remains fairly stable. The Devil is always lurking, but with a shifting set of followers at different times.

Erikson assumes a constant tendency in social systems to see the Devil (deviance) lurking "somewhere" and to engage in ritual ceremonies which define moral boundaries by punishing deviants. But, the shape of the Devil (deviance) shifts in response to internal and external changes. Drawing on the logic of the preceding quotation, it can be inferred that variations in the behavior, availability, and protection of traditional targets or enemies can affect the need for new enemies. When traditional, easily discerned enemies disappear (e.g., Indians) or gain new protection (e.g., Quakers), attention shifts to enemies that are harder to discern because they are found among "the wonders of the invisible world" (Mather 1693). The specific circumstances that "make [the Devil's] presence felt" more intensely at some times than others and the full range of "occasions" that might trigger looking for him have yet to be specified.

Erikson's basic argument can be organized to follow a functionalist logic. Witch hunts are instances of institutionalized ritual violence that arise when moral consensus or communal solidarity declines (i.e., a decline in the value of the homeostatic variable, which leads to a structured response). Such ritualistic punishment functions to bring the community together and rejuvenates moral solidarity or equilibrium (i.e., the response functions to reenhance the homeostatic variable).

In an experiment dealing with the rejection of deviance, Pat Lauderdale (1976) formalizes and adds to Erikson's functional model through a set of propositions that precisely follows the logical structure of a functional explanation:

1. an external threat to a corporate social system produces an initial, momentary loss of solidarity since the constituents become unsure of the continued existence of the system;
2. in order to insure its existence as a corporate structure and reestablish its solidarity, the system increases its rejection of the deviants, thereby shifting the moral boundary;
3. the rejection of the deviant and movement of moral boundary reduce the extent of the internal threat (the deviants) by placing the deviants further from the moral boundary;
4. the rejection of the deviants and movement of the boundary also prepare the system for repulsion of the external threat by bringing divergent (but not deviant and nondeviant) parts into a unified whole, thereby reestablishing solidarity and reaffirming the purity of the nondeviants and the moral boundary of the social system, as well as insuring the corporate existence of the system. (663)

Lauderdale's theory includes all of the elements of functionalist explanation. A "threat" (T) leads to a momentary decline in solidarity (the "homeostatic" variable, H), which leads to an increase in the rejection of deviants (S), which reestablishes solidarity (an increase or reinforcement of H).

To test such a boundary maintenance theory of deviance rejection, Lauderdale created two experimental conditions. Groups in one condition experienced an outside threat with a deviant confederate present, and a second set of groups experienced no threat with a deviant confederate present. Lauderdale reports that the groups experiencing an outside threat experienced a momentary decline in solidarity. Moreover, compared to the nonthreat groups, the groups experiencing a threat tended to reject the deviant and exhibit greater intolerance of deviant positions. Furthermore, he reports that, over time, the solidarity of the groups was reestablished and was actually increasing at a faster rate in the threat condition than the nonthreat condition. Overall, Lauderdale claims to have provided considerable support for the boundary maintenance perspective on the functions of deviance.[2]

Lauderdale's use of an experimental model necessitated specific hypotheses and clear application of the logic of a functional explanation. In contrast, Erikson was quite ambiguous about the disruptions that threatened homeostasis (T), the system need that was threatened (H), the selection of a particular response (S), and whether the response functioned to reestablish homeostasis. Although two general "disruptions" are suggested, specific threats to homeostasis that cause shifts in the perceived deployment or shape of deviance are only vaguely discussed. Moreover, circumstances that affect the selection of targets are hinted at, but never formally proposed as part of the theory. In fact, evidence that the punitive response was "functional" is never presented. In studies of witchcraft in southwestern Germany, H. C. Erik Midelfort (1972) argues, "Society was not made stronger and more cohesive by such trials, but weaker and more torn by suspicion and resentment" (4). John Demos (1982: 308) states that witch hunts affected the behavior of New Englanders but through fear of becoming a target of witch hunts (i.e., deterrence) rather than through renewed moral solidarity or consensus. Elaine Breslaw (1996) believes that "instead of bringing the community together and rejuvenating an ethic of neighborliness, the New England Puritans almost destroyed their sense of communal purpose" (104). Witch hunts may have had consequences that were functional for the interests of some members of the community, or they may have displaced the most immediate anxieties of the people, but it does not appear that they served a reintegrative function.

Additional criticisms of Erikson's approach have been elaborated by Marxist critics, and his version of functional theory can be contrasted with a variety of theories that discuss witch hunts more specifically in the language of group conflict and persecution. When the focus shifts to group conflict and persecution, greater emphasis is placed on the characteristics and interests that differentiate the parties to the conflict. Moreover, the victims are likely to be realistic threats to those supporting war against them, rather than just the next set of deviants ready to serve the functional needs of the collective.

Witch Hunts as Strategic Persecution

In Erikson's (1966) *Wayward Puritans*, deviance serves functions for a social system that explains why, even in a "society of saints," deviance persists. The deployment pattern of that deviance shifts in response to internal and external disruptions or crises, which generate "waves" of ritual punishment. Such waves, however, constitute shifts in attention among types of deviance rather than increases in the volume of deviance in a system.

In sociological discussions of theory, such "functionalist" perspectives are typically contrasted with "conflict" perspectives as alternative paradigms for understanding social organization and social change in human society. From such perspectives, witch hunts are veiled instances of persecution, with the targets of such persecution real or symbolic threats to the values or interest of groups with the power to persecute. Witch hunts are viewed as a strategy for maintaining power or as one tactic employed in contentious politics.

In 1976, William Chambliss, one of the foremost conflict theorists in the study of crime and social control, described the theoretical debate involving the two perspectives as "a gigantic struggle between the previously dominant, functional paradigm and the emergent conflict paradigm" (1). Typically, functionalist perspectives are identified with the Durkheimian legacy and conflict perspectives with an alternative Marxian legacy.

The contrast between the two is illustrated by Chambliss's critique of Erikson's theory of "crime waves," including the Salem witch trials. Theorists operating from a Durkheimian functionalist perspective attempt to explain recurrent witch hunts in terms of the functions they serve for a general, homeostatic property of society or the community. Theorists operating from a Marxist conflict perspective attempt to explain the same phenomenon but in terms of the interests or values of powerful groups or strata in society. For example, within a Durkheimian functionalist perspective, the trial of Anne Hutchinson is considered a ritual that functioned to reestablish moral solidarity when that homeostatic characteristic of the Puritan community was disrupted or threatened. In contrast, from a conflict or Marxian perspective, the same event is viewed as an attempt to reaffirm patriarchal religious authority threatened by Anne Hutchinson. The conflict perspective assumes conflicting interests among socially differentiated groups competing for power; the Durkheimian approach assumes collective problems and common community interests that are served by collective rituals.

It is unfortunate that the term *functionalism* is linked so intimately to the Durkheimian tradition since the emphasis on the struggle between a functionalist paradigm and a conflict paradigm ignores the fact that both Durkheimian and Marxist theories incorporate a functionalist-causal logic.[3] As defined by Arthur Stinchcombe (1968) Marxist explanations of social phenomena involve "functional arguments in a system of unequal power" (93).

Functional models are a specific type of causal model in which consequences of a phenomenon for some homeostatic property of a social system explain the recurrent nature of that phenomenon. Durkheimian functional models emphasize consequences for the community or system as a whole. Marxist models emphasize the consequences of a particular phenomenon for the values or interests of differentiated groups within society and the power of different groups to bring about or sustain arrangements that are functional for them. Thus, both consensus-oriented theorists and conflict-oriented theorists are functionalist. A more appropriate designation for the struggle discussed by Chambliss would be "consensus functionalism" versus "conflict functionalism."

The conflict perspective developed into the dominant perspective in most sociological scholarship on the law and social control beginning in the late 1960s. The responses of dominant groups to real and symbolic threats from other groups and the use of law to protect the interests of elites have been central to the explanation of vagrancy statutes (Chambliss 1964), Prohibition (Gusfield 1986), juvenile law (Platt 1969), law and law enforcement in general (Quinney 1970), and an array of additional examples of efforts to control problem populations.

On the surface, explanations that link law and law enforcement to the values or interests of specific groups and identify the reasons that the targets of such activities constitute a threat to those groups seem more empirically defensible than theories that invoke vague, ill-defined properties of whole systems such as "moral crises" or "boundary crises." It is specific groups whose values or interests are threatened and that define the situation as a moral crisis. Such groups are responding to identifiable threats from other groups. Threats involve discernible groups and the activities of those groups. Responses are attempts by other discernible groups to deal with those threats (i.e., strategic persecution).

Conflict functionalist explanations focusing on specific conflicts appear more empirically defensible than consensus functionalist explanations invoking vague collective properties because the groups and conflicts involved can be specified in detail and the struggle documented. Even when the focus is phenomena that do not appear to be part of a clearly defined struggle for power, such as crime control, the characteristics of the targets of control can be shown to differ from the characteristics of those who shape the law and influence its enforcement. Explanations of changes in law and law enforcement over time can be anchored in identifiable changes in the perceived magnitude of threats and "measured" by the size and visibility of threatening groups.

However, the empirical specificity of such conflict functionalist explanations is often illusory. Considerable ambiguity can be discerned in the process of linking specific laws and enforcement activities to the interests or values of specific groups. Just as consensus functionalist explanations start with known "outcomes" and then proceed to specify related threats and vague, systemic problems resolved by those outcomes, conflict functionalist explanations of specific instances of law and law enforcement are post hoc interpretations as well. For example, if a decrease in imprisonment occurs in the population, a conflict functionalist can explain it in terms of the labor supply. When industry needs labor, fewer people are imprisoned. When there is a surplus of labor, more people are imprisoned (e.g., Rusche and Kirchheimer 1939; Greenberg 1977; Berk et al. 1981). If people are withholding their labor during a labor shortage, vagrancy statutes and wage restrictions are established to keep costs down (Chambliss 1964).

Yet, the deinstitutionalization and diversion of offenders during times of relatively high unemployment is "explained" in the same terms. Steven Spitzer (1975) argues that it is in the interests of capitalists and the capitalist system to "normalize" as much crime as possible because of the high cost of imprisonment. Because group interests are as loosely defined and as vague as system needs, interests quite consistent with totally contrary outcomes can be discerned after the fact.

The most recent statement of a conflict theory of witch hunts is Jon Oplinger's (1990) *The Politics of Demonology*. Oplinger proposes "A Theory of the Mass Production of Deviance" expressed in the following set of statements:

1.0 The higher the level of external demand, the higher the rate of deviance production.
1.1 The greater the perceived threat to the status and resources of dominant groups, the higher the level of external demand.
2.0 The less a social control system is subject to accountability and organizational restraint, the greater the potential for deviance production.
2.1 The potential for the exercise of accountability is inversely related to the concentration of power within society.
2.2 The greater the immunity of the resource base of an apparatus of social control to the inroads of other organizations, the greater the resistance to the exercise of accountability.
3.0 The potential for the mass production of deviance is greatest in societies characterized by great concentration of power, a high level of external and internal demand, and an unrestrained social control system.

4.0 Within a society that is normally characterized by a restrained social control system, the advent of a high level of external demand will foster a relaxation of both accountability and organizational restraint.
4.1 Over time, the maintenance of a high level of external demand will bring about changes in procedural law that will enhance the ability of dominant groups to manufacture deviance.
5.0 The broader the perceived threat to status and self-interest, the more likely it is that powerful groups will act in concert.
5.1 The more concerted the actions of powerful interest groups, the higher the level of external demand.
5.2 The more concerted the actions of powerful interest groups, the less potential there is for the exercise of accountability (as per 4.0).
6.0 Coalitions of interest groups will tend to break down in the absence of the perception that they are facing a common menace. (31–32)

Oplinger devotes his monograph to explicating such propositions, and his elaborate treatment will not be reiterated here. His theory is intended to apply to a variety of historical episodes where deviance is "mass produced," including witch hunts. His argument falls within the conflict-persecution tradition in that the focus is on the interests of dominant groups and threats to those interests.

Although more formal and precise than prior theories, Oplinger's theory does not lead to any specific predictions relevant to the timing or distribution of witch hunts. For example, propositions 1.0 and 1.1 imply that witch hunts should be most likely to occur when the status and resources of dominant groups are threatened. With no limits on what constitutes a threat to the status of dominant groups, some sort of threat can be discerned retrospectively to explain known episodes of the mass production of deviance. Just as there is always something that can be declared to be a crisis prompting the functional sacrifice of an endless supply of deviants, there is always some way in which the status, resources, and interests of dominant groups can be defined as threatened.

Difficulties in delineating the actual nature of the threats to elite interests represented by witch hunts can be illustrated using Chambliss's (1976) interpretation of the New England crime waves. The targets of two of the crime waves, Anne Hutchinson and the Quakers, were visible threats to Puritan authority. Hutchinson challenged prevailing Puritan doctrine and was punished for that challenge. Quakers arrived in the colonies and challenged Puritan authority as well. Such groups were real, visible, and confrontational threats to ruling elites. In contrast, the people punished in the Salem witch hunts are depicted by Chambliss as "symbolic" threats to ruling elites, with no explanation given for such a shift or for the elite interest that was served through such symbolic ritual violence.

In one of the few articles on witch hunts in a sociology journal, Nachman Ben-Yehuda (1980) proposes "a sociologist's perspective on the European Witch Craze" which combines elements of both functionalist and conflict interpretations of witch hunts. Among other questions, Ben-Yehuda attempts to deal with why witch hunts began when they did, why the targets were women, and why they ended when they did. He attributes the beginning to the vested interests of the new Dominican order that defined the nature of the witch threat, a decline in the authority of the Catholic Church, and devastating disease epidemics. He argues that women were the targets not only because their inferior status made them ready scapegoats but because their movement into the labor force "produced a virulent misogynic ideology" (21). The termination of the witch hunts is attributed to the official recognition of religious pluralism, symbolized by the Peace of Westphalia and the end of the Thirty Years War. He elaborates on these arguments in *Deviance and Moral Boundaries* (1985).

Historians have proposed numerous theories of witch hunting that emphasize persecution, and several have proposed that the common link among the three waves of witch hunting in New England was that they all involved female-linked threats to male religious authority. Through a detailed analysis of characteristics of the possessed, accusers, the accused, and the severity of response, Carol Karlsen (1987) presents convincing evidence that the Salem witches shared numerous characteristics with the victims of the prior two waves of persecution. Hutchinson, the Quakers, and the Salem witches all represented challenges to patriarchal control of women. John Demos (1982) had noted such similarities in earlier research, but Karlsen strengthens the case through statistical evidence of certain biases at each stage of processing and through a comparison of the different actors involved in the witch-hunting process.

Discussing witch hunt research in general, Anne Llewellyn Barstow (1994) criticizes prior historical theories, including those that emphasize persecution, for inadequately attending to witch hunts within the context of a history of *sexual* violence against women. When details of the torture and punishment of women as witch suspects are detailed, the witch hunts can be conceived of as institutional sexual assault. She argues that "having a female body was the factor most likely to render one vulnerable to being called a witch. The sexual connotations and the explicit sexual violence utilized in many of the trials make this fact clear. Just which women were targeted and under what circumstances reveals much about the status of women in early modern Europe" (16). Barstow notes that, while Christina Larner's study of witch hunting in Scotland provides all the details that suggest that witch hunting is part of the "sex war" and a ruse for persecution by gender, she directs our attention away from that issue to more traditional political issues. However, as already noted, Larner (1981) defines witch hunting in general in a manner that equates it with persecution.

Because persecution theories involve arguments about motives and intentions, they can be depicted quite readily using Gibbs's definition of *social control* as intentional attempts at manipulation of one party by another party through a third party. In fact, the differences among witch hunt theories tend to involve differences in *who* is attempting to control *whom* by punishing *witches*? In Barstow's theory, men (the first party) are attempting to control women (the second party) via the definition and punishment of women as witches (the third party). The women most likely to serve such motives are symbols of deviation from patriarchally defined gender roles.

Robert Muchembled's (1977) theory of witch hunts involves attempts at social control at two levels of aggregation. Christian political and religious elites (the first party) were attempting to undermine commitment of peasants (the second party) to non-Christian cultural beliefs by defining and punishing those women witches (the third party) who best symbolized those beliefs. Since it was women who were most crucial to reinforcing such beliefs and socializing the young into peasant culture, peasant mothers were a more specific target of control (second party) at a lower level of aggregation.

Gunnar Heinsohn and Otto Steiger (1982) propose that the persecution of witches was part of a "pronatalist" campaign by church and state to overcome population shortages generated by plague, famine and war. Abortion, infanticide, and birth control all came under attack together with witchcraft. Not only was the stereotypical witch the antithesis of the reproductive wife, but one of the categories of women most likely to be suspected—the midwife—was a bastion of knowledge about birth control. Witches were viewed as threats to children, enthralled with nonreproductive and illegitimate sex, and a potential source of problems of infertility. Thus, the church and state (the first party) were attempting to encourage women (the second party) to marry and reproduce by punishing witches (the third party) who were symbolic enemies of reproduction.

Rodney Stark (2003) is the most recent advocate of a conflict perspective on the witch hunts. In *For the Glory of God*, he proposes that

> the frequency and intensity of witch-hunting will have been highest where and when: (1) Serious efforts are made to *suppress* magic and sorcery, and there was

> a high probability that *satanism would be imputed* to such activities, *and* (2) there was substantial conflict among religious groups representing credible threats to one another's *institutional power*, causing the withdrawal of tolerance for religious nonconformity, *and* (3) *weak* central ecclesiastical and/or political governance prevented 'national' elites from *curtailing local enthusiasms*. (255)

Stark claims to have "dispatched" arguments that the witch hunts were a response to real witches or witch cults, directed at people who were mentally ill; a product of social change, sexism, or misogyny; a product of greed or fanatical clergy; or a symptom of mass collective psychosis.

It should be noted that Stark focuses on declines in tolerance as a product of religious conflict and does not couch his arguments in terms of persecution or scapegoating. Catholics and Protestants threatened each other's institutional interests, but they looked for enemies in their own ranks. They did not target their enemies. For Stark, witch hunts are more of an outgrowth of shared intolerance across groups, with each group trying to enforce conformity within their own group. He does not invoke the notion that the people targeted were distinct as real or symbolic threats to their groups.

His theory is difficult to classify because he does not attempt to explain why religious conflict should reduce tolerance for nonconformity, nor why they would invoke witchcraft as the type of nonconformity the group cannot tolerate. He rejects Erickson's functionalist explanation but gives no explanation of what intolerance does for the contending parties. Does it displace anxiety for group members? Does it help the group to win? Do witches function as scapegoats carrying away the anxieties of the people? In short, why should intolerance grow?

The attempt to suppress magic is taken as a precondition, as is *satanism* as an official demonology in Stark's perspective. Muchembled attempts to explain the suppression of magic as a strategy directed at peasant women (a strategic persecution theory). Satanism as an official demonology endorsed by the church depicted women as particularly vulnerable, and they were the most likely targets. Why did it depict women in that fashion? Whose interests were served? If the underlying assumption is that groups in conflict have to narrow their moral boundaries, then the theory is similar to Erikson's functional theory; that is, groups tighten their boundaries when threatened. In short, although the theory is couched in terms of conflict, with witch hunts most virulent when contending groups are threatening each other, the theory could be interpreted as a sacrifice theory, a persecution theory, or a scapegoating theory.

Persecution theories tend to embody a functionalist logic with the interests of ruling groups as the homeostatic condition, a threat to realizing those interests (e.g., a labor shortage; an increase in the threatening behavior, size, visibility or power of other groups), and a response intended to reaffirm that group interest or lessen the threat (ritual violence aimed at real or symbolic enemies). Of course, since "interests" are as ambiguous as "system needs," and the response that can realize those interests can occur indirectly through punishment of symbolic enemies, the evidence for any particular perspective can be quite conjectural. Indeed, just as Erikson provided no evidence that ritual punishment solved collective problems, little evidence has been provided that witch hunting served particular group interests. For example, *if* witch hunts were stimulated by a labor shortage, and *if* witch hunts were a means of encouraging reproduction, thereby increasing the labor force, then it would be reasonable to expect marriage and fertility rates to have increased following witch hunts. If no such effects can be discerned, then the theory must address the reasons that such ineffective control techniques were repeatedly used.

It may be that the activity itself is what matters, as in Gusfield's (1986) interpretation of prohibition as a symbolic crusade. Witch hunts may have been one means of expressing group hatreds and reaffirming interests or group values, even if such moral campaigns did not have their intended effects. However, if a theory proposes that witch hunts were a tactic or strategy for realizing certain interests or goals and that such a response recurred over a considerable period of time because it served those interests, some evidence relevant to that argument should be expected.

Witch Hunts as Scapegoating

Social scientists and historians have proposed scapegoat theories for everything from prejudice (Berkowitz 1962a) to war (Levy 1989), and any review of the literature on witch hunts will encounter numerous claims that the early modern witch trials involved "scapegoating." For example, Trevor-Roper (1967) posits that just as the Jews were the scapegoats for the Black Death, witches were the scapegoats of the Wars of Religion. Jeffrey Victor (1992) proposes that "rapid change in a society results in widespread dislocation in people's lives, and the resulting frustration, fear, and anger cause a great many people to seek scapegoats" and that "the internal enemy can be a useful proxy target . . . a stand-in for conflicts between powerful elements within a society" (10). Among such instances are moral crusades pursuing subversives, heretics, witches, and Satanists. Richard Dunn (1979) argues that the ruling class needed scapegoats "to meliorate the impact of social disasters for which they had no remedy" (8–9). Barstow (1994: 57) extends this argument to suggest that elites directed hostility toward women as scapegoats, a plausible strategy considering that female competition for scarce jobs was thought to heighten misogyny in the male-dominated labor force.

Scapegoat theories are extremely common, but researchers have paid relatively little attention to the meaning of *scapegoat* and how it differs from *persecution*. Since the actual targets of ritual violence in persecution theories are, typically, symbolic of the "real" targets, persecution theories bear a resemblance to scapegoat theories. Someone is taking the blame for a crisis that is threatening group interests. However, the victims are symbolic of a group or category that constitutes a real or potential threat as defined by the persecutors. In theories depicting witch hunts as the persecution of women, those persecuted were symbolic of a female threat to patriarchy. In pronatalist theory, women are not reproducing, and the victims are threats to reproduction.

In contrast, the targets of ritual violence in scapegoat theories take the blame for problems either as an intentional diversionary tactic or as a cathartic displacement of anger and frustration. Elements of group persecution may be relevant to explaining how certain groups become vulnerable as targets, but in scapegoat theories, attributions of blame are not part of an intentional strategy for dealing with threatening groups. For example, Dunn's argument that the ruling classes needed scapegoats to meliorate the impact of disasters that they could not remedy is an example of a diversionary theory of witch hunts. The search for witches diverted blame that otherwise would have been directed at the ruling class. Of course, diversion could go hand-in-hand with persecution. The victims selected could be symbolic of threatening groups and provide a convenient diversionary target at the same time.

In his *Cows, Pigs, Wars, and Witches*, Marvin Harris (1974) presents a typical diversion theory: "the poor came to believe that they were being victimized by witches and devils instead of princes and popes. . . . Preoccupied with the fantastic activities of these demons, the distraught, alienated, pauperized masses blamed the rampant Devil instead of the corrupt clergy and rapacious nobility" (205). In this type of scapegoat theory, witch hunts are a means of dispersing and fragmenting "latent energies of protest" (207) that would result in rebellion otherwise.

Dunn, Harris, and others argue that the witch craze was an instance of scapegoating as an elite strategy to shift or displace anger or blame. Other versions of scapegoat theory link witch hunting to a more general inclination to search for scapegoats when there is a need for cathartic displacement of anger and frustration. For example, Jeffrey Victor's (1992: 10) statement that "rapid change in a society results in widespread dislocation in people's lives, and the resulting frustration, fear, and anger cause a great many people to seek scapegoats" does not require that scapegoats be part of a diversionary strategy. Rather, anger or frustration generated by other social forces and events is displaced on scapegoats. Just as the scapegoat carried away sins, as a cathartic displacement, the scapegoat carries away anger and emotion. Targets of ritual violence as cathartic displacement may be selected from among relatively powerless or disadvantaged groups regardless of any need to persecute or control the groups from which they are drawn. Of course, a history of conflict and persecution may make certain groups attractive targets for displacement.

In contrast to diversionary scapegoat theories of witch hunts, scapegoating as cathartic displacement may serve collective ends rather than constituting a veiled strategy for realizing or protecting group interests. Demos (1982: 373–79) summarizes the "harms" (disease, bad weather, famine, fires, hard times) and "signs" (comets, eclipses, earthquakes) that prompted anxiety in seventeenth-century New England. He proposes that variations in such sources of distress are relevant to fluctuations in witchcraft accusations and witch hunts over time. Collective anxiety and distress could be alleviated through ritual violence against witches who, even if not accused of causing those specific harms, were symbolic of Satan's presence and God's disfavor.

Hans Sebald (1978) posits a cathartic displacement version of scapegoat theory in his functionalist explanation of witch hunts:

> Whatever function the witch had, she certainly served as a scapegoat. In other words, her stigma facilitated channeling of all sorts of free-floating anger and anxiety. The epitome of scapegoating took place during the seventeenth century when thousands of witches were condemned and executed to purge the community of distrust and anxiety. It gave desperate emotions, generated by unusual disturbances, a focus. (187)

Witch hunts allow the displacement of crisis-induced or disturbance-induced anger onto scapegoats, and that displacement "keeps the community on an even keel" (193).

Sebald's argument illustrates the use of scapegoating as an explanation of witch hunts within the framework of a functionalist perspective. In contrast to Erikson's functionalist perspective, where deviants are recruited into a role that helps define moral boundaries or reinforce moral consensus, the witch carries away free-floating anxiety and serves cathartic functions. Since the shape of deviance changes in response to disruptions and crises in Erikson's perspective, he could have incorporated the scapegoat into his theory. However, scapegoating is intimately linked to notions of cathartic release and diversionary tactics, neither of which is central to Erickson's explanation. In Erikson's theory, such episodes recur because they are functional in maintaining moral boundaries. In cathartic scapegoat theories, they displace and alleviate anxiety.

Scapegoat theories, like persecution and ceremonial sacrifice theories, are after-the-fact interpretations, and their empirical implications have not been explored. For example, if the pursuit of witches were a diversionary strategy to provide a target for anger and frustrations that would otherwise result in rebellion (and that strategy worked), then rebellion and witch hunts should occur under similar conditions but at different times; that is, they should be negatively related to one another. John Demos (1982), Erik Midelfort (1972), E. William Monter (1976), and Ruth Martin (1989) all suggest that both war and internal rebellion tended to inhibit witch hunts as a peacetime activity. Witch hunting may have inhibited rebellion as an example of successful elite distraction, or rebellion may have inhibited witch hunting by providing real enemies. Of course, Stark proposes a positive relationship between religious conflict and witch hunts, an issue that will be addressed most specifically in chapter 5.

The range of crises and disruptions that led to witch hunts as a means of displacing anger are rarely specified, and diverse crises are often lumped together. For example, Geoffrey Scarre (1987) notes that there is a "rough temporal coincidence between energetic phases of witch prosecution and natural or man-made disasters" (38–39). However, citing Midelfort's and Monter's findings that witch hunting was a peacetime pursuit, he concludes, "The case for any direct causal connection between disaster and witch prosecution therefore remains weak." Some disruptions, crises, and disasters may be positive correlates of witch hunting, while others may be negative correlates. Human society seems to experience "rapid change," and people experience "dislocation" so perennially that such general notions are of little predictive or explanatory utility. Disruptions, crises, disasters, dislocations, and rapid change can always be found when virtually anything can qualify.

Conclusion

This chapter initiated the pursuit of more precise hypotheses about certain features of early modern witch hunts. Specification of the underlying functionalist logic à la Stinchcombe, whether Marxian or Durkheimian, forces a consideration of variables that might constitute threats to social systems, communities, or elites, prompting witch hunts as one mechanism for reestablishing homeostasis and/or eliminating the threat.

Most theorists are quite vague about the circumstances constituting threats and how the ultimate response functioned to solve the problem or realize the group interest that was threatened. If threats are introduced at the general level as disruptions, crises, stresses, dislocations, disturbances, unsettling social change, and such, then the explanation is unfalsifiable since something that could qualify can always be found. Moreover, such a general categorization of threats ignores the fact that some phenomena encompassed within such general categories may enter into quite contrary relationships with witch hunts.

Because conflict theories tend to view the targets of attack as the actual threat or, at least, symbolic of a threat to the values or interests of groups with the power to shape and use institutional machinery, they direct attention to changes or events that affect the magnitude of that threat. For example, the selection of women as targets and the initiation of witch hunts via demonology is interpreted by Barstow, Heinsohn and Steiger, Midelfort, Ben-Yehuda, and others as indicative of a change in the behavior or status of women that threatened patriarchy. Its sexual content was a reflection of patriarchal misogyny, pronatalist opposition to nonreproductive sex, or baggage that accompanies the concept of heresy when moved to women. It is assumed that witch hunting ended when the threat was brought under control or the goal attained. Even fluctuations in the course of the craze might be explained in terms of fluctuating economic conditions that heightened perceptions of women as threats. While no data directly relevant to the factors that would make women a variable threat are presented, such conflict theories do point in a concrete direction. Conflict theories direct research toward characteristics of the targets and circumstances that affect the targets' variability as a threat to other groups.

Theories in which the targets are scapegoats used in a displacement strategy or for general catharsis cannot be falsified unless there is some attempt to specify the circumstances generating such a need. References to broad categories of "possibilities" are problematic for the reasons discussed earlier. Moreover, although potentially relevant to temporal variation, such theories still need to explain why new scapegoats are selected or why shifts occur among scapegoats.

Some of these theoretical discussions contain hints of specific testable hypotheses, and historians have already taken positions on some correlates of witch hunts. Erikson's statement that the wayward Puritans looked for the Devil in a new hiding place, because he had given up his familiar disguises and no longer entered into pacts with Indians, Quakers, and other heretics, actually implies that the Devil changes disguises depending on the availability and/or protection of other enemies. It could be taken to imply that war and clearly defined internal conflicts inhibited the traditional early modern witch hunt, a position advocated by a number of historians. Erikson does not provide specific reasons why the Devil's "presence was felt everywhere." To some degree, Demos fills that void with specific positions on the "harms" or "signs" that would ordinarily precipitate witch hunts were it not for the inhibiting impact of these other variables. Of course, one of Demos's inhibiting variables, charter threats, is introduced by Erikson as one of the reasons the Devil's presence was felt everywhere.

One of the works mentioned in chapter 1 avoids the criticisms applicable to most theoretical perspectives discussed thus far: Stanislav Andreski's (1982, 1989) syphilitic shock theory of early modern witch hunts. Andreski proposes a specific threat that can be treated as a variable over time. He links that threat to witch hunts as a specific response tied to the sexual nature of the disease and the selection of women as targets. He defends the theory in competition with other theories that, he argues, do not provide as good of a fit to the facts as his syphilis theory.

Such specificity is admirable because it is actually possible to identify those findings that would cause problems for the theory. General statements explaining witch hunts in terms of vague categories of threats, crises, and disruptions do not risk falsification. When theorists advance specific hypotheses invoking potentially measurable historical variables, they risk falsification, but they also push inquiry toward more precise research and a consideration of other testable hypotheses stated at a similar level of abstraction.

Chapter 3 moves beyond the general categories or paradigms summarized in this chapter to theory and research relevant to specific independent variables (e.g., disease and war) that have been cited as somehow relevant to the explanation of early modern witch hunts. The word *somehow* is used because when scholars do get specific about variables relevant to dimensions of the panic, contending positions still exist. However, when dealing with contending positions about specific variables, the questions posed lead to a quantitative social history. What is meant by "war" when introduced into explanations of witch hunts? Can war be transformed into a measurable variable over the early modern period? How did syphilis and other diseases vary over time? Are other variables that can or have been measured over the early modern period relevant to testing the theories discussed in the last two chapters? Most theories cannot be tested in their present form and data relevant to many of these theories are not likely to be found. Yet, progress toward the explanation of early modern witch hunts will proceed a few hypotheses at a time.

Notes

1. Divergent positions have been expressed concerning the meaning of "for Azazel" as applied to the scapegoat (Smith 1977). One interpretation is that the sacrifice "for Jehovah" combined with the scapegoat accomplishes a "complete" atonement or sending away of sins. Azazel may also refer to a place or a deity. Azazel was one name for the Devil and may derive from a Canaanite god of the desert (Russell 1977: 188). Regardless of its original ceremonial meaning, the concept of a scapegoat has come to incorporate the notion of blame and is invoked whenever people are punished for problems that they did or could not cause. Moreover, the attribution of blame to scapegoats is typically conceived to be a diversionary tactic to avert blame or a means of displacing anger and anxiety.

2. It should be noted that Lauderdale's experimental design does not allow him to assess whether the rejection of the deviant confederate "functioned" to reestablish solidarity since the presence of the confederate was a constant. Solidarity might rebound following a threat-induced decline, regardless of the presence of the deviant confederate as a target of rejection. Solidarity might rebound due simply to the passage of time. A test of the full functional model would require that both the threat and the deviant confederate be varied. If groups subject to threats to their survival with a deviant confederate present recovered no more quickly or decisively than threatened groups without such a target, then the functional explanation of rejection would be suspect.

3. Similarities between functionalism and dialectic or conflict theories have been noted by numerous scholars. For example, Pierre van den Berghe (1963) argues that both functionalism and conflict theories converge on an equilibrium model, with long-range tendencies toward integration.

CHAPTER THREE

Apocalyptic Variables

Disease, War, and Famine

From Albrecht Durer's *Apocalypse*, Nuremberg, 1498. Reprinted with permission of Dover Publications.

Three of the Horsemen of the Apocalypse, War, Pestilence, and Famine, were the "scourges of God" in a common seventeenth-century saying (Langer 1978: 13). Accompanied by their companion on a pale horse, Death, they were God's tools to carry out divine judgment. Moreover, "God's Three Arrows" (Gouge 1631) were intimately linked to conceptions of sin and evil (Slack 1985). Such apocalyptic crises were commonly interpreted as punishment for sin on a large scale. God allowed Satan and his servants to use some of these tools as well, destroying crops, inhibiting fertility of the fields and spreading disease and illness. As Cotton Mather (1693) proclaimed, "Tis the Destroyer or the Devil that scatters Plagues about the World."

Not only are disease, war, and famine associated with one another in Western cultural imagery, they are typically discussed as correlated phenomena in historical scholarship as well. Frederick Cartwright (1972) states, "Pestilence, famine and war interact and produce a sequence: war drives the farmer from his fields and destroys his crops; destruction of the crop spells famine; the starved and weakened populace fall easy victims to the onslaught of pestilence" (3). Warfare could drive farmers from fields and destroy crops, contributing to famine. The movement of soldiers and the displacement of populations from area to area could help spread disease as well. When people sought refuge from war, their movement and the increase in density of the population could further spread and intensify disease epidemics. Famine could weaken resistance of the population to disease and contribute to its spread through the movement of beggars and the importation or shipment of grain from one area to another (Slack 1985: 77–78). In sum, a complex variety of direct and indirect mechanisms can link war, disease and famine.

The three apocalyptic variables are obvious candidates for the types of threats or crises to individual and communal survival that, according to perspectives discussed in chapter 2, are supposed to generate witch hunts. However, as noted in the previous chapter, it is misleading to categorize all forms of crises or disasters together because they may not correlate in the same fashion with witch hunts. Of course, such caution seems inconsistent with the views of war, famine, and disease as "interrelated" crises. If they are highly correlated, they should enter into similar relationships with witch hunts. Yet, prior research has suggested that one of the three, war, is negatively related to witch hunts.

There are several possible resolutions to this dilemma. For one, crises may be correlated but not "highly" correlated with one another. If related apocalyptic conditions vary independently of one another, then they could enter into quite different relationships with witch hunting. Second, disease is a broad category, and some types of disease may not be highly correlated with famine and war. Yet others may be weakly correlated or unrelated. For example, Paul Slack (1985) concludes that plague epidemics in England "were not visibly dependent on conditions of civil war or of food shortages for their ravages, and they did not cease when war stopped or harvests improved. They were not readily predictable phenomena as famine fevers were, but strokes of fortune, to be explained satisfactorily only as acts of God" (75). Jack Goldstone (1991: 30) implies the same sort of independence between economic factors and disease-induced mortality, noting that long-term mortality movements were determined primarily by disease. Mortality rates from pestilence were higher among the disadvantaged than the well-to-do, but that difference appears to have been a product of their ecological concentration near routes of importation and the density of their living arrangements. Pestilence was a scourge for the well fed as well as the hungry. Finally, since the fleas that spread plague are adversely affected by cold, some climatic conditions that can precipitate poor harvests may actually inhibit plague.

In this chapter, disease, war, and hardship are examined as variably correlated problems that may enter into individually distinct relationships with witch hunts over time. Moreover, when disease is considered, several possible candidates need to be examined. Pestilence and syphilis were prominent among epidemics during most of the early modern period, and each has been proposed as a potential correlate of witch hunts. Stanislav Andreski's (1982, 1989) theory attributing the witch hunts to syphilitic shock and speculation linking witch hunts to plague will both be considered in this chapter. Ergotism and sleeping sickness have also been introduced to explain the Salem–Essex County witch trials, and these conditions will be examined in chapter 7.

Epidemic Disease and Early Modern Witch Hunts

A wave of bubonic, septicemic, and pneumonic plague referred to as the "Black Death" swept Europe between 1348 and 1352, wiping out between one-quarter and one-half of the population (Gottfried 1983: xiii). One of the responses to the epidemic was the mass persecution of Jews (Trachtenberg 1943; Gottfried 1983). Since the cause of the plague is now well-known, such mass attacks are viewed as scapegoating. As summarized in chapter 2, *scapegoating* refers to the displacement of blame, anger, or anxiety on people who are not actually responsible for a problem but provide convenient targets of attack because of other characteristics that they possess.

It is widely recognized that plague recurred in a series of epidemics in the sixteenth and seventeenth centuries, and it is one of the circumstances of the early modern period cited in support of crisis-persecution-scapegoat theories. However, the strongest advocacy of a theory linking disease to witch hunts is Andreski's (1982, 1989) attribution of the early modern witch craze to the importation and spread of syphilis in the late fifteenth and early sixteenth centuries.

Andreski (1989) argues that "all hitherto advanced explanations are either inadequate or simply false, as well as mutually contradictory" (41). For example, he notes that theories linking witch hunts to war (e.g., Trevor-Roper 1967) are confronted with the problem that detailed historical research generally supports the conclusion that witch hunting was a "peacetime" activity (e.g., see Midelfort 1972; Monter 1972; Demos 1982). In addition, theories focusing on the shift to capitalism and its impact on village-level accusations (Macfarlane 1970a; Thomas 1971) identify transitions that occurred after witch hunting was under way and do not fit apparent societal variations. In contrast, Andreski proposes that the syphilitic shock fits the timing (1500–1700) of the witch hunts "perfectly" and that it explains the targets (e.g., mostly women, midwives[1]), the content (e.g., sexual depravity), societal variations (e.g., low intensity in Spain, Russia, and England), and several other features of that historical episode.

How well does the timing of the syphilitic shock coincide with early modern witch hunts? An assessment of the thesis that there is a "perfect" correspondence between the syphilis epidemic and the witch craze requires some consideration of criteria for determining temporal synchronization. It seems eminently reasonable to propose that "a perfect fit" over time would be one where both phenomena began at about the same time, fluctuated together over time, and ended at approximately the same time.

The dominant opinion about its beginning in Europe is that syphilis appeared as an epidemic disease after Columbus's voyage to the New World, although some debate persists over whether it was actually imported or was a mutation of other imported or endemic diseases. Andreski and others date the epidemic as beginning sometime between 1493 and 1495.

However, when considering the duration of the epidemic, much greater ambiguity is found. Andreski argues that "there is little doubt there was a terrible epidemic from the beginning of the sixteenth century until the second half of the seventeenth century" (1982: 15; see also 1989: 41). Elsewhere Andreski cites William McNeil's (1976: 194) classic work, *Plagues and Peoples*, to the effect that syphilis had begun to recede or to take on a less virulent form by the end of the sixteenth century. Although no precise year or even decade can be identified unequivocally as the termination of syphilis as an epidemic, one scholar (Quétel 1990: 50) limits its virulent form to as little as ten years, with a shift to a milder form of the disease occurring within the first quarter of the sixteenth century.

There is also some disagreement in depictions of the severity of the epidemic in the literature on syphilis. Andreski states that there is little doubt of a terrible epidemic from the sixteenth to the mid-seventeenth centuries, but McNeill (1976), the authority on syphilis cited by Andreski, states that the demographic impact "does not seem to have been very great" (194). Moreover, Claude Quétel (1990) states that public fear had abated within a quarter of a century as well. In his history of syphilis, Fielding H. Garrison (1929) proposes that by the seventeenth century, syphilis, in its less virulent form, had become a "fashionable disease," experienced by most of the outstanding figures of that "Age of Gallantry."

In *The Columbian Exchange: Biological and Cultural Consequences of 1492*, Alfred W. Crosby Jr. (1972) describes the course of the epidemic as follows:

> 1. 1494–1516. In this period the first sign of the disease in a patient was small genital ulcers, followed by a wide-spread rash of various character. (This rash is vividly illustrated in all the early depictions of the disease, including one by Albrecht Dürer, dated 1496). As the disease spread through the victim's body, palate, uvula, jaw, and tonsils were often destroyed. Large gummy tumors were common, and the victim suffered agonizing pains in muscles and nerves, especially at night. General physical deterioration followed and often culminated in early death.
>
> 2. During the period 1516 to 1526 two new symptoms were added to the syphilis syndrome: bone inflammation, characterized by severe pain and eventual corruption of the bone and marrow; and the appearance in some sufferers of hard genital pustules, resembling warts or corns.
>
> 3. A general abatement of the malignancy of the disease marked the period 1526 to 1540. The number of pustules per sufferer decreased, and we hear more of gummy tumors. Inflamed swelling of the lymph gland in the groin became common. Loss of hair and teeth became common, but this may have been caused by mercury poisoning, mercury having been used as a remedy.
>
> 4. From 1540 to 1560 the diminution of the more spectacular symptoms of the malady continued. Gonorrhea, which by this time and for centuries afterward was confused with syphilis, became "the most common, if not perpetual symptom" in the early stages of syphilis.
>
> 5. Between 1560 and 1610 the deadliness of the malady continued to decline, and only one new symptom was added: noise in the ears. (151–52)

Were the description of the course of the syphilis epidemic in the literature correct, then it would correspond quite poorly with the history of witch trials even in rather broad terms. Does it make sense to argue that a short-term syphilitic shock that began in 1493, that peaked sometime in the next ten to twenty-five years, and that had ceased to take epidemic form no later than middle of the sixteenth century turned a minor, sporadic search for witches into a witch craze that peaked over one hundred years later in the seventeenth century? This viewpoint reveals serious problems of synchronization, including the beginning, end and temporal variations during the course of the craze.

Although there is considerable leeway for determining when the witch trials actually became a "craze," the beginning of the syphilis epidemic can be deemed to fall within a very narrow span between 1494 and 1500. Andreski notes that the witch trials had occurred for as much as a century prior to the arrival of syphilis and that the most influential document on witchcraft and witch hunting, the *Malleus Maleficarum*, had been published a decade earlier in 1486, with at least eight editions by 1500. However, Andreski (1989) dismisses this potentially problematic discrepancy by deeming its authors, the Dominican inquisitors Heinrich Kramer and James Sprenger, to be "eccentrics," stating that "at any particular time there are number of eccentrics who attempt to propagate all kinds of out-of-the-way opinions" (57). Such a flippant dismissal is surprising since it was a 1484 papal bull from Innocent VIII that declared the spread of witchcraft to be a grave problem and accorded these two eccentrics the necessary religious authority to help stamp it out. Political authority was extended in 1486 by Maximilian I, emperor of Germany, according them full civil powers as inquisitors. Moreover, later editions of the *Malleus Maleficarum* were published together with Dominican Johannes Nider's *Formicarium*, written in 1437 and published in Augsberg in 1475. The *Malleus Maleficarum* organized popular and elite beliefs into an official "demonology" that reflected earlier trials and earlier writing.

Not only was the view of witches as women established before the syphilis epidemic, but, according to Richard Kieckhefer's (1976: 100–147) study of witch trials, the percentage of trials involving women had reached 72 percent in 1350–1399 and 78 percent in the second half of the fifteenth century. Prior to 1350, 72 percent of the trials involved men. In sum, the shift from male targets to female targets had already occurred. As Susanna Burghartz (1988) argues, "demonologists writing from the late fifteenth century onwards simply assumed that women were numerically preponderant among the tribe of witches, justifying this assumption on the basis of practical experience in witch-trials" (61). Such an assumption grew out of trials held before syphilis ever appeared.

Noting these problems, Andreski suggests that even if the witch stereotype and misogynist fundamentals of demonology were in place prior to the syphilis epidemic, syphilis transformed a sporadic small-scale search for witches into a major craze. However, that argument is problematic as well. For example, H. C. Erik Midelfort's (1972) data for southwestern Germany show witch trials for fourteen communities prior to 1493, one trial in 1495, and no trials between 1495 and 1504. Seven trials were held from 1505 to 1515 and four trials between 1515 and 1526. In sum, these detailed data from the heartland of epidemic witch trials reveal no evidence that the syphilis epidemic escalated witch hunts. The period of time when witch trials are considered to have reached panic proportions for the first time is 1560, with the major climax between 1620 and 1660 (see Trevor-Roper 1967). Summarizing prior research, Christina Larner (1981) notes, "During the first half of the sixteenth century it looked as though witch-hunting might be dying out. There were outbreaks in Como in Italy and in Basque country, but very little elsewhere. France and Germany, which had been the epicenters of the witch-hunt of the late fifteenth century and were to be so again in the later sixteenth and seventeenth centuries, seemed almost to have forgotten witchcraft" (54). Thus, not only can we question whether the short-lived syphilitic shock was associated with any unusual escalation of witch hunts, but to support Andreski's thesis, we would have to attribute major panic phases of the craze to a short-lived phenomenon that occurred 50 to 150 years earlier.

Finally, since the witch craze subsided in the second half of the seventeenth century with some late resurgence in peripheral countries (see Ankarloo and Henningsen 1993), the termination of the witch craze does not coincide with any notable variations in the syphilis epidemic. Syphilis had shifted to a nonvirulent form between 1526 and 1540 and continued to decline through the second half of the sixteenth century.

In sum, (1) witch trials and the shift to a preponderance of women as targets precede the syphilis epidemic, (2) the most virulent phases of witch hunting occurred more than a century after the epidemic phase of syphilis, and (3) the witch craze ended while syphilis persisted in its endemic, nonvirulent form. The temporal synchronization of these two phenomena is so far from perfect that no caveats about nonlinear or local effects can discount the discrepancies as minor anomalies to a general correlation of trends. The syphilitic shock is not a good candidate as an explanation of the early modern witch craze.

An Alternative Candidate: Plague

Although Andreski's arguments contain too many discrepancies to accept syphilitic shock as an explanation of temporal dimensions of the European witch craze, they do apply quite well to another epidemic disease—plague.

Andreski touched on the possibility of a relationship in his arguments, but he dismissed plague as the most probable candidate. One of the rationales he gives for advocating the syphilitic shock as a correlate of the witch craze as compared to plague is the sexual nature of much of the imagery developed and applied to witches and witchcraft. Andreski (1989) argues, "It was the sexual nature of the disease that directed the search for scapegoats against women, while during other plagues religious or ethnic minorities suffered. (The outbreaks of bubonic plague were regularly followed by massacres of Jews)" (44). He believes that "it is difficult, however, to imagine a mental process which would link the abhorrence of pleasure with the plague which, true enough, was commonly regarded as God's punishment for sins in general, but was not believed to be caused by enjoyment of carnal pleasures, as was the case with syphilis" (44).

Actually, it was quite common in the Middle Ages and early modern Europe to link disease with sexual excess and hedonism. Leprosy was viewed as a punishment for unchastity and was associated with lust in poetry (Richards 1990: 160). Flagellism following plague outbreaks centered around self-inflicted pain and an abhorrence of sex. "Sex was proscribed, and any male flagellant who said even a word to a woman had to kneel before the master and do penance" (Gottfried 1983: 70). Richards (1990: 32) states that the Black Death was attributed by ecclesiastic and popular preachers to "the judgement of God on mankind for its sexual irregularities," and Robert Gottfried (1983: 113) includes "lust with old women" as one of the causes of plague cited by medical authorities in the fifteenth century.

Disease metaphors were commonly associated with discussions of heresy. "Pestis" and leprosy were used in the twelfth century in the theological condemnation of heretics (Richards 1990: 20), and the papal bull, according to Heinrich Kramer and James Sprenger (1486), to deal with witchcraft refers to the "disease of heresy." The *Malleus Maleficarum* reflected and reinforced tendencies to link disease, both literally and figuratively, with sexual depravity and religious dissent.

The link between sexual deviance and witchcraft was well in place before the syphilitic shock as well. In fact, the element that was added to the imagery of witch hunts and associated with their epidemic form was "diabolism," the depiction of witchcraft as an organized contractual conspiracy led by Satan. Thus, it was the redefinition of witchcraft as heresy that facilitated the greatest witch panics. This observation is crucial to understanding the sexual content of the witch stereotype because the same imagery had been applied to all forms of heresy, regardless of the actual behavior or beliefs of the groups so categorized.

In *Sex, Dissidence and Damnation*, Jeffrey Richards (1990) argues that a common imagery as sexual deviants was applied to minority groups under the rubric of heresy. Whether the category under attack consisted of Jews, lepers, homosexuals, or witches, the focus of elites was on sexual deviance. Indeed, charges of sexual license, debauchery, orgies, and perversion were common in early attacks on Christians and, subsequently, were applied by the Roman church to ascetic religious movements such as the Cathari, Waldensians, and Beguines.

The demonization of heresy and involvement of heretics in obscene individual and group sexual activities in consort with Satan were all in place no later than the twelfth century (Cohn 1975; Russell and Wyndham 1976: 2). In short, the sexual content of depictions of witches is the sexual content of the depiction of all heretical groups. Thus, the central issue is not why sexual perversion was a dimension of the persecution of witches, but why there was a transformation of witchcraft into heresy, carrying with it prior conceptions of sexual perversion.

Numerous rationales can be proposed suggesting an increase in the availability and suitability of women as targets (e.g., greater frequency of mental or behavioral aberrations among widowed survivors, an increase in female involvement in trick-or-treat situations, disrupted sex ratios, higher number and visibility of women who fit the stereotype of the witch, etc), but changes in the availability or vulnerability of traditional targets may have been involved in the transformation of scapegoats as well. Jews had been the primary scapegoats of the early outbreaks of plague, with over 350 massacres (Gottfried 1983: 74). Their persecution had limits because they were executed in huge numbers and driven to Poland and Russia. Jews were also sporadically protected by authorities, primarily when their economic skills and commercial ties were valuable to political elites. While all heretic groups might be persecuted in times of crisis, their relative availability, visibility, and vulnerability could affect their selection as targets. New enemies are invented when old enemies are scarce or protected, and those new enemies are pursued and persecuted in terms of the same traditional metaphors. (This topic will be a major focus of chapter 6.) Moreover, because other devalued categories of people had been the traditional targets of persecution when epidemics were spreading, it can be posited that it would take some time to shift targets and construct the heretic witch. The pursuit of such coconspirators through invocation of laws and legal mechanisms means that legal prerequisites exist as well. Given certain facilitating prerequisites, waves of persecution could come to coincide with waves of plague.

Although numerous theoretical rationales for proposing plague as a correlate of witch hunts have been put forth, its relevance has been questioned by several historians. For example, Alan Macfarlane (1970a) dismisses plague as a correlate of witch hunts based on information about the events leading to witch accusations in Essex, England, and the lack of coincidence between high mortality and execution of witches in three sample villages. He notes that witches were rarely accused of spreading the disease. Rather, the typical situation leading to charges of witchcraft involved personal conflicts—"trick-or-treat" situations where a solicitation of charity or aid was followed by a rebuke and personal hostilities (1970a: 61). Keith Thomas (1971) and Joseph Klaits (1985) argue that universal crises required universal enemies, while charges of witchcraft stemmed from individual misfortunes.

E. William Monter (1976), studying Switzerland and France, and H. C. Erik Midelfort (1972), studying southwestern Germany, are less certain about the lack of a relationship. They both note the general correspondence between outbreaks of plague and periods of virulent witch hunting. Monter observes that witch hunts and plague vanished together in western Europe but that witch hunts were subsiding before the decline in plague (39, 68). Moreover, some of the most dramatic trials in Switzerland specifically involved charges of spreading the plague. Midelfort plotted the number of German cities with plague outbreaks over time, and those data suggest some sort of general correspondence between witch hunts and plague. However, Midelfort states that "outbreaks of plague did not always trigger witch hunts. Between 1633 and 1636, the German Southwest experienced its worst and most widespread plague. . . . Yet this period of the middle 1630s was also one of rapid and general *decline* in witch hunting. One would have to conclude either that the plague had nothing to do with witch hunting or that a new social process was at work during the second wave of plague, inhibiting the witch hunts" (123). Since the major discrepancy falls in the middle of the Thirty Years War, it may not be as perplexing as it seems. Indeed, this anomaly fits John Putnam Demos's (1982) argument wherein war neutralizes the impact of disease and other harms on witch hunting.

Robin Briggs (1996b) raises this same issue, stating that "infectious disease appears as one of the several factors which combined to intensify fear and anxiety, yet there is no direct link to witchcraft; indeed, far the worst outbreaks of plague came between 1633 and 1636, just as the witchcraft trials virtually ceased across the region" (307). Again, if war and plague were positively related but related to witch trials in contrary directions, then a multivariate analysis is needed to untangle countervailing influences over time.

Other Diseases

As Fernand Braudel (1992) notes, "different diseases break out simultaneously," and plague "was only one disease among others, intermingled in their frequent travels and contagious as a result of social mixing" (81). Other diseases might qualify as apocalyptic crises as well, and Demos (1982: 346) notes that the first witchcraft cases in New England emerged in the context of the first general outbreak of illness in 1647–1648 (likely influenza). Smallpox and measles epidemics were severe in the years immediately preceding the Salem witch hunts as well. Although such epidemics did not generate the level of mortality associated with plague, they were included among the events interpreted as "Cataracts of Wrath" by religious leaders (Silverman 1985: 56–57; Godbeer 1992: 75).

Epidemics other than plague might help explain some historical anomalies noted in the discussions of the relevance of plague to witch hunts. For example, Larner questions the relevance of plague to Scottish witch hunts because Scotland experienced its last national panic in 1661–1662, while plague had ceased to be a problem by the end of the 1640s. However, mortality statistics for Scotland (Flinn 1977: app. A, 484), show a 40 percent jump in mortality in 1660 and 1661 after several decades of stability and below-average mortality. This jump is attributed by demographers to a smallpox epidemic. In sum, disease epidemics other than plague might be relevant to the explanation of variation in witch hunts.

Finally, waves of plant and animal diseases conceivably could be reflected in waves of witchcraft accusations as well. Detailed descriptions of the microlevel events giving rise to charges of witchcraft often center around the death, illness, or strange behavior of livestock and other animals. Cipolla (1980) notes that "in medieval and Renaissance Europe, epizootic diseases were no less frequent or disastrous than epidemics" (100–101). Surges in animal diseases could increase the types of microlevel frustrations and suspicions reflected in witchcraft charges. When livestock suffered from inexplicable ailments, it was common for New Englanders to suspect that it had been "bewitched" and to resort to countermagic as a remedy (Godbeer 1992: 43). Demos (1982: 145–46) argues that in New England men were particularly sensitive to the threat of witchcraft to livestock, with accusations of cattle witchery and assaults by animal familiars distinguishing their charges from those of women. Of course, problems with livestock are also commonly noted in discussions of village-level witchcraft suspicions in Europe (e.g., see Sebald 1978).

War and Early Modern Witch Hunts

Most historians express doubt about a connection between plagues and witch hunts, but they tend to agree that war and witch hunts are related. Prompted by the quantitative studies by Midelfort (1972), Monter (1976), and others, the dominant opinion is that involvement of an area in actual warfare inhibits witch hunts. Both Midelfort and Monter view witch hunting as a peacetime activity, abruptly halted by warfare. Moreover, the end of the major war in the areas they studied did not bring about an end to witch hunting. Commenting on Switzerland and northern France, Monter argues that for a period of time after the Treaty of Westphalia ending the Thirty Years War, the region suffered from postwar exhaustion and no witch hunts were conducted, but witch-hunting was soon resumed "in a big way." Midelfort suggests that it was regions of the German Southwest which had been bruised by war that were "subsequently afflicted with witch panics of major proportions" (123). Demos (1982) proposes the same tendency in New England, arguing that clearly defined external threats as well as clearly defined internal conflicts inhibited witch trials. Although actual battles, invasions, and occupation might inhibit witch hunts, there might still be a general correspondence between periods of war and witch hunts. H. R. Trevor-Roper's (1967) arguments about witches as scapegoats of the Wars of Religion (102) and the persecution of witches as "part of the same process as the persecution of the Jew" (104) implies such a correspondence.

Observing that invading armies tended to halt the persecution of witches "in many cases" during the Thirty Years War and that witch hunts continued in their most devastating form after the war ended, Nachman Ben-Yehuda (1980) gives an overall impression of a positive association:

> The coincidence of the termination of the craze with the termination of the Thirty Years' War in the Peace of Westphalia is not just a chance occurrence. This peace, no doubt, gave official recognition to religious pluralism and symbolically ended the European struggle to redefine the social system morally. . . . The internal stresses, insecurity, and instability experienced by persons living in the stricken areas during the invasions of various military groups and armies provided fuel to the burning furnace of the final phase of the witch craze. (23)

Ben-Yehuda's discussion illustrates the difficulty in reaching conclusions about the relation between "war" and witch hunts. If witch hunts were prompted by the *threat of war*, occur *during war* with interruptions due to invasion "in many cases," and continue in their most devastating forms *after a war*, then it is questionable that any claim of a positive correlation between war and witch hunts could be falsified. When war is viewed as a reflection of underlying tensions and conflicts that precede and follow overt conflict, then it is difficult to determine the boundaries of war and, hence, the association with other phenomenon.

Although he presents no new data and relies on the same historical reports that have been used to claim a negative correlation with war, Rodney Stark (2003) dismisses the view that witch hunting was a peacetime activity. As noted in chapters 1 and 2, he attributes witch hunting to the intolerance of nonconformity associated with religious conflict. He acknowledges that actual warfare would inhibit witch trials but argues that periods of intense religious conflict were also periods of intense witch hunts.

If war were defined in terms of actual warfare, then it would make sense to argue that war inhibited witch hunts. Witch hunts were not vigilante actions but, rather, were carried out through state and ecclesiastical legal machinery (Levack 1987). They required support from the church and/or state and the expenditure of considerable time and resources. Invasion would disrupt such machinery and the inclination to use it. In addition, involvement in war itself would also discourage witch hunts, whether it involved actual invasion or not. Why pursue ill-defined "hidden" enemies when there are clearly defined opponents who pose a direct and immediate threat? Witches and political enemies might both be "enemies" of God and coconspirators with the Devil, but war should direct attention toward the most immediate threat. The period of general religious warfare might still be associated with the period of virulent witch hunts in a more general sense, or witch hunts might increase following actual warfare. The aftermath of war could be very similar to the aftermath of plague, prompting the same mediating facilitating mechanisms proposed for plague in the previous discussion (e.g., increases in widowed women, "trick-or-treat" social encounters, etc.).

Moreover, war on the fringes of a social system might constitute a type of "diffuse" external threat prompting collective anxiety and uncertainty about individual and communal survival and, hence, increase the probability or severity of witch hunts. In his recent work on *Witches and Neighbors*, Robin Briggs (1996b: 308) argues, "When outbursts of witchcraft persecution can be related to warfare, it is usually on the fringes of conflict or when its impact was less overwhelming. The German cases already discussed may well fit this pattern, belonging to a period when war was intense, but people were suffering serious indirect repercussions rather than full-scale devastations." During times of apparent "peace" within a system, witch hunts might correlate positively with the extent of warfare outside or on the fringes of the system.

The complexity of the relation between war and witch hunts is suggested in Godbeer's (1992) discussion of the impact of the Indian Wars on colonial witch hunting: "Whereas earlier crises . . . had originated within the colonial community, the dangers that faced New England toward the end of the century intruded upon the colonies as emissaries of a hostile outside world. . . . All of these interrelated, alien, and intrusive forces, which the colonists equated with witchcraft, converged on a local level in Essex County" (186, 197). Those hostile, alien, invasive outside forces included Indians, their allies, the French, and Quakers. However, Quakers were extended protection by the new charter from England mandating religious tolerance before the Salem witch hunts. The Indian threat was most intense before the Salem witch hunts as well, between 1689 and 1691. Indians, the French, and Quakers were Satan's allies, but it appears to be during respites from direct threat when traditional enemies were unavailable or protected that Salem turned inward to pursue the heretic witch. As John Hale ([1702] 1973) wrote, "Among Satan's Mysteries, this Witchcraft is one of the most difficult to be searched out by the Sons of Men" (8–9). It is much less difficult to define one's real enemies as servants of Satan than to search out imaginary enemies, even when most of the work constructing the imagery of those internal enemies had been completed much earlier.

Emile Durkheim's (1958) "Society of Saints" (see chapter 2) suggests the same sort of transition. People are most likely to begin searching for internal threats that require definitional work to transform them into a serious problem when more serious, clearly defined threats have abated. Energy previously directed at external enemies will be redirected inward, especially if reminders of those external threats continue to generate collective anxiety.

Famine and Related Variables

"For God in His Justice using the devils as his agents of punishment inflicts the evils which come to us in this world. Therefore, with reference to the Psalms: 'He called a famine on the land, and wasted all their substance of bread'; the gloss says: God allowed this evil to be caused by the bad Angels who are in charge of such matters; and by famine is meant the Angel in charge of famine" (Kramer and Sprenger [1486] 1971: 147). Famine completes the triumvirate of apocalyptic variables and will be considered together with two closely related variables, climatic and economic hardship. All three are included among precipitating "harms" indicative of God's displeasure in Demos's (1982) account of witch hunts in New England.

Famine per se has not been as central to explanations of witch hunts as general variation in economic hardship. Anne Llewellyn Barstow (1994: 97) argues that the rise in witchcraft charges and a steep rise in inflation can be charted from about 1550 and that overpopulation coupled with food shortages, hunger, and unemployment facilitated witch hunts. "This brutal combination had occurred before," she adds, "notably in the early fourteenth century, but had not triggered a witch hunt. The earlier crisis had been diverted by massive deaths caused by bubonic plague (the Black Death). . . . No such Malthusian salvation rescued Europe two hundred years later when it faced the same squeeze" (100).

Witchcraft accusations are depicted as "a method for resolving social tensions." According to Barstow, women were the most likely targets because they were competitors for scarce jobs and because they were the first to be forced out when times grew hard. Competition heightened misogyny, and poverty drove women to begging and activities that increased their vulnerability to witchcraft accusations.

Barstow's statement that there were not Malthusian forces at work to counter overpopulation during the span of virulent witch hunts requires comment. Malthusian forces were definitely at work in the heartland of the witch craze during the sixteenth and seventeenth centuries. Plague recurred numerous times and, coupled with war, decimated the German population (see figure 3.1). Moreover, although the Black Death may have been a Malthusian salvation from overpopulation and shortages, it was associated with crazes, panics and persecution as well.

Theories attributing trends in witch hunting to overpopulation, competition, and surpluses of labor stand in marked contrast to brands of theory emphasizing population stagnation and labor shortages. Gunnar Heinsohn and Otto Steiger (1982) depict the demographic circumstances leading to the first witch hunts in terms quite contrary to those emphasized by Barstow and others. They argue that witch hunting was one of a variety of strategies used by church and state to get women to reproduce, concluding that "the *malleus maleficarum* (*The Hammer of Witches*) was nothing other than the *Hammer of Birth Control*." The focus on midwives, the witches' ability to inhibit procreation, sexual debauchery, infanticide, and child sacrifice are interpreted as giving rise to the moral enterprise necessary to condemn nonreproductive sex and encourage population growth through fertile marital relations. Such population policies paved the way toward "the 'asexual' woman and 'innocent' child of the eighteenth and nineteenth centuries" (211).

Thus, two quite different tales have been constructed relevant to the role of population and economic hardship in the explanation of witch hunts.

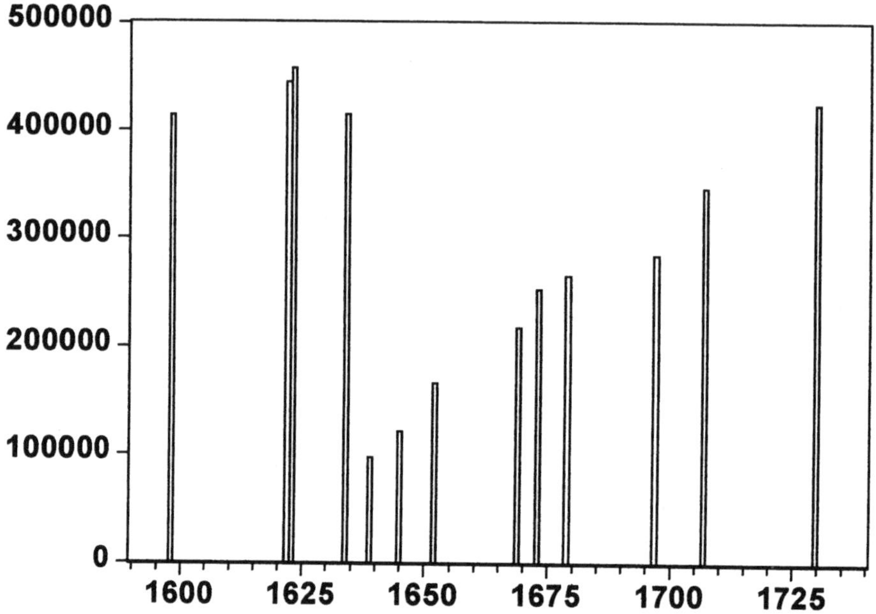

Figure 3.1. Estimated population of the Duchy of Württemberg (from Wilson and Parker 1977: 192).

From one perspective, it is population growth coupled with economic hardship and competition that generates pressure for witch hunts. From another, it is population stagnation or decline that generates a population policy to stimulate population growth and replace a decimated labor force.

The same patterns may not be found in all settings, but there are estimates of components of population change for Augsburg, Germany, a city on the edge of the heartland of the witch craze. Martha Pass (1979) reports a 36 percent increase between 1500 and 1618 in the population of Augsburg, but she finds that it is attributable entirely to immigration. There was no natural increase, and deaths exceeded births. While fluctuating within that span of time, birthrates experienced no overall increase relative to marriages or in marriages. The crude fertility rate "exhibited a downward trend over the century" (48). Between 1501 and 1620, only three decades saw births exceeding deaths: 1531–1540, 1551–1560, and 1611–1620. The three apocalyptic variables—disease, war, and economic hardship—were the major factors explaining fluctuations within that span. Immigrants tended to come from rural areas where the ratio of births to deaths was more favorable.

Pass's analysis of harvest and price data show that "bad harvests far outnumbered the good harvests in the sixteenth century since the primary independent variable was the weather" (144). Prices trended upward due to decreases in supply. Famine could stem from wet conditions at the time of winter plowing and sowing. In addition, cool, wet summers could prevent grain from developing and ripening. In fact, most famine crises were associated with wet weather, not with cold or dry weather (Pounds 1990: 257).

The trends in wages for urban and rural workers did not keep up with prices, and their standard of living was declining. In contrast, large-scale farmers prospered from an upward trend in prices, while day laborers' real wages declined. The urban middle classes prospered as well. In response, laborers "turned to cottage industry, primarily weaving, to supplement their income. . . . The abundance of these rural weavers . . . kept their wages down [as low] as those of the urban weavers with whom they competed" (Pass 1979: 145). Urban weavers increased from one-ninth of the tax-paying workforce in 1474 to one-fourth by 1615. Hence, competition did increase in some sectors of the workforce, and the real standard of living was declining due primarily to shortages in supply.

Not only did competition increase, but foreign competition led to a decrease in demand for the type of textiles that urban weavers produced. They could not compete with higher-quality cloth from Westphalia and the Rhineland or with English woolens. Moreover, the price of flax kept them from shifting to a lower-quality linen. Guilds responded by restricting membership, and the number of looms declined. In short, the competitive situation and real wages worsened for the day laborer. There were no improvements in agriculture to shift the supply-side factors and help the laborer until the nineteenth century.

In his historical geography of Europe, Pounds (1990) indicates that in the sixteenth century "the population of Europe was beginning to increase after the declines of the fourteenth century and the fluctuations of the fifteenth" (218). However, the seventeenth century through the mid–eighteenth century was a period of contraction. While slow growth continued in Great Britain, the United Netherlands' and Scandinavia's population was declining in the seventeenth century. In Germany, the Thirty Years War may have reduced the population by 40 to 50 percent.

Figure 3.1 summarizes population estimates for the Duchy of Württemberg at various intervals between 1598 and 1730. The effect of the multiple crises associated with the Thirty Years War is clearly indicated with a precipitous decline between 1634 and 1639. The population rebounded but did not reach the levels of the late sixteenth and early seventeenth centuries until 1730. Population estimates for Stuttgart between 1400 and 1700 (Keyser 1962) follow a similar course, with 4,000 people in 1400, 9,000 in 1589, and a drop to 8,327 by 1631. By 1648, the population of Stuttgart was 4,500, one-half the 1589 estimate. The population rebounded to 13,000 by 1698.

Since the course of population growth was quite variable across the centuries in which the witch stereotype was constructed and witch hunts mounted, the validity of the different hypotheses about population growth and witch hunts depends on the period selected. For example, Heinsohn and Steiger's theory applies quite well to the period following the Black Death and the mid–fifteenth century when the witch stereotype was assembled, and charges of witchcraft shifted from men to women. The Black Death and successive waves of plague had decimated the workforce by the end of the fourteenth century, and the stereotype of the heretic was shifted to the witch during a period of stagnation or fluctuation. However, witch trials began to take epidemic form during the sixteenth century, a century of growth. They reached their peak in Germany during a century of stagnation as plague, war, and famine decimated the population. Moreover, the population rebounded in the aftermath of the witch hunts. Thus, Heinsohn and Steiger's theory may apply to the *social construction* of the heretic witch as a threat to fertility and reproduction, while theories emphasizing population growth may apply to *the initiation of the epidemic phase of the craze*. Whether the witch hunts were a factor promoting replacement following demographic disaster cannot be determined. In sum, no one simple conclusion about population pressures or stagnation and witch hunts can be reached when the full span of time is considered.

No simple conclusion about climate is possible, either. Weather can affect apocalyptic variables in contrary ways. For example, it is common to link fluctuations in climate to famine and fluctuations in famine to health. Yet, it appears that susceptibility of the population is largely irrelevant to the spread of plague. Plague affected the poor more than the rich, but that differential appears to be a product of the location and density of the population rather than variations in nutritional or other forms of well-being (Slack 1985). On the other hand, since plague is spread by fleas, the movement and intensity of the disease can be greatly affected by the weather.

The flea functions best between 15 and 20 degrees centigrade and 90 to 95 percent humidity. Cold weather will restrict its activity, and warm temperatures will inhibit reproduction. Low humidity will kill fleas. Thus, some conditions associated with crop failure can be favorable to fleas (wet weather), while others that can lower productivity are unfavorable to fleas (e.g., cold). Thus, such climatic "crises" as the "Little Ice Age" could have countervailing consequences for the population. Extremes of cold could lower mortality by slowing or halting the spread of plague (as well as slowing or halting war) while contributing to mortality via famine. Since mortality was driven more by disease than famine, the net effect of long periods of cold could be a *decline* in mortality and increases in the population.

Conclusion

This chapter takes a step closer to testable hypotheses about correlates of early modern witch hunts, although available scholarship presents contrary opinions, potential countervailing mechanisms, and considerable ambiguity. It does lead to several specific observations. For one, the "syphilitic shock" is not a promising candidate for explaining the timing of early modern witch hunts and has to be considered in comparison with other disease epidemics. Second, in contrast to arguments that war is a positive correlate of witch hunts, most historians compiling data on witchcraft trials and cases argue that actual warfare and violent religious or class conflict in a region inhibited witch hunts. Stark challenges this interpretation, although no new data are compiled or presented.[2] The adjudication among contending positions may rest with a consideration of Briggs's argument about war on the fringes. Finally, the witch stereotype was assembled and witch hunting peaked during periods of population stagnation; witch hunts were common during periods of population growth, labor competition, and economic recession as well. Hence, contrary claims may apply to different dimensions and phases of the early modern witch craze.

A review of the literature provides guidelines for the empirical pursuit of relationships. Not only is it clear that apocalyptic variables should be distinguished from one another because they do not necessarily enter into the same relationships with witch hunts, but a multivariate analysis is mandated by the fact that some of the variables are correlated with one another. If the historical observation of strong correlations between war and disease epidemics is correct, then any assessment of their relation to witch hunts must attempt to untangle those relationships, especially given the prospect that they are related to witch hunts in contrary directions.

Variables such as climate, economic conditions, population growth, and competition for scarce resources are introduced rather casually as long-term trends relevant to the witch craze in general but with little attention to issues of timing or fluctuations during the course of the craze. For example, the beginning of the Little Ice Age, which spanned the period from about 1560 to 1850, coincides with the beginning of the most virulent witch hunting. Yet, as Emmanuel Le Roy Ladurie (1971) notes in his *Times of Feast, Times of Famine*, "the little ice age was no more a single entity than the French

Revolution" (313). It is introduced as a relevant variable for explaining everything from witch hunts to revolution but never treated as a variable fluctuating over time.

The next step in the pursuit of the path of the Devil is likely to be controversial in that there are few guidelines or examples to follow, and what examples there are in sociology have already generated criticism. In a critique of Goldstone's work on revolutions and rebellions, Lawrence Stone (1992) states that "the conversion of such fuzzy and unreliable data into hard statistics and graphs is a misuse of the scientific method of quantification to dress up an intriguing exercise of the sociological imagination." The implication is that the same conclusions could have been reached without such analysis. Testing hypotheses about disease, war, and hardship as correlates of early modern witch hunts will require some precision about the meaning and measurement of such variables and the use of data sources that yield measures that can be challenged as fuzzy and unreliable.

Notes

1. The view that midwives were likely to become targets in witch hunts is a source of controversy and will be discussed in chapter 6.

2. Mary Beth Norton (2002) has revived interest in war as a positive correlate of witch hunts in her monograph on the Salem-Essex witch trials in 1692. Her argument will be examined in chapter 7.

CHAPTER FOUR

A Discourse on Measures

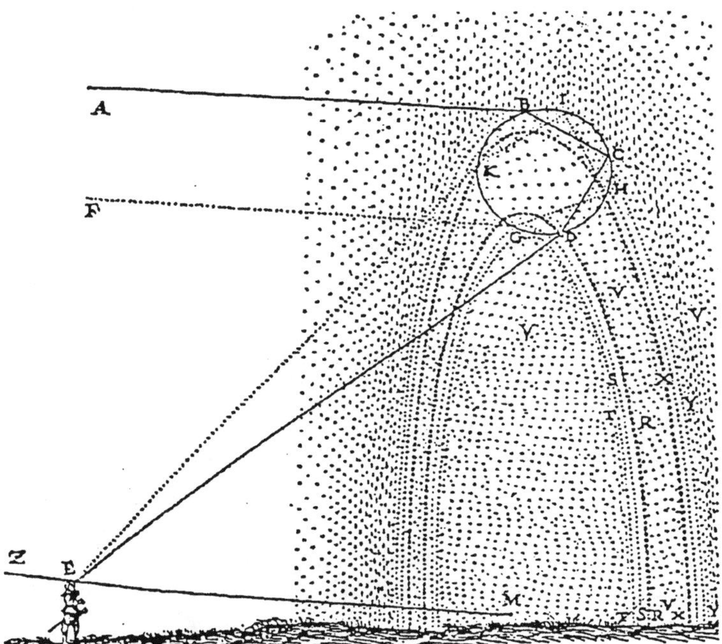

From Descartes's *Discourse on Method* (1637: 251).

Theories of the early modern witch craze in sociology and history view witch hunts as attempts at social control prompted by (1) crises that necessitate functional sacrifices, (2) realistic conflict among contending groups, and/or (3) crises that necessitate a search for scapegoats. Regardless of the form of the theory, all types link surges and variation in witch hunts to crises or threats to society or powerful groups within society. However, precise research on witch hunts has mandated a careful differentiation of crises that can encourage witch hunts from those that inhibit them. Sweeping generalizations attributing witch hunts to vaguely defined "stresses" and "strains" have been found inadequate in view of evidence on specific crises and specific strains. References to "rapid social change" and "widespread dislocations" have yielded to arguments about specific changes and their temporal correspondence with variations in the early modern witch craze.

Although the compilation of detailed data on trials and executions by historians has elevated the level of debate about causes and correlates of witch hunts to increasingly precise issues of timing and variation, data on variation in those potential correlates has been introduced primarily in a discursive manner. For example, support for the view that witch hunts are inhibited by war is based on detailed data on variation in witch hunts coupled with general observations about war. Similarly, potential sources of stress spanning considerable periods of time such as the "Little Ice Age," "population growth," "rising prices," or "falling wages" are introduced as general conditions, corresponding in a crude fashion with the whole era of intense witch hunts. With the exception of Midelfort's consideration of epidemic disease, researchers have made little effort to quantify potential explanatory variables.

Yet, demographers, economists, climatologists, historians, and a variety of social scientists have accumulated a mounting amount of data pertinent to more precisely measuring some of the circumstances that are supposed to encourage witch hunts. This chapter will lay the foundation for the analysis of several proposed correlates through an exploration of data relevant to the more precise measurement of variation over time in disease, war, and hardship.

Such an exploration should heed warnings by historians about the perils of quantification and overprecision. Listing quantification as one of the contributions of the social sciences to the study of history, Lawrence Stone (1987) cautions that such methods should be used "with discretion and common sense" and that "no amount of quantitative methodology, however sophisticated, will compensate for misinterpreted or defective data" (18, 33). Social scientists are warned to be particularly wary of attempting to be overly precise when using data compiled before the mid-twentieth century.

Because there is no authoritative methodological "cookbook" to define the discrete and commonsense use of quantitative methods for studying social history, the best way to heed these warnings is by taking standard scientific precautions. Such precautions require (1) an exploration of relationships among alternative indicators whenever possible, (2) identification of known problems with available data, and (3) comparisons of the variations discerned with discursive depictions of historical patterns. Moreover, as with all forms of social scientific analysis, alternative explanations for any patterns observed as well as for the failure of expected patterns to emerge must be considered.

The attempt to discern quantitative variation in some variables is not meant to imply that nonquantitative variables or circumstances that were relatively stable during the course of the witch craze are irrelevant to its explanation. For example, elite "demonology" set the stage for intense witch hunts, and abandonment of that belief system was associated with its demise. Concern about witchcraft did not generate panic waves of executions until it was defined as involving a pact with Satan. Charges of witchcraft did not escalate into witch hunts unless the focus shifted from the "maleficia" attributed to witchcraft to a conspiracy of heretics led by the Christian devil. Given cultural, legal, and institutional prerequisites that facilitated the escalation of charges of witchcraft into mass trials and executions, this chapter will concentrate on conditions that varied quite markedly over time and the degree to which those variations coincide with variations in the intensity of witch hunts.

Witch Hunts

In their introduction to *Early Modern European Witchcraft: Centres and Peripheries*, Ankarloo and Henningsen (1993) argue that "the European witch persecutions had so many traits in common that they must be regarded as a single, unified phenomenon" (9). They note that (1) the persecutions touched most of Europe to varying degrees between 1450 and 1750, (2) the victims were disproportionately women, and (3) the persecutions intensified when defined in terms of a widely invoked demonology. Yet, there were variations in timing, frequency, and intensity during this span as well. Ireland was spared, and relatively mild episodes occurred in Calvinist Holland, Bavaria, the lower Rhine, Italy, Spain, and England. Parts of New England, Poland, Sweden, Norway, Finland, Russia, and Hungary took part primarily at the tail end of witch hunting in the late seventeenth or early eighteenth centuries.[1]

As noted in chapter 1, there is a growing body of data on trials, accusations, cases processed, places of confession, and executions, adding to several classic compilations of information from earlier in the century. Figure 4.1 plots estimates of the number of executions for witchcraft in six settings: (1) the Jura; the French-Swiss border area, including Geneva (Monter 1976: apps. 1 and 2); (2) Bavaria (Behringer 1987: appendix); (3) southwest Germany (Midelfort 1972: appendix); (4) England (Notestein 1911); (5) Scotland (Black 1937); and (6) the New England colonies (Demos 1982). The

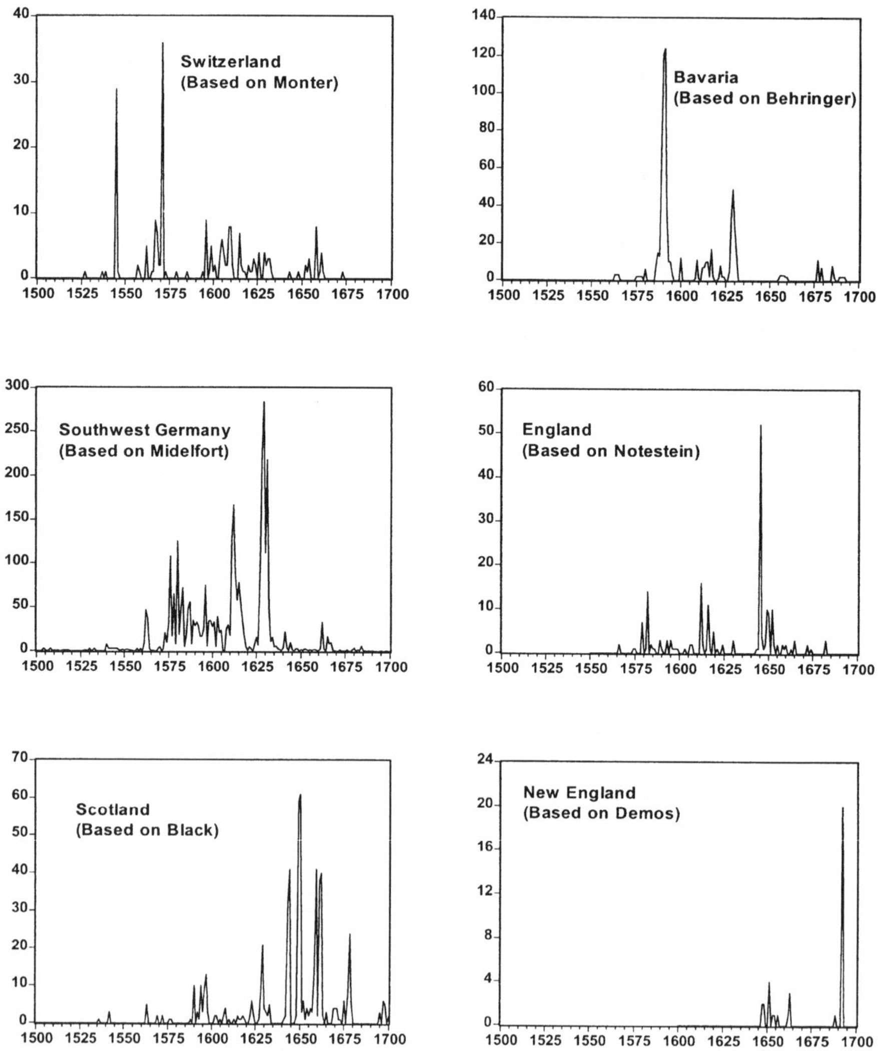

Figure 4.1. Executions for witchcraft in six settings.

six graphs are ordered from the earliest apparent peak in the set of six settings (Switzerland) to the latest (New England).

The data for Switzerland are based on all executions reported in the three appendices to Monter's (1976: 207–28) study, which include three states in the Jura region. Moreover, they include estimates of executions for four *engraisseur* panics (1545, 1567–1568, 1571, and 1615). These panics involved charges of "plague spreading" as a special form of diabolic witchcraft. Charges of a diabolic conspiracy to prepare and spread "quintessence of plague" had first been lodged in Geneva in 1530, and Monter notes that "local traditions of witch-hunting and plague-spreading conspiracies preceded the Reformation" (45). The years characterized by plague-spreader panics are years in which plague was ravaging the area. The year 1571 is the peak year for executions, and the executions in the plague-spreading years account for two to three times the number of executions (about eighty) as occurred for the entire period from 1573 to 1662 in Geneva (twenty-nine). Apart from those panics, about seventy executions took place between the Reformation and the last known trial in Geneva.

Wolfgang Behringer (1987, 1997) has compiled a detailed record of witch trials in southeastern Germany (Bayern or Bavaria). In the original version of his work, he compiled an appendix listing estimates of number of victims and places involved for witch trials from 1343 through 1792. Ninety percent of the trials and 98 percent of executions occurred between 1560 and 1730. Behringer (1997) notes that developments in southeastern Germany "were in some senses untypical" in that nearly one-half of executions fell between 1586 and 1595 (36). Another 14 percent were burned between 1628 and 1630 (35). He classifies the "core period" for witch hunts in Bavaria as 1586 through 1631 but stresses that "the witch hunt of 1590 was crucial to the region" (64).[2]

Southwestern Germany was the epicenter for witch hunts in Europe and is referred to as "the heartland" of the early modern witch craze. The Baden-Württemberg region (see figure 4.2) was the focus of H. C. Erik Midelfort's (1972) widely cited and acclaimed study of witch hunts, and his analysis has shaped most statements about historical variation in witch hunts for this region of Europe. In the appendix to his work, he lists witch hunts chronologically, based on secondary sources and archival collections.

The number of executions, summarized in figure 4.1, is striking when contrasted to neighboring Bavaria. Although similar in population, there were four times more executions in southwestern Germany than Bavaria. There was a small surge around 1590 in Germany, but the most prominent peak in that area occurred in 1629. Between 1626 and 1631, close to a thousand

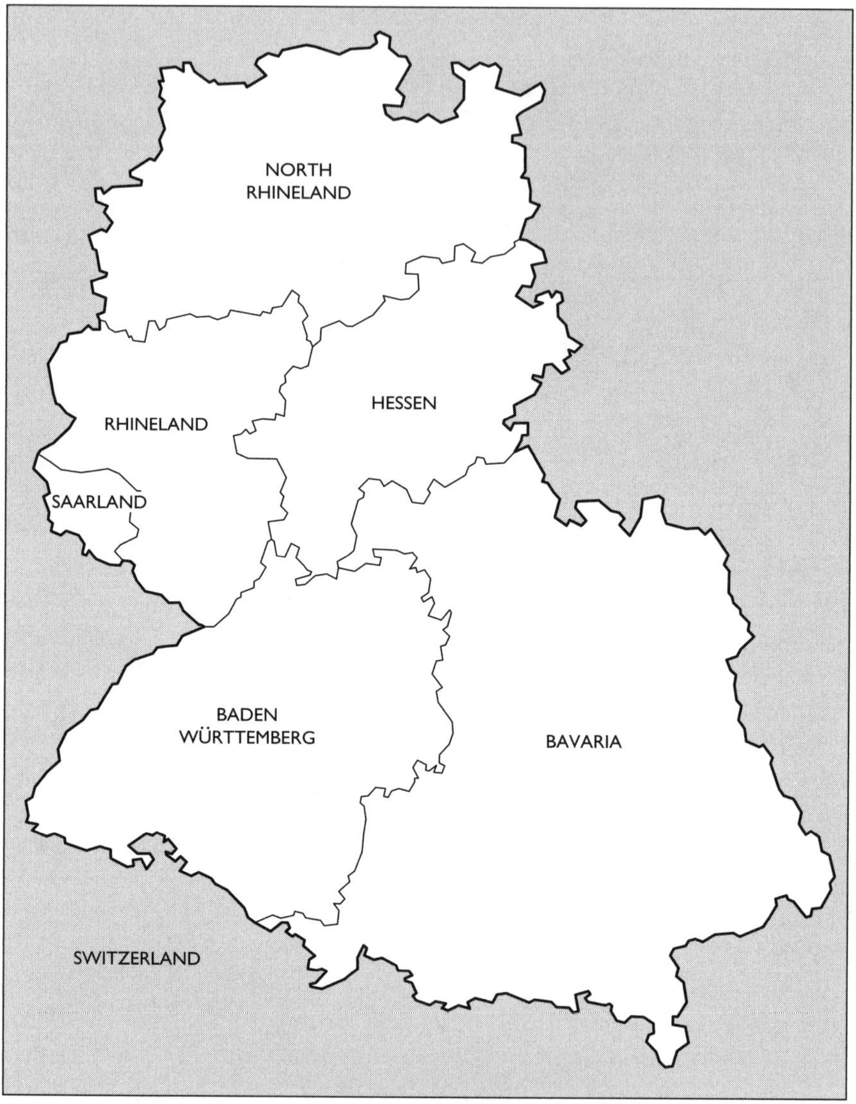

Figure 4.2. Regions of Germany coded for conflict and disease.

executions occurred in southwestern Germany, which exceeds the estimated total for all years in Bavaria.

The data on executions in Scotland are based on George Black's (1937) *A Calendar of Cases of Witchcraft in Scotland*, and executions in England are based on Wallace Notestein's (1911) compilation of historical detail on witchcraft in England for 1558–1718. Witch hunts were comparatively mild in England compared with the continent, a fact generally attributed to (1) common law traditions precluding torture (Currie 1968), (2) scarcity of the conception of witchcraft as heresy involving a diabolic conspiracy, and (3) centralized control over local justice (Levack 1992, 6: ix–x). Witch hunts focused on individuals and small groups, with only one large-scale hunt in 1645–1646. In contrast, six major witch hunts occurred between 1590 and 1662 in Scotland. The average for Scotland was about four per year, with a maximum of sixty-one in 1650. The average for England was less than one per year, with a maximum of fifty-two in 1645. Since England is estimated to have had twice the population of Scotland, the number of executions per capita was several times greater in Scotland than England. This difference has been attributed to (1) use of torture despite its illegality, (2) acceptance of the diabolic conspiracy theory, and (3) relative autonomy of local justice (Levack 1992, 6: ix–x; 1996). Yet, Scotland does not come close to the intensity of executions for southwestern Germany, which yielded an average of about twenty-one executions per year.[3]

The Salem witch trials occurred toward the end of the early modern witch craze in 1692, but there had been earlier smaller-scale witch hunts in New England in 1647–1648, 1651, 1653–1654, and 1661–1662 (Demos 1982: appendix). However, the number of executions during the Salem episode (nineteen) exceeded the number estimated for all of New England in all earlier cases combined. With a population of about fifty thousand in New England, the total of thirty-six executions yields a rate about twice that of the county of Essex, England, where it is estimated that seventy-four witches were executed between 1580 and 1680. The rate for all of England, three hundred to one thousand executions for four million people, may have been one-tenth the rate estimated for New England. Relative to the size of its population, the intensity of witch hunts in New England is more nearly comparable to the rates for Scotland than for England.

In a comparison of the course of witch hunts across several settings, Behringer (1997) argues, "The increase and apex of the western European enthusiasm for persecuting witches was not perfectly synchronic, but did follow an unmistakable rhythm" with a shared surge around 1590 after which "the witch craze broke down into regional patterns" (405, 407). The argument for a shared rhythm is based on the apparent coincidence of witch trials in Scotland, Bavaria, and southwestern Germany in the 1590s. He suggests other shared temporal patterns for Scotland, England, southwestern Germany, and Bavaria as well: "The number of trials for witchcraft rose sharply after 1560, peaking around 1600. Just as they peaked in other geographically disparate regions around the mid-1580s" (1997: 13). He argues that theories about the witch hunts "will stand or fall on their ability to explain the great wave of persecutions from 1585 to 1595" (13).

Explanations for that shared peak will be examined in chapter 5, but it should be noted here that no actual statistical evidence concerning correlations among societies over time was presented. Although there may be some shared peaks in executions across settings, they are sufficiently rare that the correlations for England, Scotland, Germany, and Swiss-Jura are all insignificant, ranging between +.10 and –.05. There was a significant correlation between Behringer's estimates of number of victims in Bavaria and Midelfort's data on number of executions (+.30), but neither of these estimates was significantly correlated with executions in other settings, including Scotland. There may be occasional shared surges across time in executions, but the overall correlations are quite weak, except for the two German neighbors.

Because data on other properties of early modern witch hunts are available for a number of settings or societies, Behringer's observation of a shared peak "around 1590" across three settings can be examined using other indicators. Figure 4.3 plots the number of places listed with witchcraft cases for Bavaria, southwestern Germany, England, and Scotland between 1500 and 1700. When this measure of the prevalence of witch hunting is used, there are significant correlations across the three for 1500 through 1700, ranging from +.56 for Bavaria and southwestern Germany to +.17 for England and Scotland.

There is a shared surge in 1590 in the number of different places with trials for Bavaria, Scotland, England, and southwestern Germany as observed by Behringer. Yet, shared surges occurred across other spans of years for several settings in the seventeenth century as well. The most notable is 1628–1629, when both executions and number of places exhibit a surge in Bavaria, southwestern Germany, and Scotland. Shared surges also are noted in 1615 and between 1660 and 1665 in several settings.

Behringer argues that shared rhythms reflect the common impact of rising prices, declining real wages, climatically induced hardship, and disease epidemics during the sixteenth century, attributing the surge in 1590 to such crises. An assessment of the overall relevance of environmental and economic circumstances as well as the impact of war on witch hunts will require

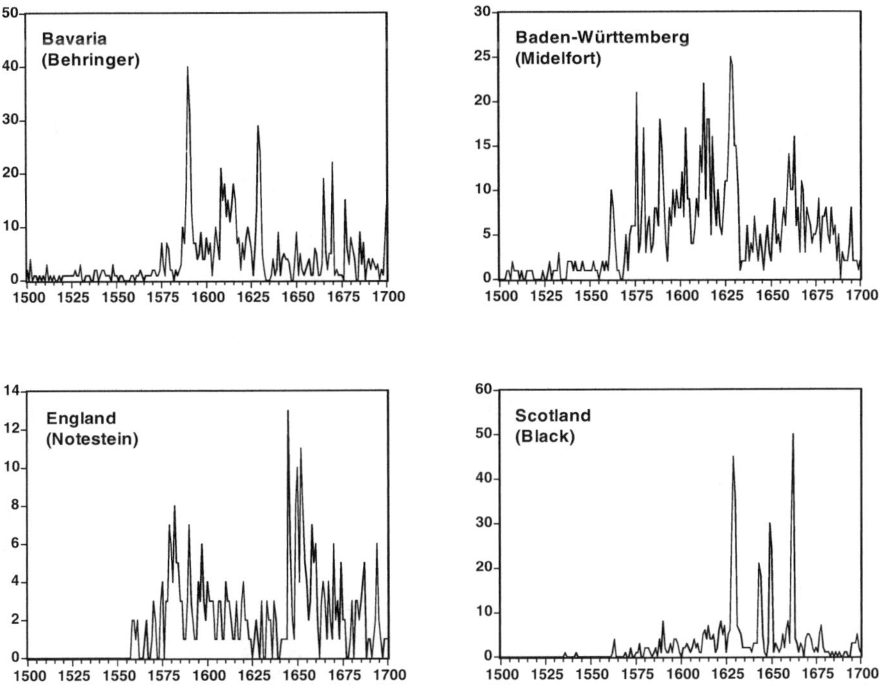

Figure 4.3. Number of place names in witch trial data for Bavaria, Baden-Württemberg, England, and Scotland, 1500–1700.

data that tap variations in such circumstances over time. This chapter will concentrate on the measurement of disease, war, climate, and hardship in Germany, paying special attention to the "heartland" of the witch craze, southwestern Germany. Behringer's argument about the importance of the 1585–1595 witch hunts for theories will be examined in chapter 5, together with analyses of two specific witch hunts that appear to challenge common historical patterns.

Disease

Midelfort (1972: 123) plotted the number of different communities experiencing a disease epidemic in his monograph using Keyser's state books for the Baden-Württemberg region and reported that between 1500 and 1680, 200 of 299 towns in the Baden-Württemberg state books made reference to a disease epidemic in community records. It was that graph that prompted him to observe a "general" correspondence between epidemics and witch hunts, coupled with perplexing anomalies.

Keyser's historical and demographic yearbooks summarize information from community records for six regions of West Germany: North Rhineland, Rhineland, Hessen, Saarland, Bavaria, and Baden-Württemberg (see figure 4.2). The six yearbooks include variable amounts of historical data on 921 communities, ranging from 15 communities in Saarland to 299 in Baden-Württemberg.

Any attempt at comparisons among regions must recognize that there may be considerable variation in (1) the degree to which the set of communities encompassed in a given yearbook constitutes a representative sample of the historic base of communities in that area, as well as (2) the number and representativeness of communities over time. However, if some patterns of variation among regions make sense in terms of other sources of historical information, confidence that the data are capturing meaningful patterns will be enhanced.

The number of communities with a recorded reference to pestilence or other diseases for all regions combined is plotted in figure 4.4, and the percentages of base communities with such references for the five areas studied are plotted in figure 4.5. The "pestilence" and "other disease" series are highly correlated with one another ($r = +.88$), but with references to pestilence exceeding references to all other diseases combined by about two to one. In the Baden-Württemberg communities, the most common disease reference was to "pest" with pestilence referred to in the records of 63 percent of the 200 communities that had a disease reference (or 42 percent of the 299 communities in Keyser's book for Baden-Württemberg).[4] Of course, the absence of a community record does not preclude the possibility that a community did experience plague, just as a variety of diseases might prompt mention of an epidemic. Among other diseases referred to in community records were smallpox, measles, typhus, the "English sweats," dysentery, and diphtheria. General terms such as *fever* and *epidemic* were used as well. For purposes of this analysis, the focus will be on pestilence data, recognizing that fluctuations in pestilence are highly correlated with fluctuations in other diseases.

Since plague epidemics spread throughout Europe, fairly strong correlations over time among pestilence records for these regions should be expected, and it seems plausible to expect that correlations would be stronger for adjacent than nonadjacent regions. The correlations are, indeed, quite high for adjacent regions (see table 4.1). For example, the correlation between pestilence series for Hessen and Baden-Württemberg is +.81. The correlations for the adjacent pairs (1) Hessen and Rhineland-Saarland and (2) Baden-Württemberg and Bavaria are +.69 and +.70. The weakest correlations are for the most distant pairs, with a +.36 for North Rhineland and

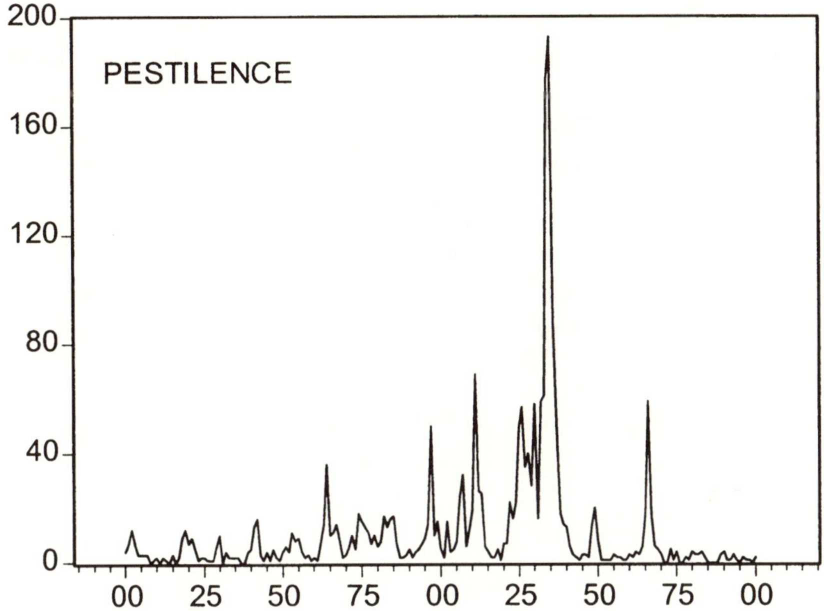

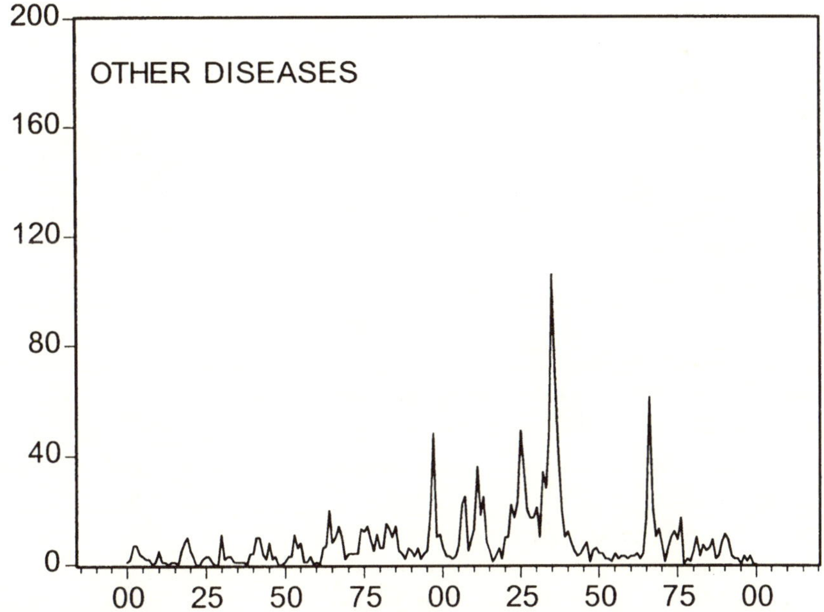

Figure 4.4. Community references to pestilence and other diseases (all regions).

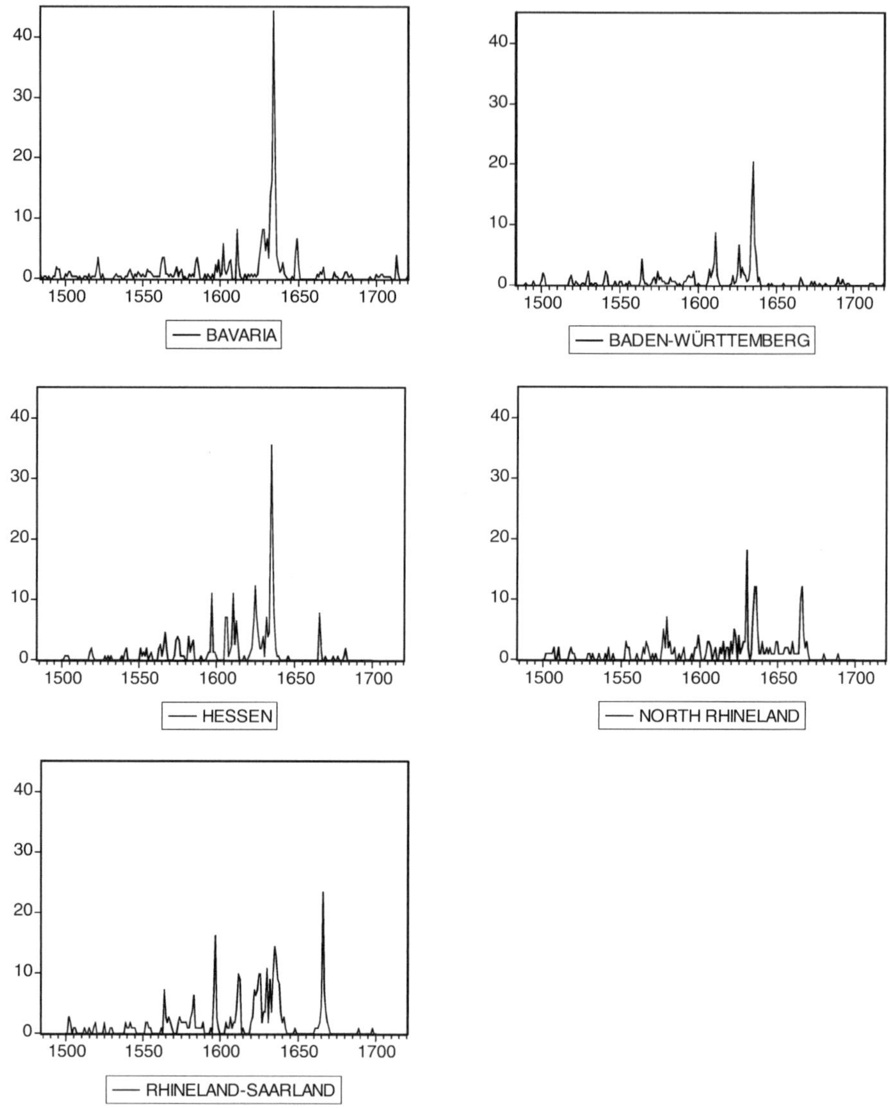

Figure 4.5. Percentage of base communities with a record of pestilence by region.

Bavaria and +.41 for Rhineland-Saarland and Bavaria. For all adjacent pairs, the average correlation is +.62 as compared to +.40 for nonadjacent pairs. In sum, measures of pestilence over time are more likely to follow the same pattern for pairs of neighbors than when comparing pairs for more distant regions. The fact that the data yield such plausible patterns suggests that they are capturing variations that behave in a meaningful manner.

Table 4.1. Correlations for Pestilence

	Bavaria	*Rhineland-Saarland*	*North Rhineland*	*Hessen*
Baden-Württemberg	+0.70	+0.55	+0.44	+0.81
Bavaria	—	+0.41	+0.36	+0.45
Rhineland-Saarland	—	—	+0.63	+0.69
North Rhineland	—	—	—	+0.53

Bivariate analysis can be misleading, but the plots of pestilence references for all regions and for Baden-Württemberg do bear a resemblance to the plot of executions. Two major outbreaks of plague in Baden-Württemberg are centered around 1610–1611 and 1626–1628, which puts them in close temporal proximity to two peaks in major epidemics of witch executions in 1611–1613 and 1628–1632. The peak in places with pestilence is reached in 1635, which, as Midelfort noted, is not accompanied by serious witch hunting (five executions estimated for that year), and there is a small surge in 1641, with twenty-two executions. The anomaly for 1635 could reflect the intensity of war in Baden-Württemberg, which peaked between 1632 and 1635. A multivariate analysis will be required to untangle the effects of positively correlated variables that may have contrary effects on witch hunts.

War

Several attempts have been made to measure dimensions of war or violent conflict (e.g., see Wright 1942; Levy 1983), but most of them are too general to taken as an estimates of such variables for this specific region. Hence, war was measured in much the same fashion as disease by coding communal records referring to violent conflict, rebellion, war, and war-related variables. References to events such as plundering, capture of the city, troops, occupation, sackings, uprisings, besiegement, battles, destruction, war losses, devastation, and a variety of related terms were used to code communities as "experiencing" or perceiving violent conflict or war in a given year. The number of communities with a conflict reference in a given year is used to estimate the prevalence of war.

The percentages of base communities with a record referring to war or conflict are summarized in figure 4.6. In all regions except North Rhineland, the period from about 1560 to 1635 is relatively peaceful, especially in Baden-Württemberg and Hessen. It should be noted that witch hunts were still quite intense (but declining) during some spans of time when war references were quite high. In fact, the overall bivariate relationship is quite weak

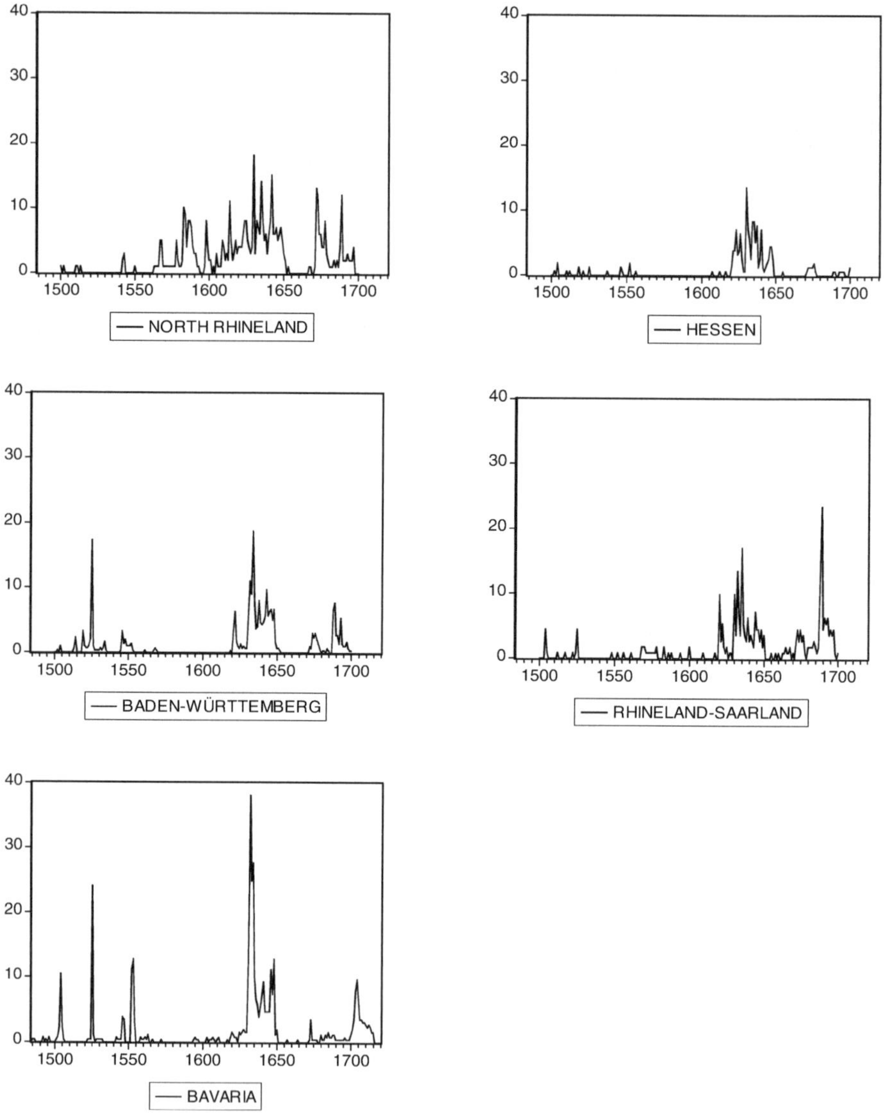

Figure 4.6. Percentage of base communities with a war reference by region.

because of such disparities. However, just as the relation of pestilence to witch hunts can be affected by a positive correlation with war, the anticipated inhibiting impact of war can be masked by its association with pestilence.

As was the case for pestilence, war in any one region is a correlate of war in other regions (see table 4.2). The correlations tend to be stronger for ad-

Table 4.2. Correlations for War Scores

	Bavaria	*Rhineland-Saarland*	*North Rhineland*	*Hessen*
Baden-Württemberg	+0.78	+0.58	+0.38	+0.52
Bavaria	—	+0.44	+0.27	+0.52
Rhineland-Saarland	—	—	+0.55	+0.48
North Rhineland	—	—	—	+0.54

jacent pairs (+.63 on the average) than nonadjacent pairs (+.46). It should also be noted that there is a positive correspondence between war and plague, with correlations between the two series ranging from +.23 for Rhineland-Saarland to +.61 for Bavaria. The correlation between war and pestilence for Baden-Württemberg is +.33. The most serious plague epidemic in Baden-Württemberg and other regions (see figures 4.5 and 4.6) overlaps with the most serious period of conflict.

Additional sources of historical data can be used to assess the sensitivity of these measures to variations discerned by other means. For example, reports of the location of battles and troops during the Thirty Years War can be used to assess the patterns suggested by community war references. Langer's (1980) summary of major battles suggests that war references for the northern region of Baden and other northern regions should be more prominent in the early phases of the Thirty Years War than for the more southern regions. As illustrated in figure 4.7, this pattern does, in fact, appear in the series for specific regions. For communities in southern Baden, war references for the early phase (1618–1625) are one-third as common as in the later phases. For northern Baden, a spike in war references during the early phase is quite prominent and comparable to later phases of the war. Similarly, war references for Rhineland-Saarland, North Rhineland, and Hessen are more comparable to later phases of the war than is the case for Württemberg, South Baden, or Bavaria.

Prior attempts have been made to measure war in this general area, and the relationship between the community-based measure and other measures were examined. A standardized score summing the number of different Central European countries involved in wars of any kind from 1500 to 1700 using Wright's (1965: tables 31–34) data from *A Study of War* is plotted together with similar scores based on total number of community references in Keyser's works for all six regions in figure 4.8. There is a close correspondence between the two series, with a correlation of +.68 between Wright's measure and the community-based measure. Together with specific variations in battles and phases of the Thirty Years War, the correspondence with alternative

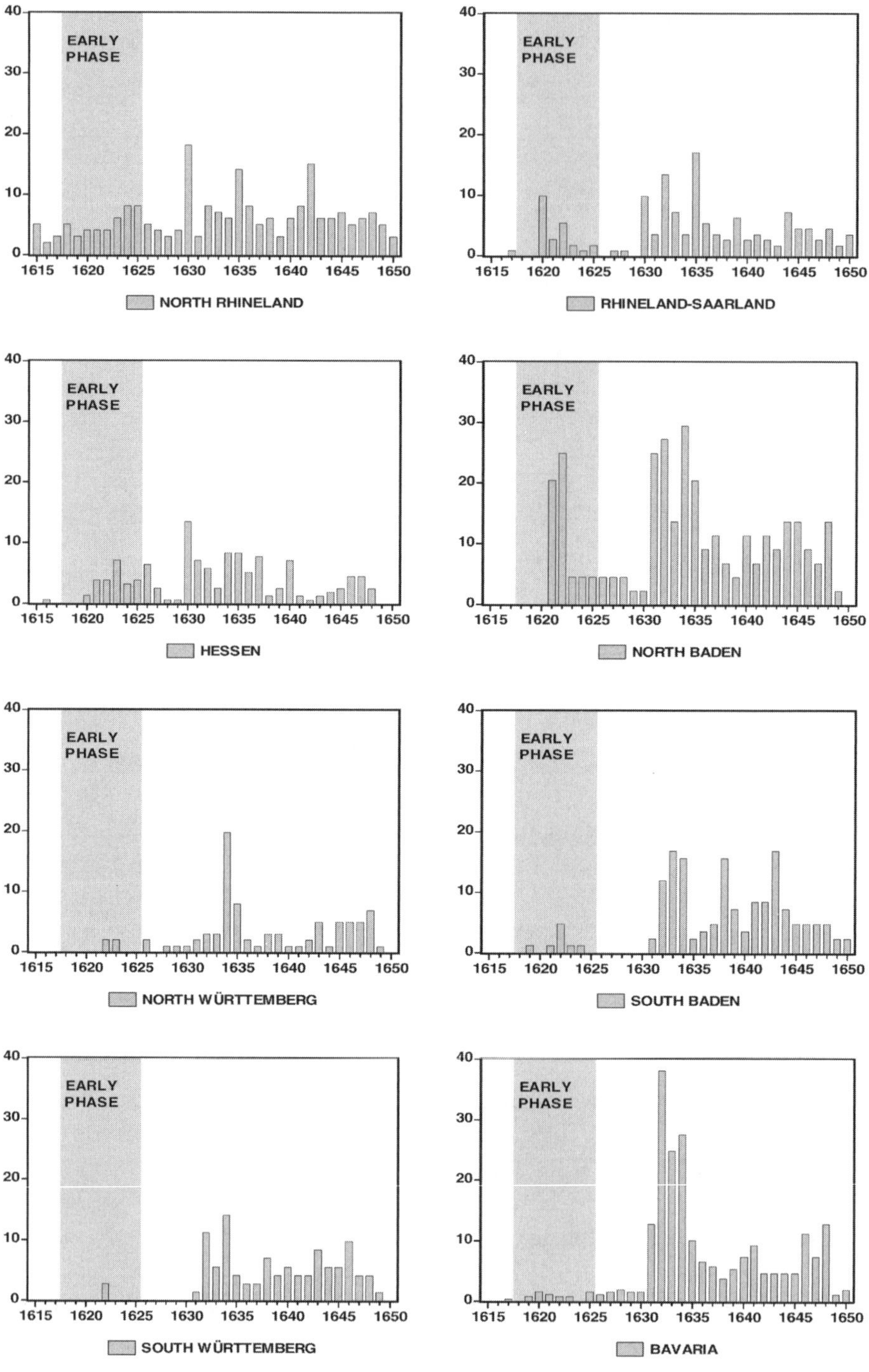

Figure 4.7. Percentage of communities with references to warfare during the Thirty Years War.

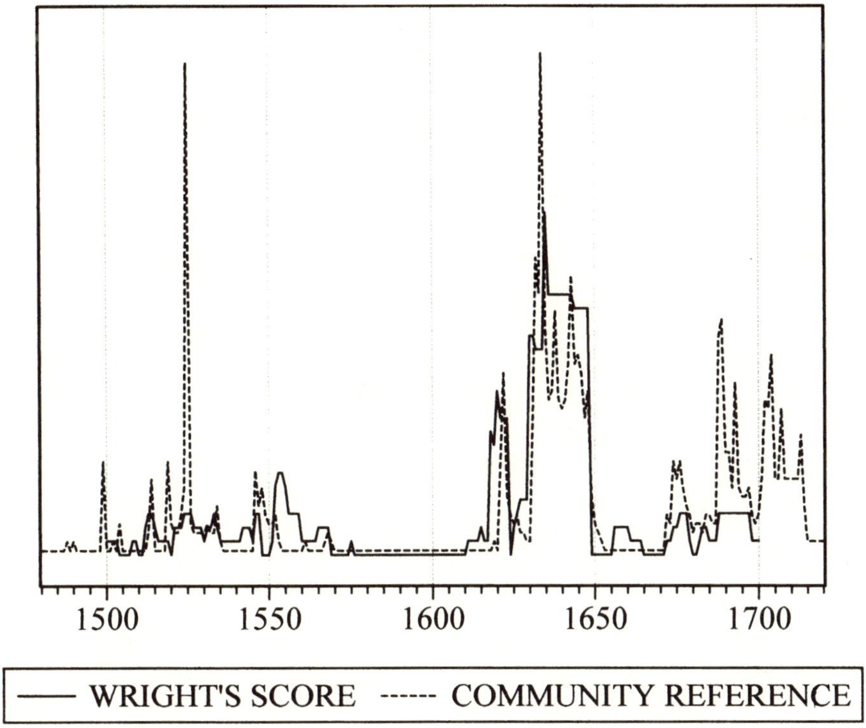

Figure 4.8. Wright's measure and the community reference measure of war.

measures suggests that the community reference data are tapping similar underlying events over time.

Hardship

A considerable volume of literature by historians and climatologists attempts to estimate climatic variation over long periods of time before humans began compiling systematic measures (e.g., see Ladurie 1971; Lamb 1977; Rotberg and Rabb 1981). Researchers have used indicators ranging from concentrations of carbon isotopes affected by solar output and gravitational fields, to the accumulation of pollen in sediments, tree rings, and dates of wine harvests. Three measures will be examined here: (1) the width of tree rings, (2) days to first wine harvest (from September 1), and (3) wheat prices. In general, narrow rings and late harvests have been taken as evidence of austere climatic conditions and high wheat prices as evidence of economic hardship for a population.

Tree Rings

Because harvest dates and wheat prices were more readily influenced by human activities and decision making (e.g. war, optimal profit) than the growth of trees in the early modern period, the width of tree rings would seem an ideal measure of climatic crises and stresses over time. However, such data are difficult to interpret because wide tree rings can reflect (among other things) the amount of sunlight received, temperature, and/or wetness. Unusually wet weather during some times of the year is bad for crops, and wide rings can indicate unfavorable climatic conditions for food production. Wide rings can also indicate above-average temperature or sunlight and be indicative of conditions favorable for food production. There is some indication that under arid conditions, tree ring thickness reflects variations in rainfall, while in northern latitudes tree ring thickness reflects temperature. For moderate latitudes, rings may reflect both temperature and rainfall.

Two series of tree ring measures are available for Germany, one for west of the Rhine near Trier (Hollstein 1965; Lamb 1977: 595–98) and one for the Spessart Forest area in the northern part of Baden-Württemberg (Huber and Giertz-Siebenlist 1969; Lamb 1977: 599–602).

Standardized annual scores and twenty-nine-year moving averages for the two series over a seven-hundred-year span of time (1200–1900) are plotted in figure 4.9. The plot for the Spessart tree rings is especially interesting because it shows the period from 1560 to 1675 to be the longest sustained span of below-average ring width in the history of the series. Moreover, the scores reach a historic low in very close proximity to the height of witch hunting in southwestern Germany (1620–1635). The pattern for the Trier rings is less apparent but consistent with the observation suggested by the Spessart tree rings. There are major valleys in the fourteenth, seventeenth, and nineteenth centuries, and record-narrow rings fall in the same span of time as the most virulent witch hunting.

Although the two series do not coincide perfectly over this seven-hundred-year span of time, they are correlated with one another overall (r = +.54), and annual variations in each "detrended" series (i.e., first differences) have a very high probability of coinciding as well (r = +.72). The Spessart rings exhibit the most dramatic pattern vis-à-vis the early modern witch craze, but the pattern observed for the Trier rings using moving averages coincides as well. Further evidence relevant to the validity of these measures as indicators of climatic hardship will require comparison with other potential indicators—a topic that will be addressed later in this chapter.

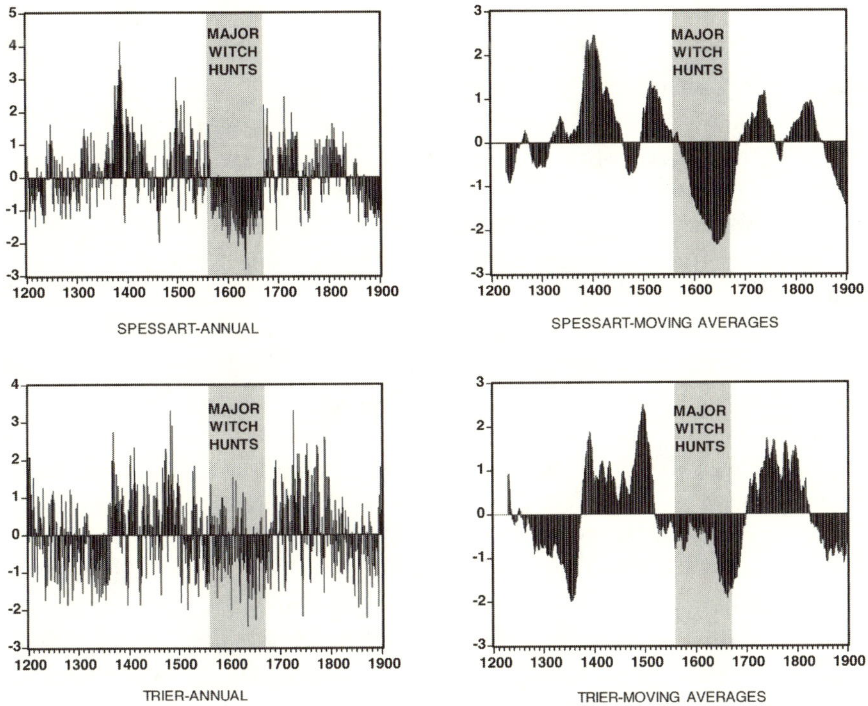

Figure 4.9. Width of tree rings, 1200–1900 (standard scores—annual and moving averages).

Harvest Dates

Ladurie and Baulant (1981: 262) have created a measure of average days to first wine harvest (with September 1 as the reference date) based on data from northeastern France, French Switzerland, and South Rhineland for 1484–1879. They report a correlation of –.86 between Parisian temperatures and this measure of global harvest date during the span of time when the two types of data overlap. They conclude that early harvest dates are indicative of warmer weather and that they appear to be most strongly correlated with temperatures in May and June.

Harvest dates involve human decisions and can reflect numerous circumstances other than the weather during the growing season. In his early work with these series, Ladurie (1971) argued that the long-term trend in mean harvest dates was upward in the sixteenth and seventeenth centuries as wine growers sought a grape richer in sugar. Pfister (1981: 95) notes that an early frost or snowfall could trigger harvests in years when the grapes were slow in maturing. It may be that other variables such as war or labor supply affected such decisions as well.

In an analysis of Ladurie and Baulant's (1981) updated global harvest dates, astronomer Barbara Bell (1981: 271–78) reports that the mean did not begin a long upward trend until after 1720. Hence, the period for which harvest dates are available and do not have to be adjusted for that "viticultural revolution" or transition includes the same span of time as the data on witch hunts, 1484–1720.

Annual data and moving averages for harvest dates are plotted in figure 4.10. The span of time from 1550 to the mid-1580s is characterized by later and later harvest dates, with a gradual movement toward earlier harvests from that peak to the late 1600s. There is relatively little change in level for the series over time, and the series does not exhibit any unusual variability during the span of time encompassing the most intense witch hunts.

Although the late harvests coincide with the "agrarian crisis" emphasized by Behringer and reach their worst years just prior to the major witch hunts in Bavaria, the overall correspondence with witch hunts in southwestern Germany is quite poor. Neither the annual data nor moving averages vary in a manner that would make sense of fluctuations in early modern witch hunts, other than the peak in 1590.

Precise data on annual fluctuations provide additional grounds for questioning the use of harvest dates to estimate climatic hardship. Ladurie (1971: 43–44) notes that there was a period of alternating hot and cold weather between 1530 and 1541, generating a sawtooth pattern in tree ring data and harvest dates. As graphed in figure 4.11, that exact pattern is reproduced for all three series for 1529 through 1541. The correlation between harvests dates and Spessart rings is +.80, the comparable correlation is +.70 for Trier rings, and the correlation between the two ring series during that brief span of time is +.88.

Ladurie cites the shared sawtooth pattern as support for the view that the two different types of data are measuring similar variations, but further analysis of these series shows that span of time is unique. For sixteen twenty-year intervals between 1480 and 1781, the correlation for the span encompassing 1529 through 1541 is larger than any other interval. Thus, it would be misleading to take that span of years as representative of the relationship over time in that the correlations between harvest dates and ring width are considerably weaker over other spans of time. For example, for 1501 to 1520, the correlations are +.22 for harvest dates and Spessart rings and +.12 for Trier rings (+.24 and +.23 when first differences removing trends are used). Be-

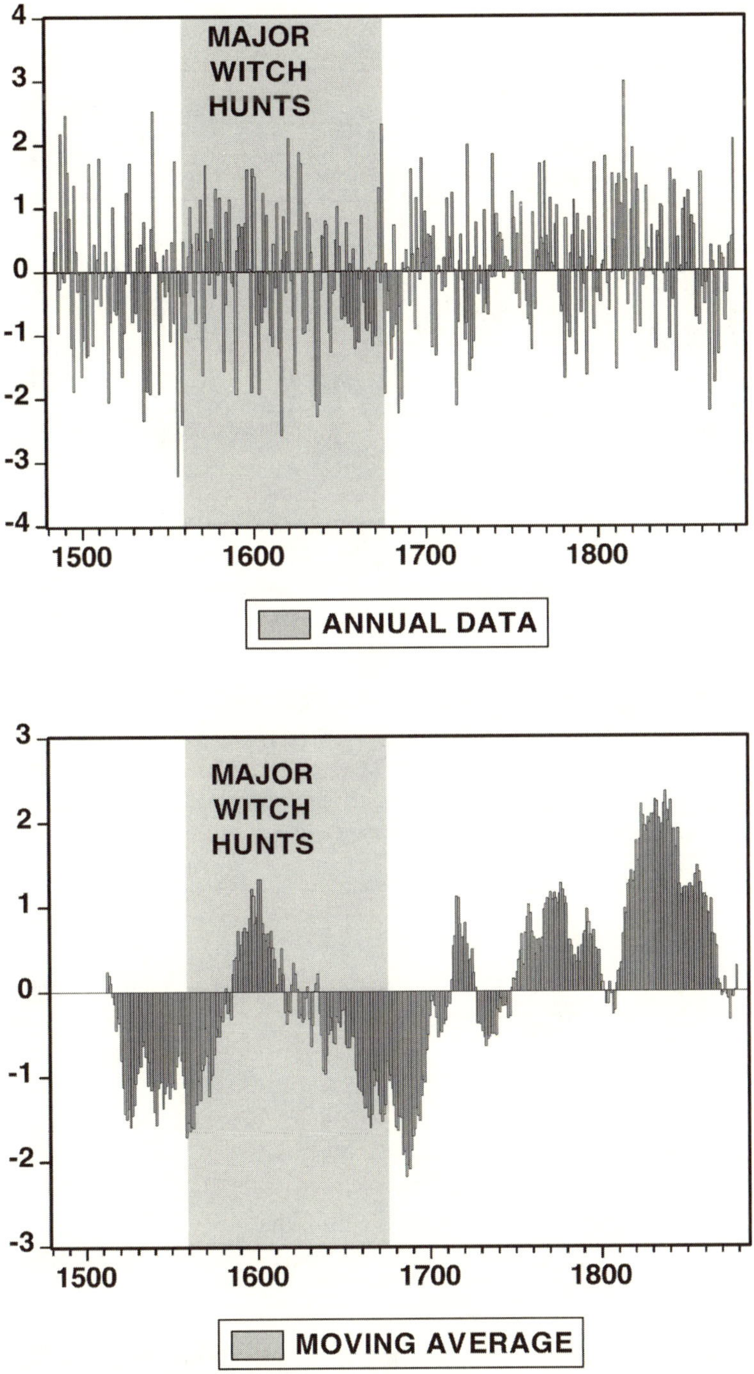

Figure 4.10. Days to first wine harvest from September 1, 1484, to September 1, 1879 (standard scores—annual and moving averages).

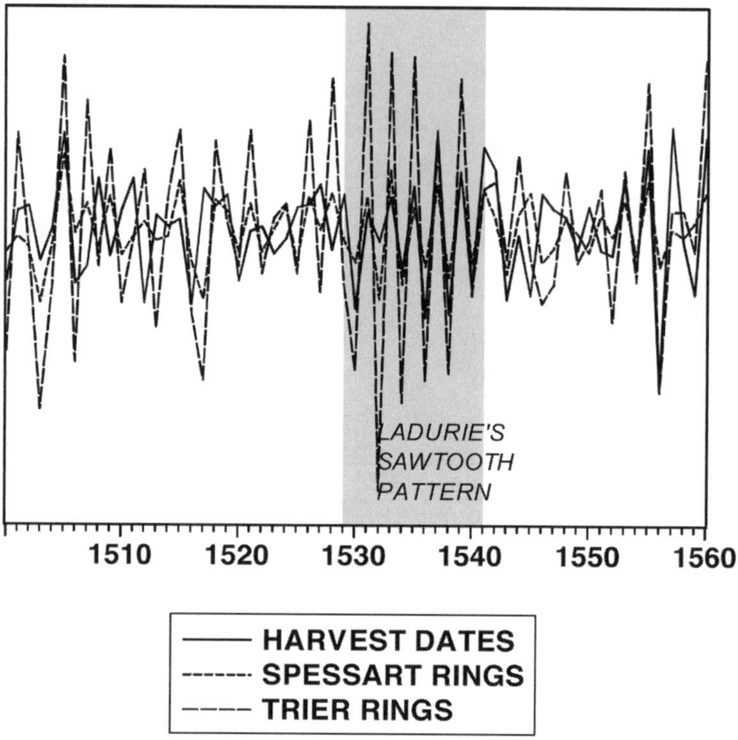

Figure 4.11. Wine harvest dates and tree ring width (1500–1560).

tween 1561 and 1580, the correlations are even weaker (+.07 for undifferenced Spessart rings and +.38 for first differences; +.10 for undifferenced Trier rings and +.33 for first differences). For the entire span of years, 1484 to 1781, the correlation is +.14 for Spessart rings and +.29 for Trier rings (+.31 for each when using first differences). In sum, there is a positive correlation, but it is quite small in comparison to the time period selected by Ladurie.

The fact that the relationships are positive is perplexing were late harvest dates and narrow rings to be taken as indicative of cold temperatures. Late dates coupled with narrow rings (i.e., a negative correlation) would be expected were they both measures of summer temperature. However, other research with these series suggests that narrow rings may indicate low levels of moisture or drought (see Lamb 1977: 223). If the link between tree ring width and harvest dates reflects moisture/drought, then the positive correlation makes sense.

Wheat Prices

Another measure potentially relevant to hardship is German wheat prices. Although they are not based specifically on Baden-Württemberg, data on wheat prices are available for 1531–1785 for Cologne (northwest of the region) and for 1484–1617 for Augsburg (southwest of the region).[5] The estimated wheat prices are plotted in figure 4.12 together with English and French wheat prices.[6] The series in all three settings are highly correlated: +.72 for France-England, +.87 for Germany-France, and +.87 for Germany-England. In all three settings, prices began an accelerated upward movement around 1550–1560, with a surge in the last two decades of that century. Prices fluctuated markedly in the seventeenth century with little sustained relief until the 1650s. Prices started up again around 1670. As plotted in figure 4.11, the most virulent early modern witch hunting spanned the same period of time as the sustained upward movement in prices (1560–1650). Moreover, the surge in prices in the 1580s and 1590s does precede the surge in witch hunts noted by Behringer in his research on Bavaria.

Several scholars have claimed that the period of most intense witch hunting was a period when wages did not keep up with rising prices. Hence, increases in prices can be considered indicative of increases in hardship. Van Bath (1963: 199) has estimated real wages for day laborers in Germany for twenty-five-year intervals; those data are summarized in figure 4.13. The span of time encompassing the witch hunts is a period of declining real wages, and the most intense witch hunts occurred in the span of years when real wages were extremely low. With the decimation of the population in the Thirty Years War, real wages rebounded between 1650 and 1675 but fell again at the end of the century.

Relationships among Measures

An examination of patterns of relationships among a variety of measures of climatic variation and other variables might help identify the most promising measures of hardship. For example, climatic conditions ought to affect wheat prices. German wheat prices are negatively correlated with ring width at Spessart (–.51) but not Trier (–.07), and days to first wine harvest are very weakly correlated with wheat prices in Germany (+.08), France (+.08), and England (+.07). In fact, harvest dates and Trier ring width fail to enter into significant relationships with either measures of war or plague. In contrast, Spessart ring width is significantly related to war in both Baden-Württemberg (–.20) and Bavaria (–.22) as well as to the prevalence of plague among communities in these two settings (–.26 for Baden-Württemberg;

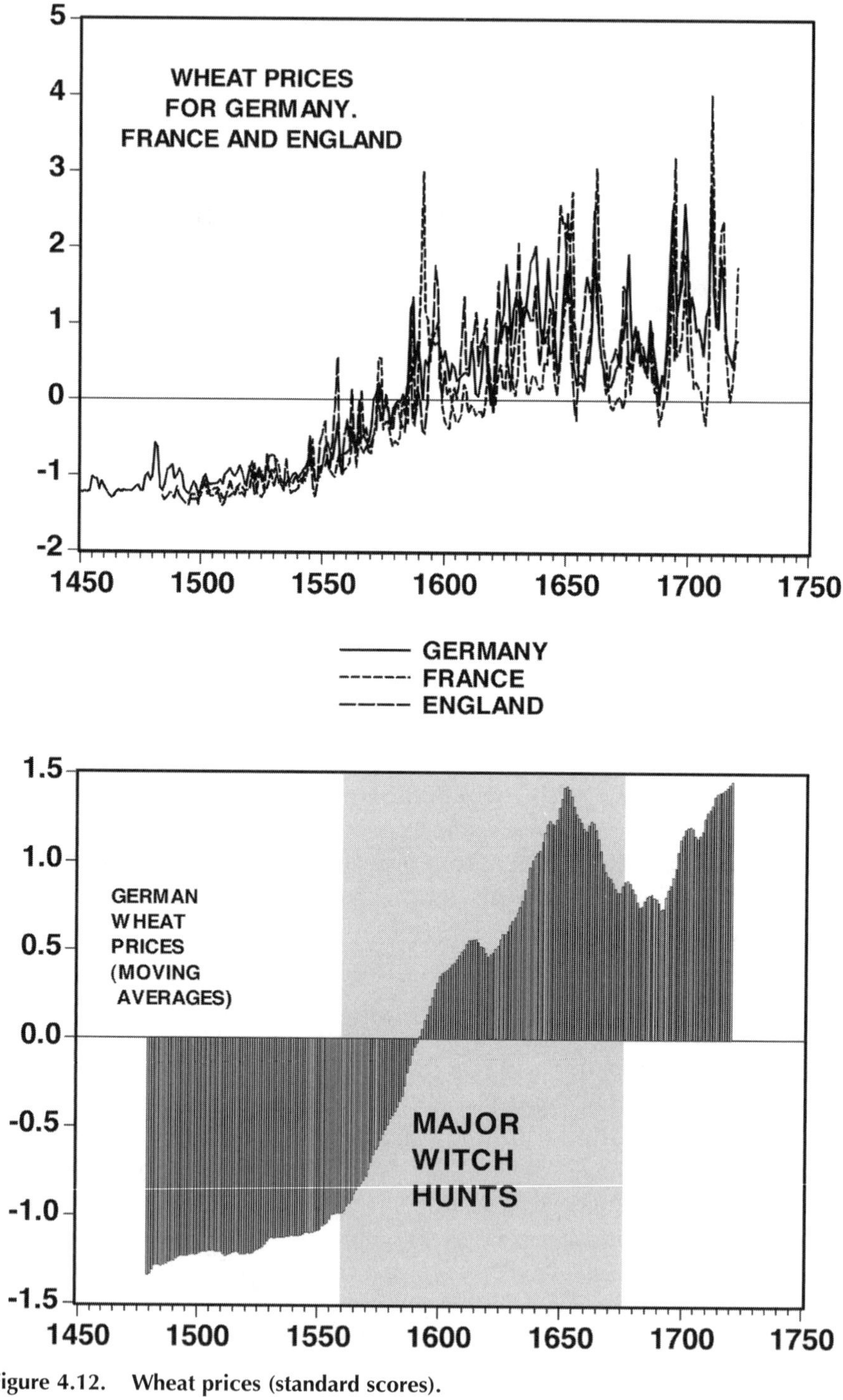

Figure 4.12. Wheat prices (standard scores).

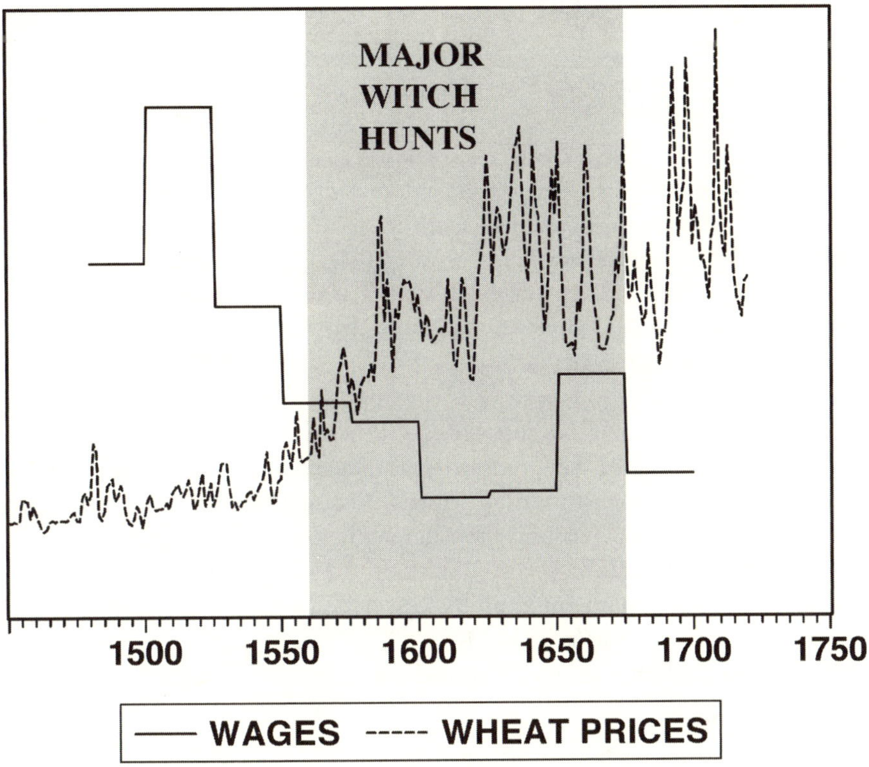

Figure 4.13. Estimated real wages for a German day laborer and wheat prices (standard scores).

–.26 for Bavaria). Similar relationships were found for German wheat prices, with high prices positively correlated with war and plague. In short, Spessart rings and wheat prices enter into relationships with other variables that are consistent with historical observation, but harvest dates and Trier rings do not.

J. R. Bray (1978) has examined the relationship between volcanic activity and measures of climate between 1500 and 1970, including poor grain harvests and periods of glacial advance in the Alps. He concludes that poor harvests and glacial advances both tend to follow volcanic eruptions. Using the harvest data for Western Europe and England and the data on glacial advances in the Alps, he determined that the correlation between eruptions and poor harvests in England was +.23, with a one-year lag for 1500 to 1720, and +.10 for Western Europe, with a two-year lag. Glacial advances are correlated with eruptions as well but with a three- to five-year lag (+.17, +.15, and +.14). In sum, poor harvests in England and Western Europe follow volcanic eruptions by one or two years, and glacial advance follows eruptions by three to five years.

Eruption data might help identify the most promising measures of hardship, and the relationships between Bray's eruption scores and first differences in the width of oak tree rings for Spessart and Trier and first differences in harvest dates were examined. There is a significant negative correlation (–.13) between ring width for Spessart oaks and volcanic activity, with a one-year lag consistent with Bray's findings. Eruptions tend to be followed one year later by narrowing rings. However, no relationship for tree rings near Trier could be found, and there was one significant correlation for harvest dates, with increases in harvest dates following eruptions by seven years (+.14). Hence, of these three potential indicators of climatic hardship, the only measure behaving similarly to Bray's analysis using first differences was tree ring thickness in Spessart. Together with the findings on relationships with measures of war and plague, the Spessart rings are the more promising indicator of climatic hardship than harvest dates or Trier ring width. German wheat prices and Spessart ring width will be included in the analysis in chapter 5 together with measures of war and plague.

Conclusion

This chapter described data relevant to the measurement of variations in witch hunts, disease, war, and hardship. As is well-known, the four horsemen did ride together with sufficient intensity in the seventeenth century to consider it a century of apocalyptic crises. Indeed, if the various plots for war, disease, and climatic and economic hardship are considered together, then there is rarely any span of time free from problems. The period of most intense witch hunts was a period of rising prices, increasing cold, periodic war, and epidemic disease. Yet, although the apocalyptic horsemen often rode together in early modern Europe, they also made independent forays. Plague and war are correlated with one another, but there are periods of relative peace characterized by repeated outbreaks of pestilence. Moreover, both war and pestilence were sporadic crises occurring in the context of a general upward movement in prices, peaking around the end of the Thirty Years War, and a downward trend in temperature that bottomed out sometime between 1650 and 1680.

Even a casual inspection of the data in this chapter challenges some interpretations of the witch craze and provides preliminary support for others.

Andreski's syphilitic shock is a poor candidate for explaining variations over time in the intensity of witch hunts in southwestern Germany. It did precede the beginning of the intense witch craze but by a considerable number of years, and it does not make sense of any other dimension of temporal variation. Moreover, syphilis is rarely mentioned in compilations of community records, while plague and other diseases are perennially documented. Plague appears to vary in a manner far more coincident with the severity of witch hunts than syphilis, with the most obvious anomalies during periods of war.

Of the potential measures of climatic hardship, the long-term trends in tree ring width (especially Spessart rings) fit the conception of this period as the most intense span of the Little Ice Age. The longest span of below-average ring width in a full seven centuries is found for 1560–1670. In general, the narrower the tree rings, the more intense the witch hunting. In addition, more intricate analyses suggest that the Spessart tree ring data are the most promising as a measure of climate hardship for more precise analysis in that they are the only data that behave as expected when examined in relation to the dust veil index and wheat prices. Data presented in earlier research as evidence that tree rings and harvest dates reveal comparable temporal patterns are misleading in that the pattern reported was specific to a short span of time and was inconsistent with the interpretation of wide tree ring width as indicative of favorable climatic conditions.

However, even harvest dates and Trier rings suggest a pattern of hardship that spans the same time as the most virulent witch hunting. Harvest dates grew progressively later beginning in 1560 and did not return to the early dates of the mid-sixteenth century until 1660. Trier ring width was narrower between 1560 and 1700 on the average than any time since the mid-fourteenth century. In short, there is general agreement among indicators that 1560 through 1670 was fraught with hardship.

In chapter 5, the relationships between measures of apocalyptic crises and the severity of witch hunts at several levels of temporal precision will be examined. A consideration of different levels of precision is mandatory not only in view of warnings about being overly precise in the analysis of historical data, but because theories are often formulated to explain general trends or patterns of change rather than more intricate variations. As will be argued in a preliminary discussion, recent analyses of time series data in sociological and criminological literature are not appropriate models for testing most hypotheses about covariation in historical phenomena. Neither quantitative nor qualitative social historical analysts have paid much attention either to the different ways in which phenomena can covary over time or to the fit between the theory under discussion and the type of statistical analysis conducted.

Notes

1. See Scarre (1987), Barstow (1994), and Levack (1996) for summary reviews and statistics.

2. In the appendix to his work on witch hunting, Midelfort (1972) lists witch hunts chronologically, based on secondary sources and archival collections, encompassing a total of 274 different places of confession. Those data allow estimates of several properties of witch hunts. Two to be examined here are number of people executed and number of different places of confession. The number executed in a given year will be taken as a measure of the intensity of witch hunting and the number of different places of confession in a given year will be considered as a measure of the communal prevalence of witch hunting in that area. When executions occurred during an interval, cases were distributed evenly over the interval. If there were overlapping intervals, the cases were first distributed over the intervals and then added together to estimate the number for a given year. When the number was unknown and the designation "several" was used, the number of cases was coded as three. When the designation "many" was used, the number of cases was coded as six.

3. Since executions were comparatively rare in England as compared with Germany, the designation "several" was coded as two executions rather than three as with Midelfort's data. That designation was used only four times in Notestein's compilation of English witchcraft cases and has no significant impact on correlations or comparative statements about the intensity of witch hunts among societies.

4. In addition to references to pestis, references specifically to the "Black Death" or the "Great Death" were counted as pestilence. General references to an "epidemic" were coded under "other disease" epidemics. The effect of including general references to epidemic together with plague references was examined, and the correlation between the "pestis-only" measure and the more general measure including epidemics was +.96.

Three different coders were assigned to the same data on pestilence in Baden-Württemberg to assess the degree of agreement for time series generated by different coders. The correlations among measures of plague over time for different coders ranged between .93 and .98. While diseases other than plague may be included under the general category "pest," that variable can be measured reliably over time.

5. The regression equation relating the two series for overlapping years was used to generate estimates for Cologne wheat prices for 1484 through 1530 (for the years when the two series overlap, the correlation is +.65). The Augsburg price series is from Paas (1979: app. K) and the Cologne series is from Goldstein (1988: appendix).

6. French wheat prices are from Goldstein (1988: appendix) and English wheat prices are from Hoskins (1964, 1968).

CHAPTER FIVE

Relationships over Time

Title page of Ulrich Moliter's *De lanijs et phitonicus mulieribus,* Cologne, 1489. Reprinted with the permission of Dover Publications.

Two broad questions guide the construction of precise hypotheses about temporal variations in the prevalence and intensity of witch hunts. Given the necessary cultural and institutional prerequisites for witch hunting, what conditions encourage a "percolation" of grievances and anxieties from below as well as "receptivity" to respond to such grievances as a matter for formal social control from above? Second, what conditions inhibit the search for, or punishment of, witches as hidden, internal enemies or interrupt the course of such hunts when in progress? Historians and social scientists interested in witch hunts tend to pay more attention to the "peaks" than to the "valleys" in the search for explanations, with valleys implicitly attributed to the absence of the conditions generating the peaks. Yet, valleys may reflect the transcendence of problems that necessitate a redirection of resources, despite the persistence of forces that encourage peaks under other circumstances.

A consideration of the social structure of witch hunts and the circumstances that could affect the distinct parties to such local conflicts leads to several hypotheses that would make sense out of temporal (and, ultimately, spatial) variations, including both valleys and peaks.

Because witch hunts were organized and structured with distinctive characteristics and networks of (1) the bewitched, (2) accusers, (3) accused, and (4) gatekeepers for formal control, variables affecting propensities in each category could affect the prevalence and intensity of witch hunts. For example, conditions that facilitated mental or behavioral problems could increase cases of possession or "strange" illnesses, thus increasing the number of people who might be defined as bewitched. Local conflicts and factions among neighbors and within communities could increase sensitivity to strange behavior as well as enhance any tendency to attribute misfortune and problems of family members to internal enemies as scapegoats. More people would be willing to lodge accusations. The availability and visibility of potential "witches" liable to accusation could be affected by some of these same conditions (i.e., increases in mental and behavioral problems and increases in factional conflict among neighbors). A perceived increase in witches could be affected by circumstances that increased the supply of people who fit the witch stereotype or that enhanced the intensity of their interaction in the community. Finally, since gatekeepers at the local level were the primary "gate openers" for the institutional processing of witches, the same communal or neighborhood circumstances that affect other parties in a witch hunt (the bewitched, accusers, and the accused) could also affect the gatekeepers. Additional "motives" and aims for formal control may be relevant. and any circumstances that increase the perceived need by formal gatekeepers to intervene at the local level or to encourage the upward percolation of local grievances would increase the prevalence and intensity of witch hunts.

The review of scholarship on early modern witch hunts in chapters 1–3 suggests several hypotheses about the course of witch executions and witch trials over time that should be amenable to test using the measures described in chapter 4. Emile Durkheim's "Society of Saints" thesis, Kai Erickson's extension of his thesis to colonial witch hunting, and historians' compilations of quantitative data on witch hunts all imply that *war and other forms of overt structured conflict within a territory should be inversely related to the intensity of witch hunting*. People are not likely to invent and pursue "imaginary" enemies when coping with more serious, direct and identifiable threats to their survival. In contrast, Rodney Stark (2003) argues for a positive relationship between religious conflict and witch hunts, and Robin Briggs (1996b) raises the possibility that war on the fringes of a society might facilitate witch hunts while more proximate wars might inhibit them.

As demonstrated in chapter 3, syphilis is not a good candidate for explaining most of the temporal variations in the intensity of early modern witch hunts in contrast to the spread of plague. Although there are divergent opinions on the issue, the second hypothesis to be tested is that *plague epidemics within a territory are positively related to the intensity of witch hunting*. Plague and smallpox, major sources of mortality crises in the early modern period, were interpreted as a sign of disfavor with God. Moreover, some of the early trials specifically involved charges of plague spreading, an accusation that had led to the persecution of Jews two centuries earlier.

Economic hardship and subsistence crises are often mentioned as possible correlates of witch hunting, and variation in climate was the major source of such problems in the early modern period. Bad weather could ruin crops and reduce yields, drive up prices, and increase the hardships experienced by the populace. Such problems could contribute to witch hunting through a variety of the persecution and scapegoating mechanisms outlined in earlier chapters. The third hypothesis to be tested is that *climatic and/or economic hardship are positively related to the intensity of witch hunting*. Since the only measures of climate or hardship that behaved in a consistent and interpretable manner were Spessart tree rings and estimates of German wheat prices (see chapter 4), those data will be used to estimate hardship.

It would seem to be a simple matter to test these hypotheses. Potential indicators have been explored, and a plausible case has been made for their validity. Yet, a search of the literature for examples of the appropriate techniques for testing hypotheses about relationships over time yields no one simple guide to provide instructions on the proper way to conduct such tests, especially when they involve relationships over long spans of history. Indeed, it will be shown here that examples in the research literature that would appear to be plausible sources of rules for conducting such analysis have paid scant attention to issues that must be considered before proceeding. One of the most basic issues is widely ignored: specification of the time-variant properties of the phenomenon to be explained. Before these hypotheses can be tested, questions about the appropriate *historical scale* for such tests as well as the effects of certain standard statistical procedures for analyzing data over time on the "history" of that series must be considered. A key question is whether the tests are appropriate to the historical scale addressed by various theorists. In short, questions about "temporality" or the conceptions of time in social history must be addressed.

Time and Social History[1]

In a special issue of *A Journal of Quantitative and Interdisciplinary History* (Winter 1997), Larry Isaac cites Phillip Abrams's classic work on *Historical Sociology* (1982: xvi) where Abrams observed that "time" was a neglected concept among historical sociologists. A full decade later, Ronald Aminzade (1992, 458) advanced a similar claim, arguing that "temporal concepts do not figure prominently in the vocabulary of the discipline of sociology." Most recently, Doug McAdam and William Sewell Jr. (2001: 89–125) make the same observation about time in the study of social movements and propose that "It's about Time" that the full temporal dimensions of collective phenomenon be identified.

Issac (1997: 5) also observes that historical sociologists have "begun to take time seriously." Isaac and Griffin (1989) and Griffin and Isaac (1992) have been critical of "ahistoricism" in time series analysis and propose that relations between variables have to be considered in historical context. Aminzade (1992: 456) identifies "duration," "pace," "trajectory," and "cycles" as key issues involving time and temporality that are the "building blocks" for historical sociology. Building on the ahistoricism critique, Isaac and Leicht (1997: 28–45) add the notion of "analytic" regimes as broad historical periods shaping relationships among variables at more precise temporal scales. I have proposed (Jensen 1997: 46–57) that relationships can vary at different temporal fractal scales and that theories that appear corroborated at one scale may not be supported at a more precise scale. Finally, McAdam and Sewell (2001: 89–125) believe the time-related notions of "transformative events" and "cultural epochs" need to be added to long-term change and protest cycles as temporal concepts important to the analysis of social movements.

Although some of these issues have been raised in specific critiques of quantitative "time series analysis," they are relevant to an assessment of both discursive and quantitative social history of various kinds. Two consequences of "atemporality" in historical analysis are (1) capricious shifts in levels of temporal aggregation (e.g., mixing the discussion of eras together with more precise fluctuations) as scholars defend favored theories and criticize alternatives and (2) the selection of statistical methods that greatly limit the "history" of the variables studied. Before hypotheses about correlates of early modern witch hunts can be tested, the specific issue of atemporality in quantitative historical sociology must be examined and an attempt made to identify the dimensions of temporality that must be considered in our analysis of early modern witch hunts.

A problem of atemporality in historical sociology can be illustrated by Jack Goldstone's (1991) explanation of state breakdowns and subsequent statements about precision in his award-winning monograph, *Revolution and Rebellion in the Early Modern World.* His central concern is "how to explain periodic waves of state breakdown in the early modern world." Since the crises Goldstone attempts to explain occurred as part of the "general crisis of the seventeenth century," and all within a few decades of each other, he argues that they had common causes. State breakdowns in England, France, and China were driven by population growth coupled with a variety of other structural and economic conditions: elevated prices, generated state fiscal crises, elite competition, and increased mass mobilization potential. Goldstone provides specific formulas and very precise graphs of pressures toward crisis (which he labels "psi"), the accumulation of which is supposed to precede revolutions and rebellions in several societies.

The use of such terms as *periodic* and *cyclical* and the idea that "waves" of rebellion and revolution can be explained by the conjunction of measurable demographic and structural conditions both imply a level of precision and a concern for timing beyond that characterizing prior historical analyses. Indeed, one of the reasons the work is unique among works on rebellion and revolution is its precise specification of formulas and the use of quantitative data to support a common explanation in three societies. Yet, more than halfway through the book, Goldstone (1991) proposes that

> it would be a grievous error to be overly precise in defining the periods of general crisis brought about by demographic pressures. For example, I focus on the English Revolution of 1640. Yet the entire period from 1540 to 1640 was marked by recurrent political difficulties in England. . . . Similarly, in France Wars of Religion in the late sixteenth century arguably constituted a more severe crisis than the Fronde in the mid–seventeenth century. I would thus prefer to consider the whole era of rising population and prices, and of turbulent

> social mobility and falling wages—an era that began in both countries in the early sixteenth century and culminated in the mid–seventeenth century—as prone to state crises, and then oppose that whole era to the period of stability that followed in the late seventeenth and early eighteenth centuries. (345)

In short, after several hundred pages attending to precise timing, sequences. and detail, Goldstone warns that it would be a grievous error to be "overly precise" in defining periods. Instead, an "eras" approach to theory testing is advocated. Although Goldstone may not have intended to advocate a specific position on temporal variables in historical analysis, he implicitly adopts an epistemological rule about cross-temporal relationships—that is, that a correlation at a high level of temporal aggregation is preferable to a correlation based on a more precise periodization of crises and their causes.

Goldstone's position is perplexing for several reasons. For one, there is no a priori reason to prefer one level of aggregation over another. If the data used to test an explanation allow a greater level of precision than whole "eras," there is no methodological rule that a higher level of aggregation or periodization is inherently superior. Second, if the analysis is shifted to the level of correlated "eras," the span encompassed by the era will still have to be specified. When does the era of rising population and prices begin and end as compared with eras of stability and crisis? Is there a beginning and end to eras of rebellion and stability? Third, if support for the theory merely requires crudely correlated eras, then the range of alternative theories greatly expands, and alternatives cannot be dismissed based on issues of specific timing.

The standard of precision required to challenge or support an argument is determined by the level of specificity in the argument. It is not a grievous error to be precise, if theory requires or suggests it, and the data allow such precision. It is important to identify the level of aggregation characterizing an interpretation and to specify the reasons that relationships might vary at different levels. But, given data that can be defended as valid at the level of precision used, there are no grounds for preferring an "eras" approach, unless that is the level at which the theory is proposed.

Goldstone's caveat about precision and time is perplexing in comparison with his statements about relationships at the micro and macro structural scales as well. He proposes that social structures are near-"fractal" (1991: 46), showing similar features on macro-micro scales. Yet, his statement on precision is based on the assumption that relationships involving historical time are not fractal, that an "eras" argument is more likely to support his theory than more precise categorizations of historical time. The preference for eras as the proper unit for the periodization of time implies that relationships at one level will not be replicated on other levels.

In response to criticisms of his use of quantitative analysis by Lawrence Stone, Goldstone states that "a really robust process will stick" (quoted in Hall 1993: 4). If that is the case, a really robust process should "stick" at a variety of levels of temporal precision. At a minimum, the levels of temporal precision intended for a theory should be specified. If a theory is intended to apply to eras, then more precise quantification is, as Stone proposes, an attempt "to dress up an intriguing exercise" (Stone 1992: 1). If the structural scale at which variables are related is fractal, then we need an explanation for the sudden revelation that relationships are to be found at one temporal scale but not at another.[2]

This caveat on precision may explain why Goldstone's work presents the latent variable "psi" and does not carry out a more intricate multivariate analysis. Complex techniques were used to create his measure of psi, but there appears to have been no attempt to isolate the independent and/or interactive influence of independent variables to explain variation in a dependent variable over time. Rebellion is supposed to occur when a variety of circumstances converge, as measured by psi, but the span of time when such an outcome should occur is not specified. Moreover, no actual evidence is provided concerning the significance of variables comprising the measure of societal tension either individually or in interaction with each other. Psi begins moving downward primarily because one of its components, population, declines as a product of civil war. In sum, Goldstone's attempt at quantification does appear as "window dressing" in the sense that he does not actually follow through with a precise analysis and shifts fractal temporal scales with no theoretical or empirical justification.

Because Goldstone's approach cannot be used as an adequate model for more precise analysis, it seems reasonable to examine examples of time series analysis in the fields of deviance and control to discern the proper procedural rules to follow. Yet, such an examination reveals similar capricious shifts in scales of time. Numerous examples of scholarship involve variation over time where researchers adopt a particular conception of the time-variant processes to be explained for statistical reasons without addressing the level at which the theory was proposed. Consider Gartner and Parker's (1990) study of the effect of changes in the age structure and homicide rates in five nations. They cite literature proposing a relation "between trends in the age structure of a population and that population's crime rate" (351). They identify features of the data that can lead to erroneous statistical conclusions by developing ARIMA models. They observe that "ARIMA analysis begins by modeling and removing components that could produce a spurious correlation" (360) and that among such components are "between series variation caused by trend" (356). Each series is modeled, identified, and diagnosed to assess whether each has been purged of trend and autocorrelation. The resulting residuals become the time-dependent processes to be analyzed. When they use such techniques, they find few significant effects of age structure on crime rates. Of course, their findings no longer apply to the relation between "trends" or long-term shifts in the age structure of a population in relation to "trends" in crime rates. Such trends are "purged" because they can generate spurious correlations. But, in the process of purging that history, the conception of the temporal historical phenomena addressed by the proposition changes. When the researchers shift to other statistical techniques (i.e., generalized least squares), they find stronger relationships. In fact, their ultimate conclusions are based on the least squares analysis. They attribute the difference in findings to the "stringency" of ARIMA techniques but fail to note that the very conception of the historical variations to be addressed changes when such techniques are used. This shift is not problematic provided that it is recognized and appropriate limits in testing theories using such techniques are specified. The time-dependent processes addressed by a theory should guide the form of analysis used.

The same shift in the conception of historical phenomena is found in ARIMA analyses of lynching and race-related forms of social control. Massey and Meyers (1989) report that they "use time series techniques to explore trends in the repressive social control of blacks, and the interrelationship among these control mechanisms in Georgia during the post-Reconstruction years" (459). One of the hypotheses to be tested (461) is based on Donald Black's (1976) work—"extralegal and legal punishments should be negatively correlated over time." They induce the appropriate stationarity in variance, model and filter out shifts in level over time, and find no support for the hypothesis. Of course, since the explanations of historical patterns of social control to be tested addressed trends, such findings may be irrelevant to the original theoretical argument. There might be a very strong inverse relation between trends in each variable, but that aspect of historical change is removed for statistical reasons. The method of analysis chosen involves a particular conception of the historical variation to be studied, and such choices should be justified in relation to the theory.

Lack of attention to temporality can be noted in a recent article on unemployment and pretrial incarceration. D'Alessio and Stolzenberg (1995: 350–59) use ARIMA techniques to test Rusche and Kirchheimer's (1939) theory that the oversupply of labor increases the use of imprisonment. They note that their preliminary bivariate analysis supported the theory but that "after adjusting for time-dependent factors" (356) the relationship was insignificant. Yet, they do not specify the fact that the adjustments made shift attention to the residual fluctuations that remain after modeling and removing trends. The theory is not supported when the focus is on the fluctuations remaining after adjustments are made for other time-dependent factors. As was the case with other analyses reviewed earlier, those findings are irrelevant to Rushe and Kirchheimer's theory to the degree that their hypothesis applied to the relation between trends in unemployment and trends in imprisonment. As time series analysts warn, a wide range of variables may exhibit correlated trends—a fact that allows a wide range of alternative explanations. Definitive crucial tests may not be possible under such circumstances. However, as used in this analysis, the ARIMA adjustments have the effect of limiting the test to one very specific conception of the temporally related properties of history to be explained.

The fact that ARIMA analyses fail to support well-established theories in a variety of areas is a challenge to those theories to the degree that they address the specific fluctuations remaining after filters are imposed. Braudel (1992) notes that "economists are on the whole interested in short-term developments" (70–78), and the use of ARIMA techniques by sociologists has tended to limit attention to such fluctuations as well. In contrast, some economists, sociologists, and other social scientists have been interested in trends, long-term waves, and cycles (for examples, see Bergesen 1983; Taylor 1988; Boswell 1989). The focus is on the components of variation that are filtered in ARIMA analysis, and such analysts have little interest in short-term residual fluctuations. In fact, scholars interested in the longer-term patterns tend to view that residual variation as random noise. If the residual variation remaining after imposing filters were the most "fuzzy and unreliable" component of a series, then methods that make such residual variation crucial to tests of theory would tend to generate negative results. Patterns and correlations at higher levels of aggregation may have a higher probability of being spurious, but they may also turn out to be less fuzzy and more reliable depictions of history.

Basic Principles for Analyzing Relations over Time

The studies reviewed so far do not provide the type of guidelines needed for testing theories or hypotheses about relationships among variables over time. However, recognition of problems of atemporality can aid in the development of guiding principles. First, scholars should be explicit about the properties of temporal phenomena addressed by a theory (e.g., the beginning and/or end, correlated eras, trends, fluctuations around trends, etc.). If there is no specification, then the theory should be assessed in terms of the full range of temporal issues. Second, when comparing explanations, the same standards should be applied to all theories, and the competitive edge should be accorded on the basis of dimensions of timing "explained" and the persistence of relationships across a range of temporal scales. Third, the methods used should be appropriate to the temporal dimensions of a phenomenon addressed by the theory. If a method filters dimensions of the "history" of a phenomenon that were to be explained by a theory, then the terms or conditions of that test should be clearly specified.

Other guidelines for integrating history and sociology are already growing in prominence in the literature. In their article on "Ahistoricism in Time-Series Analyses of Historical Process," Isaac and Griffin (1989) argue, "Most time-ordered analyses are rendered 'ahistorical' because the premises that direct quantitative inquiry obscure changing historical relations through time" (873). As one recommendation for progress in the integration of sociology and history, they call for greater attention to historical circumstances that affect relationships among variables over time.

Isaac and Griffin's discussion points toward a fourth guiding principle. A proper sociohistorical analysis of relationships over time should attempt to identify and, if possible, empirically specify the historical circumstances that condition the relationship. Such specification may be discursive and qualitative, building a logical case that certain cultural and structural prerequisites had to be in place for a recurring phenomenon such as witch hunts to be possible. Given historical circumstances that establish the necessary prerequisites for a phenomenon to occur, changes in magnitude or intensity might be explained by other variables. Such specification can also be quantitative in that the convergence of certain measurable historical circumstances might determine the span of time in which variables are related.

Degrees and Levels of Temporal Correspondence

Historians, sociologists, and other scholars are often interested in explaining trends over considerable spans of time and, although they may deny being "quantitative," engage in processes of mental averaging when discerning patterns and linking phenomena to one another. Figure 5.1 includes plots of twenty-nine-year centered moving averages for executions, number of cities with trials, pestilence, width of Spessart tree rings, wheat prices, and war references.[3] "Eyeballing" these relationships, they appear to support the basic

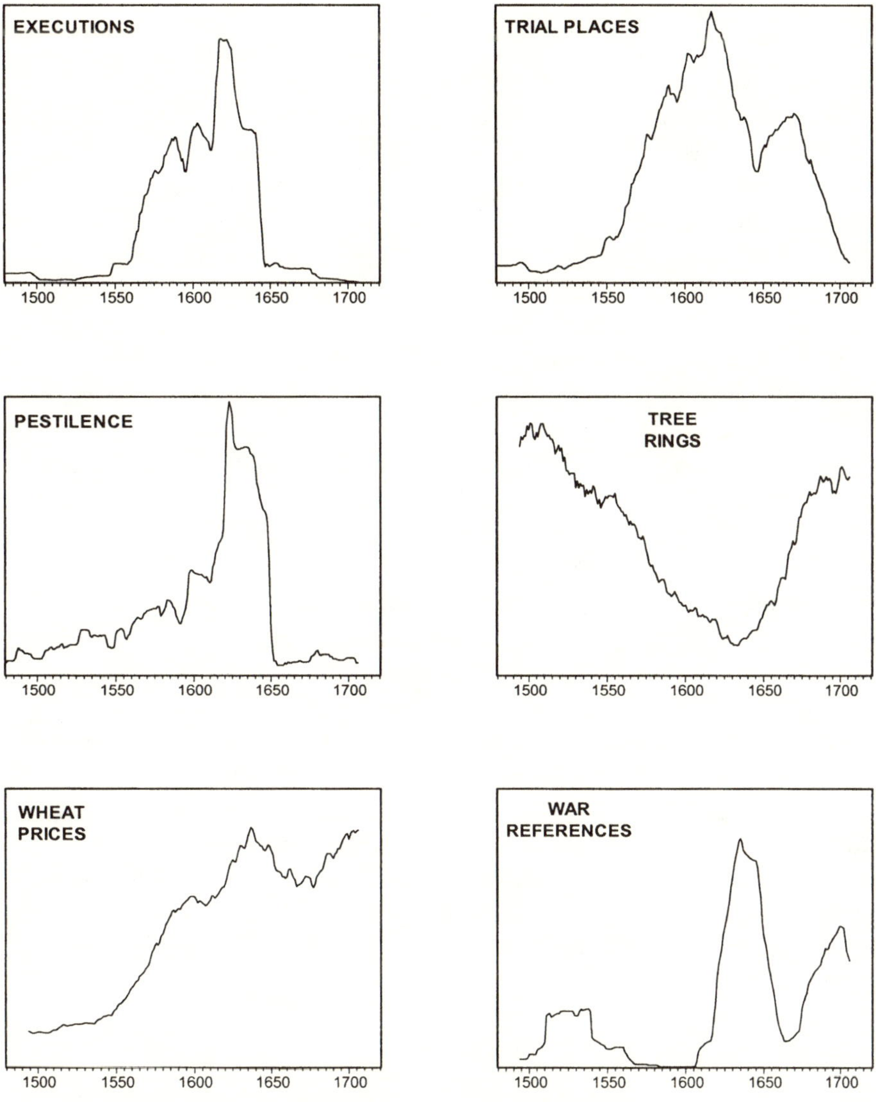

Figure 5.1. Twenty-nine-year moving averages for all variables.

hypotheses. However, when statistical analyses are conducted, the relationships vary in strength and statistical significance. For executions, the most prominent bivariate relationships involve plague (+.81) and Spessart ring width (–.79). The greater the intensity of plague, the greater the execution of witches. The wider the tree rings, the fewer the executions. Wheat prices are positive correlates of both trial places (+.65) and executions (+.38) as well. In contrast, war fails to enter into significant bivariate relationships with either executions (+.10) or places with witch trials (+.07).

Were the historical relevance of plague, hardship, and war to the prevalence and intensity of witch hunts to be determined by examining these bivariate relationships alone, the hypothesis about the effect of war would be rejected and the intensity of witch hunts "explained" by plague and economic or climatic hardship. On the other hand, the individual effects of such variables cannot be determined by merely eyeballing charts. As noted repeatedly, complex countervailing relationships cannot be untangled without some form of multivariate analysis.

A multiple regression analysis of these data indicates that moving averages of executions or number of trial places can be predicted with considerable accuracy using moving averages for plague, war and wheat prices with tree rings added as a significant correlate for number of witch trial places (see table 5.1). Although consistent with the bivariate analysis for plague and hardship, the multivariate analysis yields a very different observation about the relevance of war. War is now a significant and negative correlate of witch hunting. At this level of temporal aggregation, all three hypotheses are supported. Because war is positively correlated with plague and indicators of hardship, both of which are positive correlates of witch hunting, the bivariate relationship was misleading. When these countervailing effects are taken into account, the data are consistent with historical observations.

Predicted and measured witch hunting are graphed in figures 5.2 and 5.3 Although the overall fit between the predicted and observed data is quite good, there are spans of time for each measure of witch hunting where systematic misprediction can be found. For example, there are fewer executions in the 1660s and 1670s than these measures of plague, hardship, and war

Table 5.1. Regression Analysis of Twenty-Nine-Year Moving Averages

	Executions		*Trial Places*	
	Coefficient	*Probability (t-Statistic)*	*Coefficient*	*Probability (t-Statistic)*
Plague	+8.764	.0000	+0.683	.0000
War	–2.746	.0000	–0.486	.0000
Rings	+0.025	.430	–0.136	.0000
Prices	+.0449	.0000	+0.016	.0000
Adjusted R2	.905			.940
Durbin-Watson	.218			.109

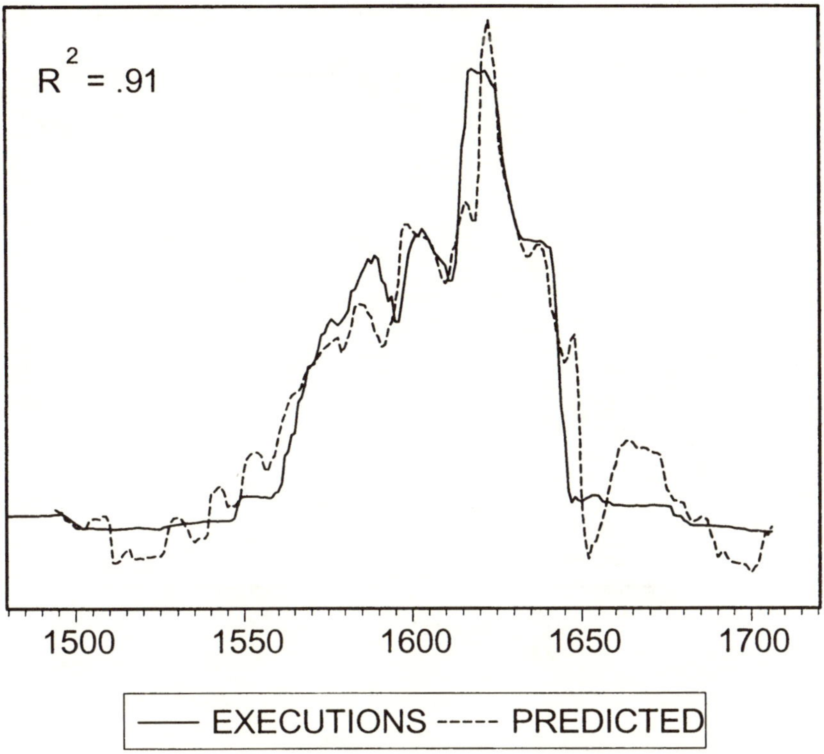

Figure 5.2. Predicted and actual executions based on plague, wheat prices, and war (twenty-nine-year moving averages).

would have us predict. In contrast, there is a close fit between predicted and observed witch hunts when number of places with trials is the focus. It may be that the Thirty Years War disrupted institutional machinery, leading to an accumulation of grievances and cases that were processed only after the end of the war. Yet, when communities began processing witchcraft cases once again, such trials did not result in the lethal consequences that characterized such hunts prior to the war and during lulls in war. The "postwar exhaustion" postulated by Monter may have suppressed executions despite the recurrence of conditions that would prompt new trials and the processing of accumulated cases.

A More Precise Analysis

The multivariate analysis of moving averages supports all three hypotheses and reveals an inhibiting impact of war that could not be discerned in a

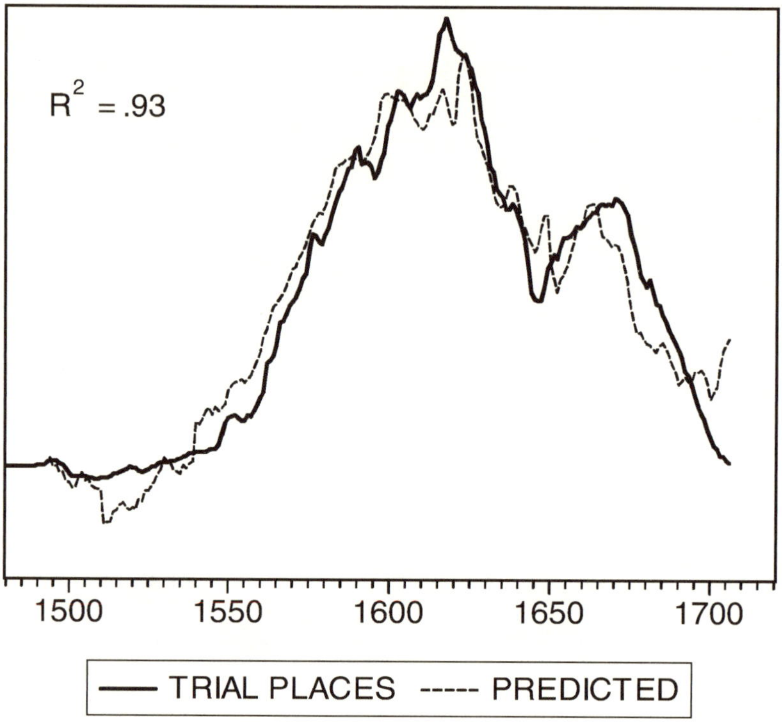

Figure 5.3. Predicted and actual trial places based on plague, ring width, wheat prices, and war (twenty-nine-year moving averages).

bivariate analysis. However, the use of moving averages generates some statistical problems since such averages intentionally "spread" variables over time and, thus, compound the problem of systematic misprediction (i.e., correlated errors or residuals). More "precise" annual data should allow an assessment of such problems as well as facilitate the proper adjustments for them. But, as noted, prior research suggests a high probability of rejecting hypotheses when extensive statistical filters and adjustments are made. In short, the research record suggests that an intricate analysis of "fuzzy" data tends to lead to disconfirmation of hypotheses that appear plausible at higher levels of temporal aggregation or "fractal" scales. On the other hand, that research record implies that a time series analysis yielding results consistent with the hypotheses stated above should be even more convincing because disconfirmation is the rule.

Table 5.2 summarizes the bivariate correlations relating each of the variables to executions and trial places using annual data. Were these data used to make statements about the correlates of witch hunting, hardship as measured by tree ring width and wheat prices would be the strongest correlates (especially for number of trial places), plague would be related to executions as expected (but not trial places), and war would be related to number of trial places as expected (but not executions). Of course, these bivariate relationships can change considerably when a multivariate analysis is conducted. Moreover, a more precise analysis leads to questions about the escalation and internal dynamics of witch hunts.

Most time series analysts use statistical filters to remove "trends" on the grounds that numerous variables can explain the same trends, increasing the odds of spurious relationships. In the case of witch trials and witch executions, historical research suggests that they occur in waves or epidemics with an internal dynamic of their own. If witch hunts have an internal dynamic, independent of the conditions that might facilitate or inhibit them, then we should expect systematic error in our mispredictions (i.e., correlated residuals). Witch hunting spread among communities in epidemic fashion, and executions or trials in one setting or time could increase the probability of further executions. In that sense, executions and trials in one year could "cause" executions and trials in subsequent years. Since trials could span several years in a set of communities, trials in one year are not independent of trials in subsequent years.[4]

One procedure for eliminating the impact of witch hunts on witch hunts would be to impose filters on the dependent variables in advance of analysis. However, such a procedure risks the elimination of temporal variations that can be explained by other variables in our model. The procedure adopted for this analysis will be to include all variables in the analysis, examine the residuals, and introduce those adjustments that are necessary to generate random residuals into the analysis.

Table 5.2. Bivariate Correlations

	Executions		*Trial Places*	
	Correlation	*Probability*	*Correlation*	*Probability*
Plague	+.142	.0000	+.050	.0000
War	–.042	.0000	–.132	.0000
Rings	–.291	.0000	–.457	.0000
Prices	+.202	.0000	+.431	.0000

Table 5.3 summarizes the results of several analyses. Column A begins with a simple multiple regression analysis, regressing the measure of executions on plague, war, ring width, and wheat prices. Using annual data, all of the relationships are in the direction expected, with plague and wheat prices positive correlates and war and ring width negative correlates. However, only war and ring width were significant correlates. Of course, the results of tests of significance may change when the problem of correlated residuals (suggested by the Durbin-Watson statistic of 0.784 in column A) is addressed.

The first step in addressing that problem is reflected in column B, which introduces a lagged effect of executions (EX_{t-1}). That addition did not eliminate the problem (as indicated by the LM test-statistic, $F = 5.387$, Prob = .005). An examination of the residuals indicated that executions_{t-2} and executions_{t-16} were needed to solve the problem. The sixteen-year lag reflects the fact that the two major peaks in witch executions are about sixteen years apart. As summarized in column C, plague is a significant positive correlate of executions and war is a significant negative correlate. Neither ring width nor wheat prices were significant correlates of executions in this model, although they are related in the direction expected. A test for serial correlation when using lagged endogenous variables (Breusch-Godfrey LM) is not significant, indicating that the tests of significance are not biased. Because the LM test was only marginally insignificant, alternative models were examined that could generate a more impressive LM test-statistic. Lagging plague one year generated a LM with a probability of .261 and improved the R^2 from .460 to .533. The coefficients for this model are summarized in column D.

The results for number of trial places differ at each stage from the results for executions. As summarized in table 5.4 (column A), war, ring width, and wheat prices are significant correlates and are related in the direction expected. Plague is not a significant correlate and the sign of the relationship is contrary to expectations. Introducing lagged trial places (TP_{t-1}) does not alter these results (column B), and its introduction did not eliminate the problem with correlated residuals (i.e., the LM test-statistic was significant). However, introduction of trial places_{t-2} and trial places_{t-3} solved that problem. Those adjustments slightly altered the results (column C). In the final model, all variables are related in the direction expected, with war, ring width, and wheat prices significant correlates of number of trial places.

Several conclusions seem justified by this rather precise analysis. First, plague appears more relevant to explaining variations in the severity of witch hunts as measured by executions than the number of different trial places. Such epidemics may heighten the intensity of witch hunts rather than the

Table 5.3. Analysis of Executions (EX), Annual Data

A			*B*			*C*			*D*		
Coefficient		*Probability*	*Coefficient*		*Probability*	*Coefficient*		*Probability*	*Coefficient*		*Probability*
Plague (PG)	+2.04	.072	PG_{t-1}	+3.05	.012	PG_{t-1}	+2.23	.016	PG_{t-1}	+2.67	.003
War (WR)	−2.21	.018	WR	−2.00	.024	WR	−1.63	.019	WR	−2.53	.001
Rings (RG)	−1.04	.001	RG	−.983	.002	RG	−0.38	.079	RG	−0.05	.418
Prices (WP)	+0.21	.122	WP	+.018	.152	WP	+.009	.257	WP	+0.01	.303
						EX_{t-1}	+0.621	.000	EX_{t-1}	+0.44	.000
									EX_{t-2}	+0.21	.000
									EX_{t-16}	+0.24	.000
R^2	.094			.108			.460			.533	
DW	.784			.778							
LM (F, Prob)						5.387,.005			1.353,.261		

Table 5.4. Analysis of Trail Places (TP), Annual Data

A			*B*			*C*			*D*		
	Coefficient	*Probability*		*Coefficient*	*Probability*		*Coefficient*	*Probability*		*Coefficient*	*Probability*
Plague (PG)	+0.06	.348	PG_{t-1}	–0.14	.181	PG_{t-1}	+0.36	.390	PG_{t-2}	+0.26	.029
War (WR)	–0.55	.000	WR	–0.53	.000	WR	–0.35	.001	WR	–0.39	.000
Rings (RG)	–0.20	.000	RG	–.199	.000	RG	–0.11	.002	RG	–0.07	.024
Prices (WP)	+0.01	.000	WP	+.010	.000	WP	+.005	.002	WP	+.004	.017
						TP_{t-1}	+0.491	.000	TP_{t-1}	+0.32	.000
									TP_{t-2}	+019	.005
									EX_{t-3}	+0.15	.013
R^2	.329			.331							
DW	1.111			1.102							
LM (F, Prob)							7.747, .001			0.191, .909	

prevalence of such events. The finding that surges in witch hunting appear to follow surges in plague by one or two years may provide support for theories that emphasize the demographic and/or social psychological aftermath of plague epidemics. Second, measures of hardship appear more relevant to explaining the prevalence of trials than their intensity as measured by executions. As hardship increases, the prevalence of trials increases. Finally, war (as measured by community references to violent conflict) behaves as proposed by Midelfort for both trial places and executions, when the confounding effects of other variables are taken into account. Communities are less likely to search for hidden internal enemies when confronted by overt violence and traditional enemies. With some qualifications, these data are consistent with the hypotheses stated at the beginning of the chapter.

Specification

In chapter 3, we noted that some conflicting theories of early modern witch hunts might be reconciled were they interpreted as addressing different aspects and/or phases of the early modern "craze." For example, the pronatalist theory of witch hunts stresses heightened concern about witches and witchcraft allegedly as an elite response to the hazards of population stagnation or decline. The demonological conception of the "heretic witch" was assembled from prior images of heretics in the fifteenth century, but, as Briggs (1996b) notes, the persecution of witches "was astonishingly slow to take off, with something like 150 years separating the appearance of the recognizable stereotype from the beginnings of widespread action across much of Europe" (404). In short, the "demonological" belief system that transformed the treatment of local conflicts in future "bad times" was assembled in times that may have been bad for elites (rising wages, full employment, little competition among laborers) but good for peasants and villagers. However, once an official demonological ideology was in place, the stage was set to allow village-level conflicts and tensions to be treated as heresy, provided local gatekeepers were receptive.

Small-scale "endemic local persecution" (Briggs 1996b: 401) began in the late fifteenth and early sixteenth centuries and grew during times of increasing competition for scarce jobs, population growth, and declining real wages in the second half of that century. The small-scale witch hunts may have been facilitated by "worsening" conditions relative to prior "good times," coupled with small outbreaks of plague. This growing relative deprivation of the sixteenth century was followed by a deterioration of life circumstances to new absolute lows in the seventeenth century. Climatic crisis was compounded by "epidemic" waves of plague, beginning in the late sixteenth century but peaking in the seventeenth century. As others have noted, this resurgence of the "Black Death" coincides roughly with "epidemic" witch hunting. Indeed, it may be that "epidemic" plague was a facilitating factor primarily during the "epidemic" or crazelike era of witch hunting in the seventeenth century.

One means of assessing whether different crises affect witch hunts during different spans of time is called *recursive regression* (Isaac and Griffin 1989). In recursive regression, coefficients are recomputed for each variable in a model as years are cumulatively added to the analysis. Variables that were significantly related to witch hunts in the overall analysis may have been related only during limited spans of time. On the other hand, variables that were not significantly related in the overall analysis may have had a bearing during certain limited spans of time as well. In short, a recursive regression analysis can yield evidence relevant to historical specification for both significant and insignificant correlates.

Recursive coefficients with executions and trial places in Baden-Württemberg as dependent variables are plotted in figures 5.4 and 5.5. Those plots support the view that the different variables may have been relevant during different spans of time. Whether dealing with executions or trial places, (1) wheat prices are a significant correlate in the second half of the sixteenth century, (2) plague becomes a significant correlate in the first half of the seventeenth century, and (3) war is a significant (but negative) correlate early in the sixteenth century (reflecting the German Peasant's Revolt) and beginning in the middle of the seventeenth century (reflecting the Thirty Years War). The data seem to support the view that plague was primarily a factor affecting "panic" witch hunts. Not only is the relationship most prominent in the seventeenth century, but, as noted in earlier analysis, it is more strongly related to the intensity than to the prevalence of witch hunts.

Replication

In "*Many Reasons Why*: Witchcraft and the Problem of Multiple Explanations," Briggs (1996a) observes that "the more we know about any subject, the harder it becomes to generalise about it" (49). This warning applies to the analysis reported earlier in that attempts to assess the historical "robustness" of the relationships leads to qualifications of what would otherwise be a simple set of conclusions about the relevance of plague, hardship, and war to early modern witch hunts. Of course, in addition to historical specificity, the findings may be specific to the "heartland of the witch craze."

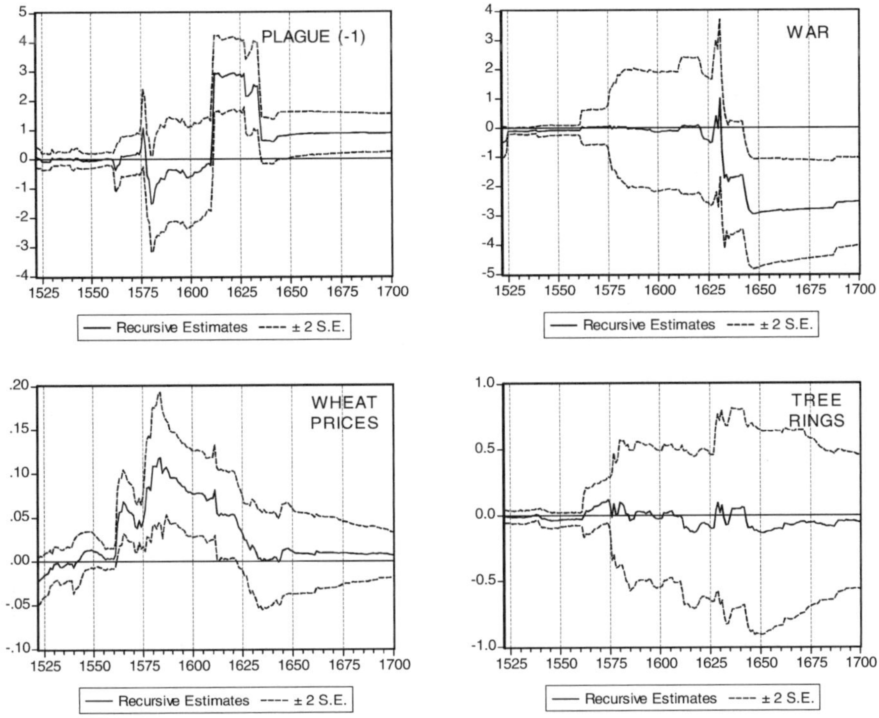

Figure 5.4. Recursive regression coefficients for executions.

In chapter 4, it was observed that the course of witch hunts in neighboring Bavaria differed from southwestern Germany despite the fact that the plague, hardship, and war were highly correlated across the two settings. With the exception of the surge late in the sixteenth century, witch persecutions were rare and did not spread in an epidemic, contagious fashion. Viewing the wave of persecutions in the 1590s as a "regional test of fire," Wolfgang Behringer (1997) notes that "the persecutory paradigm was applied for a short time, but was soon abandoned" (392).

Obviously, additional circumstances have to be introduced to explain variation in the relevance of the "persecutory paradigm" in different settings, and Behringer identifies several factors that help account for constraint:

> First of all, the judicial apparatus was characterized by an advanced state of centralisation, guaranteeing that the dictates of the central authorities guided

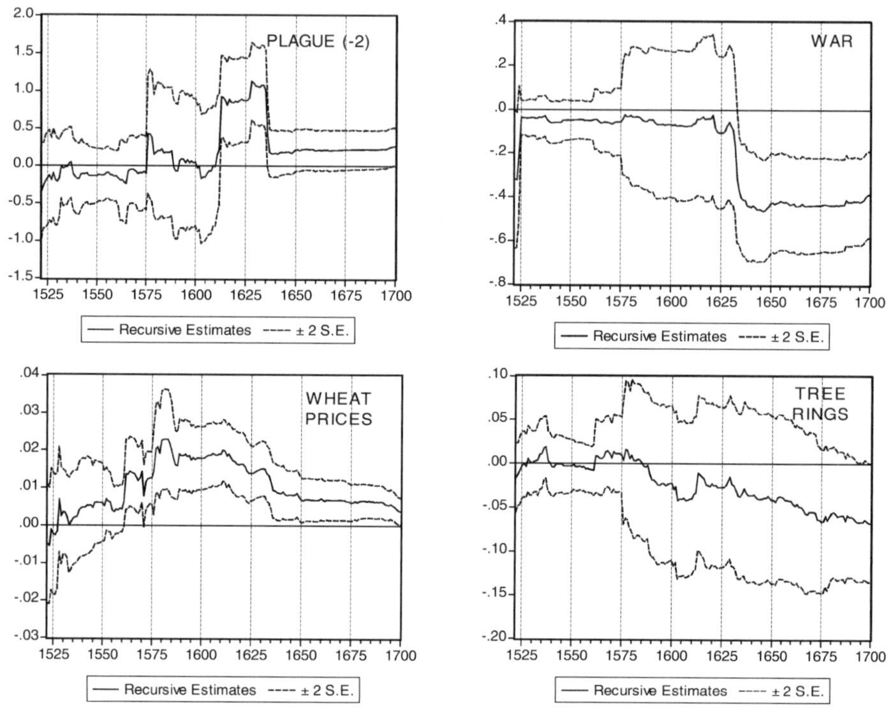

Figure 5.5. Recursive regression coefficients for trial places.

> witchcraft policy. Local officials, regularly accused by authors since Friedrich Spee of supporting trials for reasons of financial, sexual or personal gain, did not play a deciding role in this region. In fact, central authorities were quick to punish any excesses they uncovered. Secondly, strict evidential criteria were imposed during most trials for sorcery or witchcraft, resulting in incalculable risks for accusers or denunciators. (392)

He also suggests that the fact that the region was "almost purely Catholic" after 1590 is relevant to disparate patterns in adjacent settings. Although witch hunts did not, in general, cross confessional boundaries, they may have been facilitated by confessional diversity within a region.

Behringer's interpretation is consistent with the view that political and judicial centralization helped constrain epidemic witch hunting while local control allowed escalating and contagious surges of local justice. In contrast to Bavaria, the political and religious fragmentation characteristic of southwestern Germany allowed witch hunts to escalate and spread as a local option. They could grind to a halt when confronted with war but escalated and spread in a contagious fashion when people were faced with disease and subsistence crises with no brakes applied by higher authorities.

Behringer proposes a plausible explanation for differences in witch hunting between the two systems and posits "shared rhythms" encompassing, at a minimum, southwestern Germany, Bavaria, and Scotland in the late sixteenth century. However, the argument for shared rhythms is not based on an actual analysis of data across systems. If witch hunts were in closer synchronization in the late fifteenth than in the sixteenth century, then (1) witch executions and number of places with trials should be more predictable when regressing data from one system on another in intervals of the sixteenth than of the seventeenth centuries, and (2) recursive coefficients relating properties of witch hunts in one system to another should be more prominent in the sixteenth century than the seventeenth century.

Behringer's argument refers specifically to the later part of the sixteenth century, and the first hypothesis can be tested by examining relationships within twenty-five-year spans for 1575–1599, 1600–1625, and 1625–1649. Evidence in support of that Behringer's argument would take the form of stronger relationships with shorter lags in the 1575–1599 interval than during other periods.

The analysis fails to support that hypothesis. The most prominent relationships predicting either executions or trial places across systems are found for 1625–1649, followed by 1600–1624 and/or 1650–1674. For example, the correlation between executions in Bavaria and southwestern Germany is .90 (no lag required) as compared with an insignificant .05 for 1575–1599. There is a significant correlation between executions in southwestern Germany and Bavaria in 1575–1599, with Bavaria lagging behind ten years (.42), but even that correlation is less prominent than that found for 1625–1649 or any of the other spans of time. The results were similar for number of trial places although there was a significant correlation of +.42 in 1575–1599. The comparable correlation for 1625–1649 was +.72. The results were quite similar using measures for Scotland and in the analysis of recursive coefficients over the 1550–1700 span as well.

If stronger relationships with shorter lags are acceptable evidence of shared rhythms or "synchronization," then the data provide little support for the argument that there were shared rhythms in the later part of the sixteenth century but regional divergence in the seventeenth. There were shared rhythms in spans of both centuries, but they are more prominent in the seventeenth century than in the sixteenth century.

The recursive coefficents relating executions in southwestern Germany to executions in Bavaria revealed significant relationships in two spans of time, 1576–1586 and 1628–1700. For places with trials, the relationships were significant for the entire 1576–1700 span of years. In short, there were shared rhythms between the two adjacent settings, especially for number of trial places. In fact, when time is "aggregated" by using moving averages, the same variables operate in the same way for Bavaria as for southwestern Germany.

Moving averages for number of different locations with trials for Bavaria and predicted witch trials based on plague, war, and wheat prices are presented in figure 5.6. Despite the view that Bavaria did not have sustained panic witch hunts, moving averages of the same type of variables that "predicted" moving averages of executions and trial places in southwestern Germany do a reasonably good job in this setting. Plague and wheat prices are positive correlates, war is a negative correlate, and the R^2 is .84. The same model applies to moving averages of executions in Bavaria, with the war score a negative correlate and plague and wheat prices positive correlates, although the fit between the observed and predicted averages is much closer for places with trials than executions (R^2= .42). The same societal characteristics that Behringer cites as barriers to epidemic witch hunting when comparing systems may also operate to dampen or inhibit the intensity of panic surges that are prompted by disease and hardship in more fragmented settings such as southwestern Germany.

As noted earlier, Behringer (1997) suggests a typical collage of crises that are supposed to be relevant to the major epidemic in the 1590s in Bavaria:

> There was no lack of events that could be blamed on witchcraft. In times of inflation, when diet deteriorated and the risk of disease increased, suspicions of witchcraft accumulated. Often they were directly associated with damage to crops . . . ; often "unnatural" sickness or other events that are hard to attribute to inflation provided the impetus, so that one had to speak in terms of a general increase in susceptibility to the influence of witches in times of misfortune. (160)

Because the analysis of annual data for the German southwest suggested that variations in wheat prices were more relevant to explaining witch hunts in the sixteenth than seventeenth centuries, with plague and war more consequential (albeit, in different ways) in the seventeenth, recursive coefficients for similar models were examined using the Bavarian data. Recursive

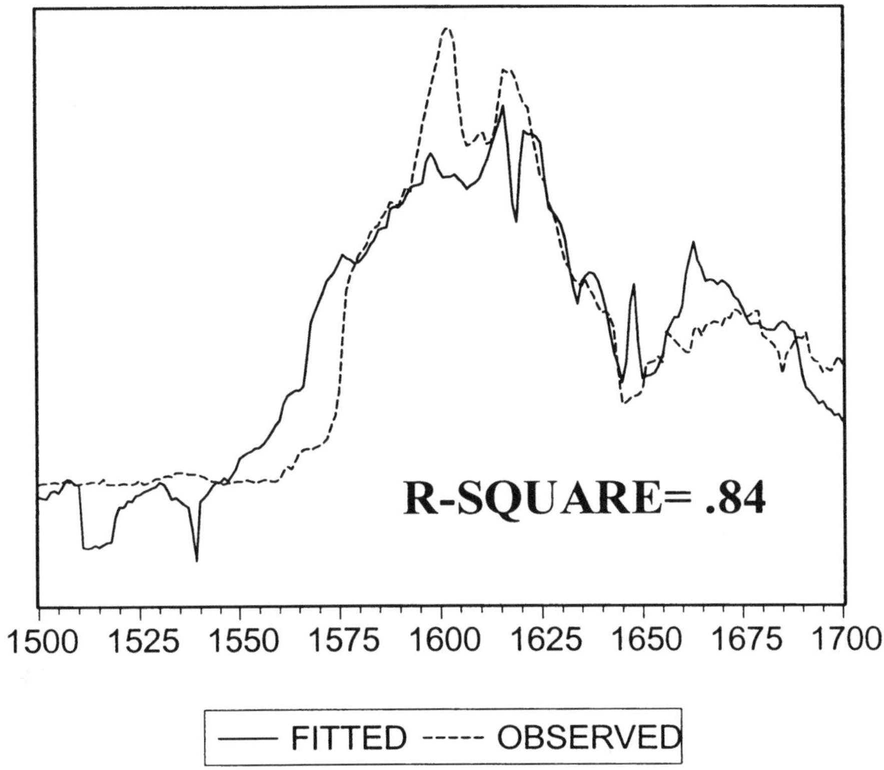

Figure 5.6. Moving averages of places with trials observed and fitted, Bavaria.

coefficients relating Bavarian executions to wheat prices were found to be significant from 1586 to 1596 and from 1596 to 1624 for trial places. Plague is a positive correlate of witch executions in the 1580s and early 1590s but is unrelated to trial places. War comes close to being a significant inhibiting force around 1630. In short, the variables that appeared relevant to explaining intense witch hunting in southwestern Germany in the seventeenth century do not apply to the mild witch hunts in Bavaria during this time. However, the finding that rising wheat prices are associated with the major witch hunt in Bavaria in the late sixteenth century is consistent with the findings for southwestern Germany.

Behringer argues that any sound theory of witch hunts must be able to explain the surge in witch trials in Bavaria and other settings in the late 1500s—a surge that he attributes to a global agrarian crisis and related misfortunes. Consideration of shared rhythms suggests that this was not a particularly unique span of time in terms of global patterns of witch hunting, but the fact that recursive coefficients for plague and wheat prices indicate significant relationships during that specific span of time prompted a closer examination. With the analysis limited to 1550–1599, the variables suggested by Behringer do predict witch executions. As summarized in table 5.5, a surge in wheat prices and plague is followed by a surge in witch executions with a four-year lag. In contrast, the community measure of war is a significant negative correlate. Similar results were found for number of trial places with two exceptions. Although the coefficient relating war to number of trial places was negative, the probability was only .08, which is not statistically significant. Moreover, while both trial places and executions in one year are positively correlated with themselves in the next year ($t - 1$), the correlation for executions turns negative the following year (executions$_{t-2}$). Such a pattern suggests that witch executions may have been self-limiting, with an accelerated panic exhausting a backlog of suspects and/or dampening enthusiasm to continue the persecution. Not only was the Bavarian panic limited to a narrow span of time, but it was a relatively short-lived panic as well. On the other hand, the same types of variables that helped explain variation at the level of moving averages appear to be relevant to explaining Behringer's surge in application of the persecutory paradigm.

Table 5.5. Regression Analysis of Bavarian Witch Hunts (1500–1599)

	Dependent Variable				
	Executions			*Places*	
Independent Variable	*Coefficient*	*Probability (t-Statistic)*		*Coefficient*	*Probability (t-Statistic)*
Executions $_{t-1}$	+1.160	.0000	Places $_{t-1}$	+0.778	.0000
Executions $_{t-2}$	–0.468	.0000			
Plague $_{t-4}$	+1.128	.0000		+1.128	.0024
War	–2.746	.0000		–0.141	.0805
Prices $_{t-4}$	+0.045	.0000		+0.044	.0000
Adjusted R^2	.830			.707	

Note: Wheat prices had an effect when first differences identifying surges above trend as well as the undifferenced data were included. The coefficients reported here are for first differences. Q-statistics and tests for serial correlation revealed no problems with residuals for these models.

War "on the Fringes"

As noted in chapter 3, there has been growing consensus that violent conflict with identifiable enemies inhibits witch hunts within a social system. However, it was also noted that the "threat of war" as evidenced by conflict in surrounding areas has been mentioned as a potential source of collective anxiety, ultimately reflected in an increase in witch hunts. Briggs (1996b) proposes that surges in witchcraft persecution were likely "on the fringes of conflict . . . when war was intense, but people were suffering serious indirect repercussions rather than full-scale devastations" (308). Such speculation suggests that during times of apparent "peace" within a system, witch hunts would correlate positively with the extent of warfare outside or on the fringes of the system. Of course, adequate tests of this hypotheses require specification of "the fringes" of the system and identification of the specific wars or types of war that might generate such indirect repercussions or prompt collective anxiety.

One possible operational definition is community references to war and violent conflict in those regions of Germany immediately adjacent to Baden-Württemberg—Bavaria, Rhineland-Saarland, and Hessen. An analysis of the relation between witch executions and references to violent conflict in community records for the regions of Germany surrounding Baden-Württemberg (after the variation explained by other relevant variables for each span of time has been removed) is consistently contrary to the hypothesis that war on the fringes intensifies witch executions. This conclusion stands for separate analyses in the sixteenth and seventeenth centuries as well as for both centuries combined. The signs of the relationships were all negative, but none reached statistical significance.

Since war "outside a system" can encompass distant as well as proximate neighbors, we explored other measures of war as well. In *War in the Modern Great Power System, 1495–1975*, Jack Levy (1983) provides a list of wars with intensity defined in terms of casualties relative to the European population. The measure used here is intensity per year, which was created by summing the annual intensity scores across all wars in a given year. A second measure is Joshua Goldstein's (1988) measure of the intensity of "great power wars" based on battle deaths from his study of *Long Cycles: Prosperity and War in the Modern Age*. These two measures are highly correlated ($r = +.75$) and moderately correlated with the community war references in Baden-Württemberg ($r = +.53$ with Levy, +.54 with Goldstein). However, neither of these measures was significantly related to executions when added to the analysis. Whether using measures of war in the world system or war in surrounding territories, there was no support for the view that war outside the system encourages witch hunts.

Although neither war in the immediate area nor global measures of war increased witch hunting net of other relevant variables, it may be that wars with a distinctively "religious" dimension might constitute such a threat. Trevor-Roper's (1967) view that witches were scapegoats of the Wars of Religion has been criticized on the grounds that witch hunting was a peacetime activity when examined within specific societies. However, there is overlap between the French "wars of religion" and sixteenth-century variation in witch hunts in Baden-Württemberg. Using Wright's dates for the Huguenot wars, peaks in witch hunting which exceed predictions based on other variables are found to be coincident with five of the seven wars: 1562 (the first war, 1562–1563), 1573 (the fourth, 1572–1573), 1575–1576 (the fifth, 1575–1576, the sixth, 1576–1577), and 1580 (the seventh, 1580). When the Huguenot wars are coded (0 = no war; 1 = war), there is a significant positive relationship with the residual variation in executions and places with trials. Witch hunting was unusually intense in Baden-Württemberg when Protestant and Catholic municipalities and factions were at war in France.

On the surface, the findings on religious civil wars are consistent with Briggs's argument about war on the fringes. Yet, both specific measures of war in the surrounding regions of Germany as well as more global measures of war were not related to witch hunting in southwestern Germany. Moreover, the findings on the French religious wars may reflect a tendency for internal conflict to escalate following international wars with the form of that internal conflict varying among societies. Witch hunts escalated during times of relative peace in southwestern Germany, while more structured, internal conflicts (i.e., civil wars) escalated in France. Witch hunts may be most intense during times of relative peace, following structured external and internal conflicts. This topic will be explored further in chapter 6, which considers possible links between the structure of social conflict and the organization of societies.

Exceptions That Prove the Rule?

Few scholars would expect to find the same variables playing the same role in all settings and spans of time or for each specific witch hunt. Two "anomalies" involving variables examined in this chapter will be addressed here: (1) the postplague surge in witch executions and trials in Scotland and (2) the surge in witch executions and trials in England during the English Civil War. The first anomaly challenges the relevance of plague as a positive correlate and the second challenges the role of war as a negative correlate.

The Scottish Witch Hunt of 1661–1662

Plague disappeared as a demographic problem earlier in Scotland than in England or Germany, and this early demise is problematic for arguments introducing epidemic diseases as a correlate of witch hunts. Indeed, in *Enemies of God*, Christina Larner (1981) questions the relevance of plague to Scottish witch hunts because Scotland experienced its last national panic in 1661–1662 while plague had ceased to be a problem by the end of the 1640s. In short, plague ended over a decade before the last big witch hunt in Scotland. Famine, scarcity, and "lean years" did not end, but none of these problems is listed by Larner as a factor behind the 1661–1662 national panic.

Was the Scottish witch hunt of 1661–1662 one of the outbreaks where variations in subsistence crises and disease epidemics are irrelevant? Scottish mortality data for 1615–1700 are available from *Scottish Population History* (Flinn 1977), allowing an examination of variations during the span of time in question. The fact that plague ended too soon to explain the national panic in 1661–1662 does not preclude the possibility of an association with other types of mortality crises. Figure 5.7 plots data for Scotland on mortality, wheat prices (based on England), witch executions, and places with trials. Those data show that mortality rates did increase in 1657 and surged again in 1661–1662. The net effect of these surges was a doubling of mortality in just a few years. In short, although plague had ended, the Scots experienced a major mortality crisis after several decades of stable and below-average mortality.

These data point toward a mortality crisis of some kind that cannot be explained by plague. However, other diseases might prompt a similar degree of panic and anxiety to that generated by plague. In fact, the surge in mortality preceding the 1661–1662 witch hunts is attributed by demographers to a smallpox epidemic (Flinn et al. 1977: app. A, 484). There is evidence of a subsistence crisis as well in that wheat prices exceeded the mean for the two prior decades by 1656 and peaked in 1661. Larner does not list "famine" as a relevant "calamity" for this particular witch hunt and rules out plague as a consideration, but this analysis indicates that this span of time was characterized by both a surge in smallpox-related mortality and a reappearance of subsistence problems.

Although a casual inspection of the data is consistent with the hypothesis that renewed bouts of hardship and mortality were accompanied quite closely by a renewed surge in witch hunting, an assessment of the independent effect of these two "problems" requires a multivariate analysis. If smallpox and a subsistence crisis were both relevant, then both a surge in wheat prices and a surge in mortality should have an effect on witch executions and

Figure 5.7. Witch hunts, prices, and mortality in Scotland, 1651–1672 (standardized scores).

witch trials. Were mortality varying only because of a connection with wheat prices, then it should not have an independent effect when introduced together with prices. Using time series techniques appropriate for the small range of years and the small number of events (i.e., "count" models), both the surge in wheat prices and the surge in mortality were found to have independent lagged effects on both the intensity and prevalence of witch hunting during this span of time.[5] The surge in wheat prices and the surge in mortality are followed one year later by a surge in witch executions and witch trials. Some "problem" other than the escalation of wheat prices escalated mortality during that short span of time. Hence, given the prior speculation by demographers, it is quite plausible to propose that smallpox was the culprit. Thus, plague may have been ruled out as a proximate correlate, but the other major epidemic disease of the era may have played a similar role.

The English Witch Hunt of 1645

The measures of war used for southwestern Germany and Bavaria were quite precise in that they were based on references to the activities of war in community records, and they supported the common observation that witch hunts were a "peacetime" activity (i.e., that they tended to be inhibited or delayed by war in a region). In southwestern Germany, witch hunts were most intense in the "interstitial" span of time between phases of the Thirty Years War. A "wave" of activity followed that war as well, although it resulted in few executions. It may be, as several scholars have suggested, that local grievances accumulate during war, resulting in a surge of formal cases when resources are once again available to address those grievances. In addition, interstitial and postwar waves might be generated by increases in grievances, increases in the types of interaction that generate local conflicts, and/or increases in the "kinds of people" that engage in such interaction. Whatever the mechanism involved, when direct and immediate threats arise from well-defined enemies, few resources are invested in the search for imaginary enemies.

Yet, the largest witch hunt in England occurred in 1645 in the middle of the span of years designated as the English Civil War, 1640–1649. In fact, it was this overlap that prompted Goldstone (1991; see chap. 1) to suggest that witch hunts may have been generated by the same circumstances as rebellion. The general rule may be that structured conflict among contending groups inhibits witch hunts, but it is possible that overlap is more likely for internal wars than international or defensive wars. In both civil wars and witch hunts, the enemies are internal "heretics." This possibility will be examined further in chapter 6, which addresses variation in scapegoats and shifting enemies.

Another prospect for making sense of this anomaly emerges from a specific consideration of the spatial and temporal movement of war. J. P. Kenyon and J. Ohlmeyer (1998) note that the English Civil War "was a war of striking contrasts. Some counties—Kent, Cambridgeshire, and much of mid-Wales, for example—saw much of troop movement but not significant battles, skirmishes, or sieges" (36). In fact, the 1645 witch hunts took place in counties in which no battles had been fought to that point in time. The Battle of Naseby in which the Royalists overwhelmed the king's army is considered the most important decisive battle of that war, and it was fought in June 1645—one month before the largest surge in witch executions in English history. Moreover, it was the only battle to take place within one hundred kilometers of London.

Although it is considered a "civil" war, the English Civil War involved England, Scotland, and Ireland with different concentrations of battles, campaigns, sieges, and towns captured at different times. In fact, of seven battles listed for 1645 in *An Encyclopedia of Battles* (Eggenberger 1985: 135) as part of the first English Civil War, six were fought in Scotland. There were no battles or campaigns anywhere near the center of witch hunting (Suffolk, Middlesex, and Norfolk) between the June 1645 battle at Naseby and the 1648 battles at Maidstone and Colchester near London. The Royalists surrendered at Colchester in August 1648, and Charles I was executed in January 1649.

Using maps from *The Cambridge Illustrated Atlas of Warfare* (Black 1996: 78–85), battles and towns captured during each year of the course of the civil wars were counted (1) within Scotland's boundaries and (2) southwest of latitude and longitude coordinates of 54 degrees north and 2 degrees east for England.[6] For example, the battles of Turnham Green, Edgehill, Adwalton Moor, and Tadcaster are counted as instances of war close to the regions encompassing witch hunts in 1645. There were no battles or towns captured in Scotland in 1642 or 1643. In 1644, seven battles were fought in southeastern England, while three towns were captured and one battle was fought within the boundaries of Scotland. By 1645, the fighting shifted to Scotland, with seven battles or captures as compared to only one in southeastern England—the Battle of Naseby in June. There were shifts back to England in 1646 (five events vs. none in Scotland) and 1648 (two in England, none in Scotland). In 1650, there was one battle at Dunbar, Scotland, and one battle in England in 1651 (Worcester). In 1647, 1649, and 1650, the so-called civil war was confined primarily to Ireland.

The most striking contrast for Scotland and England in terms of estimates of witch executions is revealed by comparing executions in 1644 and 1645. With the war concentrated in England in 1644, there was only one execution (based on Notestein's lists) as compared with forty-one executions in Scotland (based on Black's calendar). In contrast, when the war shifted to Scotland in 1645, there were no executions in Scotland but fifty-two in England! Table 5.6 presents the results of an analysis spanning 1635 through 1655, which does imply that more precise measures of war could "explain" what appears as a major anomaly when war is defined in terms of a span of time alone.[7] From 1635 through 1655, executions in England are positively related to battles fought in Scotland and negatively related to battles fought in southeastern England. When executions in Scotland are considered, the results are reversed. Executions in Scotland are positively related to battles in England but negatively related to battles in Scotland.

These findings are quite consistent with Briggs's proposal that war "on the fringes" increases anxiety and tension, increasing the probability of witch

Table 5.6. Civil War Events, Executions, and Trial Places, England and Scotland, 1635–1655 (Poisson Count Models)

	Coefficient	*z-Statistic*	*Probability*
Executions in England			
Civil war events in England	–.353	–2.738	.0109
Civil war events in Scotland	+.465	13.420	.0000
Executions in Scotland			
Civil war events in England	+.227	7.596	. 0000
Civil war events in Scotland	–.183	–4.094	. 0000
Places in England			
Civil war events in England	–.176	–2.478	.0065
Civil war events in Scotland	+.200	4.021	.0000
Places in Scotland			
Civil war events in England	+.118	3.477	.0000
Civil war events in Scotland	–.085	–1.662	.0483

Note: Each model included executions or places at t – 1. Tests for overdispersion were not significant, justifying use of Poisson models. *Q*-statistics revealed no problems with correlated residuals.

prosecutions in an area. When Scottish territory was directly involved in war, the Scots were reluctant to pursue witches, although they were quite willing when the war was confined to England. When southeastern England was directly involved in the conflict, the English were reluctant to hunt witches, but, when it shifted to Scotland, they mounted the largest witch hunt in their history.

Conclusion

This chapter has covered a wide range of issues involving theories of early modern witch hunts. The analysis was generally consistent with hypotheses about the relevance of three "apocalyptic" variables—pestilence, hardship, and war—to the prevalence and intensity of such episodes. An examination of broad general trends and moving averages for the heartland of the witch craze—southwestern Germany—revealed that increases in plague and hardship were associated with increases in the prevalence and intensity of witch hunts, while war in the region inhibited such activity. Moving averages of trial places and executions could be predicted with considerable accuracy using similar averages for plague, hardship, and war. Moreover, despite the fact that witch hunts were less prevalent, less intense, and limited to shorter spans of time in Bavaria, the same model applied at that level of temporal aggregation, especially when predicting number of trial places. More precise analyses of data for southwestern Germany supported the hypotheses about plague, hardship, and war, but with wheat prices most consequential in the sixteenth century and plague (+) and war (–) most consequential in the seventeenth century.

Hardship, as indicated by wheat prices, may have been more relevant to the generation of the relatively mild witch hunts of the sixteenth century in Germany, with epidemic disease facilitating the intense panic crazes of the seventeenth century. Wheat prices and tree ring width indicate that Germany had reached record levels of hardship by the early seventeenth century, and climatic conditions were about as bad as they could get. When major plague epidemics emerged to compound the sustained subsistence crisis of the seventeenth century, they appear to have facilitated major panics in politically and judicially fragmented southwestern Germany, with war acting as a periodic brake on the process. However, the fact that the same general model applies to executions of witches in Bavaria in the seventeenth century suggests that plague (+) and war (–) were relevant factors elsewhere as well, even when political and judicial organization tended to discourage crazelike panic prosecutions of suspected witches. Different crises may be relevant at different times, but the data are quite consistent with theories emphasizing disease and subsistence crises as factors affecting witch hunts. Moreover, consistent with emerging arguments about war and witch hunts, it is clear that war should be distinguished from disease and economic hardship as a crisis since it acts as a barrier to or a brake on witch hunting.

The results for "war on the fringes" were mixed in that measures of war in the regions surrounding Baden-Württemberg did not enter into significant relationships when other sources of variation were controlled. Yet, two specific findings were consistent with the "fringes" argument. When the French were involved in religious wars, southwestern Germans were likely to be hunting witches. This relationship could be taken as support for the argument that "war on the fringes" acts as a source of collective anxiety, facilitating witch hunts. An alternative interpretation is that the conditions generating religious warfare in France generated witch hunts in southwestern Germany.

Similarly, when the location of battles and towns seized in the English Civil War is taken into account, the most intense witch hunts in Scotland occurred when the war was being waged in England and were brought to an abrupt halt when the war shifted to Scotland. The effect of the war events was the same in England, with few executions carried out when the war was confined to England, followed by a huge surge in witch executions when the war shifted to Scotland.

In short, more precise measures of spatial as well as temporal variations in war suggest that the impact of war on witch hunts varies considerably, depending on the definition of war. Witch hunts (1) are most intense in relatively peaceful years, (2) are most intense during spans of time that have been characterized by periodic wars, and (3) can both surge and stop, depending on the proximity of actual warfare.

The analysis in this chapter concentrated on temporal variations; other issues involving war will be considered in the next chapter. For example, if war acts as a barrier to witch hunts, then it is possible that war might be relevant to explaining societal variations in witch hunts. The more years a nation or region was preoccupied with war, the less prevalent or intense the witch hunting. Similarly, the fact that the French were persecuting religious heretics while the Germans to the north were hunting witches may be relevant to the generally mild nature of witch hunting in France. The pursuit of imaginary enemies may be inhibited by the pursuit of other types of enemies.

Notes

1. Parts of this chapter appeared in an article by the author, "Time and Social History: Problems of Atemporality in Historical Analysis with Illustrations from Research on Early Modern Witch Hunts," *Historical Methods* 30 (Winter 1997): 46–57.

2. Goldstone (1991: 46) uses the term *fractal* to refer to relationships that persist at different societal scales along a macro-micro continuum. When referring to time, *fractal relationships* are those that persist across temporal scales, which can range from the coincidence of long-term trends and cycles to short-term fluctuations.

3. There is no single standard for choosing the number of years to use in creating moving averages. Twenty-nine-year centered moving averages were computed in this study so that they would be centered on an exact year with the data for that year, the fourteen preceding and fourteen following years used to compute the average.

4. Witch hunts have been argued to be self-limiting as well. Historians have suggested that such episodes may subside as acceptable targets are eliminated and when accusations begin to be lodged at people who do not fit the mold. Moreover, to the degree that such episodes are instances of persecutory or communal scapegoating, they may subside as "homeostasis" is reestablished. The most lethal panics in terms of executions may be particularly self-limiting. In fact, at least one historian has suggested a periodicity to witch executions, reflecting the time required for new targets and grievances to accumulate (see Midelfort 1979).

5. See Harvey and Fernandez (1989) for a discussion of count models and Quantitative Micro Software (1994–1997: 455–64) for specific tests and procedures. Tests for overdispersion using Poisson count methods were not significant, and there were no significant correlations among residuals using Poisson count models. Since the

focus was on specific anomalous surges, first differences of wheat prices and mortality were used. The models included a lagged effect for executions or places. The coefficients for executions were .025 (p = .0000) for executions$_{t-1}$, .023 (p = .0006) for mortality$_{t-1}$, and .003 (p = .000) for wheat prices$_{t-1}$. The coefficients for places were .064 (p = .0000) for places$_{t-1}$, .059 (p = .0000) for mortality$_{t-1}$ and .003 (p = .0000) for wheat prices$_{t-1}$. Pseudo-R^2 was .30 for executions and .57 for places.

6. The selection of the zone to be considered as in close proximity to witch hunts in England was, admittedly, arbitrary. Several procedures were considered, including scores based on hundred-kilometer zones (100, 100–200, >200) from London. The conclusions were not affected by the procedure. Battles in Ireland were not included in the measures of civil war for England or Scotland.

7. These findings are based on the procedures described in note 6. Additional details are noted in the footnotes to table 5.6.

CHAPTER SIX

The Selection of Targets

Scapegoating, Collective Conflict, and Victimology

Witches making an ointment to be used for flying to the Sabbath. (Hans Baldung Grien, Strassburg, 1514)

Three broad perspectives on early modern witch hunts were presented in chapter 2, each emphasizing distinct features of the early modern witch hunts. From functionalist, ritual-sacrifice perspectives, witches are pursued as a means to reestablish communal norms or boundaries. In conflict-strategic persecution perspectives, witches are pursued as a means of controlling threatening persons or groups. Finally, according to scapegoat perspectives, witches are pursued as a communal catharsis or as a diversionary strategy by elites to structure and deflect blame. Some aspects of each or several of these perspectives are introduced into any given treatment of the topic, and the early modern witch trials are routinely "explained" as instances of persecution, scapegoating, or social conflict.

These theories and most historical research on witch hunts focus on events, crises, or social changes that generate an increase in the "demand" or need for scapegoats, symbolic sacrifices, or persecution at certain times in history. When misfortune strikes, people "need" to sacrifice others as an atonement for sins, a way to blame others within the system as scapegoats, or a strategy to deflect blame. Moreover, demand for scapegoats is likely to be greatest when people are uncertain about the source of the misfortune or need to construct an explanation for misfortune that displaces or externalizes blame.

Exactly "who" they select is another matter. In fact, in contrast to speculation about the circumstances and prerequisites for surges in demand for targets, relatively little attention has been paid to the "supply" side of the equation. This imbalance may reflect an assumption that there is a constant "supply" of potential targets; that is, a sufficient supply of scapegoats is always available. Hence, variation in demand is the most important consideration. Yet, factors affecting the "supply" of targets and the relative "costs" of selecting targets are crucial to understanding certain features of the history of scapegoating, ritual sacrifices, or strategic persecution over time.

Although it seems to be widely accepted that the most likely targets for scapegoating come from relatively disadvantaged and stigmatized groups, that fact by itself does not yield an explanation for shifts among groups. Nor does it provide any clues about changes in the degree to which members of those groups constitute plausible targets. However, the foundation for a more precise theory can be found in a combination of research by psychologists on "the stimulus qualities of scapegoats," theories of victimization in criminology, and theories of collective behavior or social conflict in sociology.

This chapter will attempt to weave together ideas from each of these specialties to propose an explanation for (1) the emergence of the image of women as a source of organized, heretical witchcraft, enemies of God, or

"Servants of Satan" (Klaits 1985); (2) the selection of certain types of women as targets; (3) shifts among different categories of people as potential targets; and (4) variations among societies in the "opportunity" for scapegoating. Although the discussion will be couched in terms of "scapegoating," the focus could be on the selection of targets for persecution or, even more broadly, the invention or selection of certain types of internal groups as threats or enemies. Attempts to develop specific hypotheses about scapegoating lead to a consideration of qualities of targets that make them both credible as a symbolic threat as well as vulnerable as a target for scapegoating. Similarly, a focus on witch hunts as a type of institutionalized, internal conflict aimed at a type of "internal" enemy will help us make sense out of sequences of different types of conflict.

In prior chapters, war with external enemies as well as internal, "civil" wars were found to inhibit the search for hidden internal enemies. An important implication of this observation is that the sheer "opportunity" for witch hunts (whether conceived of as sacrifice, scapegoating or strategic persecution) is affected by war and, thus, can covary with any state characteristics that correlate with war. Ideas elaborated in three distinct disciplines or substantive academic specialties help make sense of the selection and shifts among targets on a wide range of "fractal scales" (see chapter 5).

The Stimulus Qualities of the Scapegoat

In their discussion of "the stimulus qualities of the scapegoat," the experimental psychologists Berkowitz and Green (1962), note that frustration-aggression theory provides the motivation for the scapegoating process, but that those ideas alone do not explain "why a particular minority is attacked when a number of groups are available" (293). They propose several variables that need to be taken into account in developing such an explanation, including (1) similarity to the instigator, (2) probability of retaliation, (3) preexisting prejudices, and (4) prior conflicts.

On the surface, the first variable, similarity to the instigator, would seem to run counter to the view that members of stigmatized or "dissimilar" groups were common targets. However, Berkowitz and Green argue that those people most likely to be used as scapegoats are of "intermediate" similarity to the instigator—that is, sufficiently similar to function as a plausible substitute, but sufficiently different to be discerned as a plausible "enemy" or target. The targets of persecution or scapegoating are, after all, members of the social system, and, historically, the most vicious and demonstrative forms of both institutionalized and vigilante punishment have been directed at "internal" enemies. Moreover, witch hunts, like civil wars, are forms of internal conflict, although, unlike civil wars, the internal enemy in witch hunts is much harder to detect.

Berkowitz and Green also propose that among those targets with intermediate similarity, those most likely to be used as scapegoats will be those characterized by a relatively low probability of retaliation, the objects of preexisting prejudices, and groups or individuals who have been involved in prior conflicts. There is a subtle, but far from irreconcilable, inconsistency between two of these variables, low probability of retaliation and prior conflicts. For a group or individual to be a party to conflict presumes some perceived capacity to "retaliate." This presumption means that the most qualified "scapegoats" or targets of persecution are unlikely to be totally powerless. In fact, the notion of "intermediate similarity" can be extended to imply that the most credible targets are found among those who have demonstrated some degree of power (i.e., a capacity for conflict) but are, as stated by Berkowitz and Green, relatively low in "probability of retaliation." One implication of this argument is the notion that people or groups have to "qualify" as credible internal targets of blame.

A similar set of variables to those identified by Berkowitz and Green can be derived from a theory in a quite distinct academic or substantive discipline. "Routine activities" theory in the academic specialty of criminology is a "supply-side" theory of victimization developed by L. Cohen and M. Felson (1979) and Cohen, J. Kluegel, and K. Land (1981). From this perspective, the events generating a criminal victimization require the "convergence" of *motivated offenders*, *suitable targets*, and *lack of guardianship*. Variations in risks of victimization among social categories and territories can be explained in terms of availability (exposure and proximity to motivated offenders), guardianship, and target attractiveness.

Although routine activities theory focuses on the characteristics and distribution of victims or targets of crime over time and space, and the selection of targets by "offenders," the concepts used are quite general and can be extended to the selection of targets for institutional and group rituals of punishment, persecution, and scapegoating as well. Routine activities–opportunity theory directs us to consider the availability, guardianship, and attractiveness of the targets of aggression, whether that aggression is carried out by motivated offenders, groups or officials.

Routine activities theory can be integrated with Berkowitz's and Green's works on the stimulus qualities of scapegoats to help explain the selection of targets. First, a prerequisite for selection as a scapegoat is availability. On the surface, the relevance of availability to the witch hunts might seem problematic, since women would be "more available and more visible" than Jews, heretics, or other potential targets. Berkowitz and Green's proposition implies that the most attractive targets for scapegoating are members of internal, marginalized, and stigmatized groups or categories of people. Yet, their depiction also suggests that the most promising scapegoats would be drawn from groups with sufficient visibility and power to be *credible targets of blame*. For example, targets with absolutely no power would involve the least risk of retaliation. However, they are not the most credible candidates for displacing blame. The most powerless members of a social system would not be plausible candidates for accepting credit or taking blame for matters as consequential for human society as plague and subsistence crises. If Berkowitz and Green were correct, then those groups and people most likely to function as credible scapegoats are of intermediate similarity to those pursuing them and have a sufficient history of conflict to qualify as a target. In short, there are prerequisites to qualifying as a credible scapegoat.

Indeed, women were not credible targets as scapegoats until it was possible to conceive of them as credible allies of Satan, together with Jews and heretics. Women had to be viewed as worthy of Satan's recruitment and as possessing the capacity for secret arrangements with him. *In short, they had to be viewed as capable of collective, organized, and conspiratorial arrangements.* Moreover, before women could be conceived of as "organized for evil," they had to be conceived of as capable of organization per se; that is, before women could be credited with the same collective evil as other threatening groups, there had to be historical instances of actual collective organization that could be transformed or "demonized." Convincing evidence of *independent and collective real-world organization* was a necessary prerequisite for women to qualify as credible heretics.

If Margaret Murray's thesis that witches were members of enduring pagan cults were correct, then women would have been on par with Jews and heretics as potential targets. Evidence of cult activity would be evidence of a significant threat comparable to that posed by these other groups. However, that thesis has been seriously challenged (see chapter 1), and it does not explain why it took so long for the heretic witch to be invented and targeted. If such groups were, in fact, real and had endured for hundreds (if not thousands) of years, the witch should have been targeted as early as other organized threatening groups.

As an alternative to the view that actual witch cults made women credible targets, it can be proposed that the likely precursors of such a conception would be instances of collective female organization in the conventional world. Carlo Ginzburg (1991) takes exactly that approach, suggesting that "an agrarian cult of an ecstatic character," the "benandanti," provided a real-world basis for the construction of the heretic witch stereotype:

> Men and women who defined themselves as "benandanti" affirmed that, having been born "with a caul" (that is, enveloped in amnion), they were compelled to go four times a year, at night, to battle "in spirit," armed with bundles of fennel, against male and female witches armed with stalks of sorghum: at stake in these night battles was the fertility of the fields. Visibly astonished, the inquisitors tried to fit these tales into the pattern of the diabolical Sabbath. (9–10)

However, since the benandanti were *men* battling witches, and women took part only through a supporting procession, it is difficult to believe that this inverted version of real groups could have provided the real-world foundation for the development of a belief that women could enter into collective conspiracies.

A more plausible candidate as a real-world precursor for development of a credible belief that women could form independent collectivities are the Beguines. The Beguines were townswomen who lived in "beguinages," and they were the only female religious community not under the control of the church. Indeed, Jeffrey Richards (1990: 63) notes that the name for these groups of independent women may have been derived from the Albigensians, a heretic group. The Cathari and Albigensians (as Cathari were known in southern France) were a relatively nonhierarchical, gender-egalitarian, and ascetic religious movement that came under attack by the church in the early thirteenth century. They were effectively decimated by the early fourteenth century when the church turned its attention to the Beguines and their male counterpart, the Beghards.

The Beguines consisted of independent women who committed their lives to austerity, chastity, and service to others, including assistance to the sick (Anderson and Zinsser 1988: 222). They emerged in the towns of northern France, Belgium, and western Germany, and estimates of members are as high as two thousand for the city of Cologne (Ranft 1996; Richards 1990), about 15 percent of the women in the city.

The most prominent leader was Marguerite Porete (1999), whose book, *The Mirror of Simple Souls*, was declared heretical in 1310—the same year she was burned to death. Beguines were condemned in the Papal Inquisition of 1332 but remained a perennial threat to the Catholic Church. Bonnie Anderson and Judith Zinsser (1988: 226) note that both Dominican and Franciscan religious orders "vied with each other" in condemning the Beguines, and they were still being pursued as heretics in Basel and Mainz in 1405 and 1406. Moreover, when prosecuted as heretics, they were forced to admit to the very type of practices that had been attributed to other heretics and Jews.

Hence, by the fifteenth century, women had joined the ranks of viable scapegoats by demonstrating that they were capable of an independent, organized group existence and that such organization was not under the control of the church and men. Given historical connections with heretic groups, it was relatively easy for the church to transform female collective organization into a conspiracy of witches. That transformation served two functions. Patriarchal control of evil was salvaged by according Satan (a male) the role of underlying instigator and leader, while women became a plausible collective threat as his servants (see chapter 2). A patriarchal view of both order and disorder was preserved and the organization of women for evil could be depicted as, ultimately, a male accomplishment.

Some features of the history of Beguines add to the credibility of this argument. Descriptions of the distribution of Beguines fit some of the patterns noted for the distribution of witch hunts among societies. In *Brides in the Desert*, Saskia Murk-Jansen (1998) notes that the movement was almost exclusively confined to mainland Europe and was most prominent "along the Rhine, in Germany and in Flanders, and less strong in France" (31–32). This description of relative strength is quite similar to descriptions of the relative intensity of witch hunts. Southwestern Germany was the heartland of the witch craze. French Flanders (Muchembled 1993: 142–43) and the County of Namur (Monter 1976: 49) were sites of relatively intense witch hunts for that region as well. Moreover, Namur was characterized by a very high proportion of women as victims (Monter 1976: 119). Although rare in England, Murk-Jansen observes that "there may have been Beguines in east Anglia, particularly in Norwich" (31). Of course, East Anglia was the setting for the English trials documented by Gilbert Geis and Ivan Bunn (1997: 9) and for the most severe witch hunt in English history led by Mathew Hopkins. The belief in a conspiracy of women organized for evil would be most plausible in settings where there was evidence of prior organization per se.

It is important to remember that this social construction of the witch as a heretic and part of a hidden conspiracy led by Satan was a social construction imposed by religious, intellectual, and political elites. The types of local grievances, hostilities, and conflicts that generated charges of witchcraft were based on interpersonal problems and local misfortunes, and the interpretation of such instances as part of the larger demonological conspiracy was largely imposed by official gatekeepers. Thus, the demonization of female collective organization was a prerequisite to development of an official template that transformed local interpersonal conflicts into a much more serious problem involving conflicting allegiances, fomenting evil on a larger scale.

The argument that some degree of organization, power, or conflict involving women was a prerequisite for women to "qualify" as credible scapegoats allows a reconciliation of two disparate views of the link between the status of women and witch hunts. In "Witchcraft and the Status of Women," Alan Anderson and Raymond Gordon (1978: 171–84) argue that the low status of women in some societies made them more "credible" targets. More specifically, they argue that witch hunts were less intense in England than on the continent because women were, as a group, higher in status in that country. The higher the social status of women as a group, the less credible they were as targets of witch hunts. This perspective highlights the protective influence of status as a barrier to the use of a group as a source of scapegoats or as targets of persecution. A similar argument about the selection of specific women as witches was summarized in chapter 1. Donald Black (1976: 56–59) cites the selection of relatively defenseless women as targets of witch hunts as support for the proposition that law is more likely to be directed at people who are powerless. Consistent with routine activities theory, people with the resources to guard themselves or to be guarded by others are less likely to be subjected to arbitrary persecution or scapegoating.

On the surface, this argument would seem to run contrary to the perspective emerging from Berkowitz and Green's discussion of the stimulus qualities of the scapegoat. If women as a group had to qualify as a credible, collective threat before the heretic witch could be constructed and aggressively pursued, then increases in the independence and collective power of women were a prerequisite for their selection as scapegoats. The same impression emerges from all of those perspectives that attribute witch hunts to women as an emerging threat to male (patriarchal) power or economic dominance.

When the focus shifts to the selection of specific women, a similar contrasting conclusion emerges. Several studies have concluded that the conception of the victims as "powerless" is an oversimplification (e.g., Karlsen 1987; Hester 1996; Willis 1995). The women most likely to be accused of witchcraft wielded some degree of power and thus could constitute a threat to both men and women in a gender-structured economy. However, they did not wield sufficient power to avoid accusations when in conflict. In his discussion of witchcraft in the Gelderland, Hans de Waardt (1991) proposes the witch "was found preferably among people with whom one already had a fundamental difference of opinion, the history of which had nothing to do with witchcraft" (148). The most marginal members of a community would be unlikely to accumulate a history of fundamental, unresolved conflicts. Robin Briggs (1996b) implies a similar pattern when he states, "Witchcraft was an idiom of conflict between closely matched rivals, rather than between those at opposite ends of spectrum of wealth and power" (304). Anne Llewellyn Barstow (1994) suggests a similar theme when she states that "certain women were suspected of witchcraft, not because they were powerless, but precisely because they were seen to have a great deal of power" (119). In summary, the same characteristics of women as a group or as individuals that have been argued to *protect* them from scapegoating in one line of argument may increase their *attractiveness*, or credibility, as scapegoats in other lines.

In *The Devil in the Shape of a Woman*, Carol Karlsen's (1987) analysis of the backgrounds of the women accused in New England witch trials leads her to conclude that accusations were aimed "primarily at older women, who like their accusers' own mothers vied with men for land and other scarce material resources. Whether as actual or potential inheritors of property, as healers or tavern-keepers or merchants, most accused witches were women who symbolized the obstacles to property and prosperity" (217). She also notes that although "most observers now agree that witches in the villages and towns of late sixteenth- and early seventeenth-century England tended to be poor, . . . they were not usually the poorest women in their communities." Yet, a paucity of resources to ameliorate the outcome of charges of witchcraft made some women liable to successful prosecution and, ultimately, execution. Karlsen observes that "unless they were single or widowed, accused women from wealthy families . . . could be fairly confident that the accusations would be ignored by the authorities or deflected by their husbands through suits for slander against their accusers" (80).

These two lines of argument can be reconciled by proposing a "nonlinear" relationship between status or power resources and the prospects of selection as a scapegoat, at either the collective or individual level. Those who constitute a moderate or modest threat but lack the resources necessary to fully protect themselves from targeting are most likely to become targeted. People and groups on the "bottom of the heap" are not a sufficient threat to be attractive as scapegoats, despite the lack of resources to avoid successful labeling when targeted. In contrast, those "on the top" might make credible scapegoats, but they generally have the resources to avoid successful targeting. Barstow (1994: 53) summarizes some of the witch trials in Offenberg, Germany, between 1557 and 1630 and notes that some trials "stand out" because of the way they "were directed at important families." However, she notes that it was primarily "elite women" who were targeted: "The use of elite women as surrogates for their powerful husbands exposes the strange value of women in an early bourgeois setting: powerless to defend themselves against witch charges, still they had *counted* in the political struggles of the Rat." The trials did come to encompass a male member of the Rat (the ruling council of the city), but his execution in 1629 "so shook the town that Offenberg killed no more citizens on the charge of witchcraft" (54).When witch accusations did encompass powerful families, women were both credible and vulnerable as targets.

Some scholars have argued that stereotypes of likely witches would break down during severe witch hunts as the pool of people who fit the stereotype was exhausted (Midelfort 1979). As that pool of credible candidates dwindled, accusations elicited under examination, threats of torture, or actual torture spread to an expanding range of suspects. But, when accusations began to spread to less credible candidates—people with sufficient resources and social standing to challenge such charges—it was difficult to sustain a witch hunt. For example, Robinson (1991: 230–31) argues that as accusations during the Salem witch trials spread to leading citizens (e.g., Philip English and his wife, Captain John Alden, Dudley and John Bradstreet), "a general fear swept through the upper echelon of society," and they began to express bitter opposition openly. H. C. Erik Midelfort (1979) argues that "Salem Village saw its traditional stereotype of the witch break down as women of high repute . . . and men fell prey to accusations" (287). This pattern parallels earlier witch hunts in Rottenberg, Germany, where he observes that "as soon as members of the elite were charged . . . the trials often came to a halt" (1979: 281). Trials would end when the supply of credible targets was exhausted and accusations began to stray into well-guarded social categories.

Transportable Stereotypes and Shifting Targets

The pursuit of the heretic witch represented more than a shift *to* a new target. It represented a shift *away* from other, more traditional targets of collective persecution as well. Several historians have noted that the pursuit of witches was less intense when traditional groups, periodically assaulted as internal enemies, were available. For example, Midelfort (1968) proposes, "With Jewish or Moorish elements to eliminate, Spain could hardly waste time on witchcraft" (381). Barstow (1994) argues that as internal religious heretics "were tamed, the inquisitors, especially in Germany, turned on fringe groups such as witches" (62). Ruth Martin (1989) suggests that with the lessening of the intensity of Protestant-Catholic conflict, the Catholic Church "began to look within itself rather than to any external threat, and there it found a mass of pagan ritual and superstition" (218). Such statements imply that variations over time and space in the selection of scapegoats or the targets of persecution are determined by the relative availability of a set of potential target categories.

Among the circumstances associated with the massive persecutions of Jews were epidemics of plague. Jews are commonly acknowledged to have been scapegoats of the Black Death which swept Europe from the Mediterranean from about 1347 to 1350 (Trevor-Roper 1967). They were charged with spreading plague by contaminating wells and corrupting the air (Gottfried 1983). Jews were either expelled or massacred. Gottfried (1983) observes, "By 1351, 60 major and 150 smaller Jewish communities had been extirpated, and over 350 separate massacres had taken place. The effect, an important legacy of the Black Death, was to encourage the eastward movement of the remaining northern European Jewry to Poland and Russia, where they remained for close to 600 years" (74).

By the end of the fifteenth century, Poland was regarded as "the safest country in Europe for Jews" (Johnson 1987), and Jewish communities in Germany were confined to Ratisbon, Frankfort, and Worms. Heiko Oberman (1984) cites 1520 as marking the point of dramatic decline in expulsions of Jews from German towns. Between 1388 and 1520, Jews were expelled from about ninety cities. Moreover, after 1500, most of the expulsions occurred in northern and northeastern regions of Germany (*Encyclopaedia Judaica* 1971). Consistent with this line of argument, little persecution of witches occurred in the northeastern region (Levack 1987), with the most intense and prevalent witch hunts in the German southwest. Moreover, as plotted in figure 6.1, there is some overlap between attacks on Jews and witch trials, but it appears that witches had replaced Jews by the late 1500s.[1]

Another variable shared between Berkowitz and Green and routine activities theory is the degree to which a group can protect itself or is protected by capable guardians. For example, considerable evidence indicates that the geographic center of the German Jewish population shifted north so that they were less available as targets. However, Jews were also "guarded" or protected at some times and places as well. Financial acumen, commercial skills, and ties to other regions could make them valuable allies, especially during times of war. They became useful allies for Catholic leaders in conflicts with Protestants, especially following Luther's fierce efforts to get them expelled from Protestant areas. At the Peace of Augsburg Jews were allowed to remain in ecclesiastical states, and Charles V protected the Jews from expulsion at diets of Augsburg (1530), Speyer (1544), and Regensburg (1546). In his *A History of the Jews*, Johnson (1987) notes, "When war came . . . the need to win it—or just to survive—took precedence over ideology, religion, race or

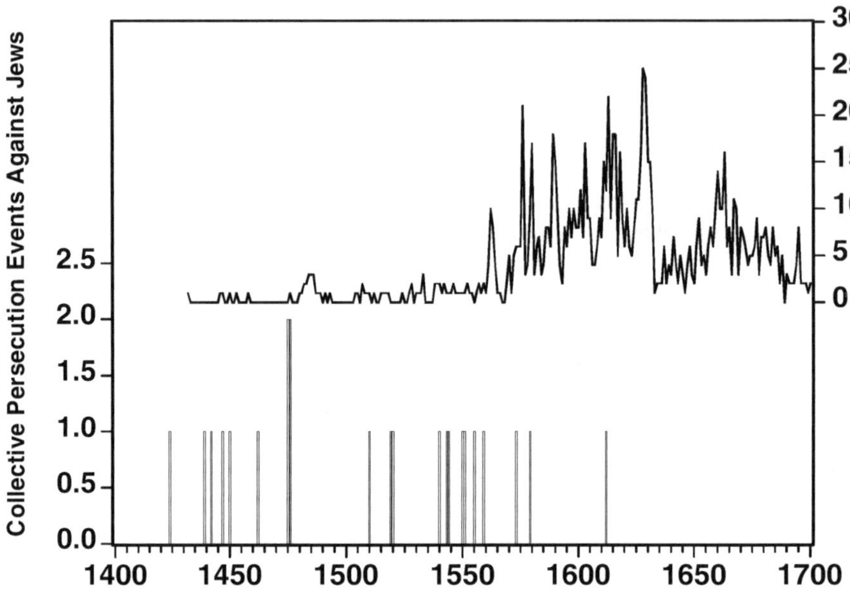

Figure 6.1. Persecution events targeting Jews and places with witch trials.

tradition. The Jews, with their extraordinary capacity to get their hands on scarce supplies and raise cash in a bleak and hostile world, soon made themselves indispensable to all sides" (255).

There are other parallels between the persecution of women as witches and the earlier persecution of Jews consistent with this general line of argument. In "The Jew as Witch Figure" Venetia Newall (1973: 95–124) draws a variety of parallels between the characteristics and behavior attributed to Jews and the characteristics and behavior of the stereotypical heretic witch. Both were charged with the sacrifice of children to the Devil, working spells and poisoning, contra-cultural mocking and reversal of Christian rituals and secret organized efforts to undermine Christian society. Newall notes that both were charged with spreading plague as well.

The heretic witch was assembled not only from materials provided from popular folklore about witches and traits invented in attacks on earlier heretics, but also from characteristics of Jews linked to Christian anti-Semitism. A variety of groups were linked together as threats to medieval and early modern Christian society, all sharing a similar stereotype. Jeffrey Richards (1990: 21) argues that six groups—Jews, witches, heretics, homosexuals, prostitutes and lepers—all shared the stereotype of "the lustful deviant" whose carnal desires made them vulnerable to Satan's influence. Not only did these groups share insatiable carnal desires, but they were depicted as entering into organized conspiracies with each other and with other threatening groups.

Several historians have proposed a sequence in persecution among such groups over time. In his iconoclastic work on *Europe's Inner Demons* (1975), Norman Cohn documents the origins of the official stereotype of the witch in the stereotypes that had been developed in attacks on heretical groups such as the Albigensian Cathari and Waldensians. Carlo Ginzburg (1991) refers to "persecutory waves" with altering targets in the sequence: "lepers-Jews, Jews, Jews-witches" (71). Heretic religious groups emerge as targets at various times in the sequence between lepers and the satanic witch as well.

Activities attributed to witches such as poisoning, infanticide, host desecration and secret meetings to worship the Devil had been attributed to Jews and to earlier heretic groups in Europe. Jews had been executed for alleged plots to poison the public as early as 1161 in Bohemia (Trachtenberg 1943) and had been accused of stealing and sacrificing Christian children in the twelfth and thirteenth centuries. In 1243, Jews were accused of host desecration in Belitz and burned for the crime. What Richards calls "the customary mixture of sex, Satanism, and the Jews" was standard by the twelfth century.

The fact that the construction of the satanic witch incorporated materials elaborated in the Christian persecution of Jews can be illustrated with late medieval and early modern art. It was common to link Jews to the goat, a symbol of fertility that came to symbolize satanic lust in Christian art. As Joshua Trachtenberg (1943) observes, "A fifteenth century sculptured figure in a Flemish church shows a Jew astride a goat, facing its rear; the animal's hind hoofs are cloven, and its forefeet end in claws" (47). The goat was a favorite disguise, and Satan was typically portrayed with goat horns.

The Christian motif connecting Jews, Satan, and the goat is later reproduced in depictions of witches. Instead of a Jew riding backward on a goat, the witch was depicted as sitting backward on a flying goat (see the opening illustration of this chapter). The broomstick ultimately replaced the goat, and witches were depicted as facing forward while flying, sometimes with the handle forward, but often with the handle backward. Witches, like Jews, were often depicted as mocking Christian ceremony by inverting or reversing some aspect of it.

The connection between Satan, lust, and the Jew was also maintained through laws requiring that they wear distinguishing clothing or a symbol badge for identification. The horn was central to both forms of identification: "Jews were actually obliged to appear in public with the distinguishing horn somewhere on their garb. In 1267 the Vienna Council decreed that Jews must wear a 'horned hat' (*pileum cornutum*), a provision which later councils sought to strenuously enforce; and Phillip III required the Jews of France to attach a horned-shaped figure to the customary Jew badge" (Trachtenberg 1943: 44).

In German and French mystery plays of the fourteenth century, Jews were to be clothed in Jewish garb with a Jew badge and peaked hat, reinforcing the connection between Jews, lust and Satan for an ever-growing audience. Such plays heightened anti-Jewish sentiment and solidified persecutory stereotypes. To quote Trachtenberg (1943), "The effect of these plays upon the passions of the mob may be gauged from the action of the Frankfurt City Council, in 1469, establishing special regulations for the protection of the Jewish quarter during the period when such play was being presented" (37).

Ruth Mellinkoff (1993) also notes that "concentration on the grotesque imagery of Christ's enemies and attempts to create stereotyped Jews of them were typical of fifteenth and sixteenth century German art" (152). The connection between Satan and Jews was further reinforced by medieval art when Jews were depicted with a hooked nose and warts or other skin blemishes (Mellinkoff 1993: 126–28). Such characteristics were built into Devil's masks and artistic depictions of Satan, and, although the old hag with a hooked nose and warts was only one cultural motif for depicting the witch, that version shared many of the characteristics that had been built into popular imagery of Jews and Satan as well.

In her study of artistic depictions of "Outcasts," Mellinkoff (1993) speculates that on occasion Jews' hats may have "functioned as independent negative attributes strong enough to transfer their derogatory significance to other persons, groups, and ideas" (91). She notes that Hungarian legal codes of 1431 required that first-time offenders charged with sorcery or witchcraft were required to wear a "peaked Jews'" hat in public (a fact noted by Trachtenberg as well). Artistic depictions of unbelievers, hypocrites, heretics, pagans, and demons were sometimes depicted with Jew hats as early as the thirteenth century.

Jews, Satan, and witches were tied together via the depiction of secret meetings of witches as "sabbaths" or "synagogues" as well, a term that had also been used to describe assemblies of heretics. Not only were witches and other heretics linked to Jews, but the conception of a conspiracy led by Satan had roots in earlier accusations against Jews as well. Ginzburg (1991: 80) argues that an "obsessional image of a plot directed against society" was reflected first in charges leveled against lepers and Jews in 1321. During the Black Death (1348), the same imagery was reproduced in accusations directed at Jews. It was applied to depictions of other heretic groups and male and female witches by the beginning of the fifteenth century. Geographically, Ginzburg (1991) argues, "It was precisely from the western Alps, where the charge against the Jews of having spread the pestilence had first appeared, that approximately half a century later a new persecutory wave commenced. But this time the role of the victim, having briefly touched the Jews, fell to others" (68). He proposes that the witch stereotype was almost complete by the beginning of the fifteenth century and would not change for 250 years.

In sum, there are certain common elements to the early modern cultural motif depicting the internal deviant enemies of Christian society. The enemy, whether Jews, heretics, lepers, homosexuals, or witches, is horny and driven by lust, is involved in secret conspiracies and deviant group activities, is led by Satan who has many of the same physical features as his compatriots, and works evil through magic or supernatural means. This image or belief system is reflected in waves of persecution with the specific targets varying depending on availability and guardianship.

Although the specific set of enemies, the exact content of enemy stereotypes, and the people so labeled varies among social settings, the tendency to merge and shift characteristics among enemies and to level accusations at those with links to old enemies may be universal. The primary perceived threats for the wayward Puritans were the French, the Indians, and the Quakers. It was after the Quakers were protected by a new charter, and during lulls in Indian wars, that the wayward Puritans mounted the fiercest campaign against satanic witchcraft in their midst. However, Richard Godbeer (1992) and others have noted that "many of the accused also lived in close proximity to the Quaker community situated between village and town" (198), and "a significant number of the accused were connected to Quakers by ties of kinship or friendship" (199). Just as Christian stereotypes of Jews came to be reflected in depictions of Satan and his compatriots in Europe, the version of Satan feared by the wayward Puritans took on native American traits, and suspects were likely to be found among people with links to the Indians: "Any association with native Americans, however tenuous and whether or not connected with native religion, could be used to incriminate a witch suspect" (Godbeer 1992: 192). According to Cotton Mather, the Indians and Quakers were part of a common assault on geographic and spiritual frontiers. Others suggested that wild Indian dances were similar to the Quaker "quaking" and that both were diabolically inspired. In sum, the selection of targets varies depending on supply and guardianship with new targets defined by borrowing from old stereotypes.

This argument does not preclude the inclusion of variables that might have increased the motivation of people in a social system to select women as targets. However, it does require attention to questions about variations in the supply of women susceptible to witchcraft and/or witchcraft charges as sources of variation in witch hunts, variations that might be attributed to such forces as heightened misogyny, economic competition, or elite attacks on female peasant culture. For example, one of the consequences of plague may have been to increase the pool of potential targets by increasing the availability of women who threatened traditional patriarchal gender roles as well as increasing the availability of relatively unprotected categories of women such as widows, the bereaved, spinsters, and barmaids. War might have similar consequences, except for the fact that it directs hostility at more obvious enemies and may counteract the selection of invisible enemies. However, witch trials could make a resurgence in the "aftermath" of war for some of these same reasons.

The Midwife Issue

One of the most widely noted perspectives on witch hunts among feminist theorists is Ehrenreich and English's (1973) conflict theory in which the witch trials are depicted as a form of strategic persecution supported by the growing male medical establishment (with the support of the ruling class) to undermine the power of female midwives and healers. Ehrenreich and English argue, "The great majority of them [witches] were lay healers serving the peasant population, and their suppression marks one of the opening struggles in the history of man's suppression of women as healers" (8). Although they emphasize conflicts with the medical profession, their view is quite consistent with Muchembled's. He also viewed wise women and other women with special peasant knowledge as targets of the witch hunts. From his perspective, peasant women with special cultural knowledge were attacked as symbolic representatives of peasant culture in a spreading attack on peasant culture and paganism by church and state.

Several witch hunt scholars have challenged the view that midwives were prime targets compared to other categories (Estes 1983; Scarre 1987; Quaife 1987; Briggs 1996b). In her work on *Malevolent Nurture*, Deborah Willis (1995) reiterates the fact that women were frequently the accusers and rejects the view that English witch hunts were "merely an excuse to wipe out midwives, female healers, widows with property, or women suspected of sexual transgression" (5). In a detailed analysis of witch hunts where such motives have been posited, David Harley (1990: 126) challenges "The Myth of the Midwife-Witch." He notes that "there can be no question that references to the existence of midwife-witches occur in writings of demonologists," but he finds only fourteen cases in all of the instances that have been cited as support for that theory (about the same as the number of members of nobility accused). He argues, "The midwife witch is a stereotype that has passed straight from the works of demonologists into the works of historians" and that "they have tortured a few facts to fit the Procrusean bed of an obsolete theory" (25). Harley reminds us that "not one New England midwife was tried for witchcraft and only one was suspected, for largely unrelated reasons" (24). Critics do not challenge the more general view that women charged with witchcraft "regularly step out of place and become usurpers of the male role," or that women in "atypical" positions and circumstances may be vulnerable" (Willis 1995: 6).

Although sometimes attacked or criticized by the male medical profession, midwives were routinely called on by ecclesiastical and political authorities in formal proceedings involving women because of their expertise on female biology. Harley (1990) notes that midwives served as "expert witnesses" in cases involving "rape, bastardy, and infanticide, and even cases of witchcraft itself" (4). In England and Europe, midwifery appears to have been a respectable female role: "Local communities . . . had to have midwives whom they could trust and medical practitioners had to be able to collaborate amicably with them" (7–8).

Of course, activities specific to women could increase their liability for blame when children died or became ill, such as wet nursing or "lying in." Willis (1995) states, "Female networks of shared mothering involved competition and conflict as well as mutual support," and "Women's conflicts circulated in and through narcistically charged objects closely associated with the maternal function—children, hens, butter, cows, milk, and so forth—and women competed with other women in a world where priorities were set largely by men" (36). Were this argument valid, then we could propose that conflicts among women and violations of expectations about how women should act, rather than a threat to men by women in certain occupational roles, is central to understanding the local dynamics generating witchcraft accusations.

The trial of Amy Denny in Lowenstoft, England, described by Geis and Bunn (1997: 40–41), illustrates the role of conflicts involving childcare as a source of accusations of witchcraft. Dorothy Durrant asked her elderly neighbor, Amy Denny, to watch her son for a penny while she ran an errand. One means of pacifying the child was to allow him to suckle, but sucking air could lead to discomfort. Denny suckled the boy despite instructions not to do so, making the mother very angry. The child fell ill that night and remained ill for weeks.

Two years later Durrant's ten-year-old stepdaughter suffered from similar symptoms, and Durrant reported that she found Denny in the house when she returned from the apothecary. She kicked Denny out, and Denny told her that the girl did not have long to live. The girl died in a few days. The son remained ill for several years and died thirteen months after Denny was found guilty of bewitching him. Another son had died in the interim (but Denny was not accused) and Durrant reported that she herself had gone lame as well. These events, Denny's "scalding tongue," and a prior reputation as a "witch" were key ingredients leading to her hanging as a witch. Denny was neither a midwife nor a healer. She was elderly and widowed but routinely involved in the lives of neighbors. She did violate numerous gender expectations in interaction with both men and women, but it was her violation of expectations in relation to the children's mother that ultimately brought her down.

The argument presented earlier concerning the credibility of women as targets of blame can be applied to the midwife issue. When Barstow (1994) stated that "certain women were suspected of witchcraft, not because they were powerless, but precisely because they were seen to have a great deal of power," she was referring to "wise women," "cunning women" or "healer-diviners." Barstow believes that references to such women as "midwives" is both misleading and narrow (111). There were a variety of activities involving women requiring special knowledge and experience in healing that did not involve birth or women who would be defined as midwives. She was not specifically addressing Harley's critique when she made that statement, but it is clear that his focus was on women who could be categorized in a specific, identifiable occupational role. Harley's analysis suggests that midwives were rarely the targets of witchcraft accusations. The midwife was suspect in the writings of demonologists, but, as Richard Horseley (1979) notes, "The peasantry did not share the learned belief that midwives were instruments of the Devil" (709). Moreover, midwives were subject to both ecclesiastic and political controls. They were required by the church to swear oaths precluding the use of magic (Horsley 1979: 709), were elected to such positions in some settings, and were subject to government ordinances and ecclesiastic licensing in others (Harley 1990: 4–5). The midwife might be liable to targeting during crises that could increase problems associated with pregnancy and childbirth, but she was also protected through a variety of mechanisms defining and constraining her role.

Women occupying the more nebulous status of "wise woman" may have been unusually vulnerable to targeting, but there are differences of opinion on that issue as well. Since years of experience were required to accumulate special wisdom, wise women were likely to be older women and many may have been relatively free from male control or guardianship compared to other women. They may have been relatively unprotected targets. Moreover, their special skills included the ability to detect and invoke supernatural forces as well as to prepare and use folk remedies to deal with illnesses and maladies. That special knowledge was accorded respect by peasants and witch hunters as well. Women with such special wisdom could be called on by courts to search for the witches mark or other signs of involvement with Satan. Of course, that special expertise could also make them credible targets when searching for servants of Satan.

Lepers, Prostitutes, and Homosexuals as Potential Scapegoats

The perspective elaborated here on the dual roles of credibility and guardianship makes sense of the emergence of women as a credible threat worthy of collective blame as well as the selection of certain types of women as scapegoats. The most obvious transition necessary for witch hunts to develop and spread was to shift the social construct of the heretic from prior internal religious enemies to witchcraft and women as a source of secret but organized evil. This transformation was especially plausible when Satan was identified as the secret leader with women as organized servants. This transition has been stressed by a number of scholars, but without recognition of its fit with theories of scapegoating and victimization in other academic fields.

Discussions of sequences and overlap among different types of targeted "deviant" groups have included groups other than Jews, heretics, and witches. For example, Jeffrey Richards's (1990) work on *Sex, Dissidence and Damnation* highlights the similarities in the treatment and depictions of heretics, witches, Jews, prostitutes, homosexuals, and lepers. Lepers had been accused of spreading poison in wells in 1321 with the imputed motive the division of the devastated territories among themselves (161–62). Moreover, confessing lepers drew Jews into the plot and threw in a Moslem king and a sultan as financial backers. Philip V of France ordered the arrest of all lepers, but he took no action against the Jews. There were widespread massacres of the Jews, and King Charles IV ordered all Jews expelled in 1322.

Lepers, like Jews, prostitutes, and heretics, were required to identify themselves through dress or some visible signal. However, Richards also points out that, although lepers were ordered to identify themselves and to be segregated because of the contagious nature of the disease, the church stressed sympathy and compassion. Leprosy was interpreted as a punishment for sin and linked with an excessive desire for sex, but lepers were "specially favored by God," and stories about several saints emphasized the special care they gave to lepers. Thus, although there are similarities in the experiences and treatment of lepers and other minority groups, lepers were rarely targeted as an organized, collective threat in the same fashion as Jews, heretics, and witches. When they were, they were tied together with more credible targets as enemies of Christian society at the time. Finally, leprosy was fading as an epidemic disease by the fourteenth century, and lepers were neither readily available as scapegoats, nor particularly credible as a source of hidden, collective conspiracies. Conflicting themes in religious doctrine precluded the same scale of demonization that was possible for Jews, heretics, and, ultimately, witches.

Prostitutes were also subject to laws requiring identifying dress and segregation, and periodic attempts were made to regulate and control their activities. However, prostitutes as a group were never viewed as a real or imaginary collective threat and were generally tolerated as an unavoidable necessity. Women who violated gender expectations might be viewed as prime candidates for charges of witchcraft, but those who entered into prostitution as a career were playing a role that was quite well integrated into patriarchal society. The prostitute engaged in sexual activities with an assortment of men in the real world and had little reason to pursue secretive or fantastic relationships with Satan or to waste time in unpaid sabbatical orgies. Prostitution involved earthly acts and overt secular exchanges between men and women. As Silvia Bovenschen (1978) observes, "Both the mother and the prostitute were definitely of this world and under the control of men" (156). In contrast to the "natural" secular exchanges involved in prostitution, women who were charged with witchcraft often reported having been offered rewards by Satan for cooperation in sexual and supernatural intrigues. In short, prostitutes were not credible candidates for secret exchanges with hidden demons.

The treatment and depiction of homosexuals shared numerous features in common with the Jews, heretics and witches. Moreover, consistent with the findings on witch trials reported in chapter 5, Richards (1990) notes that "concern in the towns for the problem of homosexuality was exacerbated by the plague epidemic and the consequent decline in population" (145). Homosexuality, bestiality, and unnatural sexual intercourse were linked to starvation, pestilence and other natural disasters. By the mid–thirteenth century sodomites and heretics were both subject to the Inquisition and targeted by the new Medicant Orders as threats to Christian society.

E. William Monter (1981) proposes several "working hypotheses" about the repression of sodomy in Europe that have some bearing on arguments about the supply and selection of scapegoats. First, in contrast to witchcraft, sodomy was primarily a charge against males (it likely meant bestiality in rural settings and homosexuality in towns). Second, although there had been homosexual subcultures in Italian cities since the Middle Ages, Monter notes that "north of the Alps, such continuous and well-developed subcultures are difficult to find before the seventeenth century" (42). Finally, he hypothesizes that "the repression of sodomy was probably most intense during the sixteenth and seventeenth centuries, during the peak of religious zeal generated by Protestant and Catholic Reformations and during the peak of prosecutions for witchcraft, a form of nonsexual deviance that had similarly been confused with heresy" (42).

Monter supports each hypothesis with evidence from French Switzerland and provides detail that is quite consistent with the arguments outlined in this chapter. For example, he observes that "unlike most European cities, which historically contained a surplus of women, Geneva in 1560 was a remarkably crowded place with a large surplus of men, mainly young men." An imbalanced sex ratio, stemming from a surplus of women, has been introduced into the explanation of variation in witch trials in the American colonies with witchcraft accusations more common when there were surpluses of women (Pearl 1977: 195–205). Midelfort (1972: 184–85) suggests a similar pattern in his work on witch hunting in southwestern Germany. A surplus of males altered the supply of credible targets for scapegoating. In fact, in his classic work on *Witchcraft in France and Switzerland*, Monter (1976: 66) refers to "The Gentle Calvinists" because of "Geneva's remarkably low rate of convictions" for witchcraft.[2]

There is, in fact, a tendency for sodomy trials in Geneva to have occurred in years with witch trials. Between 1500 and 1700, there were eighty-seven years with a witch trial, and a sodomy trial occurred in twenty of those years (about 23 percent). In contrast, in 114 years without a witch trial, there were 12 years with sodomy trials (about 10 percent). This association is significant (Pearson's chi-square = 5.725, df = 1, p = .0167), but quite weak. Most sodomy trials did occur in witch trial years (62 percent), but witch trials were accompanied by sodomy trials only 23 percent of the time. Thus, there was a higher probability of one type occurring when the other type occurred, but witch trials were much more common than sodomy trials.

The relationship between "plague spreader" trials and sodomy trials can be considered as well. In seven years witchcraft trials involved specific accusations that the people charged were intentionally spreading plague: 1530, 1545, 1567, 1568, 1571, and 1615. Sodomy trials accompanied witch trials in three of those seven years. Hence, during 43 percent of years when there were witchcraft trials involving accusations of spreading plague, there were trials for sodomy as well. In contrast, in non–plague spreader years, sodomy trials occurred only 15 percent of the time. Similarly, witch trials occurred in 86 percent of years when charges of plague spreading occurred and only 42 percent of other years.[2] These findings are quite consistent with the examples cited by Richards, suggesting a common tendency to attribute epidemic disease to witches and homosexuals during this span of time.

Monter's Genevan data led him to propose that both witch trials and sodomy trials reflected a heightened concern about morality. However, it should also be noted that the expression of this concern targeted far more women for witchcraft than it did men for sodomy, despite what appears to be a surplus of eligible male targets in Geneva. If the same argument proposed for women (i.e., that they had to be viewed as a credible "collective" threat by elites) were applied to homosexuals, then we would expect sodomy to be treated similarly to witchcraft only if there were evidence of collective organization. In support of that thesis, Monter notes that continuous and well-developed homosexual subcultures were "difficult to find before the seventeenth century" north of the Alps. Homosexuals may not have been as credible as a source of organized conspiracy as witches, and when they were a credible target of blame, it may have been in settings where the relative supply and visibility of the different types of targets were rather unique. However, even in those settings, women were more likely to become targets of scapegoating accusations than other categories of "deviant" males.

Repertoires of Contention: War, Rebellion, and Witch Hunts

Witch hunts involved the use of local institutional machinery to manage village-level, interpersonal conflicts that were interpreted, or "socially constructed," as cases involving a larger, hidden conspiracy of internal enemies. The "enemy" in the case of witch hunts is, as Cotton Mather phrased it, among the "Wonders of the Invisible World." The demonological interpretation of witchcraft that facilitated the most severe witch hunts defined the enemy as a secretive conspiracy of witches, led by Satan, involving people (primarily women) who were putative members of the social system. It was the transformation of witchcraft into heresy (a religious, political, legal category limited to members of a social system) that set the stage for panic or "crazelike" episodes of torture, burning, and hanging. Not only were hostilities directed at a diffuse, hidden threat, but they were carried out through institutional machinery. In short, witch hunts were *a structured form of institutional violence directed at internal targets, enemies, or scapegoats.*

When viewed as a form of internal conflict or violence, witch hunts share a major characteristic in common with rebellions and civil wars. Witch hunts, rebellions, and civil wars are types of internal conflict, involving struggles among contending members of a social system. However, in contrast to witch hunts, rebellions and civil wars involve overt, noninstitutional conflicts between opposing factions or coalitions of members of a social system. Both forms of internal conflict can be distinguished from wars with "external" enemies. In fact, civil wars and internal rebellions, protests, and revolutions have been hypothesized to be negatively related to war with external enemies. Wars with external enemies can compound internal problems that generate protest after the threat subsides, thereby generating a negative correlation. Or, political leaders may be inclined toward war with external enemies as a diversionary strategy (Levy 1989: 59–88). In either case, war and internal conflict should be negatively related.

However, although witch hunts and other internal conflicts may share some features in common, a key characteristic differentiating the two is the degree to which the anxieties, anger or unrest are "structured." Indeed, when witch hunts are discussed as instances of scapegoating, the focus is on "channeling" aggression and the source of that aggression is depicted as "free-floating anger and anxiety" (Sebald 1978: 187). Hans Sebald argues that scapegoating women as witches functioned to "purge the community of distrust and anxiety" and "gave desperate emotions . . . a focus" (187). The emphasis on "free-floating anger and anxiety" and the role of the witch as "a focus" for imposing structure or blame raises questions that have not been adequately addressed: Why pursue witches as scapegoats rather than attack rulers and elites? What circumstances generate a "free-floating anger and anxiety" as opposed to anger and anxiety focused in the form of rebellion, revolution, or other forms of internal conflict among distinct contending groups?

One answer to these questions is to propose that internal conflicts between or among contending factions preclude or inhibit the type of ritual, institutionalized conflict directed at hidden enemies reflected in witch hunts. Stated quite simply, members of a social system are unlikely to search for hidden internal enemies when there are overt violent conflicts among discernible contending factions within the system, just as they are unlikely to devote resources to that pursuit when involved in wars with external enemies. In short, some forms of collective behavior may, in fact, inhibit or preclude other forms. Just as some scholars have proposed that war with external enemies can be a diversionary strategy defraying internal protest, some have proposed that witch hunts may have been part of the arsenal of diversionary strategies available to political leaders.

In *Cows, Pigs, Wars and Witches*, Marvin Harris (1974) argues, "The witchcraft mania . . . dispersed and fragmented . . . latent energies of protest" as "the poor came to the conclusion that they were being victimized by witches and devils instead of princes and popes" (207). In short, rather than attributing the witch trials to free-floating anger and anxiety, the witch trials are viewed as dispersing and fragmenting energies that, otherwise, would have been vented in much more focused forms such as protest, rebellion, or revolution. If witch hunts were a successful diversionary strategy, averting more structured forms of internal conflict, then internal wars and witch hunts would occur at different times as well.

This argument is a form of conflict theory (see chapter 2) in which witch hunts are part of a strategy for dealing with internal tensions by directing them toward scapegoats as diversionary targets. Although consistent with the view that witch hunts and other internal conflicts should occur at different times, most of the research on witch hunts in the last twenty-five years has challenged the view of witch trials as an elite strategy for deflecting blame or redirecting protest. In general, centralized political and judicial systems constrained witch hunts and, when elites played a role, it was primarily at the local or provincial level rather than at the state level. Moreover, as Briggs reminds us, the trials tended to reflect a percolation of complaints built up from below rather than a fabrication by insecure leaders. Local gatekeepers may have been more responsive to such complaints when it served their interests as a mechanism for deflecting blame, but, like conspiracy theories in general, it is difficult to muster actual evidence of such hidden motives.

A third possible route to a negative relationship between witch hunts as an emotion-laden form of scapegoating and other forms of collective behavior is suggested by Charles Tilly's (1992) basic proposition as quoted in chapter 1: "Alternative paths of state formation . . . led to different forms of resistance and rebellion" (150). Were it applied to early modern witch hunts, this proposition could be rephrased as "Alternative forms of state organization and structure led to differentially organized forms of social conflict." Combining Tilly's proposition with McAdams and Sewell's (2001:113) conceptions of "master templates," "cultural epochs of contention," or "repertoires of contention, " it can be proposed that "alternative forms of state organization and structure are conducive to different repertoires of contention" and that the application of one template or repertoire can interfere with the application of another.

For example, southwestern Germany was characterized by political fragmentation, rapidly changing and brokered alliances, loyalties, and religious orientations. In contrast, seventeenth-century France was characterized by a highly centralized state and should have experienced more frequent and intense rebellions as well as less frequent and intense witch hunts. If the structure of the state or a society's organization into contending coalitions helps structure and focus anger and anxiety, then witch hunting as a type of scapegoating would be less common in such systems. Moreover, were a society continually involved in wars of some form, then the "opportunity" for witch hunts and the need for inventing or pursuing more mysterious, internal enemies would be greatly inhibited. If witch hunts tend to be a "peacetime" activity, then the prevalence of "peace" among societies and over time within any given system should affect the intensity and prevalence of such witch hunts.

When comparing southwest Germany with France in the sixteenth century, there are two different spans of time in which conflicts involved struggles among structured and reasonably well-defined groups: the German Peasants' War (1524–1525) and the French Wars of Religion against the Huguenots (1562–1577).[3] The German Peasants' War was the largest revolt of the masses in German history and the "enemy" was relatively well defined. Thomas Munster defined the enemy as "fat cats" and greedy princelings for substantial "rich and middle-income" peasants as well as urban craftsmen who were struggling to protect their rights of self-determination. The revolt was encouraged by Reformation theology, but Luther defined the German masses involved as "thieving and murdering hordes" and sided with the princes (Kitchen 1996: 92–95). The peasants were soundly defeated with thousands of casualties and there were no comparable uprisings in that specific region during the early modern period.

In contrast, structured internal conflicts and uprisings were common in France. During most of the second half of the sixteenth century, France was involved in the Wars of Religion.

These wars involved internal religious conflicts between Protestants (especially French Calvinists—the Huguenots) and Catholics, political struggles between the crown and nobles, and periodic involvement by England, Holland, German Protestants, Spain, Savoy, and Rome. Hence, although classified as "civil wars," the Wars of Religion involved outside groups and nations, supporting or opposing different contending groups.

The losses experienced between 1560 and 1580 were substantial, especially for Protestant soldiers. James Wood (1984: 141) estimates that by the late 1570s, one-half of the Protestant male population of fighting age was "wiped out." Losses were comparable for Catholic soldiers, but Wood believes the minority status of the Protestants "must have led to the exhaustion of the Protestant movement." Deaths in battles were only part of the losses to

Protestants, with the Massacre of St. Bartholomew in 1572 resulting in over three thousand Huguenot deaths in Paris and ten thousand more in other provincial cities.

In chapter 5, we noted the relationship between the Huguenot Wars and witch hunts in southwestern Germany—a coincidence that may support Tilly's (1992) general observation about state formation and "different forms of resistance and rebellion" (150). While the French were occupied with the struggle between Protestants and Catholics, complete with their supporting and opposing sets of external friends and foes, witch hunts made their initial major surge in southwestern Germany. It is beyond the scope of the current work to mount an assessment of the causes of civil wars (or other kinds of war) in comparison to the causes of witch hunts, but the circumstances generating one form of collective conflict in one system may generate a different form of collective conflict in another system. The fragmentation of Germany made it difficult for organized conflict among contending factions to develop, but it left the door open for the pursuit of hidden enemies. The witch was a symbolic representation of the same conflicts that were expressed in a less free-floating and diffuse form among "the contentious French." Enemies were not nearly as well hidden in France as in southwestern Germany.

The same level of relatively precise data measuring the intensity of witch hunts, war and other variables are not available for France as were constructed for analysis for southwestern Germany and Bavaria. However, figure 6.2 plots Quincy Wright's data on the Huguenot conflict, other internal or civil wars, and wars involving external enemies together with Alfred Soman's (1978: 33–36) estimates of number of death sentences after appeal to the Parliament of Paris for witchcraft, and Muchembled's (1993: 142–43) data for witchcraft cases in northern France (the Nord).

Several patterns are suggested by these graphs and are supported by the appropriate multivariate analyses of these data. First, involvement of France in wars involving external enemies is negatively related to involvement in internal civil wars.[4] Members of a social system are less likely to become involved in internal conflicts with one another when preoccupied with conflicts involving external enemies than when there are no such external threats. Rebellions, revolutions, and other internal protests may be particularly common following conflicts with external enemies as a product of compounded problems generated by such wars (see Obershall 1976; Levy 1989). Second, war with external enemies is a significant negative correlate of witch hunts.[5] When France is involved in wars with other societies, there are few witchcraft cases processed and few death sentences. Finally, consistent with the view that civil war and scapegoating tend to be alternative expressions of

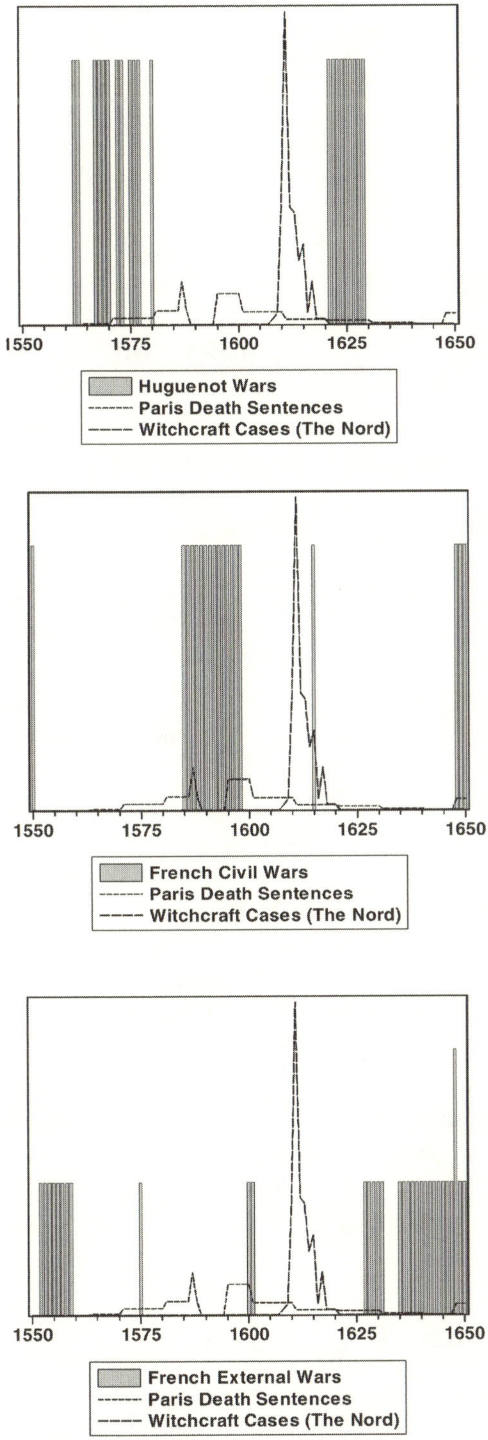

Figure 6.2. Witchcraft cases and conflicts involving internal and external enemies (France).

aggression, a negative relationship exists between civil war and witchcraft appeals or death sentences as well.[6]

The tendency for witch hunts to be inhibited by war has implications for variation at other levels of analysis. If war tends to inhibit witch hunts, then the more years a social system is preoccupied with war (especially with external enemies), the less likely the development of severe, sustained witch hunts. A comparison between Scotland and England is quite consistent with that hypothesis. Between 1550 and 1700, Scotland was involved in some form of war seven percent of the years in that span, while England was involved in war 69 percent of the time. Wright's data on war for the region of Europe with the most intense witch hunting (Baden) show that region to be involved in war only 11 percent of those 150 years. In contrast, France was involved in war 66 percent of the years between 1550 and 1700. The Netherlands was involved in war about 55 percent of that time span, while Spain was involved in war a full 93 percent of the time. If years at war were used to predict the intensity of witch hunts, then witch hunts should have been quite virulent in Scotland and southwestern Germany, followed by England, France, and the Netherlands, with the least participation in Spain. These figures are quite consistent with qualitative rankings of regions or societies in terms of the intensity of witch hunts. The most intense and sustained witch hunts were in Baden-Württemberg and Scotland, with comparatively mild outbreaks England, the Netherlands, and most areas of France, and little involvement in witch hunts for Spain.

Of course, one variable should not be presumed to account for all societal variation, especially since analyses of witch hunts in Baden-Württemberg suggest that plague epidemics and economic hardship played a role in facilitating the most intense witch hunts in southwestern Germany and Bavaria (Jensen 1997; Behringer 1997). However, that pattern of societal variations by war is quite consistent with one of the most common arguments in the witch hunt literature. Numerous historians have observed that witch hunts were most likely in areas where centralized authority was not preeminent and that when witch hunts did occur in strong nation-states (e.g., Spain, France, Italy) they tended to occur in border areas where control was weak. The opportunity for witch hunts also appears to increase when there are breakdowns in centralized control, provided such breakdowns are not accompanied by war (Monter 1976: 31–35; Klaits 1982: 148–72). Wolfgang Behringer (1996) states the general finding quite succinctly: "[G]enerally, large territories with stable, successfully centralized states tended to avoid persecutions or stepped in quickly to retard them" (77). Thus, although few scholars would disagree with Gijswitj-Hofstra and Frijhoff's (1991: 30) argument that "European witchcraft prosecution cannot be covered by one succinct explanation," the patterns involving war appear to be quite consistent across a variety of societies and suggest a possible alternative explanation to state centralization as an explanation of societal variations.

Conclusion

Academic disciplines have become so specialized that theory and research in one are rarely applied to phenomena dealt with in another. Historians tend to draw from the work of other historians, psychologists from other psychologists, and sociologists from other sociologists. In fact, scholars can become so specialized that those studying forms of collective behavior such as war, rebellion, and revolution pay little attention to other forms of collective behavior encompassed by concepts such as scapegoating or persecution.

This chapter focused on a topic that can be illuminated by drawing on ideas and theories from a variety of disciplines and specialties within disciplines—scapegoating. *Scapegoating* is the punitive or negative treatment of people or groups who are held accountable for crises or problems that they did not actually cause. Every attempt to explain the early modern witch craze introduces some version of scapegoating, lumped together with closely related concepts such as persecution. This overlap is unavoidable for the simple reason that scapegoating can be a strategy used to persecute hated groups or a strategy for structuring or deflecting hostility and blame.

When theory and research in psychology, criminology, and the sociology of collective behavior and social conflict are considered together, they allow an integrated treatment of a variety of interrelated issues that contribute to our understanding of witch hunts (and scapegoating in general) on a variety of fractal scales. When considered on a societal scale, the more years a social system is involved in violent conflict with external enemies, the less the opportunity for witch hunts directed at hidden, internal enemies to develop. People are unlikely to search for hidden, internal targets of blame, when obvious external enemies require their attention. When minority groups are targeted for repressive control during times of war (e.g., internment of Japanese Americans during World War II; persecution of Muslims during the crusades and Ottoman Wars; communists during the Korean War), it will be based on perceived ties with external enemies.

Internal wars are a form of structured conflict as well, and sociological theories of protest, riot, rebellion, and revolution have similar implications for the relation between internal conflicts and witch hunts. In societies such as France, where discernible factions can form coalitions against common, real-world foes, social conflict is likely to take the form of civil strife rather than a transformation of local conflicts into a battle with hidden forces of evil such as witch hunts. In settings where it is difficult for people to define an enemy or to coalesce in opposition to a common enemy, they are likely to pursue troublesome people within their own communities as scapegoats. Scapegoating becomes particularly intense when it is encouraged or facilitated by elite constructions or cultural templates defining the hidden cause of collective misfortune, and when gatekeepers are receptive to complaints that can be fit into that template.

Psychological theories of scapegoating propose that scapegoats are likely to be chosen from among groups and people who have been involved in prior conflicts and who are of intermediate similarity to scapegoaters. Witch hunts are directed at other members of the same social system, and those groups or people selected have to be credible as targets of blame, but vulnerable to such attack without undue fear of retaliation as well. Routine activities theory in criminology directs us to consider availability of targets as well as vulnerability or guardianship.

These ideas led to a consideration of the credibility of women as a source of hidden, organized conspiracies, and it was proposed that a precursor to the acceptance of women as a credible threat would be evidence of collective organization outside of male control in the real world, especially when that organization is defined as a threat by the learned or official gatekeepers. In terms of timing and variation in activity among social systems, the Beguines are a strong candidate as that precursor. They were the major instance of the organization of women in late medieval and early modern Europe, and reports of variation in their distribution coincide with variations in witch hunting. Moreover, they were attacked and demonized in the same fashion as earlier heretic groups.

Drawing on discussions of the stimulus qualities of scapegoats and routine activities theory, it was proposed that the relative supply and guardianship of targets of various kinds were important considerations for interpreting the timing and variation in witch hunting as well. A common sequence in persecution or scapegoating over time emphasized in witch hunt literature is Jew-heretic-witches. Witches were socially constructed as a collective threat out of the same demonological belief system that was applied to earlier groups and were not likely to be pursued when more readily accessible targets were available. Although some scholars include lepers, prostitutes, and homosexuals as targets as well, neither lepers nor prostitutes would make particularly credible collective threats and homosexuals would qualify only in a few select settings.

An ongoing debate concerns the demonization of a specific category of women as witches—midwives. From one feminist perspective, midwives were pursued as witches as a patriarchal strategy to expand male control over the female body. Others argue that midwives treated or assisted women with problems that were not a source of male status or prestige, midwives were called on by male authorities because they were viewed as having special expertise, and conflicts among women were as important for understanding witchcraft accusations as conflicts with men. Midwives were demonized in some important works defining the witchcraft problem, but only a small number of identifiable midwives are found among the accused. In contrast, wise women, healer/diviners, or older women who occasionally engaged in midwifery, healing, or devining appear to have been quite liable to suspicion when misfortune struck. The most common characteristic of women selected and labeled as witches, noted across a variety of studies of witchcraft accusations, is a history of conflicts involving accusers, a scalding tongue, or other indicators of a troublesome fit into accepted and traditional gender schemes in early modern society.

The worst battles of the early modern "witch wars" were over by the end of the seventeenth century, and, given the evidence that the witch craze itself involved a shift to a new type of internal threat, it would be reasonable to suggest that there may have been a shift to yet another category of potential scapegoats or imaginary enemies. One historian has argued that a decline in witch trials was accompanied by increasing concern about vampires (Klaniczay 1990). Klaniczay (1990: 178–79) notes numerous parallels between the circumstances associated with the persecution of witches and a surge in fear of vampires in Hungary. He reports cases of vampirism in Silesia (1591), Bohemia (1619), and Poland (1624), and he notes that in 1709, a Hungarian doctor "gave a shocking account of the number of corpses dug up and pierced by a pole or beheaded because they were considered responsible for spreading the plague." Since plague victims were often hauled away hurriedly and in mass, some may have been alive when they were buried. It is possible that some appeared to rise from the dead. Moreover, as the vampire legend spread, there were numerous cases of people with illnesses that they attributed to the bite of vampires, just as had been the case with witches. The vampire was, however, even more imaginary than the witch in the sense that no distinct, socially differentiated category of living people was implicated. Unlike the Jews, heretics, and witches, the vampire was not part of an imaginary conspiracy in league with the traditional hidden enemies of Christian society. Indeed, vampires were loners.

Klaniczay (1990) makes an interesting observation about the counterattacks on the vampire legend by Voltaire and others. He argues that "they attempted to shift public attention from mythical vampires to 'bloodsuckers' in the real social sense of the term" (187). Voltaire identified "merchants, speculators and tax-collectors" as the "real bloodsuckers" found in "very pleasant palaces" rather than cemeteries and others included "rich peasants" as the real vampires. Klaniczay concludes that "within a few decades it was no longer the blood of the exhumed corpses, but that of the 'social bloodsuckers' that was going to flow" (188). This transition would fit quite well with the thesis that fear of imaginary internal enemies declines when more secular and realistic enemies are discerned. However, no organized conspiracy on par with the demonological covens of witches appears to have emerged after the end of the witch wars. The early modern witch craze ended with late surges at the end of the seventeenth century in Sweden, Finland, and New England and some mild attacks in the first half of the eighteenth century in Hungary after the long Turkish occupation ended. Moreover, there is no evidence of a shift to a new hidden enemy.

Marijke Gijswijt-Hofstra (1999) points out, "The end of the with trials did not mean the end of witchcraft, and not even the end of witch burnings" (97). She cites a case in 1984 where a Polish woman was burned to death in her house by villagers, based on the same types of accusations that had been involved in persecutions of Jews six centuries earlier, poisoning wells and spreading epidemic disease. These episodes are rare, isolated events and take the form of vigilante "justice" rather than instances of legal, formal social control. In short, the panic or craze phases of the witch wars were limited to the sixteenth and the seventeenth centuries, with the most dramatic battles fought in the seventeenth century. Belief in witches and witchcraft persisted, but the pursuit of witches through legal machinery faded. Village conflicts continued, but formal charges of witchcraft as a solution either faded away or fell on deaf ears. By the late seventeenth century, criminal prosecution of witches was being countered by prosecutions for false accusations, slander and vigilante violence in pursuit of witches.

Among the possible explanations for the end of the early modern witch craze, Brian Levack (1996) lists the regulation of local justice, the demise of torture, new standards of evidence, increases in legal representation, religious changes, and changing environmental and social conditions as possible sources of the decline in witch prosecutions. Levack favors an explanation based on centralization of state and judicial power and argues that "the decline and end of witch-hunting, characterized by formal restrictions on the use of torture, the reversal of convictions upon repeal, and legislation that restricted the right of local courts to try witches under any circumstances, was undertaken and enforced mainly by central judicial institutions." He suggests that centralized justice inhibited witch hunts because more distant judges were less likely to share the fears of members of local communities and had more legal training. The solidification of centralized state and judicial control allegedly put the brakes on local purges.

Of course, in notable examples, distant judges appear to have shared the same fears as members of local communities. In England, judges could not hold court in their home county or the county of their birth, a policy that might be relevant to relatively mild witch trials in England, supporting the "centralization-as-brake" thesis. However, Geis and Bunn's (1997: 78) detailed study of the 1662 witch trial at Bury St. Edmunds in Norfolk, England, highlights the role that the circuit judge, Mathew Hale, played in pushing a witchcraft verdict against Amy Denny and Rose Cullender.

The Bury St. Edmund's trial involved claims that the two elderly women had bewitched several young girls, charges that were called into doubt by a "sergeant-at-law" involved in the case. The expression of such doubts by a distant official might be taken as support for the centralization argument, but Mathew Hale appears to have solicited testimony from the prominent physician Sir Thomas Browne to counter those doubts. Browne verified the reality of witchcraft for the court by citing a similar episode that had, allegedly, taken place in Denmark. In an attempt to verify that the girls were not stage acting, the court itself staged several tests. In one test, the girls were blindfolded and responded to a touch by the accused by shrieking. However, in another test, where someone other than the accused touched a blindfolded girl, it drew the same response. Instead of challenging the veracity of the accusations, the second experiment was reinterpreted to be a "ruse" by Satan. The trial proceeded and the two women were ultimately executed.

If the demise of witch trials were a product of increasing constraints imposed by elites, it is still relevant to ask why the brakes were applied, or why they were not applied at other times.

The analysis in chapter 5 suggests that, at least in the heartland of the witch craze, the end of devastating disease epidemics, as well as the beginning and fluctuations in between, coincide quite well with similar features of early modern witch trials. The early phases of the witch trials coincide with upward trends in population pressure and prices coupled with mounting environmental problems. The panic phases coincide with variations in bubonic plague during a span of time when all environmental indicators pointed to the convergence of crises into "a perfect storm."

Variations in state centralization might coincide with some patterns of regional and societal variation, as well as the temporal course of witch hunts on a broad fractal scale. But, it can also be argued that centralized states put the brakes on the escalation of local panics only when other generic pressures eased. As Briggs (1996b) suggests, "[P]olite disdain largely coincided with a growing confidence in the stability of the social and religious order" and that witchcraft's "grip on the imagination of the ruling elites faded" with that stability (408).

Other diseases may have prompted collective anxiety and set the stage for witch hunts after the demise of plague, but the only variable that fits the course of witch hunts on a variety of temporal scales is pestilence. It was much harder for fears of witchcraft and demonological conspiracies to grip the imaginations of ruling elites after the demise of the seventeenth-century epidemic. Panic witch hunts subsided after the worst source of collective anxiety in the seventeenth century disappeared. If confidence in the stability of social order was relevant to the demise of witch hunts, that stability was greatly facilitated by the end of pestilential panic.

Notes

1. The events involving victimization of Jews in figure 6.1 are based on Judah Gribetz's *The Timetables of Jewish History* (Gribetz, Greenstein, and Stein 1993). The persecution in 1614 in Frankfurt occurred during a surge in witch trials, but it should be noted that it was a mob action resulting in executions of the leaders of the mob. Although there were some instances of vigilante activity directed at witches, most witches were pursued through the courts. In contrast, Jews were the victims of attacks by mobs. This difference may reflect one or more of several contrasts between the two. For one, Jews were more readily discerned as a group than witches. With the establishment of ghettos, restrictions on land ownership, and the requirement of visible symbols to identify Jews as a group, they were more vulnerable to mob attack. On the other hand, although witches were alleged to be involved in a worldwide conspiracy with Satan, the evidence of witchcraft was based on individual grievances directed at women acting alone or in pairs. The evidence that any particular set of individuals were part of an organized conspiracy had little foundation in the real world. Rather, the notion of a conspiracy was generated from confessions and suggestions under torture. Jews lived in concentrated groups and were suspect as a group.

2. Although the associations when considering the overlap of years with sodomy trials, witch trials and plague spreader trials are all significant, the relationship between plague spreader trials and witch trials is the only significant relationship in either a least-squares regression analysis ($r = +.62$) or in count models for the series. In short, we would have difficulty predicting years with sodomy trials from years with

plague spreading trials, or predicting years with witch trials from years with sodomy trials.

3. Dates for the six Huguenot Wars, French civil wars, and wars with external enemies are all based on Wright (1965).

4. The data are years with or without war with an external enemy and years with or without war among internal enemies. Hence, the statement that there is a significant negative relationship between the two types of war is based on a Pearson chi-square (8.79, df = 2, $p = .0123$) for the cross-classification of the two types of war years. Of thirty-two years between 1550 and 1649 with a war involving external enemies, an internal war is dated as overlapping for seven of those years. In contrast, there are twenty-five civil war years during years with no wars involving external enemies. In short, death sentences are several times more likely during times of peace.

5. The correlation (Pearson's r) between Paris death sentences and external wars was statistically significant at the .01 level ($r = -.29$, $p = .0029$). However, the relationship for witchcraft cases in the Nord was significant only at the .10 level ($r = -.149$, $p = .069$). But, it should be noted that between 1550 and 1647, all thirteen years in which there were witch cases were in years with no war with external enemies. There was a small number of cases between 1648 and 1652, with the early cases overlapping with the last years of warfare. It seems reasonable to conclude that the witch trials were extremely rare during war years.

6. No witchcraft cases were held in the Nord during twenty-one years coded as the Huguenot War, and only three of eighteen cases overlapped with other internal wars.

CHAPTER SEVEN

~

The Salem Witch Hunt

A Perfect Storm

Memorial to victims of the Salem Village "witchcraft hysteria" of 1692 in Danvers, Massachusetts. Modification of author's photograph.

Anyone who has tried to make reservations to visit the colonial seaport city of Salem, Massachusetts, in October quickly discovers that all rooms have been booked for nearly a year in advance. For most of that month, Salem offers a schedule of events billed as "America's Halloween Festival" or "Salem Haunted Happenings" with street flags depicting the Halloween witch. In addition to the month-long calendar of events, tourists can visit a wax museum, a witch museum, attend plays, and view authentic documents from the Salem witch trials at the Essex Museum.

One of the most recent tourist attractions is an enterprise incorporating Wiccan themes into a depiction of the Salem witch hunts. Tourists are led by a guide (typically a young woman) through a series of scenes incorporating symbols, explanations and storylines consistent with a Wiccan interpretation of the events leading up to the witch craze. The flyer used to advertise the "Salem Witch Village" depicts the attraction as an "Indoor Guided Tour Given by Practicing Witches!" The combination of the wax museum and the Salem Witch Village are billed as "The One Stop Salem Experience."

Of course, Halloween and persecution of a Wiccan subculture have little relevance to understanding the witch trials in Salem and Essex County in 1692. The Puritans who established the town had no festivals in celebration of Halloween. Indeed, they did not even celebrate Christmas. The symbolic Halloween witch with her peaked hat, broomstick, black garb, and a hooked nose made her first appearance in children's chapbooks in the early eighteenth century in England, well after the end of the witch hunts there. Moreover, most scholars have rejected the theory that the witch wars were directed at real witch cults or practitioners of forms of pagan witchcraft. Contemporary Wiccans often link themselves to the victims of early modern witch hunts, depicting them as martyred ancestors persecuted for their religious beliefs, and call for solidarity and mutual support with the slogan "Never Again the Burning Times" (see Orion 1995). Colonists did practice folk magic, and many older women had special knowledge of folk medicine, birthing techniques, and birth control. Outbreaks of disease could increase tendencies to resort to magic and for wise women to volunteer or be called on for help. However, none of the victims of the Salem witch trials appears to have been involved in the overt, or even covert, practice of witchcraft based on any unique belief system that would clearly differentiate them from other residents of Salem Village or Salem Town. Belief in magic and folk remedies for problems was common, and some women may have been particularly well versed in that realm. However, those accused of witchcraft are not distinct in this regard from other residents of the area.

Although a perennial concern of clergy, the practice of folk magic and folk countermagic was quite common among the accused and their accusers. Many of the accused witches had conflicts with local clergy and challenged religious conceptions of ideal female behavior, but they fell far short of either rebellion or adherence to any alternative religious belief system. However, as will be detailed in this chapter, afflicted children and young people lodging accusations behaved in a manner that can (and has been) interpreted quite readily as a form of covert religious rebellion. Indeed, the concentration of "afflictions" among young girls as well as the structured nature of their behavior are more consistent with a conception of covert rebellion (see Godbeer 1992 and Karlsen 1989) than any of the contemporary biomedical interpretations. Popular medical interpretations have been based on inadequate scientific methods and data and are accorded credibility based on their "scientific" aura rather than the actual strength of their analysis.

Recent Interpretations

The Salem trials have been the subject of intensive research with new interpretations and themes still emerging. To paraphrase Midelfort's (1979) comment as quoted in chapter 1, theories about the causes of the Salem witch craze "have been sprouting . . . like mushrooms in a fairy ring." One of the most recent and novel interpretations of the episode is Laurie Carlson's (1999) *A Fever in Salem*. Carlson attributes the afflictions leading to the trials to sleeping sickness, supporting her argument with information on the symptoms exhibited, the ecology of the area, and a causal inspection of time series data on variations in wetness. She challenges earlier theories emphasizing factors as diverse as ergot poisoning (Caporael 1976) and village factionalism (Boyer and Nissenbaum 1972).

In an even more recent work, *The Devil's Snare*, Mary Beth Norton (2002) proposes another "new" explanation of the trials, asserting that "had the Second Indian War on the northeastern frontier somehow been avoided, the Essex County witchcraft crisis of 1692 would not have occurred" (298). As will be detailed later in the chapter, not only is this perspective far from new, but it ignores a considerable volume of research claiming a negative relationship between war and witch hunts. War is related to the witch craze, but in a far more complex manner than conveyed in Norton's work.

In "Many Reasons Why," Robin Briggs (1996a) warns us that "any serious interpretation of European witchcraft must be multi-factorial, relating it to a number of discrete, or at least separable, causes." He warns that "any attempt to suggest that there is a single cause, or even a dominant one, a hidden key to the mystery, should be treated with greatest suspicion" (51).

This same reservation should be applied to "new interpretations" of colonial witchcraft and the Salem witch trials. Carlson focuses on the "symptoms" exhibited by the afflicted girls and challenges the relevance of theories that focus on factional and gender conflict. Yet, an explanation of the behavior of the afflicted girls may be quite distinct from an explanation of the subsequent spread of accusations, the structure of such accusations, the ultimate execution of certain types of people, and the end of the trials. The witch trials were a socially organized phenomenon, with socially differentiated categories of people playing distinct roles in the generation of a panic (the possessed, accusers, and official gatekeepers). Indeed, as will be argued below, even personal, intimate experiences such as the "hallucinations" of the afflicted girls were socially structured, shaped, and guided by other participants as well as by common folklore about witches and witchcraft.

Norton's theory is similarly simplistic in its focus on war as the key to witch hunts. Observations in earlier chapters based on a large body of prior research led to a set of generalizations that cannot be ignored in any discussion of the Salem witch craze. Outbreaks of institutionalized witch hunting are most likely to occur following (or in close temporal proximity to) outbreaks of disease and mysterious afflictions affecting both people and animals (sleeping sickness might be one such affliction). However, witch hunting is also more likely when there is a need for scapegoats by accusers and gatekeepers. Witchcraft accusations are more likely when external enemies are not an immediate threat, when alternative internal enemies are scarce or protected, and when people who fit the preconstructed witch template are readily available, increasing in numbers, or growing in visibility. In turn, such institutionalized panics subside when sources of affliction and anxiety subside, when they spread to encompass people who do not fit the standard template, when more immediate external threats confront members of the system, and/or more immediate internal enemies are discerned.

If only one factor were required to explain witch hunts, they would have been far more frequent than they were. On the other hand, if major witch hunts were like "perfect storms," requiring the convergence of a set of discrete and separable circumstances, then the explanation becomes "multifactorial," incorporating "a number of discrete, or at least separable, causes." This approach is exemplified by John Putnam Demos in *Entertaining Satan* (1982) where he introduces a set of factors, noting, "It is only when they are considered together that a pattern of fit seems to emerge" (386). Indeed, Norton's theory runs counter to Demos's multivariate interpretation where war accounts for temporal "valleys" in witch hunting.

If, as Carlson argues, the Salem trials were prompted by sleeping sickness during an unusually wet period in the colonies, then it is reasonable to expect a correlation between variations in wetness and variations in accusations and executions for witchcraft over time in the colonies. However, the Salem outbreak was the only one of its kind in colonial New England. There was some variation in accusations and executions from the 1630s through the 1690s, and Demos has discerned and interpreted most of those peaks and valleys. Because there was only one major witch hunt, and "new" interpretations focus almost exclusively on that single event, a consideration of evidence will have to be much more discursive than the analysis in chapter 5.

On the other hand, information presented as supporting data for such theories should be more carefully considered than has been the case thus far. For example, Carlson argues that proximity to wetlands, ponds, brooks, and rivers explains the geographic concentration of afflictions. Wet years would be conducive to sleeping sickness and proximity to wet areas would explain the geography of afflicted and accused persons in Salem Village. Again, a proper test of this argument requires more than a casual reference to general location of the homes of the afflicted and accused. Carlson's argument implies that the average distance to wetlands and other bodies of standing or still water should be less for one set of people in the area than another. Such arguments should be tested systematically using data on proximity to wetlands rather than reference to rough, schematic maps.

In *Poisons of the Past*, Mary Matossian (1989) uses tree ring data from New Hampshire to support the ergotism theory. In direct contrast to Carlson, she proposes that the witch trials were prompted by unusually cold weather which would be reflected in narrow rings. She states, "The rings for 1690 and 1691 indicate unusual cold and for 1692, below normal temperatures" (119). Such climatic conditions were, she argues, conducive to ergot formation. In short, two scholars use the same types of data to make directly contrary arguments. Carlson argues that sleeping sickness associated with wide rings (indicative of wet conditions) prompted the Salem panic, and Matossian argues that ergotism associated with narrow rings (indicative of cold) was responsible.

Were tree rings wider or narrower during the span of time before the Salem-Essex trials? Was this a unique span of time compared with other years in which a major witch hunt could have occurred? If there are other spans of time when a witch hunt should have occurred based on their theories, why did no other such episodes materialize? In short, even when dealing with one event, the full set of circumstances that must converge to allow or generate a major hunt has to be examined.

Matossian parallels both Caporael and Carlson by proposing that most of the households with symptoms "were close to riverbanks or swamps" (120). Of course, no mention is made of the proximity to rivers and swamps for households without symptoms, for households in general, or for households not directly involved in the witch trials. Matossian, Carlson, and Caporael all imply that there was something "different" about the households where afflictions developed but present no data relevant to other households. They point to a quantitative variable—proximity to breeding grounds for mosquitoes or sources of moisture—that encourages ergot to develop but make no attempt to actually measure their explanatory variable. This chapter will attempt such an analysis, consider alternative interpretations of the behavior of the afflicted, and conclude with an argument for the type of convergence theory supported in the analysis of other early modern witch hunts.

Norton's war theory can be criticized on the same grounds as Carlson's sleeping sickness theory. Norton proposes an explanation for a single witchcraft crisis in 1692 but ignores other contrary arguments that posit an inverse relation between war and witch hunts. If war increases the odds of major witch trials, then witch trials should be unusually common during war. Yet, no witch trials were held during the most devastating wars in 1635–1636 and 1675–1677. There were no witch hunts after 1693 when the Indian threat was actually more immediate and direct than in the years preceding the Salem-Essex County trials. Any one of a variety of vaguely proximate circumstances can be introduced as an explanation of the witch hunt in 1692, but a strong theory has to be able to address other patterns of variation over time and space.

Before examining any data relevant to testing such theories, the key events and participants in the Salem-Essex episode should be studied. Such detail will prove to be useful in assessing theories where specific details on symptoms and hallucinations are introduced as supporting evidence. Sometimes the timing of specific events and detail makes more sense from one perspective than another. Moreover, detail cited as support may seem convincing until countered by detail that does not "fit" the explanation. Numerous facts about the background of the trials and the spread of accusations and afflictions are relevant to assessing the plausibility of various theories.

Salem: A Sociological Crucible

Most high school and college students in America encounter the Salem witch hunt as an event covered in American history courses but are most familiar with it because of Arthur Miller's (1953) play *The Crucible* and the film starring Daniel Day-Lewis and Winona Ryder. Miller's play premiered in 1953 in the context of political searches for communists and communist sympathizers both in the U.S. government and in the entertainment industry. In fact, the day before he was to begin his journey to Salem to do research for the play, his friend Elia Kazan had been forced to testify before the House Un-American Activities Committee. Kazan had directed two of Miller's award-winning plays, *Death of a Salesman* and *All My Sons*. To avoid "blacklisting" by the entertainment industry, Kazan had named people he thought to be members of the Communist Party (Martine 1993). Miller was held in contempt of Congress for refusing to cooperate when he was called to testify.

As stated by Miller in the introduction to his play, *The Crucible* was not intended to be a historically accurate depiction of the Salem witch trials. For example, in reality, Winona Ryder's character, Abigail Williams, was not a scorned teenager seeking revenge against a married lover in his thirties (John Procter, played by Daniel Day-Lewis). Abigail was eleven or twelve years of age, and John was in his middle sixties. No one has provided evidence of a sexual link between the two. A failed love affair provided convincing "motivation" for some of Abigail's charges in the play, but there is no historical foundation for such specific motives in her case. Jealousies and interpersonal conflicts of various sorts were reflected in various charges of witchcraft, but not the specific version introduced for Abigail. Miller intended his play to represent basic themes about intolerance and the consequences of panic for the disregard of human rights, and such themes are represented in the course of that historical episode. However, people who have studied the real sequence of events find the real story just as fascinating.

A Strange Affliction[1]

Betty Parris, Abigail Williams, Ann Putnam, Elizabeth Hubbard, Mary Walcott, and Mercy Lewis were friends and often spent time together. Although they ranged considerably in age, from nine to seventeen years old, they also shared much in common. Abigail was Betty's cousin and was living with Betty and her parents. Ann and Mary were cousins and often ended up at Mary's house together with their friend Mercy. Mercy's parents were dead, and she had been taken in by Ann's parents to help around the house. Elizabeth had become Mary's friend when they lived next door to each other.

Most of the girls had more than a fair share of misfortune. Only Ann and Betty were living with their natural parents. Ann was the eldest of six children, and her mother was expecting yet another child. Mary was one of ten children living with her father and stepmother (Ann's aunt). The other girls had lost their families and had been taken in by relatives or town folk who needed their help. Given their social circumstances and a shortage of potential husbands, the prospects for marriage and a secure future were bleak for most of the girls. Many of the girls had good reason to be anxious about the prospects for their future in colonial patriarchal society.

Although there are good reasons to be skeptical that such an episode was instigated by the Parris's Carib Indian slave, Tituba (McMillen 1990; Breslaw 1996), one account of the girls' activities has Abigail and Betty attempting to foretell the future using common magical folklore from England. Where they learned it is not known, but they believed that the occupation of future spouses could be foretold by watching raw egg whites form a shape in a glass of water. Allegedly, as the egg congealed, it took the shape of a coffin. Such a "message" would have frightened or terrified the girls, compounding the fact that they were involved in forbidden activity.

In *The Devil in Massachusetts*, Marion Starkey (1969: 37–39) accords this attempt at fortune-telling a role in generating subsequent afflictions. Indeed, Starkey argues that it is likely that most of the girls initially affected had taken part, although only Abigail and Betty are mentioned in the historical record. However many girls were involved, it is doubtful that they would talk about the experience with their parents. Few had parents to talk to about their fears and fascinations, and those with parents did not expect them to have a sympathetic ear. Betty and Abigail expected at least a sermon and a scolding. Samuel Parris was a "hellfire and brimstone" minister. They might even face harsh punishment were he to find out what had gone on under his own roof. He would define what they had done as a sin and an invitation for Satan to enter their lives.

In the weeks after this secret exploration with magic, Betty, Ann, and Abigail began acting strangely. They would crawl under chairs, make strange gestures, and twist themselves into unnatural positions. They vacillated between speeches in unknown gibberish and periods where they seemed to have lost their voices entirely. They complained of pains that felt like pinpricks. Although the girls had hidden much of their flirtation with magic and the supernatural from their parents and guardians, these fits and spells occurred in full view of others in the household.

Betty's father was alarmed. He presumed that Betty and Abigail had fallen ill and asked the town's only physician to examine them. One of the girls' friends, Elizabeth, was a great-niece of the doctor's wife and was living with the doctor and his wife. There were reports that several of the girls in that circle of friends were behaving strangely. The doctor could find no medical symptoms that would make sense out of their behavior and began to suspect that the girls might be "possessed." When asked who was afflicting them, the girls gave no answer.

Mary's aunt had heard of some countermagic that might break the spell the girls seemed to be under. She asked Tituba and Tituba's husband, John Indian, to prepare an old English recipe for a "witch cake." A witch cake was made out of rye mixed with the victim's urine. After baking the cake, it was fed to Betty's dog. If the dog were being used as the demon's "familiar," then the witch cake was supposed to drive any demons away. Of course, when Betty's father found out that Mary's aunt was resorting to witchcraft in the attempt to cure the girls, he was irate. In fact, he was so upset that he denounced Mary's aunt in his Sunday sermon for resorting to "diabolic" magic.

It appeared as if the countermagic had worked. The girls finally talked about what was wrong with them. Under repeated and intense questioning, the girls reported that they had been afflicted by Betty's housekeeper, Tituba, and two eccentric middle-aged women in their small town. One of the women was regarded as a community nuisance for continually begging assistance from her neighbors. The other was sick and bedridden but had been involved in a nasty legal dispute with Ann's family.

Ann and Mercy had exhibited weird behavior as well, and Ann's father and uncle, together with two other men in the community, decided to lodge a formal complaint against the three women. The three women were questioned at the village meeting house. Tituba broke down and confessed that she had practiced witchcraft and could even describe the devil that had helped her. The other two women adamantly denied any involvement, but Tituba's confession was enough for their examiners to suspect a conspiracy of witchcraft. All three women were taken to jail in the neighboring town.

The removal and imprisonment of these suspected witches did not solve the girls' problems. Their bizarre behavior continued, and ministers from neighboring communities came to assess the situation. One of the ministers found teeth marks on Mary's arm, and Abigail was observed dashing through the house as if trying to fly and grabbing logs from the fireplace to fling around the room. Ann claimed to see a yellow bird perching on the preacher's hat as it hung on a hook. By that point, Ann's mother was not feeling well and was found laying in bed after a "sore fit."

More women were accused of afflicting the girls and were brought before both the girls and the examiners. The girls reacted to the accused as if under attack. When the accused wrung her hands, the girls would scream as if being pinched. If the accused bit her lip in anxiety, the girls claimed they felt their lips being bitten. The accused had little recourse, and the number arrested and jailed grew.

A Conspiracy of Witches

It was clear to the examiners and to many leaders and parents in the community that they had uncovered a mass conspiracy of witches. Over the next several months, the accusations spread based both on the girls' identification of additional witches and new accusations from the accused witches who named new conspirators in their confessions. In fact, there were accusations of witches at work in neighboring communities, and the afflicted girls were used in examinations to help identify the culprits.

Within the nine months between the girls' explorations with the occult, their subsequent afflictions, accusations, and the trials and executions that ended the search for witches, twenty-four different communities were involved, over 150 people were accused, and 19 people had been executed. Five lives were lost in prison while awaiting trial, and one man (Giles Corey) was crushed to death as the examiners laid on a growing pile of stones in the attempt to get him to acknowledge the authority of the court to judge him.

The search for witches was brought to a halt by mounting opposition from ministers and, ultimately, an order from the new governor forbidding new trials. There had been opposition during the whole affair because the type of evidence being presented was considered a weak foundation for such ominous decisions. Moreover, accusations had spread to include people that examiners could not accept as suspects. Some doubted the authenticity of the accusations. One minister had reported that one of the girls admitted she did it "for sport." Other girls that were caught up in the craze had tried to retract their testimony and confessions at various times, but to no avail. Just one year after the affliction had begun forty-nine of the accused still in prison were acquitted, and three others were granted reprieves by the governor.

The Salem witch trials have been referred to as "the last of the classic witch hunts" (Robinson 1991: 6).[2] When the number of people who were accused, executed, or died in the course of the episode is considered in view of the size of the population (about 1,200 in the vicinity), the Salem trials certainly qualify as one of the last major battles in the war against witches. Moreover, the Salem trials may be one of the last episodes to qualify as an instance of a "witch panic," spreading quickly from community to community, climaxed by an epidemic wave of executions. As noted earlier, the episode has been intensely scrutinized and has inspired a wide range of theories. Most theories have focused on the characteristics of the victims and their relations to accusers, but two of the most recent theories emphasize the behavior of the afflicted girls, focusing on underlying biomedical causes. Because they claim to be based on scientific evidence, those theories will be examined first.

Theories Focusing on Biological Agents

The best-known theory proposing a physiological foundation for both the origin and spread of afflictions as well as the strange visions and experiences reported in testimony against the accused witches is Linda Caporael's (1976) article in *Science*, "Ergotism: The Satan Loosed in Salem?" Caporael attributes the symptoms exhibited to ergot alkaloids that grow on rye when it is stored damp or harvested in wet conditions. The evidence cited in favor of her interpretation includes (1) damp conditions prior to the outbreak, (2) the symptoms of the afflicted and accusers, (3) the proximity of accusers and the afflicted to marshlands, (4) the proximity of the afflicted to the Putnam residence, (5) the abrupt ending to the episode as the area experienced drought in 1693, and (6) a tendency for children and pregnant women to be susceptible.

Of course, the first five pieces of evidence are cited in Laurie Carlson's (1999) *A Fever in Salem* as support for encephalitis, or sleeping sickness, as the source of afflictions and hallucinations. Carlson acknowledges Caporael's theory as innovative but dismisses it based on criticisms by Nicholas Spanos and Jack Gottlieb (1976) in a subsequent issue of *Science*.

Spanos and Gottlieb challenged the ergotism theory on several grounds. For one, ergotism appears to be most severe when there is a deficiency of vitamin A. Such a deficiency is unlikely in an area where dairy products were a major part of the diet. Second, ergotism is supposed to affect young children more than adults, and only three of fifteen afflicted girls were under fifteen. Third, because most members of the households with afflicted girls would have been eating the same affected rye, psychedelic experiences should have been exhibited among others in the household. Fourth, ergotism was a recognized problem among farmers. Ingestion of ergot infested rye was known to affect livestock and would have been suspected had there been any evidence of it.

The most convincing evidence against the ergotism theory is the actual symptoms cited in the historical records as coded by Spanos and Gottlieb. A tally of symptoms among the afflicted girls does not reveal the symptoms that would point to ergotism. In 196 depositions by the girls and others, not a single reference is made to vomiting and diarrhea associated with ergotism, although Caporael claimed that such complaints were common. Gastrointestinal problems were noted for only three of the fifteen afflicted girls. In seventy-six depositions by witnesses, they found no perceptual disturbances of the kind associated with ergot alkaloids or LSD. In short, when the "symptoms" of witnesses providing testimony against the witches are analyzed, they do not support the ergotism theory. Indeed, testimony about specific events that could be deemed "apparitions" (seeing people or objects as opposed to perceptual distortions) could be based on events that had occurred several years before the trials. Spanos and Gottlieb (1976) conclude:

> The available evidence does not support the hypothesis that ergot poisoning played a role in the Salem crisis. The general features of the crisis did not resemble an ergotism epidemic. The symptoms of the afflicted girls and of the other witnesses were not those of convulsive ergotism. And the abrupt ending of the crisis, and the remorse and second thoughts of those who judged and testified against the accused, can be explained without recourse to the ergotism hypothesis.

Carlson argues that, although the symptoms do not fit with ergotism, they do correspond with sleeping sickness which is spread by mosquitoes and ticks, affecting both animals and people. As noted, she presents a graph of tree ring widths as supporting evidence. It appeared to her on visual inspection that the Salem trials were prompted by wet years, which would be conducive to this disease, and ended during a drought year, when mosquitoes would have been less prevalent. Although such data are not presented as definitive evidence for her argument, they are presented as consistent with the argument. However, this observation appears to have been made by "eyeballing" the plot with no actual examination of the detailed data. An examination of the specific years surrounding the Salem trials and the association between ring width and witchcraft accusations may yield quite different results.

Tree Rings

The data on tree ring width that Carlson used as supporting evidence for the sleeping sickness argument are plotted in figure 7.1. The ring data were compiled for a study of "The Lost Colony and Jamestown Droughts" by David Stahle and colleagues (1998: 564–67) and are based on rings from the Virginia-Maryland tidelands. These dendrochronologists were able to show that the Jamestown colony had to face a severe drought reflected in a span of unusually narrow rings. Moreover, it was quite appropriate to use rings from that area of the colonies to support their argument. In contrast, no justification for using tree rings in Maryland to support arguments about environmental conditions in Massachusetts is provided. The use of these data is particularly perplexing given the availability tree ring data for adjacent areas of New Hampshire published in Matossian's work ten years before the publication of *A Fever in Salem*.

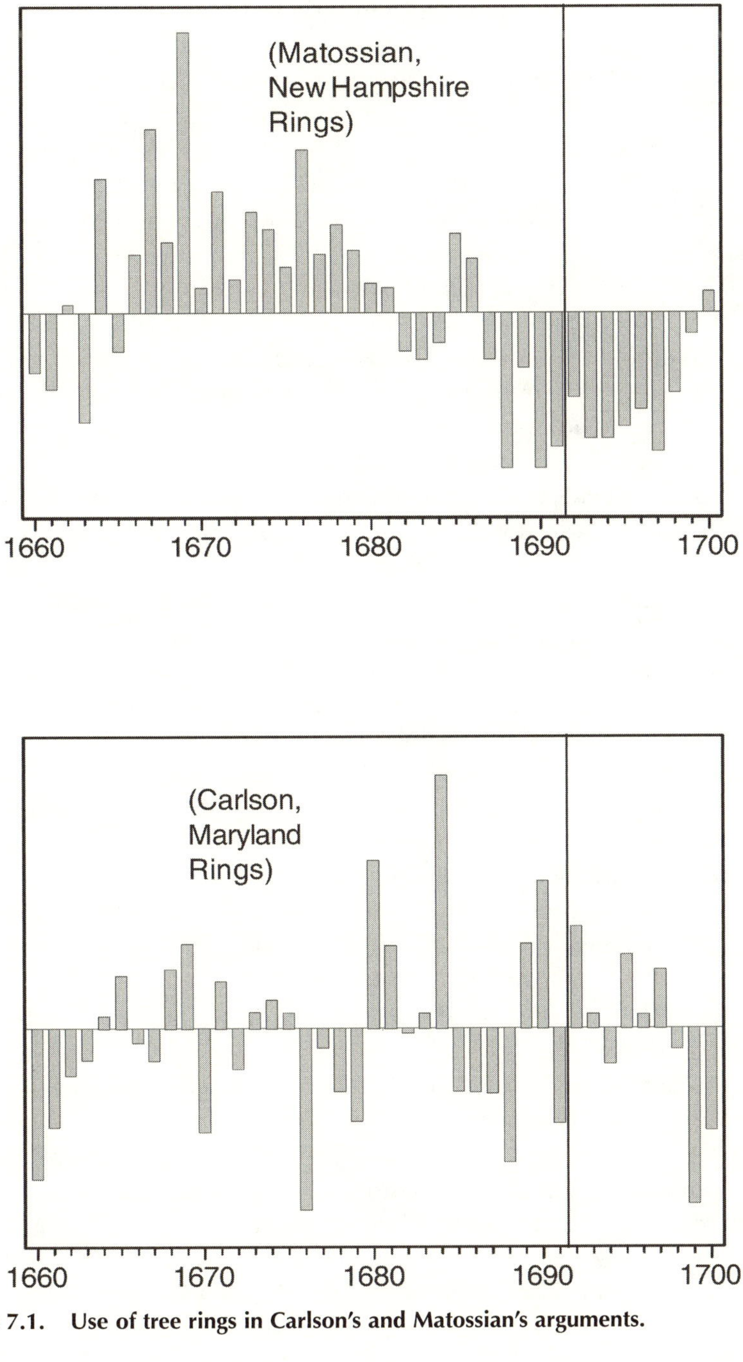

Figure 7.1. Use of tree rings in Carlson's and Matossian's arguments.

Because the girls' afflictions began in early 1692, tree rings for 1691 should have been unusually wide. To the contrary, the Carlson rings are well below the mean in 1688 (–1.84), above the mean in 1689 (1.16) and 1690 (2.02), but below the mean again in 1691 (–1.31). They are above the mean again in 1692 (1.40), close to the mean in 1693 (0.29), and below the mean once again in 1694 (–0.49). There is nothing unusual about these rings that would support the sleeping sickness argument. Moreover, there is no major drought year in these tree ring data until 1699 (–2.42). Tree rings are unusually wide in 1690, but that is the only major fluctuation suggesting wetness. In fact, the rings are narrower in the year preceding the witch hunt (–1.31) than during the alleged drought year (–0.49) that is supposed to coincide with the end of the witch hunts. In sum, not only are the tree ring data from the middle colonies, but they do not reveal any unusual pattern that would have predicted the Salem-Essex witch hunt in 1692.

The Salem-Essex episode is the only major instance of a major early modern witch hunt in the colonies, but we can consider whether years with witch trials of any magnitude coincide with unusually wide tree rings. Years with witchcraft accusations in the American colonies based on Demos's (1982: 401–9) appendix were categorized for years when the standardized ring width score was "wide" (exceeds +1.0), "narrow" (–1.0 or less), or "normal" (falls between the two cutting points). There were twelve years with narrow rings between 1635 and 1696, fourteen years with wide rings, and thirty-six years with normal rings. There were witch accusations somewhere in the colonies during eleven of the twelve narrow years, nine of fourteen wide years, and twenty-four of thirty-six normal years. Thus, during the narrow ring years, witchcraft accusations were lodged 92 percent of the time as compared to 64 percent of wide years and 67 percent of normal years. This pattern is contrary to Carlson's argument. However, it has to be noted that these variations are not statistically significant.[3] The safest conclusion is that there is no significant relationship between middle colony ring width and years with witchcraft accusations.

Carlson does express reservations about the ring width data, but she presents them because the plot appeared to be consistent with the argument. Not only do they fail to support her argument, but other sources of historical data indicate drought and excessive cold during the years leading up to the Salem witch trials. For example, Samuel Sewall's diary (p. 29) refers to prayers at John Alden's house on July 20, 1692, with the note that there were "brave showers of rain while Capt. Scottow was praying after much drought." Other accounts of the weather emphasize exceptional cold and snow during much of the 1690s (Weisman 1984: 174). Such reports do not preclude wet periods during other seasons, but the overall impression of climate is not favorable to any argument requiring an unusual surge of insect-borne disease.

As noted earlier, Matossian uses tree ring data for New Hampshire to make a case for Caporael's argument that ergot-infested rye was a source of hallucinations prompting the Salem witch hunt. In direct contrast to Carlson, it is narrow rings that are introduced as evidence for the ergotism theory. As illustrated in figure 7.1, the Salem witch trials did occur during a period of unusually narrow rings. Matossian takes narrow rings as evidence of unusually cold conditions which provided the "optimum temperature for ergot alkaloid production" (119). Such a finding is certainly more consistent with the ergotism argument than Carlson's sleeping sickness theory. But it is consistent with any theory attributing witch hunts to hardship or climatic crises as well. Although the Salem trials occurred in the middle of a stretch of narrow rings, there is no significant relationship between years with witchcraft accusations and years with narrow rings overall. Between 1660 and 1700, there were eight years with standardized ring widths of –1.0 or less, five with rings +1.0 or more, and twenty-seven years with relatively normal widths. Witchcraft accusations occurred in five of the eight narrow years, twenty of twenty-seven normal years, and all five of the years with unusually wide rings. This pattern does not constitute a significant variation from chance.[4] Matossian's theory may apply to the Salem witch hunt, but not to the timing of witchcraft cases in general.

It is interesting that Carlson's rings are more consistent with Matossian's theory than her own, and Matossian's rings are more consistent with Carlson's theory than her own. However, the safest overall conclusion is that tree ring width in the colonies is not a good predictor of witchcraft cases in general, although the only major witchcraft episode does fall in the middle of a severe span of narrow rings. This finding is quite consistent with patterns noted earlier in that the continental witch craze occurred during the worst phase of "The Little Ice Age" with a lengthy and sustained narrowing of tree rings. Although more subtle variations in climate did not help predict panic witch hunts in early modern Germany, the consistency of patterns at a larger fractal scale across settings is consistent with convergence theories of witch hunting.

Proximity to Wetlands

Both Caporael and Carlson cite proximity to sources of water, especially standing or slow-moving water, as further evidence for arguments that damp conditions had something to do with which youths were afflicted. Yet, no actual evidence that proximity to marshes, wetlands, rivers, or streams was more common for the afflicted than the nonafflicted has ever been presented. It is presumed that since the afflicted girls lived in Salem Village, they were in closer proximity to breeding grounds for mosquitoes and other insects than the nonafflicted population. Carlson argues, "Looking at the map of the Salem area, one sees that those who complained of bewitchment or affliction (or those who complained for sick relatives) lived on the west side, nearer to the forest, and in rocky, swampy terrain—a river flowed directly through the area" (138). However, the map that she shows is Boyer and Nissenbaum's map of residential patterns of the afflicted and the witches in Salem in 1692. In contrast, an inspection of a detailed historical map of Salem Village (figure 7.2), Salem Town (figure 7.3), and the surrounding area raises serious questions about this alleged correlation.

It is hard to find an inhabited area that was not in close proximity to a potential breeding ground for mosquitoes. Just south of Salem Town was the South River and the largest millpond in the area. The Salem Commons included ponds and marshes in close proximity to a substantial proportion of houses in Salem. In fact, as detailed on the map, the households that generated the most afflictions and the most accusations, Abigail Williams and

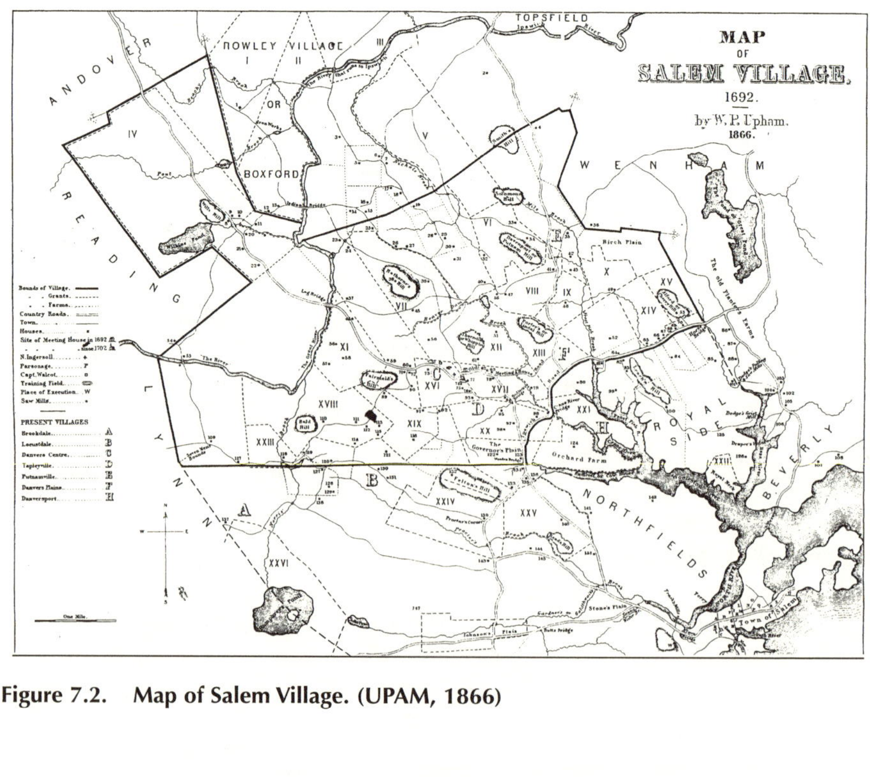

Figure 7.2. Map of Salem Village. (UPAM, 1866)

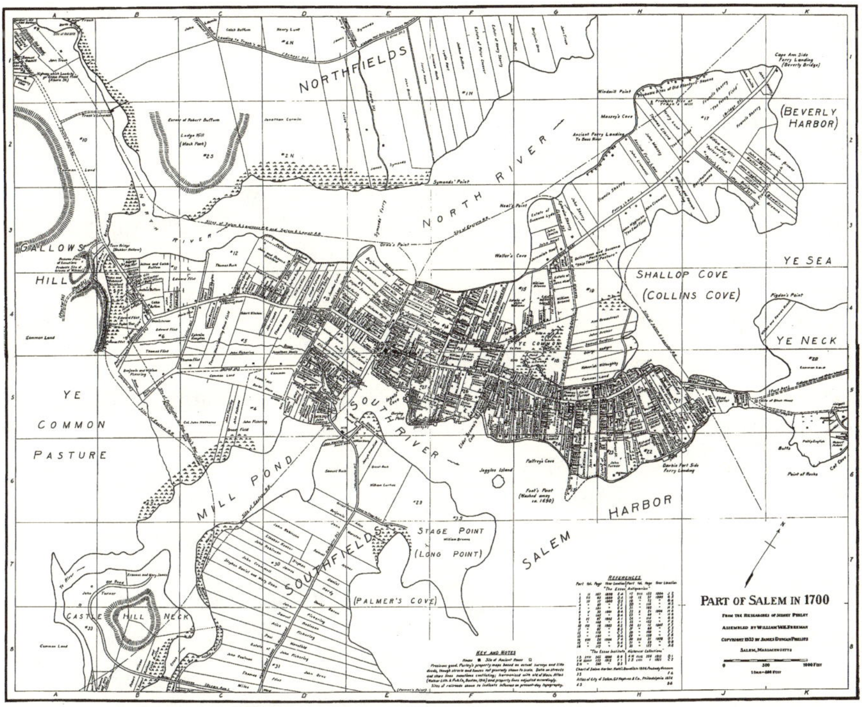

Figure 7.3. Most of Salem Town was as close to marshland and standing water as the afflicted in Salem Village. (UPAM, 1866)

Betty Parris in the Reverend Samuel Parris's parsonage and Mercy Lewis, Mary Walcott, Ann Putnam Jr., and Ann Putnam Sr. in the Sergeant Thomas Putnam household, appear to have lived farther from marshlands, wetlands, brooks, rivers, and millponds than many, if not most, of the defenders and the accused. Moreover, many of the afflicted were from the same households as the accused, further complicating the wetlands interpretation.

One way to test the hypothesis about wetlands is to estimate the distance for the afflicted girls as compared to the average resident of Salem Village. Although the distances estimated are subject to error based on imprecise location of homes on the map, as well as error in measurement of distances on the map, that error should be random; that is, there should be no more error in measurements for one set of residents than another.

The average distance to water (marsh, pond, river, brook) was 942 feet for all households on the map for Salem Village. The estimate for thirteen afflicted girls was 1,027 feet. The comparable estimate for those accused of witchcraft who lived in Salem Village was 911 feet. This difference is not statistically significant (t = .303, p = .586). In short, the afflicted lived no closer to sources of dampness than accused residents. For example, Rebecca Nurse (one of those executed) lived about 580 feet from sizable wetlands along Crane Brook. The household with the most afflicted women (the Putnam household with four afflicted) was over 1,700 feet from the nearest water source. The first household with afflicted girls (the Parris parsonage) was only 286 feet from a brook but over 2,000 feet from the nearest small marshland. In short, there is no evidence that the afflicted lived closer on the average to wetlands, brooks, millponds, or rivers than others in Salem Village. Indeed, while the difference is not statistically significant, the accused lived closer to such sources than the afflicted.

Although a few of the executed may have been poor, many of the accused were members of quite prosperous families who owned valuable tracts of land. In *Currents of Malice*, McMillen (1990) notes that John Proctor was "was sufficiently well-healed on his arrival to be able to lease one of the largest farms in the area, a 700 acre holding," that the Nurses "were definitely on the rise," but that the Putnams were "on their way down" (238). If prosperity were affected by land holdings, then the accused might have come from households that were closer to water than the afflicted and their representatives.

Households were further classified into those housing people who are listed in the indexes of major works on the Salem trials and those not included in such indexes. The average for 109 households with residents involved in some referenced capacity in the historical record is 970 feet as compared to 890 feet for 58 residents who are not listed. This difference is not statistically significant, but it does run counter to the argument about proximity to water. Those involved in the trials in some fashion lived no closer to such sources than those not involved (t = 0.753, p = .453). Thus, whether the focus is on the afflicted or those involved in the episode in some acknowledged fashion, there is no evidence that proximity to wetlands affected the roles played.

Using the average for the afflicted households, the proportion of Salem Town residents who lived a comparable distance from wetlands can be estimated. Concentric circles centered on the marshland in the Salem Common and surrounding rivers and millponds encompass most of Salem Town. A conservative estimate would be that at least 80 percent of the population of Salem Town lived as close to wet areas and mosquito breeding grounds as the afflicted. In fact, Carlson, Caporael, and Matossian might interpret this as evidence that the whole Salem area was primed for witchcraft accusations based on sleeping sickness or ergotism—an argument that would require further geographic analysis for the colonies. However, even a cursory consideration of climate and health in other colonies (e.g., the Chesapeake colonies) would raise doubts about the sleeping sickness argument since mosquitoes were a far more serious problem in southern than the New England colonies (Taylor 2001).

Tailored "Symptoms"

Other serious problems with the sleeping sickness and ergotism arguments arise when details about the symptoms, afflictions, and hallucinations are considered. Carlson uses Spanos and Gottlieb's critique of the ergotism argument to challenge Caporael's theory and proposes that the symptoms provide a better fit for sleeping sickness as the cause of "a fever in Salem" than ergotism (see figure 7.4). When matched with symptoms from a more recent, documented epidemic of sleeping sickness, the symptoms seem to match up extremely well. However, in challenging the ergotism argument, Spanos and Gottlieb use details from the historical record of the trials to question the notion that the "symptoms" exhibited reflected "any internal disease process"

1692 SALEM	1916-1930s ENCEPHALITIS EPIDEMIC
fits	convulsions
spectral visions	hallucinations
mental "distraction"	psychoses
pinching, pricking	myoclonus of small muscle bundles on skin surface erythmata on skin surface;
"bites"	capillary hemorrhaging
eyes twisted	oculogyric crises: gaze fixed upward, downward, or to the side
inability to walk	paresis: partial paralysis, neck twisted torticollis: spasm of neck muscles forces head to one side, spasms affect trunk and neck

Figure 7.4. Carlson's symptoms of sleeping sickness.

(1391). Their critique is as relevant to Carlson's theory as to Caporael's, although the internal disease process is different for each.

Any careful reading of the trial testimony raises serious doubts about a biological or physiological basis for the girls' behavior and the hallucinations. Spanos and Gottlieb argue that the behaviors exhibited and the afflictions reported were well-known as the "signs" of possession and were the "expected" behaviors of anyone playing the "role." There is considerable evidence for this interpretation in the historical description of other cases of "strange" behavior. For example, Cotton Mather had investigated a case in 1688 involving "afflicted" children. Although many of the behaviors and reported symptoms might seem to reflect some form of underlying disease such as sleeping sickness, specific details on the behaviors over time and in relation to distinct "audiences" support Spanos and Gottlieb's "role playing" interpretation.

When afflicted children were examined by a "minister," the behaviors exhibited were those that would confirm the belief that there was a deeper, underlying religious heresy and conspiracy involving witches and Satan at work. The minister did not have to impose a religious interpretation on the behavior of the afflicted. Rather, the "afflicted" tailored their behavior to fit such an interpretation. McMillen (1990) summarizes Mather's encounters as follows:

> His description of the children's "fits" is very vivid. They would bark at one another like dogs and then purr like cats. They complained of being in a red-hot oven sweating and panting, and then cried of cold water being thrown at them when they would shiver. They cried out that great cudgels were hitting them. Bystanders could not see the cudgels, but they could see the marks left upon the children in red streaks on their bodies. They flew through the air like geese. If their parents reproved them, their agonies became extreme. Sometimes, though seldom, they would not eat. If there was any discourse of God or Christ, "or any of the things which are not seen and are eternal, they would cast themselves into intolerable anguishes." When ministers tried to counsel them, they would stop up their ears with their hands, shriek and holler to drown out their voices. (142–43)

Mather took the eldest Goodwin girl into his own home, where she continued to act in a bizarre fashion. Her torments were sometimes succeeded by her "frolics" when she would talk wittily and "beyond herself." She frequently said that if she could steal or be drunk, she would be well immediately. In her frolics, Mather tried to see whether she could read. She would not read the Bible, and listening to passages being read out loud cast her into agonies. But she could read a Quaker book, a Popish book, or a jest book perfectly well. She was also able to read the forbidden Book of Common Prayer. In short, the afflicted responded to parents and other authorities by increasing the intensity of the behavior and responded to ministers in a religiously rebellious manner. Such behavior would have resulted in severe punishment were they not "possessed" or "afflicted."

It is also important to note that the Goodwins' afflictions began after the Goodwin girl had challenged a washerwoman over some missing linen. The washerwoman was the daughter of a reputed witch and an Irish Roman Catholic, Goody Glover. Glover intervened to defend her daughter. Glover confronted the Goodwin girl about the accusation and verbally attacked her. The Goodwin girl "immediately was 'visited with strange fits, beyond those that attend an epilepsy, or catalepsy, or those called the diseases of astonishment." The other Goodwin children were soon "afflicted" as well (McMillen 1990: 141). When the Goodwin girl and a younger brother were removed from her parents' home, they apparently exhibited none of these symptoms. When returned home the younger brother began having fits once again, and they were particularly severe when his father tried to take him to church. McMillen notes that the boy was quite willing when it was suggested that he attend a Quaker meeting.

Neither sleeping sickness nor ergot poisoning are required to explain the youths' behavior. Since most colonists believed in the power of witches, there was reason to be terrified about Glover's threats. On the other hand, adoption of the "role" of the afflicted or possessed was an effective strategy for revenge. Playing such a role would spread to other children through normal processes of imitation and social learning. A strategy for countering a contentious enemy on the part of one child could also become a strategy for expressing discontent and rebellion toward adult authority in general, both for the initiator as well as other children. None of the children had to invent a strategy of contention or rebellion. As Spanos and Gottlieb argue, the role of the possessed was well-known and could be adopted as a means of wielding power or avoiding punishment, provided the other parties involved were willing to authenticate it as a product of witchcraft.

The fits and torments of some of the most active "afflicted" girls in Salem exhibited a rebellion against religious doctrine and sacred texts as well (McMillen 1990: 149). Deodat Lawson reported on the behavior or "symptoms" of the afflicted girls in Salem: "It was several times observed that when they were discoursed with about God or Christ, or the things of salvation, they were presently afflicted at a dredful rate; and hence were oftentimes outrageous, if they be permitted to be in the congregation in the time of public worship. . . . They were vehemently afflicted, to hinder any persons praying with them, or holding them in any religious discourse" (McMillen 1990: 179). Lawson and Dr. Griggs ruled out disease as an explanation and proposed "possession" or the "evil hand" because of the variation in behavior in different situations. The girls behaved normally at times, claiming no recollection of their behavior during their fits. Such structure causes problems for modern attempts to attribute their fits and hallucinations to sleeping sickness and caused problems for applying a medical interpretation at that time as well. Young people appear to have been challenging parental and religious authority while possessed or afflicted, as well as countering threats from other people by exhibiting tailored symptoms.

Given their position is colonial society, possession was one of the only strategies of contention available to young women. The young could become possessed "rebels." Older participants could use religious authority to both authenticate their possession and enhance the credibility of their accusations against long time enemies. For example, Ann Putnam Sr., the most active afflicted adult in the Salem trials and mother of one of the most active afflicted girls, targeted Rebecca Nurse as the source of her torment. Putnam carried on the following dialogue with the specter of Nurse during the "fit" Deodat Lawson (a prior minister to the Salem villagers) witnessed:

> After telling the apparition to "be gone," Lawson continued to state that Mrs. Putnam seemed to dispute with the apparition about a text of scripture, although the apparition seemed to wish him not to read the text. Ann Putnam said, "I am sure you will be gone, for you cannot stand before the text." Then she was 'sorely afflicted; her mouth being drawn to one side' and her body straining violently. The apparition appeared to be commanding her not to name the text. But she declared that she would tell and at last broke forth and said: "it is the third chapter of Revelations." Lawson had scruples about reading the text, fearing that it would be using Satan's tools to fight the devil, but decided to try it for an "experiment." As soon as he began reading, Ann Putnam opened her eyes and was cured of her fit. Her husband and the spectators—there always seemed to be plenty on hand—told Mr. Lawson that she had often been so relieved. (McMillen 1990: 218)

Such structured, directed fits, complete with tailored hallucinations indicting old enemies while authenticating underlying religious purity, cannot be explained as symptoms of a disease. In Ann Putnam Sr.'s case, it was an effective strategy for revenge against people who represented long-enduring family conflicts in the community. The Townes had filed suit against the Putnams just five years earlier in a heated dispute over land boundaries and timber rights, a suit that the Townes won. The three Towne sisters—Rebecca Nurse, Mary Esty, and Sarah Towne—were all charged with witchcraft, and the Putnam women were the active accusers in the process. However, the mother's hallucinations were more complex and aimed primarily at Nurse.

The "Convergence" of Symptoms and Hallucinations

Another problem with disease interpretations of the behavior of the afflicted is the manner in which specific testimony was introduced. Tituba had shown no signs of affliction that would cause anyone to be suspicious of possession until she was forced to testify. She had her first "trance" on the stand, and it brought her ordeal to a comforting, although temporary, halt.

According to Elaine Breslaw (1996), Tituba's testimony was the key factor that steered the search for an explanation of the girls' afflictions toward a secret organized conspiracy of witches led by a mysterious "white man" from Boston. Moreover, it was Tituba who introduced a "yellow bird" as the "attendant" or familiar of accused witches. Once the yellow bird was introduced, it was "sighted" in the courtroom by the afflicted girls at strategic points when their testimony was being challenged. Sighting the yellow bird became an effective strategy for enhancing the credibility of their charges against a variety of witches, and once a tactic was found to work, others repeated and adopted it.

Tituba introduce the yellow bird as an attendant to Sarah Good, one of the first to be accused of witchcraft. "It did suck between her fingers" (Essex Institute 1938: vol. 3, 747). Tituba was questioned on March 1 and 2. On March 14, Martha Corey went to Thomas Putnam's house to find out why young Ann had accused her of witchcraft. Ann went into a fit complete with twisting, loss of sight, choking, and a distended tongue, which she bit. When she could speak, she saw the yellow bird sucking between Corey's fingers, exactly as Tituba had described it doing to Good (McMillen 1990: 201). On March 20, Deodat Lawson held a service with the afflicted girls and Corey in attendance. During the long service, Abigail Williams, one of the first afflicted, sighted Corey sitting on a beam with the yellow bird "betwixt her fingers." Ann Putnam said she saw the yellow bird on Lawson's hat that was hanging nearby, but this unexpected extension to a minister was quickly quieted by the elders present. When Corey was examined the next day, the afflicted girls reaffirmed their sightings of the yellow bird. Two months later in May, Martha Carrier of Andover was accused, and one of her sons reintroduced the yellow bird, claiming that it had appeared to him and frightened him (McMillen 1990: 422). It is difficult to explain the "sighting" of the yellow bird as a hallucination when it is sequentially incorporated to embellish and validate charges of witchcraft.

Spanos and Gottlieb note that the girls' testimony and courtroom behavior taken as evidence of witchcraft became more and more "standardized" over time. The girls played their roles in an increasingly uniform manner. They would mimic the behavior of the witch as if under supernatural control. If the accused bit a lip, they would bite a lip. If the accused protested their charges, they would respond with dramatic demonstrations of shared torment. The behavior was so patterned that others who had resisted being drawn in as afflicted accusers knew exactly what to do to move into the role of the possessed. Indeed, it was often a precautionary measure to avoid being pursued as one of the tormenting witches. Mary Warren, Deliverance Hobbs, Abigail Hobbs, and Mary Lacy Jr. all switched roles at one time or another. None of these features of the behavior of the afflicted are consistent with either a sleeping sickness or an ergot interpretation of the behavior of the afflicted.

One of the common complaints from the afflicted was that they were being "pricked" by pins, and such pricking is interpreted as a physiological symptom by Caporael and Carlson. However, a very simple and obvious alternative can be proposed based on the testimony of defenders of the accused witches. Sarah Nurse (Rebecca Nurse's daughter) testified, "On June 29, 1692, I saw Goodwife Bibber pull pins out of her close and hold them between her fingers, and clasp her hands around her knees, and then she cried out and said Goody Nurse pricked her" (Robinson 1991: 276). A crotchet needle was found in Abigail Some's apron, and, after taking it away, Mary Warren was no longer "bit" or "pinched."

In an earlier Norwegian case (Geis and Bunn 1997: 85), a fourteen-year-old boy allegedly vomited nails, needles, crooked pins, and a variety of other objects as evidence that he was bewitched. The noted medical authority, Thomas Browne, believed that these objects were introduced into the afflicted by witches (Geis and Bunn 1997: 82). These "symptoms" were exhibited in 1662 in Lowenstoft, England, where an eighteen-year-old young woman was reported to have vomited crooked pins. Another girl vomited pins daily and was found to have several pins in her hands. No one knew how they "were conveyed thither" (Geis and Bunn 1997: 72). In 1688, one of the Goodwin children studied by Cotton Mather was alleged to have swallowed a brass pin, which was removed by a surgeon (McMillen 1990: 145). The point is that, whether vomited or used to prick oneself, *the pins were real.* Both pins and pinpricks were interpreted as evidence of witchcraft, and the disease argument merely substitutes one hidden cause for another. The most plausible explanation of pinpricks is that they were pin pricks. At other times people claiming injury produced an iron spindle and a piece of a sheet torn from a specter (Weisman 1984). These pieces of evidence were not hallucinations, but real items linked with accused witches.

Rosenthal (1993: 17–18) makes the same observation in his research on the Salem story. William and Deborah Shaw testified that they found one of the young accusers, Susannah Sheldon, with her hands so tightly tied together that they had to cut her loose. Susannah reported that the specter of Sarah Good would bite her whenever she touched the binding. This event cannot be considered to be hysteria, a hallucination, or a product of illness. Her hands were bound and the Shaws cut the binding. It is a real event that cannot be explained by either real witchcraft or illness of any kind. The most plausible interpretation is that Susannah either tied her own hands or had someone tie them for her. It makes far more sense to propose that the girls were cooperating with one another to protect themselves from charges of fraud and slander and to avoid the severe punishment they would have suffered for allowing their rebellious exercise of power to be exposed.

There is evidence in testimony from the trials that some of the afflicted girls were influenced by the excitement and attention that they received. Three people present when one of the girls reported seeing apparitions of Goody Proctor reported they saw nothing. When confronted as a liar, the afflicted girl admitted that she did it for "sport" and that others had as well (McMillen 1990: 255). Initially, Mary Warren (Proctor's servant girl) had testified that the afflicted girls "did but dissemble" (McMillen 1990: 259). But, when the afflicted had fits in response to her testimony, Mary Warren started having fits and seeing apparitions as well. As McMillen (1990) notes in the case of Sarah Churchill, "We know for certain that at least one of the 'afflicted' accusing girls was faking her symptoms, for she admitted so herself" (340). Churchill had confessed to Sarah Ingersoll that she had given false testimony about herself and others. Despite the fact that this recantation was reported to the court, Churchill's original testimony continued to be used in the trials. By repeatedly exhibiting symptoms of bewitchment, the afflicted girls could avoid the repercussions that would follow were they found to be dissembling.

Spanos and Gottlieb challenged Caporael's arguments about ergot-induced hallucinations by noting that many of the events and experiences interpreted as a product of ergotism had occurred many years before. For example, John Louden testified that an apparition of Briget Bishop had sat on his stomach and choked him when he tried to free himself. She later appeared or sent a familiar in the form of a black pig and a monkey with a man's face and cock's feet. These events had occurred seven or eight years before the trials when Louden was a servant of John Gedney in Salem Town. Bishop had appeared to Richard Coman in a red paragon bodice and "laid upon his breast" while he slept with his wife. He was "so oppressed" that he could not call out to wake his wife. This apparition appeared eight years before the trials. Samuel Grey's testimony involved an apparition from fourteen years earlier that he did not initially recognized as Bishop. Christian Trask (wife of John Trask) complained that five or six years earlier Goodwife Bishop had entertained people at "unseasonable hours," drinking and playing shovelboard. Trask visited Bishop and threw the game pieces in the fire. After that episode, she began having "fits" that she only recognized as such after observing the bewitched girls. The fact that many of the experiences that could be categorized as hallucinations were distributed over a considerable span of time casts doubt on any theory that would claim them as evidence of specific outbreaks of ergotism or sleeping sickness in close temporal proximity to the Salem witch hunts.

The evidence involving tree rings, proximity to wetland, the structure and timing of the behavior of the afflicted, and the fact that real physical objects were involved are all contrary to the sleeping sickness theory. However, that evidence does not allow us to dismiss disease as a factor in the explanation of the Salem witch craze. The problem with Carlson's argument is its emphasis on the afflicted and those exhibiting "symptoms" as instances of one specific underlying medical disorder. Demos (1982: 346) notes that the first witchcraft cases in New England coincided with the first general outbreak of illness in 1647–1648 (likely influenza), and that smallpox and measles epidemics were severe in the years immediately preceding the Salem witch hunts (346). Moreover, the analysis of European witch trials supported the argument that temporal patterns of plague were associated with temporal patterns of witch executions. Such correlations may reflect increases in strange behavior on the part of those afflicted, but they may reflect increases in collective fear and suspicion among members of a community as well.

In his work on *The American Colonies*, Alan Taylor (2001) states that "although New England was remarkably healthy compared to the rest of the English-speaking world, the advantage was only relative. Especially after 1650, New Englanders experienced periodic epidemics of measles, influenza, and smallpox that proved especially fatal to children. These unpredictable afflictions called out for explanation, some attribution of cause" (183). Sleeping sickness and ergotism might be found among ailments, diseases and afflictions experienced prior to witch accusations and trials, but do not play the dominant role accorded them by Carlson and Matossian.

Variations among Colonies

Another shortcoming of the sleeping sickness theory is the distribution of witchcraft trials among the colonies. Were sleeping sickness a major correlate of accusations of possession and witchcraft, then such charges should have been more common in the Chesapeake colonies than the New England colonies. The Chesapeake colonies had far higher death rates due to disease than the New England colonies and had far more serious problems with mosquitoes and other biting insects. Yet, there were very few charges of witchcraft in Maryland and Virginia. As Taylor (2001) notes:

> Relative to the Chesapeake, the New England environment . . . permitted longer and healthier lives. In contrast to the Chesapeake tidewater with its long, hot, and humid summers and low topography, New England was a northern and hilly land with a short growing season and faster-flowing rivers and streams which discouraged the malaria and dysentery that afflicted southern planters. In New England, people who survived childhood could expect to live to about seventy; in the Chesapeake, only a minority survived beyond forty. (170)

The Chesapeake environment "shocked English bodies used to the milder pathogens, insects and climate of their temperate homeland. The intense labor of tobacco cultivation peaked with the blistering sun, soaring temperatures, thick humidity, and voracious mosquitoes of the long hot Chesapeake summer" (Taylor 2001: 143). The same observations are made about the Carolina colonies, which are described as "hot, humid and replete with biting insects" (Taylor 2001: 223). In short, if sleeping sickness were the major culprit in the etiology of afflictions and accusations, then cases of possession and witchcraft accusations should have been more common in the southern than the northern colonies.

In *Founding Mothers and Fathers*, Norton (1996: 12–13) observes that the Puritans emigrated as kinship groups or families while the Chesapeake was heavily populated with single males who came as indentured servants. About three-fourths of emigrants to the Chesapeake were English servants, and they were disproportionately young males. Men far outnumbered women and "widows were few" (Taylor 2001: 141). In 1635, only 14 percent of emigrants were women (Taylor 2001: 143). The labor shortage also resulted in a reliance on slaves who constituted about 13 percent of the Chesapeake population compared to less than 2 percent in New England.

The differences in emigration and demographic variations were reflected in features of colonies that would "structure" the direction of conflict or contention. Taylor (2001) describes the New England colonialists as "the most egalitarian in the distribution of property" (170) among the colonies and notes that "social gradations were subtle among the New English" (172). In contrast, clear-cut cleavages existed in the Chesapeake colonies. Virginia had clear lines of differentiation with an elite class of planters, a "callous and exploitative" colonial government, and a very large population of servants and slaves. In 1671, Governor Berkeley expressed concerns that the poor would revolt and opposed free schools and printing as sources of disobedience and heresy. In fact, Berkeley opposed protective measures against the Indians called for by colonialists on the frontier because of the profitable trade in deerskins that would be jeopardized.

"Bacon's Rebellion" in 1676 was led by a frontier segment of the planter elite who opposed the governor's policies and sought to enlist servants with a promise of freedom. The rebellion was quickly crushed in 1676, but Berkeley lost control of the colony to authorities of the English Crown, who used the rebellion as an excuse for invasion and for sending Berkeley back to England. The new royal government was opposed by the Virginia elite who sought to enlist the support of the discontented by supporting some of the aims of the failed rebellion: "To maintain their political ascendancy, the great planters needed to lead, rather than oppose, wars meant to dispossess and destroy frontier Indians. Such wars united the free whites by providing convenient external, alien scapegoats for internal frustrations and inequalities" (Taylor 2001: 151). As proposed in chapter 6, witch hunts are aimed at hidden internal enemies that share many of the same characteristics as those pursuing them. In social settings where there are clearly defined, socially and culturally differentiated groups with structured conflicts of interest, structured fears, and frustrations, conflict will be structured along such fault lines. In Virginia, the conflict took the form of a rebellion, which, despite its smashing defeat, redirected lines of conflict toward a new common enemy, the Indians.

Although there were divisions and conflicts among different groups of people in Salem Town and Salem Village, the colonialists shared a great deal in common, and the lines of contention were far more likely to involve disputes with one's neighbors. Indians were a common threat, but the Second Indian War was most devastating in Maine. Indeed, many of the Salem residents had moved to Salem to escape the Indian threat in the north. Thus, circumstances in Salem were similar to Briggs's interpretation of war and witch hunts in England. Indians were a serious threat, but for most of the Salem residents they were not an immediate threat. Indeed, the threat became most immediate after the trials were well under way and the threat peaked after the Salem-Essex trials.

Norton (1996) proposes another similarity between Maine and the Chesapeake colonies that could be relevant to the intensity of witch hunts as well. She states that "Maine in general resembled the Chesapeake rather than its New England neighbors: with a similarly imbalanced sex-ratio—the excess men were fisherman working for wages rather than indentured servants laboring in the tobacco fields" (16). A similar observation has been made about the paucity of witch trials in New Netherlands, which was also characterized by an excess of men.

In short, the sleeping sickness theory does not make sense out of colonial variations since it should imply more common experiences of possession and suspicions of witchcraft in the most disease ridden colonies. In contrast, theories that emphasize the convergence of a variety of social and demographic factors to explain its distribution and a variety of precipitating circumstances, including outbreaks of disease, make far more sense of the social and temporal geography of witch hunts in the colonies.

War and Witch Hunts: The Case of Salem and Essex County

The work receiving the most recent acclaim as a "new" interpretation of the Essex County witchcraft cases is Norton's (2002) *The Devil's Snare*. Norton argues that the Essex County witchcraft crisis would not have occurred had King William's War been avoided. The Second Indian War allegedly "created the conditions that allowed the crisis to develop as rapidly and as extensively as it did." Reviewers have applaud the work as "the best approach to the Salem witchcraft episode in thirty-five years," for "casting new light on the infamous witch trials of 1692," and as "the final word on an episode that has bewitched and bewildered generations of historians" (back cover of *The Devil's Snare*).

According to Norton:

> Other scholars have touched on connections to the Second Indian War but did not explore them in detail. In the 1980s, I learned from Carol Karlsen's [1987] *The Devil in the Shape of a Woman* and an article by James Kences [1984] that some of the "afflicted girls" of Salem Village were refugees from the Maine frontier. When I started my research, I expected the accuser's familial origins to prove to be important for my analysis, but I had no idea that this book would become what it has: an exploration of the history of frontier warfare and its impact on the collective mentalité of an entire region. (5)

Norton does, indeed, present more detail than previous authors, but the thesis is far from new or original. Indeed, Kences (1984) proposes the exact same relationship between the Indian wars and collective mentalities as Norton. In fact, he did more far than "touch" on the topic. He conducted a detailed analysis of the relationship between the location and date of raids and battles and subsequent witchcraft accusations. Kences documents the links between the Indian wars, the afflicted girls, their families, and other parties to the village conflicts. However, the central focus in his examination of "unexplored relationships between Essex County witchcraft and the Indian Wars of 1675 and 1689" was the effect of wars and war scares on the collective memories and fears of people in the region, fears that were reflected in the behavior of the accused, the afflicted, defenders and magistrates in the Essex County witchcraft cases.

Kences argues that "veterans" and "survivors" of massacres from the First Indian War (King Phillip's War) carried fearful memories of these prior conflicts, and "The military alliance of the Indians and the French in the 1690s added a terrifying dimension to the Indian war, because Puritans were taught from childhood the evils of Catholicism" (181–84). In this historical context:

> [War] scares imposed a significant strain upon society; daily the inhabitants scanned the horizon for signs of enemy ships and were alert to detect any suspicious activity among local Indian tribes, such as unexplained movement of very large gatherings. The crisis diminished the colonists' tolerance for antisocial behavior, and they interpreted verbal attacks against life and property as being extremely dangerous and symbolically in conformity with the actions of an enemy that had yet failed to appear. (184)

Given collective memories and fears from prior wars, King William's War led to a heightened "invasion neurosis" and "war hysteria" (Kences 1984: 191). His final conclusion was that "the 1692 witch hunt was very much a product of King William's War, which seemed not only to exacerbate village factionalism but to have promoted the further alienation of Salem Village from Salem Town." In sum, Kences proposed and defended the same thesis twenty years before Norton.

Other scholars have proposed the same relation between war and accusations of witchcraft. In *The Devil's Dominion*, Richard Godbeer (1992) devotes most of one chapter to the role of war and war scares to the Salem witch trials. He argues that "only by placing the witch hunt in immediate historical context can we understand why the people of Essex County reacted so strongly to the afflictions of Salem Village" (182). Among the features of that historical context introduced by Godbeer as crucial for understanding the Essex witch trials are King Phillip's War and King William's War. He proposes that "the traumatic events of the previous two decades had affected the entire community, clerical and lay, Puritan and non-Puritan. The witch hunt provided an opportunity to release pent-up fears and to root out persons who seemed threatening to the community" (204). The threat of "interrelated, alien, and intrusive forces, which the colonists equated with witchcraft, converged on a local level in Essex County. In particular, Salem Village and Andover, the two principal sources of witch hysteria in 1692, were prey to threatening invasive forces" (197). In short, his argument focuses on the effect of the Indian wars and other crises on the predisposition of people in Essex County to suspect that witches were at work.

In *The Devil's Disciples* (1996), Peter Hoffer develops the same thesis: "The fear of witches came to Salem from beyond its boundaries, from the woods to the west and north. These witches rode the winds of war. What began in Europe late in 1688 as a dynastic struggle escalated into a world war over religion and power. The conflict exposed the colonies to stark, unrelieved terror. Salem lay at the southern region of marsh and wood thrown open by 'King William's War' to human predation" (55). Hoffer elaborates on the effect of those wars on the collective mentality of the region and concludes that "merging the bits and pieces of stories from the north with their own imagined tales, they began to formulate a larger mythopoeic structure—a fantasy for themselves" (57):

> rumors of violence on the frontier blended into tales of witchcraft, as a set of vernacular beliefs about witchcraft, including counter-magic, merged imperceptibly at its edges into a fear that the French and Indians would drive down the coast and destroy Essex settlements. Indeed, some suspected that was the plan in the north, but the mere fear itself made Salem people readier to accept supernatural explanations for illness and misfortune. (58)

In sum, Hoffer's treatment of the relation between war and witch trials emphasizes the impact of the French-Indian Wars and memories of past wars on the collective anxieties of colonists in Essex County communities, anxieties that would facilitate escalation of witchcraft accusations.

As elaborated in prior chapters, other scholars have proposed that witch hunts are inhibited by war. Both Kai Erikson and John Demos depict witch trials as a *shift* in the Devil's hiding places or a shift in the nature of contention. To reiterate Erikson's quote from chapter 2:

> As the wilderness took on this new character, it seemed that even the Devil had given up his more familiar disguises. He no longer lurked in the underbrush, for most of it had been cut away; he no longer assumed the shape of

> hostile Indians, for most of them had retreated inland for the moment; he no longer sent waves of heretics to trouble the Bay, for most of them lived quietly under the protection of toleration; he no longer appeared in the armies of the Counter-Reformation, for the old battlefields were still too far away to excite the imagination. But his presence was felt everywhere, and when the colonists began to look for his new hiding places they found him crouched in the very heart of the Puritan colony. (157–58)

Erikson emphasizes the "retreat" of hostile Indians and legally mandated tolerance of old heretical enemies as reasons for a shift in the Devil's disguises. Colonists would not pursue an imaginary enemy hidden in their midst when directly confronted by real and familiar enemies.

John Demos (1982) advocates a similar position, arguing that conflict with clearly defined enemies inhibited the tendency to search for imaginary enemies. In his chapter on "Communities: Witchcraft over Time," he advances the simple proposition that "*Witchcraft proceedings and episodes of conflict did not appear together, in the same time and place; instead they waxed and waned, in alternating sequence*" (369, emphasis added). He notes that "the period from 1675 through 1678 represented a low point in the half-century curve of witchcraft cases" (382), despite hurricanes, fires, and epidemic illness. He argues that these predisposing influences were muted by a "massive counter force: the desperate absorption of the entire region in King Phillip's War. For the time being danger from the invisible world was superseded by combat with a host of quite present and visible Indian enemies."

On the surface, the two perspectives on war and witch hunts appear to contradict one another, one implying a positive correlation between war and witch hunts over time ("witches rode the winds of war") and the other implying a negative correlation ("wax and wane, in alternating sequence"). This contradiction was encountered in earlier chapters where it was observed that the hypothesized impact of war on witch hunts varies among scholars interpreting European, English, and Scottish witch hunts.

Both temporal and comparative analysis were consistent with the notion that direct involvement in war with clearly discernible enemies was negatively correlated with the intensity of witch hunts. The more years a nation was at war, the less the intensity of witch hunts. Moreover, witch hunting was most intense either during peacetime, or during times of "interstitial peace" in the midst of long spans of war, or in the aftermath of war. The relation between war and witch hunts is comparably complex in the colonies. For example, among colonies, the more common and severe the actual fighting, the less likely witchcraft accusations and trials were to occur. This argument is supported in the detailed treatment of Indian wars as a factor in the explanation of witch hunts. Kences (1984: 179) notes that the heaviest fighting in the Indian wars occurred in Maine and New Hampshire, not in Massachusetts. Norton repeats the same observation, attributing the surge in Essex County witchcraft cases to war on the frontier, especially Maine.

Kences's argument about displaced aggression implies a similar pattern over time. When invaded or directly involved in conflict, aggression does not need to be "displaced." However, anxiety about a possible invasion that never occurs could result in a search for internal scapegoats as a form of displaced aggression. Similarly, it is conflict *on the frontier* that helps explain Essex witchcraft trials, according to Norton and others. Thus, it would be consistent with both lines of argument to propose that witchcraft trials are more likely to occur when war constitutes a distant rather than an immediate threat.

If the precise timing of witchcraft charges is considered, witchcraft accusations do not occur during the span of time when the threat is most immediate and direct. For example, in Scituate (Plymouth Colony) in March 1677, Mehittable Woodworth accused Mary Ingram of causing her to have violent fits. Kences notes that at the time of the accusation "the town was completely free of an Indian menace." However, exactly one year earlier in March 1676, the town of Scituate had been "under constant threat of Indian attack for two months." He observes that "hysterical behavior triggered by the first or second anniversaries of critical events was the common element in both the Scituate and Salem episodes."

Many of the communities involved in the witch trials had experienced attacks in earlier wars, but King William's War did not reach Essex County. Rather, the area had all of the characteristics that have been proposed as relevant to panic witch hunts. The populace had past experience with war and was fearful of the spread of war to its area, but it was not directly involved. In fact, in documenting the threat that war deaths of eligible young males might constitute for the future of young females, Kences reports two war deaths in 1690, four in 1691, none in 1692, and one in 1693. The most "peaceful" year was 1692.

A consideration of fluctuations in King William's War is consistent with Demos's argument. For example, in 1689 and 1690 the French, aided by Indians, attacked English settlements in New York and Maine. In 1690, the English seized Port Royal, Nova Scotia, but the French recaptured it. However, in 1691 the English were victorious in their attempt to retake New York. Between 1691 and 1696, the French suffered numerous defeats in Europe and were preoccupied with their problems at home. The French were defeated by the English and Dutch at Le Hogue in 1692 and were defeated by the English off Lagos, Portugal, in 1693. In 1694, the English and Dutch bombarded French towns; in 1695, Namur, Belgium, was retaken from the French by the Dutch and English. In 1696, the French managed to hold Quebec, and the war ended the next year. In short, not only was the war a somewhat distant war during the period from 1691 through 1696, but the French threat can be argued to have subsided.

The attacks on York, Maine, on January 25, 1692, and Wells, Maine, on June 11, 1692, are introduced to support the view that the Salem trials were prompted by the immediacy of war. However, it is important to reiterate that there were virtually no witchcraft trials in Maine, where settlers were repeatedly attacked. Furthermore, the girls' afflictions began before the attack on York and the first hanging for witchcraft occurred before the attack on Wells. The fear of war was certainly relevant to the emotional climate at the time of the trials, but witchcraft accusations were very rare in the villages and towns of Maine that were most directly threatened.[5]

Factors other than the Indian War have to be introduced to explain why the craze began in a setting that had never been attacked, rather than in Maine. Indeed, in her work on *Founding Mothers and Fathers*, Norton (1996) documents features of colonial settlement in Maine that distinguished that colony from Massachusetts, features that are central to other explanations. As noted earlier, Norton observes that the Puritans emigrated as kinship groups or families, while Maine "resembled the Chesapeake" with an excess of men (16). Kences (1984) observes that the homes and farms in agricultural villages such as York were widely dispersed making them vulnerable to attack as compared to Salem Village as well. In short, both the Chesapeake colonies and Maine had major conflicts with Indians but did not experience major witch hunts.

Kences uses the experience of Glouchester, a community much closer to Salem than Wells or York, to illustrate the notion of "invasion neurosis." Glouchester experienced an outbreak of war hysteria in the summer of 1692 initiated by their minister who did not want to commit Glouchester militia to the invasion of Quebec for fear that Glouchester would be defenseless. There were reports of Frenchmen sneaking through the swamps in the area and some settlers abandoned their farms. Norton (2002) reports that a troop of sixty men from Ipswich arrived in July 1692 but found no actual threat. She states that "the Glouchester folk concluded that the attackers were spectral rather than real" (232). Kences makes the same observation in his 1984 work, claiming, "At Glouchester, the rapid shift in interpretation of the menace as first actual enemy, and then one of supernatural origin, was due in part to the memory of the 1653 and 1657 witchcraft outbreaks in the town, and also to the mind-set of Essex County in 1692" (194–96). However, these earlier witchcraft outbreaks do not appear to be associated with Indian wars. Demos notes that there were Indian scares in 1642–1643, but little new internal or external conflict erupted before the 1660s. In contrast, Kences proposes that witchcraft outbreaks in Glouchester (and other places) reflected war scares generated by the First Anglo-Dutch War in 1652–1653. Yet, the First Anglo-Dutch War did not directly involve the New England colonies. If any war involving England can qualify as a source of a "war scare," no matter how distant and indirect, then the a theory linking war scares and witch hunts is unfalsifiable.

The war theory as proposed by Norton poses other problems. For one, it makes little sense out of variations among towns in Massachusetts. For example, Glouchester and Marblehead were at greater risk of Indian attack than Salem. Yet, there was very little witch hunting in those two towns. There was a case resulting in slander charges in Glouchester in 1653 and 1667, and individual complaints in 1650, 1651 and 1657. In 1692, when Glouchester was caught up in the Salem craze, seven women were named, but no further action was taken for six of the women, and the seventh was pardoned. Although one woman from Marblehead, Wilmot Read, was executed, the complaint came from the accusers and afflicted in Salem. The accusations of witchcraft did not stem from fears indigenous to residents of Marblehead.

Glouchester and Marblehead were vulnerable to Indian attack but did not get deeply involved in the hunt, and, to paraphrase Briggs (1996a), there are many reasons why. Taylor (2001) observes that Marblehead and Glouchester were fishing towns, employing "hard-drinking and hard-swearing men with scant property and little reputation to lose." They were likely to have immigrated from the English West country (175). In contrast, the Puritans "came primarily from south-eastern England" and emigrated as families. Fisherman from Western England shared superstitions about witches and witchcraft, but most of the witch hunting in England was concentrated in the southeast. The same sorts of village and family conflicts that shaped charges of witchcraft in England were reproduced among the Puritan families in Salem and spread from there to surrounding communities through family and neighborhood networks.

As Taylor (2001) describes the community, "Loud and smoky taverns abounded in Marblehead." The residents had no church until 1684, and "when obliged to choose a faith, most fisherman preferred a relaxed Anglicanism with its ceremonies as compared to an intense Puritanism with its strict morality and long sermons" (175). In short, the threat of Indian attack does not make sense out of variations in witch hunts among communities. In fact, the communities and colonies most directly affected by Indian attack invested few resources in the pursuit of imaginary enemies in their midst.

The Salem Panic as a Perfect Storm

Claims for a "new" perspective on the Salem (or Essex County) witch craze should be received with considerable caution, especially when the focus is on a single case or cause and little or no attention is paid to the larger body of research on witch hunts in other settings or societies. Clearly, research on European witch hunts has supported that intense witch hunting is generated by the convergence of a variety of distinct and separable circumstances. The variables introduced in new explanations of the Salem episode may be quite relevant to understanding witch hunts, but as one among several precipitating, or inhibiting, circumstances in the sense proposed by Demos and others. The analogy of a "perfect storm" applies to the Salem witch hunt in that all of the circumstances introduced to explain panic-level witch hunts appear to have converged during a relatively short period of time encompassing that episode.

Although there is little evidence to justify the specific claims that sleeping sickness or ergotism led to afflictions and/or hallucinations resulting in the witchcraft accusations, all histories of the Salem witch trials agree that disease epidemics had something to do with the social climate leading to the Salem panic. There was a major outbreak of smallpox in Massachusetts and other New England colonies in 1690. Epidemics of other diseases broke out as well, with fever and measles also reported between 1687 and 1690. In fact, when all diseases are considered together, 1690 was one of the most illness-ridden years in seventeenth-century New England.

Sleeping sickness and ergotism may have contributed to the afflictions and hallucinations of some colonists as Carlson and Caporeal propose, but the data on proximity to wetlands, tree ring width, and the details on the girls' behavior cause problems for such theories. Yet, outbreaks of disease could increase the odds of witch hunts through mechanisms other than the afflictions and hallucinations that are the focus in their theories. First, epidemic illness was taken as a sign that the Devil was at work and that the colonists had fallen out of favor with God. Such beliefs could contribute to suspicions that some people were engaged in witchcraft regardless of any real afflictions. Second, women who attempted to help the sick during epidemics could be held accountable for the spread of disease or become suspects when the afflicted died. Third, a surge in illness and death rates could shift the demographic characteristics of a community in ways that affected the visibility and availability of plausible candidates for witchcraft (e.g., contentious women with inheritances and destitute women who could use fear of witchcraft in social exchanges) as well as increase the anxiety or anger of others (e.g., scarcity of potential mates).

The relative importance of actual mechanisms linking disease and witchcraft accusations cannot be empirically established at present. Moreover, the apparent consensus that disease epidemics help make sense out of temporal patterns in New England does not allow an explanation of the concentration of witch hunts in Massachusetts and Connecticut rather than Maine, the Chesapeake colonies, or the southern colonies. Other variables or circumstances have to be introduced to explain such colonial variations.

Research on European witch hunts indicates that the behavior and attitudes of official "gatekeepers" were crucial for understanding witch hunts, especially "crazelike" or panic-level witch hunts. Since witch trials involved religious and legal institutions, the accusations among contentious families and neighbors and/or the strange behavior of some villagers had to be accepted and defined as evidence of witchcraft before a panic was possible. The potential to open the institutional gates could not be impeded, and leaders had to be willing to apply such a definition to the situation. Of course, the same circumstance that could increase the potential for people to charge each other with witchcraft could increase the acceptability of such charges by gatekeepers.

Several key gatekeepers appeared in the development and escalation of the Essex County trials. Dr. Griggs played a key role in rejecting the possibility that the girls were suffering from a known disease or medical problem. Such a diagnosis could be self-serving in that it allowed an alternative to any admission of incompetence or powerlessness in dealing with the problems afflicting people. It does not appear that such a diagnosis was a veiled attack on women as healers or midwives because wise women and midwives were those most likely to be called on to search for evidence of witchcraft. Moreover, by the time of the Salem episode, Dr. Griggs could call on prior documented cases in the colonies, England, Scotland, and the rest of Europe that had been defined as evidence of possession and witchcraft in similar circumstances.

Several religious gatekeepers were directly or indirectly involved in either opening the gates for the Salem trials or assuring that they stayed open. Samuel Parris (pastor to the Salem Village parish) is the key figure in opening the gates. Deodat Lawson (a prior pastor to the Salem Parish) and Increase Mather (Cotton Mathers's father, pastor to the Second Church of

Boston, and president of Harvard) expressed views that could have helped shut the gates had their messages not been superseded by those more immediately involved.

Deodat Lawson was the third minister of Salem Village, spanning the period from 1684 to 1688 before Salem Village had a full-fledged church with an ordained minister. Lawson's ordination was opposed, and he left when his contract expired. During the witch trials, Lawson was invited to the pulpit by Samuel Parris, where he presented the events that were unfolding as products of the "Fires of Contention." Lawson proposed that Satan's malice was evident in the afflictions and accusations, but most of his message focused on the lines of contention that had driven him away from Salem and that he believed generated contentious dichotomies and scapegoating in the community. Lawson preached, "We all, even the best of us, have by sin a hand and share, in Provoking God thus to let Satan loose, in an unusual manner. Who can say he is clean?" (Trask 1992: 91). He warned the community that "there is an inclination in the best, to Charge the Sins of others, as the procuring cause of GODS Judgement and to reflect severely on the Pride, Lukewarmness, Covetousness, Contention, Intemperance, and Uneven Conversation of others; but we can hardly be brought to smite upon our own Breast, and say What have I done" (93). Throughout his sermon he warned about the advantage to Satan of a community "divided against itself," about "giving way to . . . Envy, malice, or Hatred of Neighbors and Brethen" (98). He warned "give no place to the Devil by the rash sentencing of others, without sufficient grounds, or false accusing any willingly" (100).

Samuel Parris delivered a sermon a few days later. As reported in a narrative of Parris's sermon written by Lawson, Parris preached, "We are either saints or Devils, the scripture gives us no medium," that "God would not suffer Devils in the guise of Saints to associate with us," and that "Christ knows who these Devils are" (111). Norton argues (2002) that "despite the differences in the tone of their sermon, Lawson and Parris concurred on essentials. The devil was abroad in Salem Village. Church members could be found among the witches. The afflicted were innocent victims of Satan's wrath, deserving the pity and sympathy of others" (69).

In contrast to Norton's assessment that these two sermons are similar, there is far more than a difference in tone between these two sermons. For Lawson, the afflictions are evidence that Satan is at work, but the cause of God's judgment is the lack of neighborliness, false witness, blaming others, and the envy and malice reflected in the contentious behavior of the laity. In contrast, Parris's sermon is inflammatory (Trask 1992: 110), dichotomizing the community into good versus evil, with devils attempting to pass as saints and vice versa. For Lawson, all members of the community share responsibility for the crisis and helped generate it by ignoring basic norms of neighborliness. The root of evil in the community is envy, malice, or hatred among neighbors and brethren, rash sentencing of others, and false accusations. In short, Lawson's sermon reflects the modern interpretation of the Salem episode as a product of contention among families and factions, and he appears to have been pleading for them to recognize their growing animosities.

Parris's sermon was delivered three days after Lawson's, and the timing makes sense when it is viewed as a challenge to Lawson's call for neighborliness and caution. It can be argued that Parris felt he had to counter Lawson's message that the community was being punished for shared sins and the divisions among them. Although anyone could be found to be a witch, only some members of the community were at fault according to Parris. There were real devils in their midst, and some were trying to pass as saints. For Lawson, envy was a sin that divided the community. For Parris, the envious were prone to witchcraft. It was not false accusation and malice in the community that was responsible for the afflictions, but the slander and malice of those that had been accused of witchcraft. In fact, one member of the anti-Parris faction, Sara Cloyce (Rebecca Nurse's sister), walked out on the sermon, slamming the door behind her. Quite legitimately, Parris's sermon was interpreted by his enemies as an attempt to demonize them. In contrast, although Lawson did not deny the reality of the afflictions, they were presented as punishments for the very sort of contentious behavior reflected in Parris's sermon. Lawson's sermon dramatized the political and secular roots of the craze, but Parris's sermon depicted it as a battle between real witches (members of the opposing faction) and the rest of the community.

Cotton Mather's role as a gatekeeper remains a source of controversy among historians. Mather was acting pastor to the Second Church of Boston at the time of the trials and was quite familiar with the afflictions and aberrant behavior of young people that were symptomatic of witchcraft. He had investigated the 1688 bewitchment of the Goodwin children in Boston (discussed above), attributing their problems to the witchcraft of Mary Glover, an Irish washerwoman. He reported his observations in "Memorable Providences," one of over three hundred books completed in his lifetime.

He was close friends with several of the judges in the Court of Oyer and Terminer which had been established by Governor Phips to hear the backlog of cases. Cotton Mather wrote to advise one of the judges, John Richards, about the types of evidence necessary to determine whether or not the accused was a witch. He cautioned the judges to be wary of accusations based solely on spectral evidence and argued that a confession was the best evidence that someone was a witch. His reservations about the use of spectral evidence as the sole evidence for conviction are often cited as support for the view that Mather's opinions were not responsible for escalating the witch hunts. On the other hand, he did reinforce the judges' belief that witches could appear as specters and such testimony was taken quite seriously in the trials. Moreover, Mather did not sign the letter that his father, Increase Mather, and seven other clergy prepared in August, a letter that played a role in bringing the trials to an end. In subsequent written assessments of the trials, Mather reiterated the fact that he had questioned reliance on spectral evidence. Yet, among the influential clergy, he played the greatest role in reinforcing fear of witchcraft and sustaining the call to battle in defeating them. Indeed, he sustained this call despite meetings with eight confessors who told him they had falsely confessed (Hoffer 1996: 181).

A potentially critical point where the momentum of the trials could have been halted was the hanging of George Burroughs. Standing on the gallows, Burroughs said the Lord's Prayer without error, a feat that was supposed to be impossible for a witch or wizard. In Calef's report on the trials, the audience was aroused by Burroughs's performance. Burroughs's execution was the only one attended by Cotton Mather, and, according to Calef, Mather intervened to quell any move toward mob action to free Burroughs, declaring that "the Devil has often been transformed into an Angel of Light." Silverman (1985: 110–11) notes that although it has not been established that those were his exact words, Calef's report that Cotton Mather intervened to keep the execution on course is completely consistent with Mather's animosity toward mobs and toward Burroughs. Had he not intervened, it is possible that Burroughs would have been spared and, given Burroughs's opposition to the witch beliefs used to justify the trials, a more organized countermovement might have emerged. Moreover, Burroughs fit Mather's religious template for the problem of witchcraft. He was the leader crucial to a patriarchal conception of the problem faced by New England, a secret conspiracy of women led by a clever and devious male with unusual powers.

In sum, although Mather cannot be held responsible for initiating the trials, he helped turn Parris's religiously disguised factional conflict into a cosmic war of colonial proportions, helped legitimate the use of witness testimony about specters as acceptable evidence for initiating charges, strongly defended the court and its procedures when other clerical forces were criticizing it, and intervened to sustain the momentum of the trials at a point where popular action may have stopped the trials by freeing Burroughs.

Another circumstance identified as conducive to witch hunts in European research is the relatively unfettered exertion of local authority in the absence or breakdown of centralized government. From 1688 through 1692, Massachusetts is described by Robert Calef as "between government and no government" (quoted in McMillen 1990: 128). The royal governor, Edmond Andros, had been imprisoned in Boston and sent back to England in 1688–1689 in a rebellion against English rule. Not only would this structured form of contention (local rebellion against a real enemy) detract from any need to search for imaginary enemies, but the "lack of power in the central authority" encouraged Salem Villagers "to push through a properly ordained minister of their own without outside interferences" (McMillen 1990: 129). The resulting split among families and factions set the stage for internal strife which was defined by Parris as a struggle between forces of good and evil with his opponents symbolized as Satan's confederates.

Indeed, had Increase Mather not been in England negotiating a new charter, the clerical advice that helped end the trials might have been provided much earlier than August. The lack of centralized religious intervention was accompanied by a lack of centralized political action. Governor Phips created the Court of Oyer and Terminer (to "hear" and "determine"), but promptly headed north to take part in a campaign to defeat the French and their Indian allies. In fact, Rosenthal (1993) argues, "While there can be no single explanation for the Salem trials, we may reasonably assume that something radically different would have happened had Phips stayed home" (195). Rosenthal's argument shows why it is difficult to identify a single explanation for the trials since Phips's decision to turn governance over to William Stoughton was a product of the Second Indian War in the northern frontier. Thus, Norton may be correct in reiterating Kences's argument about the impact of war on the frontier on witch hunts, but its impact could be indirect as a product of Phips's preoccupation with the war and the resulting absence of central government "brakes" on escalations of local contention.

When Governor Phips returned to Boston to resupply his troops, he discovered "a strange ferment of dissatisfaction which was increased by some hot spirits that blew the flame" (quoted in Robinson 1991: 231). He terminated the Court of Oyer and Terminer and agreed to a new court. The council elected many of the same judges and put Stoughton in charge once again, but their fervent attempt to resume the hunt was inhibited by the abandonment of spectral evidence and the recalcitrance of the subsequent juries. Only three guilty verdicts were handed down in fifty-six cases when prosecution resumed. Stoughton pushed for executions, but Phips granted reprieves. By May, 1693 Phips had ended the witch hunt.

Although it widely accepted that government centralization and control over judicial processes helps tone down witch hunts, partially explaining variations among societies and over time, there were periods subsequent to the Salem trials when cases of possession occurred and centralized control was weak, but no new witch trials occurred. Lord Bellomont arrived in 1699 as governor of both New York and New England and spent only fourteen months of a three-year reign in Boston (see Silverman 1985: 139). The government was once again in Stoughton's and a "Council's" hands, but there was no resumption of the witch wars. However, that was also the span of time (1694–1697) when the Indian wars encroached directly on towns in Massachusetts and even threatened Boston. War was a major direct threat to the area and can be argued to preclude witch wars rather than cause them. War could inhibit the search for imaginary enemies during spans of political weakness.

The Salem-Essex trials occurred in the middle of a span of severe winters and 1696 was particularly severe (Weisman 1984: 174). Yet, climatic stress and potentially related problems (e.g., ergotism) did not generate any unusual new surge of either afflictions or accusations. In 1694, Samuel Sewall wrote in his diary that there were community suspicions that a woman had died of witchcraft (Rosenthal 1993: 201). A servant in Boston, Mary Watkins, confessed to witchcraft in 1693 and was indicted, but the jury refused the bill (Weisman 1984: 182). Cotton Mather continued to be fascinated with cases of possession, but none of them escalated into witchcraft trials. Mercy Short became a public attraction in Boston with groups of five to fifty observing her trances and fits. No new witch hunts were mounted despite the persistence of climatic stress.

If Norton's theory that the trials were generated by the Indian wars or Kences's theory that they were associated with war-related invasion anxiety were to explain the end of the witch hunts, it would be quite legitimate to expect that the threat of war had declined or disappeared. Yet, King William's War continued. In fact, as noted in the discussion of Norton's thesis, there were no major events in King William's War for two years from July 1690 to the raid on Wells, Maine, in June 1692 after the trials were well under way. Durham, New Hampshire, was raided in 1694 and Haverhill, Massachusetts, was raided in 1697. The second French-Indian War (Queen Anne's War) spanned from 1702 through 1713 with a force of French and Indians attacking Deerfield, Massachusetts, in 1704. The town was burned with fifty casualties and one hundred captives. In fact, a case could be made that the second phase of the French-Indian Wars was a more severe and immediate threat to Massachusetts than the early phases involving New York and Quebec in 1690. However, whether interpreted as an immediate threat or not, it is clear that the threat of war did not disappear after 1692 and may have intensified. Yet, there was no resumption of witch hunts.

Midelfort (1972) suggests that the "'enlightenment' that ended the European trials came not from one group to another, not from books, but from the shattering realization that witch hunts could destroy all sense of community, and all inhabitants as well" (191). He concludes that "the large panic trial, the severe social purgation, was dead by its own hand" (192). The Salem–Essex County trial ended when accusations began spreading to powerful families. There was mounting opposition to the trials and it appears that key religious leaders, including Cotton Mather's own father, would have put brakes on the episode earlier were they not preoccupied with pressing issues such as the creation of a new charter. Religious opposition to the witch trials grew in strength during the trials and was even stronger after the suspension of trials. Gatekeepers were not inclined to allow another Salem panic to occur.

Outbreaks of disease are relevant to understanding variations in witch hunts, and those facilitating epidemics did not disappear after 1692. However, a fundamental shift occurred in the conception of disease emerging in the late 1600s and early 1700s, and, ironically, Cotton Mather's own writings reveal that shift in interpretations. He had attributed diseases such as smallpox to Satan, the "Destroyer," and viewed New England's epidemics as signs of disfavor with God. Colonial leaders had attributed the decimation of the Indian population by disease as God's punishment for their savage and heathen ways. When confronted with similar epidemics in their own society, they expressed similar concerns about departures from Puritan tradition.

Perry Miller (1939) argues that both Increase and Cotton Mather posited a dual nature to phenomena such as lightning, earthquakes and comets. They could have natural causes, but they could be "portentious signs of divine anger" (231). Mather considered himself to be a scientist as well as a minister and noted a twelve-year cycle to smallpox epidemics in New England. Moreover, Mather and other authorities knew that isolating the sick and contaminated slowed the spread of the disease. In addition, Mather's slave, Onesimus, was a survivor of a form of inoculation in his native Africa (Silverman 1985: 339). Cotton Mather experimented with inoculation on one of his own sons, an act that led to fierce criticism climaxed by a bomb being thrown through his chamber window. Mather championed the use of the technique in New England, a stand that generated strong opposition, but one he stood by as strongly as he had the demonological interpretation of possession and witchcraft (Silverman 1985: 336–63).

The shift in interpretation of disease as a natural rather than a supernatural problem was well under way. Not only had plague, the most devastating disease in the second millennium, run its course, but other diseases were increasingly interpreted in naturalistic, scientific terms as problems potentially subject to control by natural means. Indeed, the witch trials involved a pseudo-scientific demonology where authorities or their experts searched for empirical indicators of possession and witchcraft using existing reference books and prior court cases as guides (i.e., swimming witches, searching for devil's marks, touch tests, blindfolded responses, faults reciting the Lord's prayer, etc.). Before a search for hidden supernatural causes could begin, possible medical explanations had to be eliminated. As Leland Estes (1983) argues in his essay on "The Medical Origins of the European Witch Craze," witchcraft was a residual category to explain illnesses and ailments that were "not explicable by ordinary means" (278). Although he had obvious reasons to benefit from a demonization of his enemies, Reverend Parris first sought a naturalistic diagnosis from Dr. Griggs. Only when Griggs could not explain the spontaneity and unpredictability of the girl's systems in terms of any known ailment was that residual category used. The shift toward naturalistic explanations of illness was evident in the initial behavior of the accusers.

A central axiom in Jack Gibb's (1994) control theory of "supernaturalism" is that "among countries and for any country over time, perceived control capacity is a "negative determinant" of the "amount of supernaturalism" (80). The construct "amount of supernaturalism" is defined as "the relative prevalence of supernatural beliefs and practices in some designated population over some designated period" (193). Although attempts to control disease through some form of human action such as quarantine had been practiced for centuries, the most lethal and epidemic diseases such as plague and smallpox appeared beyond control. Plague had subsided as an apocalyptic crisis in Europe and the colonies by the time of the Salem witch hunt, but smallpox and other diseases were still serious problems. The discovery that smallpox could be brought under human control through crude forms of inoculation was a dramatic step forward in perceived control capacity. This shift is clearly evident in Mather's writings, and the religious interpretation of disease as one tactic God allowed Satan to use to punish the wayward Puritans was being supplanted by a more scientific view.

When all of the converging conditions surrounding the trials are considered, the Salem episode appears to fit the template generated in studies of other early modern witch trials. The residents had experienced war, but they were not immediately threatened. The worst outbreak of smallpox occurred in 1690, and a smaller outbreak hit New Hampshire in 1692. The trials fall right in the middle of one of the most severe periods (drought, cold, or both) experienced in new England. The panic might have occurred earlier, but gatekeepers were preoccupied with their own rebellion against the Crown's imposed government. Other traditional internal enemies were protected by

English law or had moved on to settle new colonies. Other circumstances necessary for a panic (demonology) were eroding away, and some of the most devastating sources of mortality had either disappeared or were shifting from the realm of supernatural beliefs to the realm of science. When added to the self-exhausting and negative consequences of such panics, the beginning of yet another long stretch of warfare involving real enemies, improvement in climate, as well as increases in biotic control, the foray of the Devil and his companions into the colonies had ended, and he was never to return in quite the same form.

Notes

1. This narrative description of people and events draws on a variety of sources, including Robinson (1991), Breslaw (1996), Starkey 1969), McMillen (1990), and Roach (2002).

2. For discussions of witch trials in the early 1700s, see Ankarloo and Henningsen (1993), Barry, Hester, and Roberts (1996), and Ankarloo and Clark (2002).

3. Chi-square was 3.12 with two degrees of freedom. A chi-square of 5.99 was required for statistical significance at the .05 level.

4. Chi-square was 2.35 with two degrees of freedom and was statistically insignificant at the .05 level. The Salem-Essex trials did fall in a span of years with narrow rings and that association generates a significant correlation in regression analysis relating accusations and executions to ring width. However, that relationship is due entirely to the Salem-Essex trials. There was no significant relationship when 1692 was excluded from the analysis. Other variables entered into significant relationships as well. Smallpox and war-in-the-distance were positive correlates and Andros's imprisonment and Quaker-Anabaptist controversies were negative correlates. However, all relationships were due to the inclusion of the Salem-Essex trials. Without 1692 in the analysis, there were no significant relationships. The patterns discerned with Salem in the analysis are quite compatible with those observed by Demos and in the analyses of other witch hunts.

5. Years for wars, battles, and other events are based on David Marley's (1998) descriptions in *Wars of the Americas*, John Demos's (1982) chronologies in *Entertaining Satan*, Laurence Urdang's (1996) *The Timetables of American History*, and Marilynne Roach's (2002) *Salem Witch Trials: A Day-by-Day Chronicle of a Community under Siege*.

CHAPTER EIGHT

Modern "Witch Hunts"

More Than Metaphors?

We are a society that, every fifty years or so, is afflicted by some paroxysm of virtue—an orgy of self-cleansing through which evil of one kind or another is cast out. From the witch-hunts of Salem to the communist hunts of the McCarthy era to the current shrill fixation on child abuse, there runs a common thread of moral hysteria. After the McCarthy era, people would ask: But how could it have happened? How could the presumption of innocence have been abandoned wholesale? How did large and powerful institutions acquiesce as congressional investigators ran roughshod over civil liberties-all in the name of a war on communists? How was it possible to believe that subversives lurked behind every library door, in every radio station, that every two-bit actor who had belonged to the wrong political organization posed a threat to the nation's security?

Years from now people doubtless will ask the same questions about our present era—a time when the most improbable charges of abuse find believers; when it is enough only to be accused by anonymous sources to be hauled off by investigators; a time when the hunt for child abusers has become a national pathology.

—Dorothy Rabinowitz, "From the Mouths of Babes to a Jail Cell," *Harper's Magazine* (May 1990).

This voyage along the path of the Devil has involved ideas and data from scholars representing a wide range of academic disciplines as well as several specialties within sociology. Using data compiled by historians, dendrochronologists, economists, and historical demographers, disease epidemics were found to play a role in generating the most intense witch hunts, but not in the simplistic "symptoms-of-disease" form proposed by advocates of biomedical theories. Surges in disease appear to be followed by surges in witch hunts through a variety of mechanisms, including heightened anxiety and fear and disruption of the demographic structure of society in ways that foment conflicts among neighbors and generate inheritance struggles within families.

When "war" is measured as violent conflict in a territory, it appears to inhibit witch hunts. This finding is consistent with perspectives proposed by several witch hunt historians but contrary to the most recent perspective on the Salem-Essex witch trials. However, when the location of actual conflict is considered, the "war on the fringes" theory applies to witch hunts in Salem, England, and Scotland. War on the fringes may play a role similar to disease, heightening fear and anxiety, prompting a cathartic search for scapegoats. Forms of structured conflict where real enemies can be discerned tend to stifle conflicts with imaginary enemies. Integrating theoretical notions from the psychology of scapegoating, victimization theory in criminology, and the sociology of collective behavior helps make sense of findings on war and witch hunts, shifts in targets over time, and variations among societies.

Disease and war are key apocalyptic variables for understanding the course of witch hunts within and among societies, but the most intense witch hunting in early modern history occurred during a span of time when a variety of factors converged to make life miserable. The Salem-Essex witch hunt occurred during one of the worst cold spells in the New England colonies, and the worst phases of the European witch hunts occurred during a span of time when all measures of hardship told the same story. Such "convergence" or "confluence" theories challenge single variable theorists, and for good reason. Cultural, social, and environmental variables operating at a macro- and a microlevel have to converge for intense witch wars to be fought. Local gatekeepers have to be inclined to accept and act on accusations. Central authority has to be weak or preoccupied. The prerequisite perspectives on disease, the lack of a clear structure of class conflict, involvement in actual warfare in the immediate area, and scarcity of alternative enemies are among the converging factors as well. Accusations would escalate into a panic when the conception of a conspiracy with Satan was applied and torture in one form or another was allowed, leading to escalating accusations. All of the prerequisites and precipitating sources of anxiety and fear had to fall in place. Were witch panics to be a product of a single factor, they would have occurred far more frequently than they did, and it would be difficult to explain why they ended.

Although state-supported witch hunts ended several centuries ago, the pursuit of women as witches continues in the modern world. Hundreds of women have been killed in India based on village-level accusations of witchcraft, and several thousand have been assaulted (Barman 2002). Similar reports can be found for African and Asian nations (Behringer 2004). Of course, these modern attacks are against the law, and, although founded in folk beliefs, they are not backed by a state-supported, demonological theory of satanic witchcraft, facts that help explain why they do not result in escalating panics. On the other hand, some characteristics of these modern "witch hunts" are similar to those generating accusations in the Salem witch trials.

Not only are there numerous modern instances of violence directed at witches, but contemporary episodes such as the search for witches and Satanists in preschools and "political witch hunts" are cited as *metaphorical* analogues to earlier witch hunts. Bernard Rosenthal (1993) concludes his story about Salem with the observation that the Salem witch trials "shaped our metaphors of persecution" as a paramount "episode of injustice" (212–13). He states that this metaphor is "so powerful . . . that, ironically, it has crossed the ocean back to England and caught the attention of a country with its own long record of witchcraft persecutions" (213). The specific episode depicted as fitting the witch hunt metaphor as a "modern crucible" involved charges of child abuse in England, a case analyzed in the book *When Salem Came to the Boro* (Bell 1988). Dorothy Rabinowitz (1990) expresses a similar view of child abuse cases (see the chapter-opening illustration) such as the McMartin preschool trials prosecuted in the 1980s and categorizes them together with "McCarthyism" as instances of "moral hysteria." As noted in chapter 7, Miller's *The Crucible* was written in the midst of a hunt for secret conspiracies of communists, and Senator Joseph McCarthy came to be labeled as a "America's Witchfinder General" (Oplinger 1990: 160).

In this chapter, features that these more contemporary phenomena appear to share in common with early modern witch hunts will be considered. The central question is whether the patterns involving disease, war, and other forms of structured conflict found for early modern witch hunts can be discerned in the course of the political witch hunts, the preschool panic, and witch hunts in modern India. Such phenomena have features that clearly distinguish them from the early modern witch hunts, and they might not follow the same rules as the witch hunts analyzed in earlier chapters. However, the fact that scholars propose metaphorical parallels between the early modern witch hunts and more contemporary events mandates a consideration of possible parallels. Are contemporary phenomena referred to as "witch hunts" merely instances of a broad metaphorical analogue, or do they share some generating circumstances in common?

More Than a Metaphor?

Although Salem is depicted as a metaphor for a wide variety of concepts such as "persecution," "scapegoating," "intolerance," and "injustice," the most distinct legacy of the Salem trials for American culture and political discourse is the concept of a "witch hunt" itself—a concept that embodies complicated ideas about motives and tactics that now shape contentious politics. The concept has come to refer to use of prosecutorial machinery against members of a society (individuals or groups of people) based on contrived, exaggerated and/or suspect evidence in situations where a credible case can be made that the underlying motives for such a pursuit involve one or more of the following: (1) prejudice toward targeted groups, (2) disguised attempts to gain an advantage over opponents, and (3) a need to attribute blame.

Such hunts are characterized by efforts to demonize targets and to impose a template where the people prosecuted are part of a larger hidden conspiracy of evil. Moreover, those processes of demonization are couched in terms that link the internal threat to external enemies. When a historical episode is shown to involve such processes, it is likely to be deemed an instance of "injustice." When a specific disparaged group appears to have been targeted, it may qualify as an instance of "persecution." When those pursued appear to be a target of displaced anxieties or a means of displacing attention, it may be an instance of "scapegoating."

For a historical, social scientific, or political attempt to categorize an episode as a "witch hunt" to be credible, there must be a demonstration that the magnitude of the threat prompting accusations is either fabricated or grossly exaggerated. Of course, a successful counterattack to the witch hunt strategy requires just the opposite tactic. The threat must be shown to be real and serious. Indeed, historians still disagree about the role and threat of actual witchcraft as a cause of the Salem-Essex trials or the European witch trials. If fear can be shown to exceed the actual threat, then application of the witch hunt template gains credibility.

Because the concept is applied to situations where ulterior motives are imputed, evidence to that effect will help justify application of the concept. For example, when charges are mounted by parties, factions, or individuals with histories of contention, suspicions that the attack is an attempt to gain an advantage over opponents can be raised. Such contentious politics has been documented as a plausible and credible cause of the Salem witch hunt, and successful application in contemporary political contention requires a demonstration of structure that would justify applying the concept. If the targets are disproportionately members of distinct religious, ethnic, or political groups and the accusers are members of groups traditionally hostile toward them, the application of the concept gains credibility in political discourse.

The concept can be applied retrospectively in assessing historical episodes and has been applied in discussions of a variety of contemporary events or episodes, ranging from McCarthyism to attempts by fundamentalist preachers to "demonize" feminists. Although it may seem blatantly obvious that McCarthy's zealous pursuit of hidden communists was a "witch hunt," placing McCarthy's crusade in that category has to be carefully assessed. An attempt to apply the concept can itself be a strategy for discrediting those responsible for the "hunt" as well as the sincerity of their motives. In short, in contemporary political debate, attempts to place an episode in the category is a strategy for discrediting it. Any discussion of the search for hidden communists in America as a "witch hunt" will have to address the observable features of the episode that justify that categorization whether developing a credible historical theory or discrediting the parties and factions involved.

McCarthyism: Real Enemies or a Witch Hunt?

In contemporary discourse, references to "McCarthyism" are virtually synonymous with the concept of a witch hunt. However, *McCarthyism* refers to far more than the activities of Senator Joseph McCarthy. It has become a negative, pejorative label to be applied to political strategies and tactics of investigation that parallel the Salem trials. The association of McCarthyism with Miller's play is somewhat misleading in that Miller's specific involvement in the congressional search for hidden communists was not with McCarthy and his Senate committees. Rather, Miller was among those questioned by the House Un-American Activities Committee (HUAC) in the years between World War II and the Korean War. He wrote the play during the era encompassing both HUAC attacks on artists with "leftist leanings" in the late 1940s and McCarthy's extension of the search for communists in the early 1950s. The play was completed before the height of the McCarthy phase of the search in 1953.

McCarthy reinvigorated and expanded a search for hidden enemies that had targeted Miller and others in the House of Representatives between

1947 and 1948. The HUAC had been established in 1937 to investigate subversive activities by members of groups on both the Right and the Left in America. But, under their first chairman, Martin Dies, the focus was directed away from consideration of groups such as the Ku Klux Klan to leftist groups, especially the American Communist Party. Several members of the American Communist Party had been successfully prosecuted under the Alien Registration Act that had been passed by Congress in 1940 to deal with people advocating the overthrow of the government.

Under its third chairman, John Parnell Thomas, HUAC began a major search for subversives in the film industry. The committee was able to get names of artists with leftist leanings from many of the witnesses called, but some of the artists questioned, including Miller, asserted Fifth Amendment rights and refused. Miller and others were held in contempt of Congress, and some were sentenced to six to twelve months in prison. The most severe consequence of the hearings was not the legal sanctions imposed but the reaction of Hollywood film studios. A blacklist of suspects was created, and it precluded employment of hundreds of people. Unlike Salem, the most pervasive consequences suffered were based on the secretive, informal actions of Hollywood executives rather than actual formal sanctions.

McCarthy, a senator from Wisconsin, entered the search for hidden enemies in 1950 with a speech where he claimed to have a list of personnel in the State Department who were, or had been, members of the American Communist Party. The list was not new and had been compiled by the State Department in 1946, but McCarthy used it to revive American's concerns about the threat of internal enemies who were believed to be linked to a worldwide web of communist organizations. He was made chairman of the Senate Government Committee on Operations and, with the help of information from J. Edgar Hoover's FBI, mounted a crusade to ferret out communist subversives within the government.

One of the reasons McCarthy's search has been labeled a witch hunt is the partisan nature of his activities. There were, in fact, members of the American Communist Party among the targets of both HUAC investigations and McCarthy's crusade. Moreover, the spread of communism was viewed as a threat by most Americans. However, in the course of the presidential campaign leading to General Eisenhower's election, McCarthy made speeches attacking President Truman and members of his administration, administrators associated with President Roosevelt's "New Deal" legislation, and a variety of Democrats up for election. Vice presidential candidate Richard Nixon joined in the campaign to label key opponents as "soft on communism." Even Eisenhower modified speeches to avoid upsetting McCarthy (Bennett 1988: 302).

Not only did Eisenhower-Nixon win, but many of those attacked by McCarthy lost to Republican opponents. Democrats viewed McCarthy's tactics as a "witch hunt," designed to gain an advantage for Republicans, and contemporary Democrats are likely to share that interpretation. In contrast, many Republicans viewed his initial activities as a necessary crusade against a real enemy, a crusade that required defeat of the Democrats and a cleansing of American institutions (see Buckley and Bozell 1954). Contemporary debates over McCarthyism as a "witch hunt" as opposed to a vital crusade are still divided along party lines (see Coulter 2003).

Another source of the conception of McCarthy's and HUAC's search for communists as a "witch hunt" is the fact that the search escalated from people who could be defined credibly as potential or real threats to include people who appeared to be imaginary threats. In Salem, the initial charges were leveled against Sarah Good, who fit the stereotype of the ornery beggar woman; against Sarah Osborne, who refused to play by the rules in transferring an inheritance; as well as the slave Tituba, who had ample opportunity to "afflict" the girls. However, charges began to spread to include people who did not fit the cultural template of the witch.

Similarly, the initial search for communist subversives had resulted in successful prosecution and imprisonment of leaders of the American Communist Party in 1948, convictions that were upheld by the Supreme Court. Whether those targeted constituted a serious threat to overthrow the American government is debatable, but they did belong to the American Communist Party. Like the Salem episode, the search expanded to pursue people who had any kind of association with communist, leftist, or liberal organizations at any time and to people who did not appear to be real threats to the American way of life. The search expanded to include people in the motion picture industry who were suspected of using their scripts, acting, and directorial talents to insert communist propaganda into films. McCarthy expanded the search further to include books, charging that at least thirty thousand books by communists or people with communist leanings could be found in the government's Overseas Library Program. His staff expanded the attack to include Protestant clergy who were depicted as a hidden nest of radicals (Bennett 1988: 305). In short, what began as a search for real enemies ballooned into an attack on a huge "hidden" threat with the potential of stealing the minds and souls of Americans, much like the alien "body snatching" pods in the American science fiction film *The Body Snatchers*.

Ironically, it was McCarthy's expansion of his search to include the army that ultimately halted his crusade. General Eisenhower had won the election in 1952, and an extension of McCarthy's search to include communists hiding in the army was a personal affront to military leaders and Eisenhower. Although they had played along with the attack when Democrats were the targets, Eisenhower was very concerned about this extension and asked his vice president, Richard Nixon, to begin a counterattack. Popular newspaper columnists and broadcasters joined the counterattack, and the Army-McCarthy Hearings became a media and public drama, nationally televised in 1953.

McCarthy loved the publicity and drama surrounding his crusade, but television coverage of the proceedings highlighted his pettiness and vindictiveness. A member of the army's defense team had once been a member of the National Lawyers Guild, an organization that had been a concern of the HUAC, and McCarthy was ready to go after the young man as one of his hidden communists. The army was defended by a prominent lawyer, Joseph Welch, and Welch challenged McCarthy's attempts to discredit a member of the army's team. Welch was eloquent in his attack on McCarthy's methods and intentions, but it was clear that McCarthy was already doomed. When Welch aggressively attacked McCarthy's tactics, members of the press and Congress stood up to applaud. Senator McCarthy had extended his attack too far, not so much in his attempt to assail the young member of the defense team, but through his attack on the army. He had lost credibility even before the hearings were televised, and the audience was ready to applaud a dramatic public rebuke. The Salem trials ended when they expanded to include people who could muster political support and who were not credible targets as witches. McCarthy's charges began to lose credibility when he expanded them to institutions revered during wartime and when his tactics became a threat to a new and very popular president.

The postwar era of political witch hunting is identified as "McCarthyism" although McCarthy's search was relatively inconsequential compared to the impact of the search for communists in the late 1940s. His entrepreneurial and reckless extension of the search ultimately led to its demise. Cotton Mather is remembered as a key figure in the Salem witch hunt for similar reasons. Mather defended the goal of the Salem-Essex trials even after they had been terminated by Phipps and helped sustain their momentum at a point where the evidence could have led him to intervene and end the craze (Burrough's gallows speech). McCarthy was largely unsuccessful in indicting any actual communists. In fact, the HUAC search was far more consequential in its effect on Hollywood "leftists" and the content of American films. Yet, the post–World War II search for hidden communists came to be labeled "McCarthyism," highlighting the reckless tactics that ended the state-sponsored search for the "enemy within."

The Hunt for Witches in Preschools

The various versions of the "Red Scare" exhibit parallels to Salem as a sociological crucible, but the most contemporary example of an attempt to control a "hidden threat" through the courts are the trials involving the McMartin preschool in California. The McMartin preschool case involved charges of child molestation and abuse in Manhattan Beach and remains the single most expensive trial in California history. From the initial charges to the behavior of prosecuting attorneys, the McMartin trials exhibited numerous features similar to the Salem trials. The initial complaint came from a woman who charged that her son had been molested by the son and grandson of the mother and grandmother who owned the preschool. After an initial investigation, the district attorney decided not to prosecute because of lack of evidence. There were no possessed or afflicted girls, and the initial suspect was a young male.

The event did not escalate until the chief of the Manhattan Beach police sent a confidential letter to parents of McMartin preschool children encouraging them to discuss possible molestations. Parents were alarmed and started questioning their own children for any evidence of abuse. A local television station magnified their concerns by proposing possible links to child pornography and cults. Although religious leaders had helped magnify and interpret the events in Salem as products of witchcraft, the local police and mass media played that role three centuries later. Witches and Satanists in preschools became a "news theme," picked up by popular nationally syndicated programs reaching an international audience.

At Salem, midwives and others searched for the devil's mark on the bodies of the accused, while Manhattan Beach relied on interviews between child protective workers and the children. Interviewers from a private agency concerned with child abuse ultimately diagnosed 360 children as victims of abuse. The panic spread, and as many as one hundred teachers at ten preschools or daycare facilities became suspects. Teachers were "demonized" as a secretive, hidden threat to families and society as participants in satanic rituals. Seven adults were charged with child abuse, including the son, his mother, and grandmother. Although a young male was the first major suspect, the percentage of females (85 percent) ended up nearly identical to the proportion of women in most early modern witch hunts. When children are the victims (abused, possessed, or afflicted) those that spend the most time caring for children are most likely to be accused.

The evidence of abuse was similar to the evidence of witchcraft in the Salem trials. Children were asked suggestive and leading questions in interviews and reinforced for answers that suggested abuse (Richardson, Best, and Bromley 1991). Any attempt on the children's part to recant or change their testimony was ignored. Evidence that the mother lodging the original charges had a history of similar accusations against her husband, drinking problems, and schizophrenia was not revealed by the prosecution. Accusations by the mother were bizarre, including accusations that her son had been attacked by elephants and lions while on a field trip. Similar fantastic claims were taken seriously in the Salem trials, but they would have weakened the case were they made public during the McMartin trials.

Police searched for any physical evidence that would convincingly connect the fantastic experiences reported by the children to the specific actions of defendants. They sought evidence of purported tunnels and underground rooms where rituals had been carried out but could find none. Other children who should have been involved in these rituals did not corroborate the stories told by their peers. When an assistant prosecutor broke ranks in disgust and revealed evidence that Judy Johnson had numerous problems and wild hallucinations, the case against the teachers began to fall apart. The defendants were acquitted on most accounts and jurors were split on other charges. No one was convicted, but nine preschools had closed, and the seven who had been accused were financially ruined.

There are definite parallels to the Salem witch trials, with local gatekeepers encouraging an interpretation of strange experiences as evidence of a huge but hidden problem. When parents were prompted to watch for symptoms of that hidden problem, an accumulating number began interpreting ordinary experiences in their children's lives as evidence that the problem was real, personal and extraordinary. Experts who knew that the cases they were examining had been identified as possible victims of abuse found what they suspected through leading questions and their own responses to the children's answers. They adamantly defended their interpretation, and any attempt by the children to recant or to tell a different story was ignored or dismissed. The number of accused abusers increased in a search for coconspirators, and the socially constructed interpretation was applied to an ever-widening range of cases. When higher legal authorities begin to question the credibility of the evidence and some local authorities begin to break rank, the trials were brought to an end.

Of course, there are notable differences between the Salem trials and the McMartin preschool prosecutions as well. Although most people in the community believed the teachers to be guilty of some form of sexual molestation, belief that the people involved were real witches capable of the fantastic feats described was not central to the charges because very few people would believe them. Indeed, such details were suppressed by the prosecution because they undermined the credibility of their case. During the Salem trials, such fantastic experiences were considered to be real. The police could not find evidence that the locations described by children in the McMartin case were real, adding to suspicions that children were telling stories, but similar stories were accepted as plausible in terms of seventeenth-century religious belief.

The Disease-War Model: Does It Apply?

It is beyond the scope of the current work to develop measures that would allow a full test of the hypotheses examined in chapter 5. Moreover, it must be noted that these were relatively minor searches for hidden internal enemies compared to the early modern witch hunts and may not follow the same patterns as found for the real witch wars of the early modern era. On the other hand, the possibility of such a fit can be explored.

The search for hidden communists was initiated in a time of peace following World War II and prior to the Korean "incursion." The Korean War, like the English Civil War, would appear to be an exception to the negative relationship between war and witch hunts in that it spanned the years 1950–1952 when McCarthy emerged as a communist hunter. However, the peak in his activities was 1953, after the Korean Armistice. His activities during the Korean War were largely routine politics aimed at unseating Democrats, and he was largely unsuccessful in mustering enthusiastic support in his initial attempts to ferret out communists. Were the height of McCarthyism defined as the extension of the attack to encompass enemies that required increasing amounts of imagination, then the timing of war and political witch hunting would be consistent with prior findings.

The earlier "Red Scare" in the United States had begun during peacetime (1919–1921), following the most serious polio epidemic in American history (1916) and the worst flu epidemic in history (1918–1919). Given the modern scientific and medical understanding of disease, caution should be advised in proposing links between the search for hidden enemies and these epidemics, but the proximity of the two is quite similar to the patterns found for the early modern witch craze. Outbreaks of epidemic disease may heighten anxieties and fear of attacks by hidden "invisible" enemies despite the modern medical understanding of disease.

The large gap between the post–World War I "Red Scare" and the post–World War II scare may support the notion that political witch hunts are postwar phenomena, but it may also be useful to consider whether internal forms of contention might have precluded a search for hidden enemies.

Were political witch hunts to follow patterns suggested by research on early modern witch hunts, then researchers should find less concern about hidden internal enemies when there are structured internal conflicts. For example, surges in work stoppages and strikes might frame the conflicts among groups with sufficient clarity that people do not waste energy inventing more imaginary enemies. The Red Scare subsided as a public or political concern in the mid-1950s and soon thereafter American concerns shifted to race and civil rights. Some of the lingering rhetoric from the search for hidden communists emerged in attacks on civil rights leaders, but the structure and framing of the conflict involved specific goals and well-defined lines of political contention. Such structured conflict would inhibit tendencies to search for more elusive hidden enemies. McCarthy may have, as some suggest, exhausted inclinations to the search for enemies hidden in our midst, but other circumstances may have precluded their resurrection as well.

There are similarities between the course of the search for hidden enemies and the temporal patterning of disease, war, and other types of conflict. The model may apply to the preschool cases as well. The initial accusation in the preschool case was lodged in 1983, and by 1984, hundreds of child abuse cases were attributed to cult activity. The United States invaded Grenada in 1983, but this was an extremely short and limited campaign, and the U.S. forces had departed by December, with nineteen deaths during the short conflict. It would be safe to consider the ritual abuse "panic" as a peacetime affair.

Infectious diseases had been declining in the United States, but a new epidemic, AIDS/HIV, began in the early 1980s. A few cases of AIDS were found to have occurred prior to the 1980s, but the real epidemic surge began in 1981 and accelerated quickly, with some evidence of leveling by the late 1980s (see Rushing 1995: 92–93). The AIDS epidemic did not take the form of a short-lived surge in disease comparable to those noted for smallpox, polio and influenza earlier in the century, and it is certainly legitimate to question its potential relevance to the surge in ritual abuse charges. On the other hand, it should be noted that the sexual orientation of the young man initially charged with child abuse was central to his questioning as a suspect.

William Rushing (1995) observes that AIDS appeared "when belief in the natural causes of disease was thoroughly institutionalized in the culture," but that the fact that a virus was not known to be the cause until 1984 led to considerable anxiety and wild speculation. Between 1981 and the mid-1980s, "uncertainty abounded, and a situation not unlike that of the earlier epidemics existed" (170). AIDS was defined as a gay disease and its spread was deemed to be retribution for sin. Rushing argues that the statements about

AIDS and homosexuality at the time "resemble the statements church officials had made about the Jews during the Black Death" (171). If Rushing's depiction of the period from 1981 through 1984 is correct, then the timing of the surge in public fear would be consistent with the panic search for hidden sexual deviants in our preschools.

Rushing's argument about the public uncertainty and anxiety surrounding this new disease in the early 1980s would be consistent with the timing of the ritual abuse cases. However, the case would be strengthened by evidence in media coverage, trial records, and the accusations for heightened concern about homosexual abuse of children. Such evidence would support the notion that the search for sexual deviants followed a pattern similar to earlier witch hunts as a peacetime activity facilitated by a new epidemic that heightened fears about threats to children. The AIDS epidemic prompted a surge in fear of homosexuals, and outspoken fundamentalists couched the problem as a battle with a "satanic virus" that was "eating away at the very foundations of our civilization" with our children at the mercy of pedophiles and Satan in the schoolyard (*The New Federalist* quoted at www.Larouche.com).

The satanic abuse cases were a peacetime activity that accompanied a new and mysterious plague, directing fear and anger inward toward homosexuals and others who might have the opportunity to victimize children. They did not escalate into a major sustained panic since the evidence of such an internal threat was not acceptable in modern courts of law.

Whether various types of climatic or economic hardship also affect the tendency to search for hidden internal enemies will have to be considered in future research. These modern episodes were short-lived and did not escalate into major panics. However, the fact that there is some hint that they may follow similar patterns when war and disease are considered was an unexpected surprise and other surprises may be in store as well.

Modern Violence against Witches

A common observation after any discussion of Salem and early modern witch hunts is that "real" witch hunts, not just metaphorical witch hunts, are still occurring. Murders as well as assaults upon women accused of witchcraft are a contemporary problem in third world countries. Women's rights groups have been raising public awareness of the problem in India, and several monographs have documented the problem in villages in the "tribal" areas of several Indian states. In fact, a search of newspaper and Internet reports reveals at least ten states in India that are recognized as settings for witch hunts

(West Bangal, Bihar, Jharkland, Rajasthan, Gujarat, Maharashtra, Andhra Pradesh, Madhya Pradesh, Uttar Pradesh, and Assam).

Although they are often referred to as "witch trials," or "witch hunts," the episodes encompassed under that rubric differ in several ways from the early modern version. First, the attacks are against the law. Village "authorities" may hear complaints, impose fines, and propose remedies, but those informal activities have no standing in formal law. However, their extralegal status does not mean that deliberations and informal channels are inconsequential. Rather, parties bringing witchcraft charges follow informal norms for such cases, and those successfully charged are likely to abide by the decisions made. The fact that attacks on witches are against the law plays a major role in inhibiting escalation. Second, although beliefs about demons and spirits play a role in charges against witches, those beliefs are not part of an elite demonology where witchcraft is categorized as heresy or an indicator of a larger conspiracy calling for a war against witches. The episodes involve individual charges reflecting specific individual conflicts and suspicions. Third, informal processing at the local level is oriented toward the discovery of specific causes of individual suffering with no interest on the part of local authorities, accusers, or the accused in escalating the search for hidden enemies. Accusations may surge as villagers begin to share suspicions about problems "caused" by witches, and they may take action through local authority or take action on their own, but the features of early modern Western society that facilitated escalation into major panics are missing.

Witchcraft charges may not escalate into widespread panics sustained by an official demonology, but the possibility of similarities between village-level witchcraft cases and some features of the early modern pursuit of witches should be examined. Fortunately, three studies have addressed witch hunts in India and have provided some data relevant to surges and fluctuations over time as well as details on the circumstances and characteristics of the people accused. A. B. Chaudhuri (1984) compiled data on witch killings and police interventions among tribes in West Bengal from the 1950s through the early 1980s. More recently, two studies have compiled some statistical data on witch accusations and killings in the 1990s: Mita Barman (2002) studied witch accusations and killings in West Bengal and Bihar, and Archana Mishra (2003) studied witch killings and police reports on witchcraft cases in the state of Jharkland These sources provide data on hundreds of cases over time, and all three sources provide some systematic, narrative detail on specific cases.

A surprising number of similarities between witch hunting in modern India and the patterns reported for early modern witch hunts is apparent.

Mishra refers to these events as "witch trials" because they follow established tribal procedures for bringing charges of harm through witchcraft to the attention of local tribal authorities. The attacks as well as the penalties imposed at the village level would be considered illegal by centralized law enforcement authorities were they called on to enforce the law. However, centralized authorities often prefer to avoid interfering with tribal customs involving witchcraft and are often too remote from the villages to intervene. Some killings have occurred with the police watching, but it appears that women are most often likely to receive some protection by seeking police intervention.

Among the twenty-nine cases of women killed or attacked as witches where these three researchers were able to collect detailed information, twenty-three involved accusations that the woman attacked had caused illness, disease, or death. In case after case, some form of illness is cited as the major motivation for suspicions of witchcraft. Typically, the cause of the illness is unknown, but very specific outbreaks of known diseases can lead to such charges. In one case, Mishra (2003) notes, "Within one year preceding the incident as many as fourteen villagers fell victim of T.B." In another, "the younger son of the deceased was suffering from smallpox." For another "the incident was preceded by a series of ailments in the village." In yet another, "One of his nephews died all of a sudden" (2–3). Mysterious deaths of animals could lead to accusations of witchcraft as well. In short, disease is a factor in a sizable proportion of accusations, but there is no evidence that either the witches or accusers had hallucinations or that the women attacked were acting as midwives or healers.

Not only are disease and death cited as reasons for accusations in most cases, but surges in such disease may be linked to surges in witchcraft accusations across villages. It is beyond the scope of this study to quantify all of the variables needed to test such a theory, but notable increases in disease do appear to have occurred in close temporal proximity to surges in witchcraft accusations. For example, Bihar, Uttar Pradesh, and West Bengal had major outbreaks of *visceral leishmaniasis* in 1978. This disease was particularly lethal for children under fifteen and males (World Health Organization [WHO] 1991; Bora 1999). In addition, a surge in malaria has been noted between 1976 and 1978 (Reid 2000). Tuberculosis also peaked in 1977 (Chada 2003). Chaudhuri's data on attacks on witches from 1951 through 1981 show 1978 and 1979 to be peak years for witch accusations and killings, and these are the same years encompassing surges in epidemic disease.

As reported by the Centers for Disease Control (CDC), 1994 was the year of a major outbreak of actual plague in Northern India: "A total of 693 suspected bubonic or pneumonic plague cases with positive test results for antibodies to *Yersinia pestis* were reported by India to the World Health Organization" (CDC 1994). Furthermore, a major surge in malaria occurred in the tribal areas in 1994 (Reid 2000), a surge that may have been particularly alarming since it occurred in the context of several years of decline in that disease. Both Chaudhuri's and Barman's surges in attacks on witches in the mid-1990s are consistent with this surge in disease.

A consideration of the intensity of disease among states in India suggests a relationship as well. Reports on leprosy, polio, and malaria all point to the witch hunt states as the most disease prone states in India (Shariff 1999). It is important to note that although malaria is among the diseases surging in close proximity to surges in village witch accusations, there is no evidence that it operates in the manner proposed by the sleeping sickness theory. The symptoms of malaria may be among the sources of heightened fear and anxiety in villages, and such symptoms may raise suspicions of witchcraft. However, a variety of different illnesses could lead to accusations of witchcraft.

In addition to the attribution of blame for illness, disease, and death to witchcraft by some villagers, Mishra (2003) argues that "in many cases," the accusers were relatives who were motivated by "the landed property that would have change hands" (40). Disputes over inherited property were implicated as sources of family conflict in the Salem Village witch hunts, and similar disputes appear to generate accusations of witchcraft in India. Such disputes are depicted as a mounting problem in tribal areas of India where acreage available to tribes is shrinking due to corporate encroachment. Salem villagers experienced land constraints as well as new townships were established and land was subdivided among a rapidly growing population. With increasing pressures on available land, there are increasing conflicts among relatives. Surges in death rates can lead to surges in family conflicts over the transition of land and family wealth.

The states in India most characterized by witch killings also have a disproportionate population of widows (Bose 2000: 7). West Bengal has the highest percentage of widowed women over sixty years of age at 65 percent. Moreover, three of the six states with 60 percent or more widowed women are witch hunt states, as compared to none of the states with less than 40 percent widows. This overrepresentation of widows can be conducive to violence against witches in several different ways. Their overrepresentation can be reflected in family conflicts and disputes over inheritances, resulting in self-serving charges of witchcraft. Widows with control over resources can become a target as a threat or impediment to male heirs. In contrast, widows with few resources make vulnerable targets as scapegoats in the sense that they have little or no protection from such charges.

In chapter 6, it was argued that theories of scapegoating and victimology imply that victims have to be both credible threats as well as lack the resources to resist actions against them. This same combination of factors is reflected in theories proposed by Indian witchcraft scholars. For example, in their article on "Women as Witches and Keepers of Demons," Dev Nathan, Govind Kelkar and Yu Xiaogang (1998) state, "Various studies of witch-hunting show that the victims were not just women but also those who were old and unprotected" (62). Yet, just three paragraphs later they propose that "it is where women generally have considerable authority in society that it would be necessary to attack them as the 'source of all evil.' Where women's authority has been destroyed or reduced, such a continued attack would then not be necessary." Women may be pursued as witches when they constitute a threat to the interests of male heirs, but women who have few resources to resist attack such as impoverished widows may be blamed for outbreaks of illness. This paradox can be illuminated by introducing both credibility and vulnerability into the explanation of the selection of targets.

Another feature of the witch hunts in India that coincides with prior historical research on early modern witch hunts is their location in tribal areas. The concentration of attacks on witches in tribal areas can be interpreted (1) as *cultural* in the sense that it is more common in some tribes than others, (2) as a product of *stresses on tribal populations* as corporations take over increasing amounts of land (see Communist Party of India 2002: 1), and (3) as *products of the prevalence of disease and demographic disruptions*. However, it is also consistent with the argument by several early modern witch hunt theorists that witch hunts are more likely to occur in areas peripheral to centralized governmental controls.

Barman's (2002: annexure 1) data on witch killings by district can be used together with census data on population (South Asia Research Society 1996) to create rates of witch killing for each district in West Bengal. Measuring distance to the seat of governmental control (Calcutta) in terms of the number of district boundaries that must be crossed moving away from Calcutta, there is a significant positive correlation (+.592, $p = .008$, $N = 17$, missing = 4) between distance and the rate of witch killings. The closer to the seat of government, the lower the relative frequency of witch killings. Of course, all sorts of other circumstances associated with distance from the seat of government could account for that pattern, including the prevalence of disease and the survival of tribal traditions that allow informal action against accused witches. On the other hand, this pattern is consistent with one of the most common observations by witch hunt historians studying the early modern episodes. Distance from the seat of governmental control increases the likelihood of attacks on witches.

A pattern noted for early modern witch hunts was the inhibiting influence of war on witch hunts over both time and space. Because data are available for limited spans of time and only a few settings in India, and information on war is limited to historical narratives, timetables, and newspaper articles, a definitive time series analysis of these issues is not possible. However, the timing of some major conflicts involving both external enemies and structured internal conflicts can be considered.

As noted in chapter 6, witch hunts are rare when conflict with clearly defined external enemies preoccupies people in an area, and structured internal conflicts may inhibit the pursuit of witches as well. Reviewing Chaudhuri's (1984) and Barman's (2002) data, two major concentrations of attacks on witches in the tribal regions of northern India can be discerned. The most prominent surge in witch hunting between 1950 and 1981 occurred from 1976 through 1979. Using the Hindustan Year-Books, Vijay Alok (2004) has compiled a chronology of major events, including wars and violent internal conflicts. Communist China attacked India in 1962, and the Indo-Pakistan War took place in 1965–1966. The "War of Liberation" for Bangladesh took place in 1971 with millions of refugees pouring into West Bengal. The "People's War Group" was established in 1980 in Andhra Pradesh, and a mass peasants movement spread through central Bihar (see Ahmed 2003 for a detailed report on these conflicts). Finally, the Sikh-Hindu violence spanned 1982–1984.

When Chaudhuri's witch killings and accusations are summed for the span from 1960 through 1981 and an average created for these identified "war years" as compared to nonwar years, they support the same conclusion about war and witch hunts as found for other witch hunts. The average for war years was 2.2 witches attacked as compared to 9.2 in nonwar years. Although there are only six war years and nine nonwar years, these two means are significantly different at the .01 level. There were over four times more attacks on witches in the nonwar than in the war years.

West Bengal witch killings between 1991 and 2000 peaked in mid-decade, and it is quite common to find references to the mid-1990s as years when tensions eased on a number of fronts. Tensions over border disputes between India and China had eased between 1993 and 1995. In 1993, the Indian government had settled a crisis involving a Muslim mosque and agreed to the withdrawal of troops. Indian leaders met peacefully with leaders of Muslim communities in Kashmir and released some Muslim activists from prison In 1994 Indian leaders attempted rapprochement with Pakistan in the dispute over Kashmir (Heitzman and Worden 1996). Violence and conflict appear to have escalated once again in the late 1990s (BBC News 2004).

A major source of internal conflict in Bihar, West Bengal, and other tribal areas in India began in 1967 with the "Naxalbini Uprisings" (Ahmed 2003). The resulting "Naxolism," or "Naxolite" movement, involved violent conflict between peasants, referred to in the news as "ultraleftists," and the private armies of upper-caste landlords. A thorough study of the effect of such conflict on attacks on witches is beyond the scope of this final chapter, but an exploratory survey of time lines for the conflict appears consistent with the hypothesis that the emergence of violent class or caste conflict inhibits witch attacks.

Several upsurges in internal conflict can be noted between 1967 and 1971, and there were only two witch attacks among the Santal during that span. Attacks on witches began their upward movement in 1972, peaking in 1979 at twenty. There was a dip in 1977 to three attacks compared to eight in 1976 and fifteen in 1978. No newsworthy, violent Naxolite conflicts occurred in 1978 and 1979, which were peak years for attacks on witches. Moreover, the 1977 upsurge in the Naxolite conflict coincides with that drop in witch attacks. The next major surge in witch killings between 1993 and 1995 occurred during a span of relative "peace" in this ongoing internal conflict.

Conflict surged once again in 1996, but two years of relative peace ensued (1997–1998). Major strikes began in 1999, with internal conflict escalating considerably in the first year of the new century. If witch hunting in India behaves similarly to witch hunting in prior research, witch hunts should be declining. On the other hand, should there be an increase in epidemic disease and illness and an increase in widows and conflicts involving inheritance together with a relative suspension of external and internal conflict, another surge in attacks on witches might be anticipated. Of course, as formal law and law enforcement are extended into tribal areas, the odds of any successful attacks on neighbors as witches decrease as well. Fortunately, most developments in India lead to a prediction of a decline in witch hunting in the early twenty-first century.

Another similarity between the witch accusations in India and the findings noted for Salem and other witch hunts is the fact that midwives are *not* found to play a role as victims of attacks. Not only are midwives missing from the narrative cases of attacks, but the health care situation in the tribal areas is not conducive to conflict between the growing medical profession and midwives or folk healers. Physicians are not available to villagers and have little to gain from extending their reach into tribal areas. Nor does there appear to be conflict between tribal medicine men and any of the women whose cases are documented in the available literature.

In *Beloved Witch*, a self-professed Wiccan, Ipsita Roy Chakraverti (2000), states that "the witches of olden times were learned women. They were goddess worshipers. They were doctors and wiser than the panchayat men" (220). Chakraverti's depiction of conflict between women as healers and tribal male healers parallels witch hunt theories emphasizing conflict between women as healers and the male-dominated medical professions in medieval Europe. Her depiction grows out of her study of Western Wiccan traditions and incorporates the "burning times" interpretation of witch hunts in Europe into the interpretation of the persecution of women as witches in India. Yet, although she studied numerous cases of women accused as witches, she does not report on a single case where women are accused because of efforts to heal or usurp the spiritual healing authority of tribal authorities.

In a scholarly work on "Women as Witches and Keepers of Demons," Nathan and his colleagues (1998) discuss the emergence of patriarchy in India and argue that witch-hunting was a rebellion "by men in the process of establishing authority" (58–59). They argue that "at some time . . . women did function in being spiritual mediators" but that "subsequently men established a monopoly over the higher ritual sphere" (61). Witch hunting is interpreted to have been a form of strategic persecution that enabled men to gain control over the spiritual realm, including roles that involve healing. Nathan et al. draw on tribal legends or "myths" in regions of India where witch accusations are common to propose that "witch hunting is, in this analysis, the process of establishing the authority of men" (61). They speculate that women in tribal regions continue to wield more power compared to women in caste-dominated regions and hence are more likely to be a threat to male authority. However, their argument does not lead to any expectation that midwives or female healers should be common among women attacked as witches. In sum, the same types of theories proposed in the attempt to explain the early modern witch hunts are being introduced in attempts to make sense out of attacks on women as witches in India. In the process, some of the same erroneous theories are likely to be proposed, but hints at continuity and empirical generalizations are beginning to emerge as well.

Final Comments

Although the witch wars and the execution of thousands of "Servants of Satan" (Klaits 1985) was confined to Christian societies in the fifteenth, sixteenth, and seventeenth centuries, the village-level tensions and conflicts among neighbors and relatives that result in charges of witchcraft can still be found with surprising similarities in the features of attacks on witches in tribal regions of India. In fact, in a study of newspaper reports in modern Netherlands, Willem De Blecourt (1996: 339) proposes that accusations of witchcraft may be as frequent in modern European settings as in early modern times, but that such accusations do not result in state-supported witch trials. The potential fuel for witch hunts can still be found, but the prerequisites for an escalation into panic attacks are missing.

Commenting on the transformation of village-level conflicts from minor disputes into major witch wars, Robin Briggs (1996b) notes, "It was certainly fortunate that most European rulers and their more powerful servants took such a hesitant and ultimately skeptical line." Why? Because "the exceptional cases in which restraint was abandoned . . . provide chilling warnings of how persecution by an alliance of rulers and people could spiral out of control" (406). As Jon Oplinger (1990) argues, holocausts occur when centralized authorities have successfully undermined or gained control over all other social institutions that might put a brake on persecution. When central authorities instigate or join in alliances with local authorities, choose to build on the people's conflicts, hatreds, and fears, and identify and demonize hidden internal enemies, then local panics can escalate into holocausts.

At present, tendencies toward persecution or scapegoating do not appear on the verge of spiraling out of control in the United States, although a number of instances of attempted demonization can be found. Prominent Christian fundamentalists in the United States view religious movements such as Wicca as evidence of a pernicious and growing threat to Christian society and have mounted attempts to demonize such movements, defining such movements as growing conspiracies led by Satan. However, such fundamentalists have been relatively ineffective in gaining support for their cause. Quite to the contrary, the military has recognized the right to embrace such beliefs and both government and public support for religious freedom remains sufficiently strong to counter any effort at organized persecution. Individuals may experience stigma and discrimination for their beliefs, but they are not likely to become targets of a larger witch hunt. Wiccans and neo-Pagans have been quite vocal in differentiating their environmental, "living Earth" and goddess beliefs from satanic cults (see Adler 1997; Berger 1999) and are the fastest-growing form of religious identification in the United Sates (Kosmin, Mayer, and Keysar 2001). They are a growing "threat" to some established Christian groups, but attempts to apply the satanic witch stereotype are likely to be countered by widespread familiarity with Salem and other witch hunts.

The lessons learned may act as a barrier to the invention of new enemies, but events in the near future can provide yet another test of progress in recognizing tendencies toward scapegoating and persecution during times of crises. Continual warnings of a pending, potentially devastating, epidemic of avian influenza are likely to lead to an escalation of fears of suspicious people and beliefs that there are evil groups conspiring to spread disease. Television shows depicting "worst-case scenarios" are already being aired, with an emphasis on the ineffectiveness and futility of many forms of protection. Some religious groups interpret such threats as signs of the apocalypse and warn their followers to prepare for the "End of Days." The record series of hurricanes is interpreted by some as evidence of God's anger with the reason for such anger varying from vengeance against people in "red states" to vengeance for tolerance of homosexuality to vengeance for abortions. Even liberal comics ask, jokingly, why "The Big Guy" is so pissed off. Tendencies to interpret disaster in religious terms and to interpret disease as evidence of sin are still quite pervasive. Some religious and political leaders will play on those fears and begin to construct a demonic image of the culprits responsible for casting disease around the world. These tendencies will, however, be countered by others aware of earlier historical episodes where such fears were allowed to escalate into a witch craze.

As this section was being written on Halloween (October 31, 2005), the media were warning the public to be wary of an enemy in our midst, the registered sex offender. Few will deny the importance of vigilance in protecting children from "sexual predators," and most Americans are likely to agree that rights to privacy and normal interaction should be severely restricted for such offenders. To provide such protection, numerous states are imposing curfews, mandating home confinement, and ordering sex offenders not to answer the door or give candy to children on Halloween. They are not allowed to be on the streets or to interact with children in any manner on Halloween. Critics of such requirements note that not a single instance of child molestation or sexual victimization has been reported involving Halloween trick-or-treaters.

On the other hand, defenders of the restriction argue that precautionary measures should be taken so that there is no opportunity for such an event to occur in the first place. No one denies the importance of taking steps to protect children from predators, but the extensive steps taken served to heightened parental and public fear of events that had never occurred. In contrast to the invention of satanic witches, sex offenders do exist, and they have committed offenses. Parents should supervise their children and exercise vigilance, but both the Halloween "boogeyman" hiding next door and the Halloween witch are myths.

This work began with the observation that the path of the Devil could be followed for several centuries by studying witch hunts and the wars with the mythical heretic witch. This concluding chapter suggests that more recent "metaphors" may be more than metaphors and that some of the same patterns found in the study of early modern witch hunts may be found in studying the social context and timing of more recent events. Research on early modern witch hunts has pointed to the circumstances that transform small-scale attacks on hidden enemies into panics, if not holocausts. Given knowledge of the circumstances that can facilitate such transformations, it is wise to be wary of any hints that historic demonic templates are being imposed on new hidden enemies.

References

Adler, Margot. 1997. *Drawing Down the Moon*. New York: Penguin/Arkana.

Ahmed, Nadeem. 2003. "Caste War and Red Terror." *Hindustantimes.com*, May 9, www.hindustantimes.com/news/6257_249856,0009.htm.

Alok, Vijay. 2004. *Indian Chronology*. www.hindunet.org.

Aminzade, Ronald. 1992. "Historical Sociology and Time." *Sociological Methods and Research*, special issue on "Temporality, Events and Explanation in Historical Sociology," Larry Griffin, guest ed., 20, no. 4: 456–80.

Aminzade, Ronald, Jack A. Goldstone, Doug McAdam, Elizabeth J. Perry, William Sewell Jr., Sidney Tarrow, and Charles Tilly. 2001. *Silence and Voice in the Study of Contentious Politics*. New York: Cambridge University Press.

Anderson, Alan, and Raymond Gordon. 1978. "Witchcraft and the Status of Women: The Case of England." *British Journal of Sociology* 29 (June): 171–84.

Anderson, Bonnie S., and Judith P. Zinsser. 1988. *A History of Their Own: Women in Europe from Prehistory to the Present*. Vol. 1. New York: Harper & Row.

Andreski, Stanislav. 1982. "The Syphilitic Shock." *Encounter* 58: 7–26.

———. 1989. *Syphilis, Puritanism and Witch Hunts*. New York: St. Martin's.

Ankarloo, Bengt, and Stuart Clark, eds. 2002. *Witchcraft and Magic in Europe*. Philadelphia: University of Pennsylvania Press.

Ankarloo, Bengt, and Gustav Henningsen, eds. 1993. *Early Modern European Witchcraft: Centres and Peripheries*. Oxford: Clarendon.

Ashton, John. 1882. *Chapbooks of the Eighteenth Century*. New York: Blom.

Bainbridge, William Sims. 1997. *The Sociology of Religious Movements*. New York: Routledge.

Barman, Mita. 2002. *Persecution of Women, Widows and Witches*. Calcutta: Indian Anthropological Society.

Baroja, Julio Caro. 1964. *The World of the Witches*. London: Phoenix.

Barry, Jonathan, Marianne Hester, and Gareth Roberts. 1996. *Witchcraft in Early Modern Europe*. Cambridge: Cambridge University Press.

Barstow, Anne Llewellyn. 1994. *Witchcraze: A New History of the European Witch Hunts*. San Francisco: HarperCollins.

BBC News. 2004. "India-Pakistan: Troubled Relations." Country Profiles, May 29. news.bbc.co.uk/hi/english/static/in_depth/south_asia/2002/india_pakistan/timeline.

Becker, Howard S. 1963. *Outsiders: Studies in the Sociology of Deviance*. New York: Free Press.

Behringer, Wolfgang. 1987. *Hexenverfolgung in Bayern: Volksmagie, Glaubenseifer und Staatsräson in der Frühen Neuzeit*. Munich: Oldenbourg.

———. 1996. "Witchcraft Studies in Austria, Germany and Switzerland." Pp. 64–95 in *Witchcraft in Early Modern Europe* Ed. Jonathan Barry, Marianne Hester, and Gareth Roberts. Cambridge: Cambridge University Press.

———. 1997. *Witchcraft Persecutions in Bavaria*. Cambridge: Cambridge University Press.

———. 2004. *Witches and Witch-Hunts*. New York: Blackwell.

Bell, Barbara. 1981. "Analysis of Viticultural Data by Cumulative Deviations." Pp. 271–78 in *Climate and History*, ed. Robert I. Rotberg and Theodore K. Rabb. Princeton, N.J.: Princeton University Press.

Bell, Stuart. 1988. *When Salem Came to the Boro: The True Story of the Cleveland Child Abuse Case*. London: Pan Books.

Bennett, David H. 1988. *The Party of Fear: From Nativist Movements to the New Right in American History*. Chapel Hill: University of North Carolina Press.

Ben-Yehuda, Nachman. 1980. "The European Witch Craze of the 14th to 17th Centuries: A Sociologist's Perspective." *American Journal of Sociology* 86, no. 1: 1–31.

———. 1981. "Problems Inherent in Socio-Historical Approaches to the European Witch Craze." *Journal for the Scientific Study of Religion* 20, no. 4: 326–38.

———. 1985. *Deviance and Moral Boundaries*. Chicago: University of Chicago Press.

Berger, Helen A. 1999. *A Community of Witches: Contemporary Neo-Paganism and Witchcraft in the United States*. University of South Carolina Press.

Bergesen, Albert, ed. 1983. *Crises in the World-System*. Beverly Hills, Calif.: Sage.

Berk, Richard, David Rauma, Sheldon Messinger, and Thomas Cooley. 1981. "A Test of the Stability of Punishment Hypothesis: The Case of California, 1851–1970." *American Sociological Review* 46: 805–29.

Berkowitz, Leonard. 1962a. *Aggression: A Social Psychological Analysis*. New York: McGraw-Hill.

———. 1962b. "Anti-Semitism and the Displacement of Aggression." *Journal of Abnormal and Social Psychology* 59: 182–87.

Berkowitz, Leonard, and James A. Green. 1962. "The Stimulus Qualities of the Scapegoat." *Journal of Abnormal and Social Psychology* 64: 293–301.

Berry, Brian J. L. 1991. *Long-Wave Rhythms in Economic Development and Political Behavior*. Baltimore, Md.: Johns Hopkins University Press.

Black, Donald. 1976. *The Behavior of Law*. New York: Academic Press.

———. 1979. "Common Sense in the Sociology of Law." *American Sociological Review* 44: 18–27.

———. 1983. "Crime as Social Control." *American Sociological Review* 48: 34–45.

———. 1984. "Social Control as a Dependent Variable." Pp. 1–36 in *Toward a General Theory of Social Control*, vol. 1, *Fundamentals*, ed. Donald Black. Orlando, Fla.: Academic Press.

———. 1989. *Sociological Justice*. New York: Oxford University Press.

———. 1993. *The Social Structure of Right and Wrong*. San Diego: Academic Press.

Black, George F. 1938. *A Calendar of Cases of Witchcraft in Scotland, 1510–1727*. New York: New York Public Library and Arno.

Black, Jeremy. 1996. *The Cambridge Illustrated Atlas of War, Renaissance to Revolution*. London: Cambridge University Press.

Bora D. 1999. "Epidemiology of Visceral Leishmaniasis in India." *National Medical Journal of India* 12: 62–68.

Bose, Ashis. 2000. "Demographic Transition." www.india-seminar.com/2000/488.

Bostridge, Ian. 1996. "Witchcraft Repealed." Pp. 309–34 in *Witchcraft in Early Modern Europe*, ed. Jonathan Barry, Marianne Hester, and Gareth Roberts. Cambridge: Cambridge University Press.

———. 1997. *Witchcraft and Its Transformations c. 1650–c. 1750*. Oxford: Clarendon.

Boswell, Terry. 1989. "Colonial Empires and the Capitalist World System: A Time Series Analysis of Colonization, 1640–1960." *American Sociological Review* 54: 180–96.

Bovenshen, S. 1978. "The Contemporary Witch, the Historical Witch and the Witch Myth. *New German Critique* 15: 83–119.

Boyer, Paul, and Stephen Nissenbaum. 1972. *Salem-Village Witchcraft: A Documentary Record of Local Conflict in Colonial New England*. Belmont, Calif.: Wadsworth.

———. 1974. *Salem Possessed: The Social Origins of Witchcraft*. Cambridge, Mass.: Harvard University Press.

Braudel, Fernand. 1972a. "History and the Social Sciences." Pp. 11–42 in *Economy and Society in Early Modern Europe*, ed. Peter Burke. New York: Harper & Row.

———. 1972b. *The Mediterranean and the Mediterranean World in the Age of Philip II*. London: Collins.

———. 1992. *The Perspective of the World*. Vol. 3 of *Civilization and Capitalism, 15th–18th Century*. Berkeley: University of California Press.

Braudel, Fernand, and Frank C. Spooner. 1967. "Prices in Europe from 1450 to 1750." *Cambridge Economic History of Europe* 4: 374–486.

Brauner, Sigrid. 1995. *Fearless Wives and Frightened Shrews. The Construction of the Witch in Early Modern Germany*. Amherst: University of Massachusetts Press.

Bray, J. R. 1978. "Volcanic Eruptions and Climate during the Past 500 Years." Pp. 256–62 in *Climatic Change and Variability*, ed. A. B. Pittock, L. A. Frakes, D. Jenssen, J. A. Peterson, and J. W. Zillman. London: Cambridge University Press.

Breslaw, Elaine. 1996. *Tituba, Reluctant Witch of Salem*. New York: New York University Press.

Briar, S., and I. Piliavin. 1965. "Delinquency, Situational Inducements, and Commitments to Conformity." *Social Problems* 13: 35–45.

Briggs, Robin. 1996a. "'Many Reasons Why': Witchcraft and the Problem of Multiple Explanation." Pp. 49–63 in *Witchcraft in Early Modern Europe*, ed. Jonathan Barry, Marianne Hester, and Gareth Roberts. Cambridge: Cambridge University Press.

———. 1996b. *Witches and Neighbors. The Social and Cultural Context of European Witchcraft*. London: HarperCollins.

Buchwald, Art. 1994. "Are Feminists a Bunch of Man-hating Old Witches?" *The Tennessean*, September 4, 13A.

Buckley, William F., and L. Brent Bozell. 1954. *McCarthy and His Enemies: The Record and Its Meaning*. Chicago: Regnery.

Burghartz, Susanna. 1988. "The Equation of Women and Witches: A Case Study of Witchcraft Trials in Lucerne and Lausanne in the Fifteenth and Sixteenth Centuries." *The German Underworld*, ed. Richard J. Evans. London: Routledge.

Burke, Peter. 1993. "The Comparative Approach to European Witchcraft." Pp. 335–41 in *Early Modern European Witchcraft: Centres and Peripheries*, ed. Bengt Ankarloo and Gustav Henningsen. Oxford: Clarendon.

Bynum, Jack E., and William E. Thompson. 1989. *Juvenile Delinquency: A Sociological Approach*. Boston: Allyn & Bacon.

Caporael, Linda R. 1976. "Ergotism: The Satan Loosed in Salem?" *Science* 192 (April): 21–26.

Carlson, Laurie Winn. 1999. *A Fever in Salem: A New Interpretation of the New England Witch Trials*. Chicago: Dee.

Cartwright, Frederick F. 1972. *Disease and History*. New York: Dorset.

Centers for Disease Control. 1994. "International Notes Update: Human Plague—India 1994." *Morbidity and Mortality Weekly Report* 43, no. 41: 761–62.

Chada, V. K. 2003. "Epidemiological Situation of Tuberculosis in India." *Journal of the Indian Medical Association* 101, no. 3 (March 2003), www.jimaonline.org/mar003.

Chakraverti, Ipsita Roy. 2000. *Beloved Witch: An Autobiography*. New Delhi: HarperCollins.

Chaudhuri, A. B. 1984. *Witch Killings amongst Santals*. New Delhi: Ashish.

Chambliss, William J. 1964. "A Sociological Analysis of the Law of Vagrancy." *Social Problems* 12: 67–77.

———. 1976. "Functional and Conflict Theories of Crime: The Heritage of Emile Durkhiem and Karl Marx." Pp. 1–28 in *Whose Law? What Order?* ed. William J. Chambliss and Milton Mankoff. New York: Wiley.

Chambliss, William J., and Milton Mankoff, eds. 1976. *Whose Law? What Order?* New York: Wiley.

Cipolla, Carlo M. 1980. *Before the Industrial Revolution: European Society and Economy: 1000–1700*. New York: Norton.

Clinard, Marshall B., and Robert F. Meier. 1989. *The Sociology of Deviant Behavior*. Fort Worth, Tex.: Holt, Rinehart & Winston.

Cohen, L., and M. Felson. 1979. "Social Change and Crime Rate Trends: A Routine Activity Approach. *American Sociological Review* 46: 588–607.
Cohen, L., J. Kluegel, and K. Land. 1981. "Social Inequality and Predatory Criminal Victimization: An Exposition and Test of a Formal Theory." *American Sociological Review* 46: 505–24.
Cohn, Norman. 1975. *Europe's Inner Demons: An Enquiry Inspired by the Great Witch-Hunt*. New York: New American Library.
Collins, Randall. 1988. "The Micro Contribution to Macro Sociology." *Sociological Theory* 6 (Fall): 242–53.
Communist Party of India. 2002. "Declaration of the All India Tribal Convention." *People's Democracy* 26, no. 50 (December 2).
Coulter, Ann H. 2003. *Treason: Liberal Treachery from the Cold War to the War on Terrorism*. New York: Crown Forum.
Crosby, Alfred W., Jr. 1972. *The Columbian Exchange: Biological and Cultural Consequences of 1492*. Westport, Conn.: Greenwood.
Currie, Elliott P. 1968. "Crimes without Criminals: Witchcraft and Its Control in Renaissance Europe. *Law and Society Review* 3 (August): 7–32.
———. 1973. "The Control of Witchcraft in Renaissance Europe." Pp. 344–67 in *The Social Organization of Law*, ed. Donald Black. New York: Seminar.
D'Alessio, S. J., and Lisa Stolzenberg. 1995. "Unemployment and the Incarceration of Pretrial Defendants." *American Sociological Review* 60: 350–59.
Davies, R. Trevor. 1972. *Four Centuries of Witch-Beliefs*. New York: Blom.
De Blecourt, Willem. 1996. "On the Continuation of Witchcraft." Pp. 335–52 in *Witchcraft in Early Modern Europe*, ed. Jonathan Barry, Marianne Hester, and Gareth Roberts. Cambridge: Cambridge University Press.
Demos, John Putnam. 1982. *Entertaining Satan: Witchcraft and the Culture of Early New England*. New York: Oxford University Press.
Dentler, Robert, and Kai Erikson. 1959. "The Functions of Deviance in Groups." *Social Problems* 7 (Fall): 94–197.
De Warrdt, Hans. 1991. *Toverij en Samenleving*. Holland 1500–1800. Rotterdam.
Douglas, Mary, ed. 1970. *Witchcraft Confessions and Accusations*. London: Tavistock.
Dunn, Richard S. 1979. *The Age of Religious Wars: 1559–1715*. New York: Norton.
Durkheim, Emile. 1958. *The Rules of Sociological Method*. Trans. Sarah A. Solovay and John H. Mueller and ed. George E. G. Catlin. New York: Free Press.
Eggenberger, David. 1985. *An Encyclopedia of Battles*. New York: Dover.
Ehrenreich, B. and D. English. 1973. *Witches, Midwives and Nurses*. New York: Feminist Press
Elmer, Peter. 1996. "'Saints or Sorcerors': Quakerism, Demonology and the Decline of Witchcraft in Seventeenth-Century England." Pp. 145–79 in *Witchcraft in Early Modern Europe*, ed. Jonathan Barry, Marianne Hester, and Gareth Roberts. Cambridge: Cambridge University Press.
Encyclopaedia Judaica. 1971. New York: Macmillan. Berlin: Eschkol.

Erikson, Kai T. 1962. "Notes on the Sociology of Deviance." *Social Problems* 9: 307–14.

——— . 1966. *The Wayward Puritans*. New York: Wiley.

Essex Institute. 1938. *Salem Witchcraft Papers: Verbatim Transcripts of the Legal Documents of the Salem Witchcraft Outbreak of 1692*. Salem, Mass.: Essex Institute Library.

Estes, Leland. 1983. "The Medical Origins of the European Witch Craze: A Hypothesis." *Journal of Social History* 17: 271–84.

Ewen, Cecil Henry L'Estrange. 1929. *Witch Hunting and Witch Trials*. London: Paul, Trench, Trubner.

Farrell, Ronald A., and Victoria L. Swigert. 1988. *Social Deviance*. Belmont, Calif.: Wadsworth.

Flinn, Michael, ed. 1977. *Scottish Population History: From the 17th Century to the 1930s*. London: Cambridge University Press.

Fogel, Robert William, and G. R. Elton. 1983. *Which Road to the Past?* New Haven, Conn.: Yale University Press.

Garrett, Clarke. 1977. "Women and Witches: Patterns of Analysis." *Signs* 3, no. 2: 461–82.

Garrison, F. H. 1929. *An Introduction to the History of Medicine*. Philadelphia: Saunders.

Gartner, Rosemary, and Robert Nash Parker. 1990. "Cross-National Evidence on Homicide and the Age Structure of the Population." *Social Forces* 69: 351–71.

Gay, Ruth. 1992. *The Jews of Germany: A Historical Portrait*. New Haven, Conn.: Yale University Press.

Geis, G. 1978. "Lord Hale, Witches, and Rape." *British Journal of Law and Society* 5: 26–44.

Geis, G., and Ivan Bunn. 1997. *A Trial of Witches: A Seventeenth-Century Witchcraft Prosecution*. New York: Routledge.

Gibbs, Jack P. 1966. "Conceptions of Deviant Behavior: The Old and the New." *Pacific Sociological Review* 9: 9–14.

——— . 1981. *Norms, Deviance and Social Control*. New York: Elsevier.

——— . 1989. *Control: Sociology's Central Notion*. Urbana: University of Illinois Press.

——— . 1994. *A Theory about Control*. Boulder, Colo.: Westview.

Gibson, Marion. 1999. *Reading Witchcraft: Stories of Early English Witches*. New York: Routledge.

Gijswij-Hofstra, Marijke. 1999. "Witchcraft After the Witch Trials." Pp. 95-129 In Bengt Ankarloo and Stuart Clark, eds. *Witchcraft and Magic in Europe. The Eighteenth and Nineteenth Centuries*, vol. 5. Witchcraft and Magic in Europe Series. Philadelphia: University of Pennsylvania Press.

Gijswijt-Hofstra, Marijke, and Willem Frijhoff, eds. 1991. *Witchcraft in the Netherlands from the Fourteenth to the Twentieth Century*. Trans. Rachel M. J. R. van der Wilden-Fall. Rotterdam: Universitaire Pers.

Gijswijt-Hofstra, Marijke, Brian P. Levack, and Roy Porter. 1999. *Witchcraft and Magic in Europe: The Eighteenth and Nineteenth Centuries*. London: Athlone.

Ginzburg, Carlo. 1991. *Ecstasies: Deciphering the Witches' Sabbath*. New York: Pantheon.

———. 1993. "Deciphering the Sabbath." Pp. 121–38 in *Early Modern European Witchcraft: Centres and Peripheries*, ed. Bengt Ankarloo and Gustav Henningsen. Oxford: Clarendon.

Girard, René. 1986. *The Scapegoat*. Baltimore, Md.: Johns Hopkins University Press.

Godbeer, Richard. 1992. *The Devil's Dominion*. Cambridge: Cambridge University Press.

Goldstein, Joshua S. 1988. *Long Cycles: Prosperity and War in the Modern Age*. New Haven, Conn.: Yale University Press.

Goldstone, Jack A. 1991. *Revolution and Rebellion in the Early Modern World*. Berkeley: University of California Press.

Goldstone, Jack A., and Bert Useem 1999. "Prison Riots as Micro-revolutions: An Extension of State-Centered Theories of Revolution." *American Journal of Sociology* 104 (January): 985–1029.

Goodare, Julian, ed. 2002. *The Scottish Witch-Hunt in Context*. New York: Manchester University Press.

Goode, Erich. 1994. *Deviant Behavior*. Englewood Cliffs, N.J.: Prentice Hall.

Goode, Erich, and Nachman Ben-Yehuda. 1994a. "Moral Panics: Culture, Politics, and Social Construction." *Annual Review of Sociology* 20: 149–71.

———. 1994b. *Moral Panics: The Social Construction of Deviance*. Oxford: Blackwell.

Gottfredson, M. R., and T. Hirschi. 1990. *A General Theory of Crime*. Stanford, Calif.: Stanford University Press.

Gottfried, Robert S. 1978. *Epidemic Disease in Fifteenth Century England*. New Brunswick, N.J.: Rutgers University Press.

———. 1983. *The Black Death: Natural and Human Disaster in Medieval Europe*. New York: Free Press.

Gouge, William. 1631. *God's Three Arrows: Plague, Famine, Sword*. London: George Miller for Edward Brewster.

Greenberg, D. G. 1977. "Labor Market and Imprisonment." *Crime and Social Justice* 8: 17-31.

Gregg, Charles T. 1978. *Plague*. New York: Scribner's.

Gribetz, J., with E. L. Greenstein and R. S. Stein. 1993. *The Timetables of Jewish History: A Chronicle of the Most Important People and Events in Jewish History*. New York: Simon & Schuster.

Griffin, Larry. 1992. "Temporality, Events, and Explanation in Historical Sociology." *Sociological Methods and Research*, special issue on "Temporality, Events and Explanation in Historical Sociology," Larry Griffin, guest ed., 20, no. 4: 403–27.

Griffin, Larry, and Larry Isaac. 1992. "Recursive Regression and the Historical Use of 'Time' in Time-Series Analyses of Historical Process." *Historical Methods* 25 (Fall): 166–79.

Gusfield, Joseph. 1986. *Symbolic Crusade: Status Politics and the American Temperance Movement*. 2d ed. Urbana: University of Illinois Press.

Hagan, John. 1985. *Modern Criminology: Crime, Criminal Behavior and Its Control.* New York: McGraw-Hill.

Hale, John. [1702] 1973. *A Modest Enquiry into the Nature of Witchcraft, and How Persons Guilty of That Crime May Be Convicted.* Bainbridge, N.Y.: York Mail-Print.

Hall, John. 1993. "Goldstone Wins 1993 ASA Distinguished Publication Award." *Newsletter of the Comparative and Historical Sociology Section of the American Sociological Association* 6, no. 1: 1–4.

Hansen, Chadwick. 1969. *Witchcraft at Salem.* New York: Braziller.

Harley, David. 1990. "Historians as Demonologists: The Myth of the Mid-Wife Witch." *Social History of Medicine* 3: 1–26.

Harris, Marvin. 1974. *Cows, Pigs, Wars, and Witches.* New York: Random House.

Harvey, Andrew C., and C. Fernandes. 1989. "Time Series Models for Count or Qualitative Observations." *Journal of Business & Economic Statistics* 4: 407–17.

Hassard, John, ed. 1990. *The Sociology of Time.* New York: St. Martin's.

Heinsohn, Gunnar, and Otto Steiger. 1982. "The Elimination of Medieval Birth Control and the Witch Trials of Modern Times." *International Journal of Women's Studies* 5: 193–211.

Heitzman, James, and Robert L. Worden, eds. 1996. *India: A Country Study.* 5th ed. Area Handbook, Army Department Publication 550 21. Washington, D.C.: U.S. Department of Defense.

Hester, Marianne. 1996. "Patriarchal Reconstruction and Witch Hunting." Pp. 288–306 in *Witchcraft in Early Modern Europe*, ed. Jonathan Barry, Marianne Hester, and Gareth Roberts. Cambridge: Cambridge University Press.

Hill, Francis. 2000. *The Salem Witch Trials Reader.* New York: Da Capo.

Hirschi, Travis. 1969. *Causes of Delinquency.* Berkeley: University of California Press.

———. 1973. "Procedural Rules and the Study of Deviant Behavior." *Social Problems* 21 (Fall): 159–73.

Hoffer, Peter Charles. 1996. *The Devil's Disciples: Makers of the Salem Witchcraft Trials.* Baltimore, Md.: Johns Hopkins University Press.

Hollstein, E. 1965. "Jahrringchronologishe Datierung von Eichenholzern ohne Walkante (Westdeutsche Eichenchronologie)." *Bonner Jahrbücher* 165: 1–27.

Horseley, Richard. 1979. "Who were the Witches? Social Role of the Accused in European Witch Trials." *Journal of Interdisciplinary History* 9: 689–715.

Hoskins, W. G. 1964. "Harvest Fluctuations and English Economic History, 1480–1619." *Agricultural History Review* 12: 28–46.

———. 1968. "Harvest Fluctuations and English Economic History, 1620–1759." *Agricultural History Review* 16: 15–31.

Huber, B., and V. Giertz-Siebenlist. 1969. "Unsere tausendjährige Eichen-Jahrringchronologiedurchsnittlich 57 (10-150)-fach belegt." *Sitzen-berichte I: Biologie, Mineral, Erdkunde und Verwandte Wissenschaften* 178, nos. 1–4: 37–42.

Hufton, Olwen. 1995. *The Prospect before Her: A History of Women in Western Europe.* New York: Knopf.

Hunter, James Davison. 1991. *Culture Wars: The Struggle to Define America.* New York: Basic Books.

Isaac, Larry. 1997. "Transforming Localities: Reflections on Time, Causality, and Narrative in Contemporary Historical Sociology." *Historical Methods* 30: 4–12.

Isaac, Larry, and Larry Griffin. 1989. "Ahistoricism in Time-Series Analyses of Historical Processes." *American Sociological Review* 54: 873–90.

Isaac, Larry W., and Kevin T. Leicht. 1997. "Regimes of Power and the Power of Analytic Regimes: Explaining U.S. Military Procurement Keynesianism as Historical Process." *Historical Methods* 30: 28–45.

Jensen, Gary F. 1988. "Functional Research on Deviance: A Critical Analysis and Guide for the Future." *Deviant Behavior* 9: 1–18.

———. 1997. "Time and Social History: Problems of Atemporality in Historical Analyses with Illustrations from Research on Early Modern Witch Hunts." *Historical Methods* 30: 46–57.

Johnson, Paul. 1987. *A History of the Jews*. New York: Harper & Row.

Jütte, Robert. 1994. *Poverty and Deviance in Early Modern Europe*. Cambridge: Cambridge University Press.

Kamensky, Jane. 1998. "Female Speech and Other Demons: Witchcraft and Wordcraft in Early New England." Pp. 25–51 in *Spellbound: Women and Witchcraft in America*, ed. Elizabeth Reis. Wilmington, Del.: SR Books.

Karlsen, Carol F. 1987. *The Devil in the Shape of a Woman: Witchcraft in Colonial New England*. New York: Vintage Books.

Kences, James E. 1984. "Some Unexplored Relationships in Essex County Witchcraft to the Indian Wars of 1675 and 1689." *Essex Institute Historical Collections* 120: 179–212.

Kenyon, J. P., and J. Ohlmeyer, eds. (1998). *The Civil Wars: A Military History of England, Scotland, and Ireland 1638–1660*. Oxford: Oxford University Press.

Keyser, Erich. 1956. *Deutches Stadtebuch*. Stuttgart: Kohlhammer.

———. 1957. *Hessishes Stadtebuch*. Stuttgart: Kohlhammer.

———. 1959. *Badisches Stadtebuch*. Stuttgart: Kohlhammer.

———. 1962. *Wurttembergisches Stadtebuch*. Stuttgart: Kohlhammer.

———. 1964. *Stadtebuch Rheinland-Pfalz und Saarland*. Stuttgart: Kohlhammer.

Keyser, Erich, and Heinz Stoob. 1971. *Bayerisches Stadtebuch*. Stuttgart: Kohlhammer.

Kieckhefer, Richard. 1976. *European Witch Trials: Their Foundations in Popular and Learned Culture, 1300–1500*. Berkeley: University of California Press.

Kitchen, Martin. 1996. *The Cambridge Illustrated History of Germany*. London: Cambridge University Press.

Klaits, Joseph. 1982. "Witchcraft Trials and Absolute Monarchy in Alsace." Pp. 148–72 in *Church, State and Society under the Bourbon Kings of France*, ed. Richard M. Golden. Lawrence, Kans.: Coronado.

———. 1985. *Servants of Satan: The Age of the Witch Hunts*. Bloomington: University of Indiana Press.

Klaniczay, Gabor. 1990. "The Decline of Witches and the Rise of the Vampires under the Eighteenth Century Hapsburg Monarchy." In Gabor Klaniczay (ed.), *The Uses of Supernatural Power: The Transformation of Popular Religion in Medieval and Early Modern Europe*. Oxford: Polity Press.

Kondratieff, Nikolai D. 1925. "Long Business Cycles." *Problems of Economic Fluctuations* 1: 28–79.

———. 1935. "The Long Waves in Economic Life." *Review of Economic Statistics* 17: 105–15.

Kosmin, Barry A., Egon Mayer, and Ariela Keysar. 2001. *American Religious Identification Survey*. New York: Graduate Center of the City University of New York.

Kramer, Heinrich, and James Sprenger. [1486] 1971. *Malleus Maleficarum*. Trans. Montague Summers. New York: Dover.

Kuznets, Simon. 1930. *Secular Movements in Production and Prices: Their Nature and Their Bearing upon Cyclical Fluctuations*. Boston: Houghton Mifflin.

Ladurie, Emmanuel Le Roy. 1969. "Paysans de Languedoc." Pp. 164–72 in *European Witchcraft*, ed. E. E. Monter. New York: Wiley.

———. 1971. *Times of Feast, Times of Famine*. New York: Noonday.

———. 1987. *Jasmin's Witch*. Trans. Brian Pearce. New York: Braziller.

Ladurie, Emmanuel Le Roy, and Micheline Baulant. 1981. Pp. 259–70 in *Climate and History*, ed. Robert I. Rotberg and Theodore K. Rabb. Princeton, N.J.: Princeton University Press.

Lamb, H. H. 1977. *Climate, Present, Past and Future*. Vol. 2. New York: Barnes & Noble.

Landis, Judson R. 1980. *Sociology: Concepts and Characteristics*. Belmont, Calif.: Wadsworth.

Langer, Herbert. 1980. *The Thirty Years War*. Poole, England: Blandford.

Larner, Christina. 1980. "Crimen Exceptum? The Crime of Witchcraft in Europe." Pp. 49–75 in *Crime and the Law*, ed. V. A. C. Gatrell, Bruce Lenman, and Geoffrey Parker. London: Europa.

———. 1981. *Enemies of God: The Witch Hunt in Scotland*. London: Chatto & Windus.

———. 1984. "Witchcraft Past and Present." Pp. 79–91 in *Witchcraft and Religion*, ed. Christina Larner. Oxford: Blackwell.

Lasswell, Harold. 1935. *World Politics and Personal Insecurity*. New York: Free Press.

Lauderdale, Pat. 1976. "Deviance and Moral Boundaries." *American Sociological Review* 41: 660–76.

Levack, Brian P. 1987. *The Witch-hunt in Early Modern Europe*. London: Longman.

———, ed. 1992. *Articles on Witchcraft, Magic and Demonology: A Twelve Volume Anthology of Scholarly Articles*. New York: Garland.

———. 1995. *The Witch Hunt in Early Modern Europe*. Second Edition. New York: Longman.

———. 1996. "State-building and Witch Hunting in Early Modern Europe." Pp. 96–115 in *Witchcraft in Early Modern Europe*, ed. Jonathan Barry, Marianne Hester, and Gareth Roberts. Cambridge: Cambridge University Press.

Levy, Jack S. 1983. *War in the Modern Great Power System, 1495–1975*. Lexington: University Press of Kentucky.

———. 1989. "The Diversionary Theory of War: A Critique." Pp. 259–88 in *Handbook of War Studies*, ed. Manus I. Midlarsky. Boston: Unwin Hyman.

Lipset, Seymour. 1955. "The Sources of the Radical Right." Pp. 166–234 in *The New American Right*, ed. Daniel Bell. New York: Criterion Books.

Liska, Alan. 1992. *Social Threat and Social Control*. Albany: State University of New York Press.

Macfarlane, Alan. 1970a. *Witchcraft in Tudor and Stuart England: A Regional and Comparative Study*. London: Routledge & Kegan Paul.

———. 1970b. "Witchcraft in Tudor and Stuart Essex." Pp. 81–99 in *Witchcraft Confessions and Accusations*, ed. Mary Douglas. London: Tavistock.

Mager, Nathan H. 1987. *The Kondratieff Waves*. New York: Praeger.

Mandel, Sheldon L. 1987. "Of Asklepiads, Quacks, and Early Caretakers of the Skin." *International Journal of Dermatology* 26: 610–14.

Marley, David F. 1998. *Wars of the Americas: A Chronology of Armed Conflict in the New World, 1492 to the Present*. Santa Barbara, Calif.: ABC-CLIO.

Martin, Ruth. 1989. *Witchcraft and the Inquisition in Venice, 1550–1650*. New York: Blackwell.

Martine, James J. 1993. *The Crucible: Politics, Property and Pretense*. New York: Twayne.

Massey, James L., and Martha A. Meyers. 1989. "Patterns of Repressive Social Control in Post-Reconstruction Georgia, 1882–1935." *Social Forces* 68: 458–88.

Mather, Cotton. 1693. *The Wonders of the Invisible World: Being an Account of the Trials of Several Witches, Lately Executed in New England*. Boston: Dunton.

Matossian, Mary Kilbourne. 1989. *Poisons of the Past: Molds, Epidemics, and History*. New Haven, Conn.: Yale University Press.

McAdam, Doug, and William Sewell Jr. 2001. "It's about Time: Temporality in the Study of Social Movements and Revolutions." Pp. 89–125 in *Silence and Voice in the Study of Contentious Politics*, ed. Ronald R. Aminzande, Jack A. Goldstone, Doug McAdam, Elizabeth Perry, William H. Sewell Jr., Sidney Tarrow, and Charles Tilly. Cambridge: Cambridge University Press.

McAdam, Doug, Sidney Tarrow, and Charles Tilly. 2001. *Dynamics of Contention*. New York: Cambridge University Press.

McCleary, Richard, and Richard A. Hay Jr. 1980. *Applied Time Series Analysis*. Beverly Hills, Calif.: Sage.

McMillen, Persis. 1990. *Currents of Malice: Mary Towne Esty and Her Family in Salem Witchcraft*. Portsmouth, N.H.: Randall.

McNeill, William H. 1976. *Plagues and Peoples*. Garden City, N.Y.: Anchor.

Mellinkoff, Ruth. 1993. *Outcasts: Signs of Otherness in Northern European Art of the Late Middle Ages*. Vol. 1, *Text*. Berkeley: University of California Press.

Meltzer, Milton. 1999. *Witches and Witch-Hunts*. New York: Blue Sky.

Merton, R. K. 1957. *Social Theory and Social Structure*. New York: Free Press.

Midelfort, H. C. Erik. 1968. "Recent Witch Hunting Research, or Where Do We Go from Here?" *Papers of the Bibliographical Society of America* 62: 373–420.

———. 1971. "Witchcraft and Religion in Sixteenth-Century Germany: The Formation and Consequences of an Orthodoxy." *Archiv für Reformationgeschichte* 62: 266–78.

———. 1972. *Witch Hunting in Southwestern Germany, 1562–1684: The Social and Intellectual Foundations*. Stanford, Calif.: Stanford University Press.

———. 1974. "Were There Really Witches?" Pp. 189–205 in *Transition and Revolution: Problems and Issues of European Renaissance and Reformation History*, ed. Robert M. Kingdom. Minneapolis: Burgess.

———. 1979. "Witch Hunting and the Domino Theory." Pp. 277–335 in *Religion and People, 800–1700*, ed. James Obelkevich. Chapel Hill: University of North Carolina Press.

———. 1981. "Heartland of the Witchcraze: Central and Northern Europe." *History Today* 30: 31–35.

Miller, Arthur. 1953. *The Crucible*. Viking.

Miller, Perry. 1939. *The New England Mind: The Seventeenth Century*. Cambridge, Mass.: Belknap Press.

———. 1962. *The New England Mind from Colony to Province*. Cambridge, Mass.: Belknap Press.

Miller, W. 1958. "Lower Class Culture as a Generating Milieu of Gang Delinquency." *Journal of Social Issues* 14: 5–19.

Mishra, Archana. 2003. *Casting the Evil Eye: Witch Trials in Tribal India*. New Delhi: Roli.

Modelski, George. 1978. "The Long Cycle of Global Politics and the Nation State." *Comparative Studies in Society and History* 20: 214–35.

———. 1987. *Exploring Long Cycles*. London: Pinter.

Modelski, George, and William R. Thompson. 1989. "Long Cycles and Global War." Pp. 23–54 in *Handbook of War Studies*, ed. Manus I. Midlarsky. Boston: Unwin Hyman.

Monter, E. William. 1972. "The Historiography of European Witchcraft: Progress and Prospects." *Journal of Interdisciplinary History* 2: 435–51.

———. 1976. *Witchcraft in France and Switzerland*. Ithaca, N.Y.: Cornell University Press.

———. 1981. "Sodomy and Heresy in Early Modern Switzerland." *Journal of Homosexuality* 6: 41–53.

———. 1987. *Enforcing Morality in Early Modern Europe*. London: Variorum Reprints.

Moore, R. I. 1987. *The Formation of a Persecuting Society: Power and Deviance in Western Europe, 950–1250*. Oxford: Blackwell.

Morton, R. S. 1990. "Syphilis in Art: An Entertainment in Four Parts, Part I." *Genitourin Medicine* 66: 33–40.

Muchembled, Robert. 1977. *Culture populaire et culture des élites dans la France moderne: XVe–XVIIIe siècles*. Paris: Flammarion.

———. 1993. "Satanic Myths and Cultural Reality." Pp. 139–69 in *Early Modern European Witchcraft: Centres and Peripheries*, ed. Bengt Ankarloo and Gustav Henningsen. Oxford: Clarendon.

Murk-Jansen, Saskia. 1998. *Brides in the Desert: The Spirituality of the Beguines*. Maryknoll, N.Y.: Orbis.

Murray, Margaret. 1921. *The Witch-Cult in Western Europe*. Oxford: Clarendon.

———. 1931. *The God of the Witches*. Oxford: Oxford University Press.

Nathan, Dev, Govind Kelkar, and Yu Xiaogang. 1998. "Women as Witches and Keepers of Demons: Cross-Cultural Analysis of Struggles to Change Gender Relations." *Economic and Political Weekly*, October 31, 58–69.

Newall, Venetia. 1973. "The Jew as Witch Figure." Pp. 95–124 in *The Witch Figure*, ed. Venetia Newall. London: Routledge & Kegan Paul.

Nirenberg, David. 1996. *Communities of Violence: Persecution of Minorities in the Middle Ages*. Princeton, N.J.: Princeton University Press.

Norton, Mary Beth. 1996. *Founding Mothers and Fathers: Gendered Power and the Forming of American Society*. New York: Knopf.

———. 2002. *In the Devil's Snare: The Salem Witchcraft Crisis of 1692*. New York: Knopf.

Notestein, Wallace. 1911. *A History of Witchcraft in England from 1558 to 1718*. Washington, D.C.: American Historical Association.

Ober, William B. 1989. "To Cast a Pox: The Iconography of Syphilis." *American Journal of Dermatopathology* 11: 74–86.

Oberman, Heiko A. 1984. *The Roots of Anti-Semitism in the Age of Renaissance and Reformation*. Trans. James I. Porter. Philadelphia: Fortress.

Obershall, A. 1973. *Social Conflict and Social Movements*. Englewood Cliffs, NJ: Prentice-Hall.

Oplinger, Jon. 1990. *The Politics of Demonology: The European Witchcraze and the Mass Production of Deviance*. London: Associated University Presses.

Orion, Loretta. 1995. *Never Again the Burning Times: Paganism Revisited*. Prospects Heights, Ill.: Waveland.

Ostrom, Charles W. 1990. *Time Series Analysis: Regression Techniques*. 2d ed. Newbury Park, Calif.: Sage.

Pass, Martha White. 1979. *Population Change, Labor Supply, and Agriculture in Augsburg, 1480–1618*. New York: Arno.

Pearl, Jonathan. 1977. "Witchcraft in New France in the Seventeenth Century: The Social Aspect." *Historical Reflections* 4: 195–205.

Pfister, Christian. 1981. "The Little Ice Age: Thermal and Wetness Indices for Central Europe." Pp. 85–116 in *Climate and History*, ed. Robert I. Rotberg and Theodore K. Rabb. Princeton, N.J.: Princeton University Press.

Pfohl, Stephen J. 1985. *Images of Deviance and Social Control: A Sociological History*. New York: McGraw-Hill.

Platt, Anthony. 1969. *The Childsavers: The Invention of Delinquency*. Chicago: University of Chicago Press.

Porette, Margaret. 1999. *The Mirror of Simple Souls*. Trans. Edmund Colledge, J. C. Marler, and Judith Grant. Nore Dame, Ind.: Notre Dame University Press.

Pounds, N. J. G. 1990. *An Historical Geography of Europe*. New York: Cambridge University Press.

Power, Eileen. 1975. *Medieval Women*. Ed. M. M. Postan. Cambridge: Cambridge University Press.

Purkiss, Diane. 1996. *The Witch in History*. New York: Routledge.
Quadagno, Jill, and Stan J. Knapp. 1992. "Have Historical Sociologists Forsaken Theory? Thoughts on the History/Theory Relationship." *Sociological Methods and Research*, special issue on "Temporality, Events and Explanation in Historical Sociology," Larry Griffin, guest ed., 20, no. 4: 481–507.
Quaife, G. R. 1987. *Godly Zeal and Furious Rage: The Witch in Early Modern Europe*. London: Croom Helm.
Quantitative Micro Software. 1994–1997. *Eviews 5.1*. Irvine, Calif.: Author.
Quétel, Claude. 1990. *History of Syphilis*. Cambridge: Polity.
Quinney, Richard. 1970. *The Social Reality of Crime*. Little, Brown.
———. 1977. *Class, State and Crime*. New York: McKay.
Rabinowitz, Dorothy. 1990. "From the Mouths of Babes to a Jail Cell." *Harper's Magazine*, May, 52–53.
Ranft, Patricia. 1996. *Women and the Religious Life in Premodern Europe*. New York: St. Martin's.
Reid, Colleen. 2000. "Implications of Climate Change on Malaria in Karnataka, India." Senior honors thesis, Brown University.
Reijners, Jan. 1990. *Long Waves in Economic Development*. Brookfield, Vt.: Elgar.
Reis, Elizabeth. 1998. *Spellbound: Women and Witchcraft in America*. Wilmington, Del.: SR Books.
Reiss, A. J., Jr. 1951. "Delinquency as the Failure of Personal and Social Controls." *American Sociological Review* 16: 196–207.
Richards, Jeffrey. 1990. *Sex, Dissidence and Damnation: Minority Groups in the Middle Ages*. London: Routledge.
Richardson, James T., Joel Best, and David G. Bromley. 1991. *The Satanism Scare*. New York: Aldine de Gruyter.
Roach, Marilynne K. 2002. *The Salem Witch Trials: A Day-by-Day Chronicle of a Community under Siege*. New York: Cooper Square.
Robinson, Enders. 1991. *The Devil Discovered*. New York: Hippocrene Books.
Robinson, William S. 1950. "Ecological Correlations and the Behavior of Individuals." *American Sociological Review* 15: 351–57.
Roper, Linda. 1996. "Witchcraft and Fantasy in Early Modern Germany." Pp. 207–36 in *Witchcraft in Early Modern Europe*, ed. Jonathan Barry, Marianne Hester, and Gareth Roberts. Cambridge: Cambridge University Press.
Rosenthal, Bernard. 1993. *Salem Story: Reading the Witch Trials of 1692*. New York: Cambridge University Press.
Roshier, Bob. 1977. "The Function of Crime Myth." *Sociological Review* 25: 309–23.
Rotberg, Robert I., and Theodore K. Rabb, eds. 1981. *Climate and History*. Princeton, N.J.: Princeton University Press.
Rusche, Georg, and Otto Kirchheimer. 1939. *Punishment and Social Structure*. New York: Morningside.
Rushing, William. 1995. *The AIDS Epidemic: Social Dimensions of an Infectious Disease*. Boulder, Colo.: Westview.

Russell, Jeffrey Burton. 1972. *Witchcraft in the Middle Ages*. London: Thames & Hudson.
———. 1977. *The Devil*. Ithaca, N.Y.: Cornell University Press.
———. 1980. *A History of Witchcraft: Sorcerers, Heretics, and Pagans*. London: Thames & Hudson.
———. 1981. *Satan: The Early Christian Tradition*. Ithaca, N.Y.: Cornell University Press.
———. 1984. *Lucifer: The Devil in the Middle Ages*. Ithaca, N.Y.: Cornell University Press.
———. 1986. *Mephistopheles: The Devil in the Modern World*. Ithaca, N.Y.: Cornell University Press.
———. 1988. *The Prince of Darkness: Radical Evil and the Power of Good in History*. Ithaca, N.Y.: Cornell University Press.
Russell, Jeffrey Burton, and Mark W. Wyndham. 1976. "Witchcraft and the Demonization of Heresy." *Mediaevalia* 2: 1–21.
Scarre, Geoffrey. 1987. *Witchcraft and Magic in Sixteenth and Seventeenth Century Europe*. London: Macmillan Education.
Schoeneman, Thomas J. 1975. "The Witch Hunt as a Culture Change Phenomenon." *Ethos* 3: 529–54.
Schur, Edwin M. 1979. *Interpreting Deviance: A Sociological Introduction*. New York: Harper & Row.
Scot, Reginald. [1584] 1930. *The Discoverie of Witchcraft*. Ed. M. Summers. London: Rodker.
Sebald, Hans. 1978. *Witchcraft: The Heritage of a Heresy*. New York: Oxford University Press.
———. 1981. "Franconian Witchcraft: A Discussion of Functionalism." *Deviant Behavior* 2: 349–70.
———. 1989. "Nazi Ideology Redefining Deviants: Witches, Himmler's Witch-Trial Survey, and the Case of the Bishopric of Bamberg." *Deviant Behavior* 10: 253–70.
Shariff, Abusaleh. 1999. *India: Human Development Report*. New York: Oxford University Press.
Silverman, Kenneth. 1985. *The Life and Times of Cotton Mather*. New York: Columbia University Press.
Slack, Paul. 1985. *The Impact of Plague in Tudor and Stuart England*. London: Routledge & Kegan Paul.
Smelser, Neil J. 1962. *Theory of Collective Behavior*. New York: Free Press.
Smith, William. 1977. *Smith's Bible Dictionary*. New York: Jove Books.
Soman, Alfred. 1978. "The Parlement of Paris and the Great Witch Hunt (1565–1640)." *Sixteenth Century Journal* 9: 31–144.
South Asia Research Society. 1996. "Population Explosion in West Bengal: A Survey." App. 2 in *Time for Stock Taking*, ed. Sita Ram Goel. New Delhi: Voice of India.
Spanos, Nicholas P., and Jack Gottlieb. 1976. "Ergotism and the Salem Village Witch Trials." *Science* 192: 1390–94.

Spencer, Metta. 1982. *Foundations of Modern Sociology*: Englewood Cliffs, N.J.: Prentice Hall.

Spitzer, Steven. 1975. "Toward a Marxian Theory of Deviance." *Social Problems* 22: 638–51.

Stahle, David W., Malcolm K. Cleaveland, Dennis B. Blanton, Matthew D. Therrell, and David A. Gay. 1998. "The Lost Colony and Jamestown Droughts." *Science* 280 (April 24): 564–67.

Stark, Rodney. 2003. *For the Glory of God*. Princeton, N.J.: Princeton University Press.

Starkey, Marion L. 1969. *The Devil in Massachusetts*. New York: Doubleday.

Stinchcombe, Arthur L. 1968. *Constructing Social Theories*. New York: Harcourt, Brace & World.

Stone, Lawrence. 1987. *The Past and Present Revisited*. London: Routledge & Kegan Paul.

———. 1992. "The Revolution over the Revolution." *New York Review of Books* 39, no. 11.

Summers, Montague. [1926] 1987. *The History of Witchcraft*. New York: Dorsett.

Sutherland, E. H., D. R. Cressey, and D. F. Luckenbill. 1992. *Principles of Criminology*. 11th ed. Dix Hills, N.Y.: General Hall.

Taylor, Alan. 2001. *American Colonies*. New York: Viking Penguin.

Taylor, James B. 1988. "Long Waves in Six Nations: Results and Speculations from a New Methodology." *Review* 11: 373–92.

Thomas, Keith. 1971. *Religion and the Decline of Magic*. New York: Scribner.

Thompson, Janet. 1993. *Wives, Widows, Witches and Bitches*. New York: Lang.

Thompson, William R., and L. G. Zuk. 1982. "War, Inflation, and the Kondratieff Long Wave." *Journal of Conflict Resolution* 26: 621–44.

Thurston, Robert W. 2001. *Witch, Wicce, Mother Goose*. Edinburgh Gate, England: Longman.

Tilly, Charles. 1984. *Big Structures, Large Processes, Huge Comparisons*. New York: Russell Sage Foundation.

———. 1986. *The Contentious French*. Cambridge, Mass.: Harvard University Press.

———. 1992. *Coercion, Capital and European States, AD 990–1992*. Cambridge, Mass.: Blackwell.

———. 1993. *European Revolutions, 1492–1992*. Cambridge, Mass.: Blackwell.

Toby, J. 1957. "Social Disorganization and Stake in Conformity: Complementary Factors in the Predatory Behavior of Hoodlums." *Journal of Criminal Law, Criminology and Police Science* 48: 12–17.

Trachtenberg, Joshua. 1943. *The Devil and the Jews*. New Haven, Conn.: Yale University Press.

Trask Richard B. 1992. *The Devil Hath Been Raised: A Documentary History of the Salem Village Witchcraft Outbreak of March 1692*. Danvers, Mass.: Yeoman.

Trevor-Roper, H. R. 1967. *The Crisis of the Seventeenth Century: Religion, the Reformation, and Social Change*. New York: Harper & Row.

Tylecote, Andrew. 1992. *The Long Wave in the World Economy: The Present Crisis in Historical Perspective*. New York: Routledge.

Urdang, Laurence. 1996. *The Timetables of American History*. New York: Touchstone.

Van Bath, B. H. Slicher. 1963. *The Agrarian History of Western Europe*. London: Arnold.

Van den Berghe, Pierre L. 1963. "Dialectic and Functionalism: Toward a Theoretical Synthesis." *American Sociological Review* 28: 695–705.

Victor, Jeffrey. 1992. "The Search for Scapegoat Deviants." *The Humanist* 52: 10–13.

Vold, G., and T. J. Bernard. 1986. *Theoretical Criminology*. New York: Oxford University Press.

Wallerstein, Immanuel. 1974. *The Modern World-System: Capitalist Agriculture and the Origins of the European World-Economy in the Sixteenth Century*. New York: Academic Press.

———. 1980. *The Modern World-System: Mercantilism and the Consolidation of the European World-Economy*. New York: Academic Press.

Weisman, Richard. 1984. *Witchcraft, Magic and Religion in Seventeenth Century Massachusetts*. Amherst: University of Massachusetts Press.

Wendell, Barrett. 1892. "Were the Salem Witches Guiltless?" *Essex Institute Historical Collections* 29: 129–47.

Weyer, Johann. [1563] 1991. *Witches, Devils, and Doctors in the Renaissance (De Praestigiis Daemonum)*. General ed., George Mora; associate ed., Benjamin Kohl; trans. John Shea. Binghamton, N.Y.: Medieval & Renaissance Texts & Studies.

Widdowson, John. 1973. "The Witch as a Frightening and Threatening Figure." Pp. 200–220 in *The Witch Figure*, ed. Venetia Newall. Boston: Routledge & Kegan Paul.

Willis, Deborah. 1995. *Malevolent Nurture: Witch-Hunting and Maternal Power in Early Modern England*. Ithaca, N.Y.: Cornell University Press.

Wilson, Charles, and Geoffrey Parker. 1977. *An Introduction to the Sources of European Economic History*. Ithaca, N.Y.: Cornell University Press.

Wood, James B. 1984. "The Impact of the Wars of Religion: A View of France in 1581." *Sixteenth Century Journal* 15: 131–68.

World Health Organization. 1991. *Control of Leishmaniasis*. Expert Committee Technical Report Series 793. Geneva: Author.

Wright, Quincy. 1965. *A Study of War*. 2d ed. Chicago: University of Chicago Press.

Ziegler, Phillip. 1993. *The Black Death*. Gloucestershire, U.K.: Sutton.

Zimmerman, Ernest L. 1938. "Extragenital Syphilis as Described in the Early Literature (1497–1624) with Special Reference to Focal Epidemics." *American Journal of Syphilis, Gonorrhea and Venereal Diseases* 22: 757–80.

~

Index

About the Author

Gary F. Jensen is professor of sociology and religious studies at Vanderbilt University and has held faculty appointments at the University of North Carolina, Chapel Hill, and the University of Arizona. He has published over sixty articles and chapters and authored, coauthored, or edited eight books on criminology. Jensen was installed as a fellow of the American Society of Criminology in 2001. *Path of the Devil* was completed with support from the National Science Foundation and Vanderbilt University.